£30·00

D1328176

CITIES AND SOCIAL CHANGE
IN EARLY MODERN FRANCE

Cities and Social Change in Early Modern France

Edited by
PHILIP BENEDICT

London
UNWIN HYMAN
Boston   Sydney   Wellington

Published by the Academic Division of
Unwin Hyman Ltd
15/17 Broadwick Street, London W1V 1FP, UK

Unwin Hyman Inc.,
8 Winchester Place, Winchester, Mass. 01890, USA

Allen & Unwin (Australia) Ltd,
8 Napier Street, North Sydney, NSW 2060, Australia

Allen & Unwin (New Zealand) Ltd in association with the
Port Nicholson Press Ltd,
Compusales Building, 75 Ghuznee Street,
Wellington 1, New Zealand

First published in 1989

British Library Cataloguing in Publication Data

Cities and social change in early modern France.
1. France. Cities. Development, 1500–1800.
Socioeconomic aspects
I. Benedict, Philip
307′.14′0944
ISBN 0–04–944017–9

Library of Congress Cataloging-in-Publication Data

Cities and social change in early modern France.
Bibliography: p.
Includes index.
1. Cities and towns — France — History. 2. France —
Social conditions. I. Benedict, Philip.
HT135.C57   1989   307.7′6′0944   88–27697
ISBN 004–9440179 (alk. paper)

Typeset in 10 on 12 Garamond by Nene Phototypesetters Ltd, Northampton
and printed in Great Britain at the University Press, Cambridge

Contents

List of Maps

Contributors

PHILIP BENEDICT is Associate Professor of History at Brown University. He is the author of *Rouen during the Wars of Religion* (1981), as well as of numerous articles on the social and religious history of sixteenth- and seventeenth-century France.

ROBERT DESCIMON's many publications on the social and political history of Paris from the Wars of Religion to the Fronde include *Qui étaient les Seize? Mythes et réalités de la Ligue parisienne (1585–1594)* (1983) and, with Elie Barnavi, *La Sainte Ligue, le juge et la potence: L'assassinat du Président Brisson* (1985). He is Directeur de Recherches at the Centre Nationale de Recherche Scientifique, Paris.

CLAIRE DOLAN, Professeure Agrégée at the Université Laval, Québec, is the author of *Entre tours et clochers: Les gens d'église à Aix-en-Provence au XVIe siècle* (1981) and a contributor to the collective *Histoire d'Aix-en-Provence* (1977). She is currently at work on a book on family ties and urban life in later-sixteenth-century Aix.

JAMES R. FARR is Assistant Professor of History at Purdue University. He recently completed *Hands of Honor: Artisans and Their World in Early Modern France (Dijon, 1550–1650)* and is now engaged in a study of sexuality and criminality in Counter-Reformation Burgundy.

RENÉ FAVIER is Maitre de Conférences at the Université des Sciences Sociales de Grenoble. He has published numerous articles on the social and economic history of early modern Dauphiné and is currently nearing completion of a *doctorat d'état* on the province's cities in the seventeenth and eighteenth centuries.

FREDERICK M. IRVINE received his PhD from the University of Toronto in 1980 for his dissertation 'Social Structure, Social Mobility and Social Change in Sixteenth-Century Montpellier: From Renaissance City-State to Ancien Régime Capital'. He practices law in Vancouver.

ROBERT A. SCHNEIDER, Assistant Professor of History at Brandeis University, is the author of the forthcoming *From Municipal Republic to Cosmopolitan City: Public Life in Toulouse 1478–1789*. He has also published articles on penitential confraternities and on duelling in early modern France.

List of Abbreviations

A.C.	Archives Communales or Municipales (followed by the name of the locality in question)
A.C.T.	Archives Municipales de Toulouse
A.D.	Archives Départementales
A.D.B.R.	Archives Départementales des Bouches-du-Rhône, dépôt d'Aix-en-Provence
A.D.H.	Archives Départementales de l'Hérault
A.D.H.G.	Archives Départementales de la Haute-Garonne
A.D.I.	Archives Départementales de l'Isère
A.N.	Archives Nationales (Paris)
Annales: E.S.C.	*Annales: Economies, Sociétés, Civilisations*
B.M.	Bibliothèque Municipale
B.N.	Bibliothèque Nationale (Paris)
Braudel and Labrousse	Fernand Braudel and Ernest Labrousse (eds), *Histoire économique et sociale de la France,* 3 vols (Paris: Presses Universitaires de France, 1970–77)
R.D.B.V.	*Registres des délibérations du Bureau de la Ville de Paris, 1499–1624,* 19 vols (Paris: Imprimerie Nationale, 1883–1953)

Introduction

The construction of historical knowledge involves an essential tension: between the quest to detect broad patterns of significance, and the need to root these patterns in the stubborn particularities of time and place. This volume attempts to capture this tension, and in so doing to provoke some rethinking of the history of French cities and of their changing role within the larger society of which they were a part over the course of the three centuries that the French conventionally label '*l'époque moderne*', and which shall be referred to here interchangeably as the 'Ancien Régime' or 'early modern' period. Six original archival studies, exploring important and largely neglected aspects of French urban history between the close of the Middle Ages and the outbreak of the Revolution, are preceded by a long introductory essay offering an interpretive overview of the subject.

During the late 1960s and early 1970s, the urban history of early modern France emerged as a particularly exciting area of historical investigation. Between 1967 and 1975 an impressive series of books dedicated to the social history of individual cities appeared, most notably Pierre Deyon's study of Amiens in the seventeenth century; Richard Gascon's and Maurice Garden's investigations of Lyon in the sixteenth and eighteenth centuries respectively; and Jean-Claude Perrot's analysis of eighteenth-century Caen. All of these works were massive, detailed *thèses de doctorat d'état* of the sort that were for so long, when completed successfully, the glory of French academic scholarship. (One of the periodic 'reforms' of the Ministry of Education has recently abolished the *doctorat d'état*; it remains to be seen if this change will be permanent.) Among this quartet were some of the most penetrating examinations of the history of any city at any period of time. Together they shed a sharp new light on the structure and functioning of Ancien Régime urban society.

Since 1975, the pace of research into the history of early modern French cities has slowed only slightly. Work published since then has conquered the difficult challenge of applying the demographic techniques of family reconstitution to large cities, traced the patterns and logic governing the flow of migrants to and from the city with new precision, and above all supplemented the somewhat abstract depiction of urban social structures characteristic of the urban history of the 1960s and 1970s with the more vivid evocation of patterns of everyday life and association based upon the use of

1

police and court records. But even as virtually every year has brought forth its share of new monographs or articles on the urban history of the Ancien Régime, it has also grown increasingly hard to escape the impression that the investigation of this field has experienced a certain loss of momentum. Few if any important interpretive debates have emerged to galvanize interest around specific questions. Recent synthetic works that have sought to sketch out the long-term evolution of French cities between 1500 and 1789 have been more in the nature of attractive syntheses of work to date than bold interpretations of the subject that might serve either to direct the course of future research or to inspire revision and refinement. At its best, the recent trend toward the 'thick description' of patterns of urban life, justified in the name of liberation from 'the imperialism of a certain economic and social history', has moved us closer to an appreciation of the lived realities of social interaction in Ancien Régime cities. At its worst, it has substituted anecdotal-ism for the search for meaningful patterns of long-term change.

For all that has been learned from the research of the past generation, our knowledge of France's urban history between the sixteenth century and the Revolution consequently remains uneven. First of all, it is chronologically uneven. As the Select Bibliography provided at the end of Chapter 1 makes clear, the majority of the important works have been devoted to the eighteenth century; the closer the student of early modern French cities advances toward 1789, the more abundant the literature becomes, and the progression is geometric rather than arithmetic. The reasons for the dispro-portionate amount of attention devoted to the eighteenth century are easy to adduce. The source material for this period is more abundant, the hand-writing poses fewer problems for beginning researchers, and the eighteenth century will always be a *terre d'élection* of scholars seeking to assess the causes and consequences of the Revolution. At the same time, this lopsided distribution of intellectual energy impedes a proper understanding of the long-term dynamics of social change across the three centuries of the early modern period.

Still more important, our knowledge of French cities is uneven in terms of its coverage of different kinds of cities. Nearly all of the most important studies have been devoted to the larger provincial towns, whose size suited them well to being the subject of a *doctorat d'état*. The numerous smaller towns below the rank of major provincial cities are less well served, while, like all of the great European capitals, Paris has tended to discourage historians by its very size, although a number of investigations, often collaborative in character, have explored aspects of its social structure and life.

Furthermore, even among the larger provincial towns, certain kinds of cities have attracted far more attention than others. Historical research in France has been characterized during the past decades far more by the replication and refinement of influential models of investigation than it has been by the systematic examination of large interpretive questions or theories. Several works provided inspiration for the upsurge of research on urban history – François Furet and Adeline Daumard's investigation of Parisian social structures on the basis of marriage contracts, Louis Henry's development of the demographic technique of family reconstitution – but the most influential work of all was unquestionably Pierre Goubert's masterful 1960 study of Beauvais and its surrounding region. Among its many lessons, this book underscored the centrality of textile production in the early modern economy and called attention to the sources that could be used to chart it. In so doing, it stimulated other studies of cloth manufacturing towns. Richard Gascon's study of sixteenth-century Lyon was perhaps less directly influential, but its linkage of the study of long-distance trade with the general history of Lyon in its period of greatest commercial importance nonetheless exemplifies another important stimulus to research in urban history: the strong French interest in the history of commercial capitalism. The result of such traditions is that the most detailed social histories of individual early modern French towns that we now possess are devoted to cities that were primarily commercial towns or textile manufacturing centers. Such a conflation of urban history with the history of commerce and industry – like the parallel conflation of rural history with agricultural history – is highly misleading for an era when both trade and manufacturing were increasingly penetrating the countryside while many important provincial towns were above all centers of administration and *rentier* life.

One rival tradition of scholarship of some force does exist: that of two students of Alfred Cobban, Olwen Hufton and T. J. A. LeGoff. These scholars have devoted books to, respectively, Bayeux and Vannes in the eighteenth century. Their studies draw attention to smaller towns that were predominantly administrative and *rentier* in character, in so doing offering local illustrations of Cobban's revisionist emphasis on the importance of landed elites and the weak development of capitalism on the eve of the Revolution. Unfortunately, they have less to offer the study of the dynamics of the Ancien Régime itself. Hufton's work explores only the period immediately prior to the outbreak of the Revolution, while in selecting Vannes as the locale for his case study, LeGoff chose a decaying city sapped by competition from the nearby new port of Lorient, which consequently forms an idiosyncratic basis for any broader generalizations. The fate of individual towns was intimately connected to the evolution of the larger regional systems of cities of which they were a part, and it is only when case studies of individual towns set them in the context of these larger systems that the broader significance of such studies can be grasped. Unfortunately, LeGoff's study is not alone in examining a small town without setting it in the framework of its regional urban system. The tendency of French historians to isolate single towns or micro-regions as objects of study, with the goal of their research then becoming to reconstruct the 'total history' of that town or region, has meant that they have also not yet devoted much attention to the functioning and evolution of regional systems of cities.

In assembling the studies contained in this book, a conscious effort has been made to redress these imbalances. Most of the six detailed essays are devoted to the sixteenth and seventeenth centuries or cover the entire sweep of the early modern period, rather than confining themselves to the eighteenth century. The volume thereby hopes to contribute to a better understanding of the long-term processes of change within the early modern era. Furthermore, four of the essays are concerned with towns that were provincial administrative capitals, and a fifth with Paris. The centrality of administrative activity in the life of these towns means that an underlying theme uniting most of the essays is that of the implications for urban society of the growth of the state. An attempt has also been made to include new work on the relatively neglected smaller towns, studied not in isolation but as part of regional urban networks. Methodologically, most of these essays are quite classic in their approach, resting upon the quantitative exploitation of such sources as tax rolls and notarial documents. This is a deliberate reflection of the editor's belief that these classic methods of social history remain the most valuable way to determine significant patterns of social change over time. One contribution, however, does break new methodological ground: Claire Dolan's highly innovative application of some of the techniques of micro-history to the urban artisan classes.

In order to make this volume of greatest value, the detailed archival studies are preceded by a long introductory essay summarizing the current state of our knowledge of French cities from 1500 to 1789 and setting forth an interpretive overview of the subject. This essay at once draws upon the findings of the more detailed studies and seeks to provide a context for understanding and appreciating their importance. It also tries to call attention to those aspects of the history of Ancien Régime cities still requiring further research, while offering a provisional synthesis, which future research can either confirm or revise. By combining the synthetic and the monographic, the search for broad patterns and the excitement of new discoveries, the book strives to work on both of scholarship's mutually reinforcing fronts in order to foster new understanding of the history of Ancien Régime cities in a manner that can be appreciated by both specialists and interested readers more generally.

The articles of Robert Descimon, Claire Dolan and René Favier have all been translated from French by the editor.

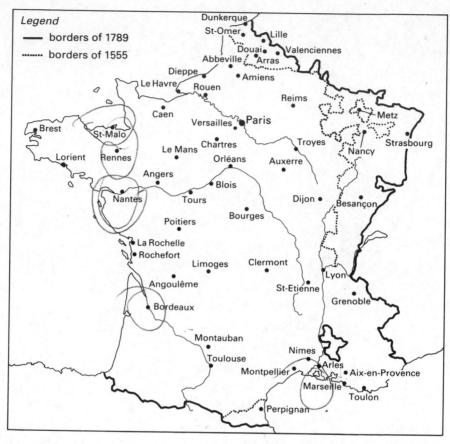

Map 1.1   Ancien Régime France: Major Cities.

1

French cities from the
sixteenth century to the Revolution:
An overview

PHILIP BENEDICT

It is a commonplace that Ancien Régime France was a society dominated by the land. On the eve of the Revolution, only twenty per cent or so of the kingdom's population lived in communities of more than 2,000 inhabitants.[1] The great bulk of the country's wealth derived from agriculture, and, as several essays in this volume will make clear, the hegemony of the rural economy extended over significant aspects of city life as well. But for all of the numerical predominance of the peasantry, and for all of the economic importance of agriculture, France's cities played a role in the society and economy of the Ancien Régime out of all proportion to their place within the total population of the country. As Hugues Neveux has recently observed, the geographic descriptions of France's regions and provinces which developed as a literary genre from the second half of the sixteenth century onward regularly devoted as much as ninety per cent of their space to describing the towns of the regions in question.[2] This reflects more than the simple fact that the most impressive architectural monuments of the kingdom were located disproportionately in the cities. Most of the institutions from law courts to episcopal sees which governed people's lives and souls were found there as well. Much of the country's wealth was, if not generated, then spent and displayed in the towns. And cities possessed exceptional significance in regional and national politics, as events from the Wars of Religion to the Revolution would demonstrate.

Furthermore, it can be argued that between the years 1500 and 1789, the dominance exercised by cities over France's economic and social life increased substantially. This did not result simply from the increase in the percentage of French men and women living in cities. Such an increase did occur – from perhaps 13–15 per cent of the population in 1550 to 20 per cent in 1789[3] – but as these figures suggest, it was only limited. More fundamentally, the growing urban dominance stemmed from broader economic, social, and even cultural changes that transformed France between the sixteenth century and the Revolution: the extension of bourgeois control over the land;

7

the growth of rural industry controlled by urban merchants; the expansion of the state and, with it, of town-based administrative elites; the movement to the cities of a significant fraction of the nobility; and the creation of new patterns of aristocratic culture and comportment that reinforced the equation of urbanity with refinement and distinction. All of these developments bound city and countryside more closely together and meant that, although France's cities were not dramatically larger relative to the kingdom's total population in 1789 than they were in the sixteenth century, their place in the country's economic and social life was very different. Furthermore, precisely because so many changes of greater significance for French society conditioned the evolution of the country's cities, the examination of urban society offers a privileged window into the course of social change in France as a whole during these years.

The first part of the essay will outline some fundamental features of early modern French urban society. Ideally, the portrait sketched here ought to be one of city life as it emerged from the Middle Ages, based exclusively on sixteenth-century sources; this would provide a baseline against which subsequent changes in French urban society might be measured. But because both the extant sources and the secondary literature are so heavily weighted toward the last centuries of the Ancien Régime, it has often been necessary to have recourse to evidence from these centuries in trying to identify basic features that would have characterized urban society in France from 1500 to 1789. The first part of the essay is thus an attempt at once to sketch the network of cities that France inherited from the Middle Ages, to describe the basic features of the urban social, political, cultural and architectural land-scape in the sixteenth century, and to diagnose certain fundamental charac-teristics of city life that would perdure to the very end of the Ancien Régime. The second half of the essay then seeks to identify the major changes transforming urban society during the course of these years.

I

Seen in comparative perspective, France possessed at the beginning of the early modern period a network of cities that placed the kingdom within the middle range of European societies in terms of its degree of urbanization. During the Middle Ages, the kingdom had not developed cities as dense or collectively important as those of the Low Countries, Italy, or the Iberian peninsula, but the percentage of people living in towns was higher than in any other part of the continent.[4] In Paris, France boasted the largest city west of Istanbul. The larger provincial towns were bigger than any city in Germany, Scandinavia, or the British Isles except London.

With population figures scarce for the sixteenth century, the best picture of the hierarchy of cities as it existed toward the beginning of our period is

Table 1.1 'Statement of the Cities of This Kingdom which the King Expects to Aid Him'. (The initial figures refer to the number of footsoldiers that the towns in question were expected to support. Figures in parentheses are estimates of the city's population for the date(s) closest to 1538, where such estimates are available for years between 1500 and 1560.)

3000 men	Paris (1550: 250,000)
1500 men	Rouen (1500: 40,000; 1550: 75,000), Toulouse (1550: 50,000)
1200 men	Lyon (1515: 41,000; 1550: 58,000)
800 men	Orléans (1550: 47,000)
600 men	Bordeaux (1500: 20,000; 1550: 33,000), Troyes (1500: 22,500)
550 men	La Rochelle
400 men	Limoges, Reims (1500: 12,500)
300 men	Dieppe, Poitiers (1550: 15,000), Rennes (1540: 13,000)
200 men	Albi (1517: 8,000; 1555: 7,000), Bourges (1557: 16,000), Chartres (1540: 12,000), Grenoble, Montauban, Nantes (1540: 16,500), Rodez, Sens, Tours (1520: 16,000), Vienne
150 men	Clermont and Montferrand, Dijon (1556: 12,500), Vannes
100 men	Agen (1528: 6,500), Angers (1540: 17,000), Angoulême, Auch, Auxerre (1515: 7,500), Bazas, Beauvais, Blois, Cahors, Castres, Châlons-sur-Marne (1517: 9,000), Chalon-sur-Saône, Condom, Langres, Le Puy, Libourne, Millau, Nevers, Nîmes (1510: 6,000), Périgueux (1500: 8,000), Saintes, Villefranche-en-Rouergue
50 men	Alençon, Aurillac, Autun, Beaune, Bergerac, Châteaudun (1550: 7,500), Dol, Evreux, Issoudun, Laon, Laval, Le Mans, Lisieux, Mâcon, Meaux, Melun, Mende, Montélimar, Moulins, Noyon, Pontaudemer, Quimper, Romans (1509: 4,000; 1557: 8,500), Saint-Brieuc, Saint-Emilion, Saint-Malo (1540: 5,000), Saint-Pol-de-Léon, Sarlat, Senlis, Soissons, Tréguier, Valence (1550: 6,500), Vendôme
30 men	Dinan, Niort (1550: 8,000)
25 men	Aigueperse, Amboise, Avranches, Bayeux, Brive, Caudebec, Château-Thierry, Châtellerault, Chauny, Compiègne, Crépy-en-Valois, Etampes, Eu, Harfleur, Honfleur, Issoire, Loches, Loudun, Louviers, Mirepoix, Montargis, Montivilliers (1550: 2,500), Pamiers, Pontoise, Provins, Saint-Flour, Saint-Jean-d'Angély, Saint-Pourçain, Tulle, Uzès, Vernon
20 men	Brioude, Clamécy, Coutances, Cusset, Fontenay-le-Comte, Gien, Gisors, Maillezais, Montbrison, Pithiviers, Sées, Thiers, Vitry
15 men	Aubenas, Crest
10 men	72 cities (e.g. Avallon, Beaugency, Luçon, Thouars)
5 men	22 cities (e.g. L'Isle-Jourdan, Loriol, Rabastens, Vire)

For the sources of the population estimates provided here, see Appendix (p. 60).

provided by a royal document of 1538 distributing the cost of 20,000 armed footsoldiers among the cities of the kingdom according to their presumed ability to pay.[5] This is recapitulated in Table 1.1, with modern estimates of the size of the cities in question for those for which such estimates exist. The assessments contained in this 'State of the towns of this kingdom which the King expects to aid him to pay for the *solde* of footsoldiers' undoubtedly involved some inequities. Paris, for instance, appears manifestly to have been under-assessed; the crown was always concerned to maintain its loyalty and so spared it wherever possible. The document also omits Amiens, Bayonne, and the towns of Provence, which were not called upon to pay this extraordinary levy. It nonetheless presents an informed contemporary appreciation of the relative size and wealth of the great majority of the kingdom's cities of any importance. As can be seen, the country's cities arranged themselves into a rough pyramid, with Paris standing out as by far the largest, followed by four provincial towns of between 40,000 and 70,000 inhabitants (Rouen, Lyon, Toulouse, and Orléans), perhaps a score of towns of 10,000 to 30,000 inhabitants, another forty or so towns of 5,000 to 10,000 people, and finally the still more numerous small towns, with several thousand inhabitants, if that. The document highlights the importance still retained in this period by such towns as Orléans, Troyes, and Dieppe, which would subsequently decline in relative size.

In all, the 'State of the towns which the king expects to aid him' lists 246 localities, and even this omits many communities that probably deserved to be considered as towns according to contemporary criteria. Just where one crossed the line distinguishing a small town from a large *bourg* or village was uncertain at the time, as it has been ever since for historians who have struggled to specify what defined a city. Size alone is an inadequate criterion, although it is often adopted in statistical studies simply for the sake of facility. Many localities in northern or central France that contemporaries considered towns contained less than two thousand inhabitants, while the more highly clustered settlement patterns typical of Mediterranean France produced numerous communities of the sort Maurice Agulhon has called 'urbanized villages' with more than two thousand inhabitants, which contemporaries nonetheless did not think of as cities. Seventeenth-century dictionaries typically stress the fact of being walled. To this criterion, which the eighteenth century would render obsolete as many cities demolished their walls (this did not prevent dictionaries from continuing to use the definition), historians in addition would usually cite the possession of certain privileges and a wider variety of occupational and social types than neighboring communities as defining marks of urbanity. The royal document of 1538 includes 11 towns in Brittany, yet 16 localities were considered cities for the purpose of sending delegates to the provincial Estates at the time, and the number of localities granted that privilege would rise to 39 by 1667.[6] However the cut-off point of urbanity is defined, small towns were numerous and their importance deserves underscoring. In 1809, the first date for which reliable information exists, 498 of 722 communities of more than two thousand inhabitants housed under five thousand people, together accounting for 30 per cent of the urban population.[7] Such towns are only beginning to attract their share of historians' attention, and a great deal remains to be learned before we will know how fully they partook of the characteristics typical of the larger cities that have attracted the bulk of historical research to date. Culturally and demographically, they may well have had more in common with surrounding

10

rural communities than with larger cities, even if their social structure was characterized by a wider range of occupations and services and more members of the professional or mercantile elites than that of adjacent villages.[8]

If the smallest towns could be hard to distinguish from large villages, the country dweller who passed through the gates into a city of any substance could hardly have escaped the feeling of entering a very different world. The ramparts themselves, more or less well maintained according to how close the city was to a border and how recently war had threatened the region; the houses packed tightly together on streets that typically measured no more than twelve to fifteen feet across; the great variety of people of differing occupations and social status going about their business; the abundance of churches and monasteries, their bells joining that of the city clocktower in a chorus of liturgical and secular messages; the spectacle of the street and the marketplace, with its intermittent parade of hawkers, itinerant acrobats and *montreurs d'ours* – all these would have marked off the urban scene as something quite different from a typical rural parish.

The human density and physical appearance of the cities varied considerably according to local architectural practices. The small half-timbered houses of Rouen rarely housed more than a single family, while seventeen people resided in the average three- or more-storied stone building typical of Grenoble.[9] Little Cavaillon crammed 575 people into each hectare in 1764, while Poitiers, a far larger city, contained just 103 inhabitants per hectare in 1790.[10] But in all towns of any significance, once one passed the gardens and monastic establishments that often provided open space near the walls, the sensation of finding oneself within a closely built world of human artifice must have been overpowering. An unbroken vista of more than a few hundred feet was rare amid the winding streets, especially in the sixteenth century when, as yet, few towns had constructed the large squares, promenades, or *places royales* that would later embellish French cities. Cemeteries and charnel houses provided some of the largest open spaces and were an important site for informal assembly and socializing, as well as a favored site of public preaching. The imposing profile of the numerous churches and religious establishments offered an irregular interruption to the succession of houses and their ground-floor shops; a few larger secular buildings or private *hôtels* might also stand out for their splendor. In many towns, the massive profile of a fortified chateau also loomed from a high point in the city, casting its shadow of royal or seigneurial authority over the town.

Each town's distinctive character was defined not only by its built environment and topography, but also by the specific mixture of occupational groups which its socio-economic character generated. 'The cities unquestionably have their attractions in our France,' wrote the Breton author Noël du Fail in 1547, 'but they are only convenient for men of the law, merchants and artisans, and it can be boldly stated that when one sees a nobleman in town,

11

he is there because he is a plaintiff or defendant, is paying off some debt or borrowing money at enormous interest, or is engaged in debauchery.'[11] His observation aptly described the northern and central parts of the kingdom during his lifetime, but a stronger tradition of noble residence in towns existed in the Midi.[12] Where a city contained a significant number of administrative tribunals, *gens de loi* pullulated. River or seaports naturally generated great numbers of merchants, boatmen, and barrelcoopers. If artisans and shopkeepers formed the largest and most variegated element of most cities' population, up to a third or more of these might cluster in a few trades in towns dominated by a single major industry, as in eighteenth-century Nîmes, where 43 per cent of the active population was linked in some way to the production of silk, while in less industrially specialized towns these individuals distributed themselves more evenly among a variety of trades.[13] One noteworthy characteristic of many French cities, especially those located in the Midi or in wine-growing regions farther north, was the sizeable fraction of the population engaged in agriculture. *Laboureurs*, *vignerons*, market-gardeners and millers accounted for 15 to 20 per cent of the heads of households of cities as large as Montpellier, Dijon, and Clermont in the sixteenth and seventeenth centuries; the figure exceeded 50 per cent in the small towns of southern Dauphiné and Provence.[14] Servants were another large group whose ranks were distributed very unevenly among towns. Good information about them only becomes abundant from the late seventeenth century onward, when capitation rolls reveal them to have been particularly abundant in aristocratic–administrative towns such as Aix-en-Provence or Toulouse, where 42 per cent of all families had at least one servant and domestics formed 10 per cent of the total urban population, as opposed to 4 per cent of the population of commercial Marseille.[15]

Last of all, clergymen abounded within city life. Nearly 900 clerics lived in sixteenth-century Rouen, and the roughly 1.5 per cent of the total population that they formed was almost certainly significantly exceeded in those less commercially and industrially dynamic cities that were much more exclusively cathedral towns. In the eighteenth century, after the great increase in the size of the regular clergy occasioned by the Counter-Reformation, the clergy formed 2.8 per cent of Rouen's population, 4.8 per cent of Chalon-sur-Saône's, and 6 per cent of that of Gray, Dole, and Blois.[16] With its numerous divisions of status and wealth, running from episcopal sees and the most exclusive religious houses, through the cathedral chapters, parish livings, and mendicant orders, down to the clerical proletariat of chaplains and mass priests, this first estate paralleled secular society in its complex hierarchy. If bishops and the members of the most prestigious monastic houses typically came from the high aristocracy, the cathedral chapters and collegiate churches offered their share of comfortable livings for the sons of the urban elites.[17] The social origins of those clerics whose activities placed them in closest contact with the urban population, the parish priests and members of the mendicant orders, remain poorly explored, but some scant evidence suggests that both of these groups were composed of individuals of middling origins who came predominantly from outside the city in which they exercised their ministry, a situation which might have made them mistrusted as outsiders but could also, in placing them beyond local connections and rivalries, have facilitated their ability to serve as disinterested moral authorities and agents of reconciliation within the urban community.[18] The sociology of these groups and their relations with the urban community at large deserve considerably more attention than they have received to date.

Although residential segregation was far less marked than it would become in the industrial city, the richer inhabitants of smaller cities typically clustered in the center of town and the poor around the periphery, while in the larger cities the patterns of social geography could become quite complex. Robert Descimon's essay reveals for the first time the sixteenth-century physiognomy of the largest and most complex city of all, Paris. The pattern he finds of multiple nodes of wealth centered on the chief commercial streets and quarters, around the loci of royal power, and in fashionable residential neighborhoods in certain fringes of the city also characterized, in a somewhat simpler fashion, Lyon and Rouen.[19] Similarly, the tendency for certain artisan groups to cluster in clearly defined parts of town, for others to distribute themselves evenly across the city, and for still others to display a degree of dispersion yet still to be more numerous in wealthier quarters than in poor, also appears to have been more generally characteristic of larger French cities.[20] The greater density of doctors, notaries and luxury craftsmen in better neighborhoods suggests a link between such trades and the presence of a significant elite element that also led these occupations to be particularly abundant in cities where that presence was strong.[21]

A fundamental characteristic of early modern cities was the considerable turnover of their population from year to year and generation to generation. A sixteenth-century town could be likened to an accordion, expanding when harvest failures or warfare led inhabitants from the surrounding countryside to seek refuge or charity behind city walls, shrinking when plagues sent the rich fleeing to the safety of their country estates or prolonged economic difficulties provoked the emigration of skilled artisans. Beyond these short-term fluctuations, a constant stream of migration steadily replenished the ranks of the permanently resident population. Forty-three per cent of the heads of households listed on Vannes' tax rolls in the eighteenth century disappear from the records within five years.[22] Marriage records consistently show that between a third and a half of the residents of any given city entering into wedlock were born outside the town.[23]

The high percentage of immigrants living in towns stemmed in part from the basic demographic characteristic of early modern cities, their inability to reproduce themselves in this era of high mortality. In an important article published in 1978, the late Allan Sharlin challenged the long-hallowed truism that pre-modern European cities devoured their population, claiming that the negative 'natural balance' evident in most cities' population statistics – that is, the excess of recorded deaths over births – stemmed uniquely from the deaths within these cities of temporary migrants. If one excluded these individuals from consideration, Sharlin claimed, the permanently resident urban population demonstrated an excess of births over deaths.[24] Sharlin's argument in fact subtly altered the terms of the position he claimed to be attacking, for among the group he defined as permanently resident were many individuals born outside the cities in question and who were thus immigrants. His article nonetheless had the merit of underscoring that only a close examination of the reproduction rates of the local-born fraction of an urban population could determine with certitude whether or not cities could reproduce themselves, and it provoked several scholars who already had ambitious demographic studies of urban populations well under way to look directly at the question of urban reproduction rates. With the publication of the recent works of Alfred Perrenoud on Geneva and Jean-Pierre Bardet on Rouen, more is now known about the urban demography of early modern France and nearby francophone Switzerland than about any other region in Europe, and it is clear that the traditional wisdom was in fact well founded. At no period between 1625 and 1810 did native Genevan families produce enough children so that, given the mortality rates of the era and the fraction of the population that would never marry, two or more children of each couple might be expected to survive until the average age of marriage and in fact marry.[25] Had all emigration been prevented by law, the city's population would have inexorably declined at the rate of 0.35 per cent per year in the seventeenth century and 0.75 per cent in the contraceptive eighteenth century. This, it turns out, was the case even though, during certain periods within these two centuries, more births than deaths were recorded in the city.[26] In other words, that traditional measure of a city's ability to reproduce itself, the 'natural balance' of its population, may in fact overestimate cities' demographic vitality, not understate it; in any case, the measure is clearly unreliable and misleading. Rouen's native population was even less able to reproduce itself in the eighteenth century than Geneva's. In the absence of migration into or out of the city, Bardet has estimated, this city's 70,000 inhabitants would have declined to 45,000 within fifty years and to 28,000 within a century.[27]

Above all else, the inability of these cities' populations to maintain themselves stemmed from their high rates of infant mortality, caused by both the notorious insalubrity of town life and the widespread habit, prevalent among town dwellers of all classes, of placing infants in the care of rural wet nurses.[28] Bardet was only able to calculate figures for child mortality in Rouen for the second half of the eighteenth century. At that period, roughly one-third of all children died before their first birthday, with the risk of death being 50 per cent higher among babies placed in the care of wet nurses than among those cared for at home. Only 45 out of 100 children lived to the age of fifteen. In Geneva, where mortality would decline between the seventeenth and eighteenth centuries, figures for the years 1625–84 were comparable. In both cities, death came far more frequently to the poor than to the rich. Mean life expectancy at birth in the seventeenth century was 35.9 years for a baby born to the Genevan upper crust, just 18.3 for a child of a semi-skilled or unskilled worker.[29] Urban demographic patterns differed from those characteristic of the countryside in other manners as well. Town dwellers, at least in the larger cities, also married later than their rural conterparts.[30] Urban populations were often characterized by a significant imbalance between the sexes, especially in those towns where the textile or needle trades offered significant employment opportunities for women, and a higher percentage of women never married in cities than in the countryside.[31] Those urban women who did marry then bore children with greater frequency than their rural counterparts, again a consequence of the widespread recourse to wet nursing, although this would change once conscious family limitation began to spread among the urban population, as it did from the later seventeenth century onward.[32]

Although much of the immigration into cities was needed to fill the ranks of populations that could not reproduce themselves, much also served to replace city dwellers who had left for other communities, for migration from city to city or back and forth between city and countryside was widespread. Emigration from a community is always one of the most difficult phenomena to measure, for individuals who leave a locality disappear from its records and must be tracked down through the records of all of the localities to which they might have moved. Once again, however, recent advances in urban demography have provided us with at least a rough idea of the extent of emigration, for the technique of family reconstitution reveals the number of couples who married in a city and began to bear children there, only to disappear from its records before the death of either spouse. Some 26 per cent of all families left Rouen after establishing a settled residence there. This out-migration was higher among merchants and legal officials than among artisans or unskilled workers. It was also considerably more common in the difficult seventeenth century than in the relatively peaceful and prosperous eighteenth century, and it was nearly twice as common among families headed by men born outside Rouen as among those headed by natives, suggesting that people who had already left their birthplace once were particularly likely to contemplate further migration in search of opportunity.[33] Among skilled workers, even national boundaries were no barrier to movement when times grew hard in one locality or opportunity called. As the Wars of Religion were drawing to a close, a *mémoire* from Lyon explained the depopulation perceptible in that city:

The workers have been obliged to leave the aforesaid city for lack of employment. Those of the silkweaver's art have gone partly to Avignon and partly to Genoa; the printers are all in Geneva; the hatmakers and other workers in wool, thread, pelts and other merchandise leave for the duchy of Milan and Piedmont to exercise their craft.[34]

For certain groups, migration was virtually a way of life, as for the journeymen of certain trades, who moved from town to town in accordance with the availability of work, or the seasonally migrant workers from the uplands of the Massif Central and Alps, who regularly descended into the cities in the fall to find employment as chimney-sweeps, masons, or water-carriers, before returning home in the spring to work their minuscule plots of land, significantly richer, or at least less poor, than their sedentary counterparts of nearby regions without such traditions of seasonal migration.[35]

Although a high degree of turnover characterized urban populations, it should not be thought that cities were consequently characterized by social disorganization and personal anonymity. Clear patterns governed much of the mobility into and out of cities. Admittedly, the powerful and even oppressive family structures and, for the poorer half of the population, the precariousness of existence often produced what might be termed 'rupture migration' – people forced by catastrophe or simply provoked by family quarrels to leave home and seek sustenance and a new life in a distant city.[36] Recent studies of migration have nonetheless revealed how well established and durable were the routes leading most people to cities. Merchants followed commercial connections; servants in aristocratic households often came from villages in which the family possessed a fief; journeymen learned of employment opportunities in new towns through an informal communications network centering in the boarding houses in which they stayed or the taverns in which they drank.[37] Above all, as Claire Dolan's contribution to this volume shows, kinsmen or neighbors had usually travelled the same route before. Many immigrants thus did not arrive as total strangers in their new towns. They could turn to relatives, fellow villagers, or family business connections for help in inserting themselves in their new communities.

A series of formal and informal institutions also enabled new arrivals to construct a network of social relationships once settled in a city. One was the neighborhood, whose significance has been underscored by several recent studies. The mobility of many elements within the urban population should not obscure the substantial degree of stability that existed as well. Urban leases typically ran for three, six, or nine years at a stretch. They could, of course, be renewed, and the average duration for which a house in Rouen was rented by a single family was fourteen years.[38] Neighborhoods thus had many stable residents, and these people knew a great deal about one another, for work, play, and conflict all regularly spilled out of cramped shops and houses into the street. Furthermore, residential proximity entailed obligations of mutual assistance, obligations that are attested to by numerous court cases which show town dwellers interceding in quarrels to protect their neighbors 'as a good neighbor should'.[39] Perhaps the most striking indication that individual *quartiers* could become urban villages is the fact that in sixteenth-century Lyon charivaris were often organized when a man took a wife from another quarter of the city and brought her home, just as was done in the countryside when somebody married outside the village.[40]

The last centuries of the Middle Ages had also witnessed the vigorous growth of more formal institutions which provided town dwellers with flexible yet powerful social bonds. Occupational solidarity was one source of these. Here, the enormous variety of situations makes generalization extremely difficult. The most characteristic expression of Ancien Régime occupational solidarity was, of course, the guild. For those artisans and shopkeepers who were members, guilds could be a potent instrument for the defense of their interests and a focus of strong loyalty. But guilds were far from ubiquitous throughout France, especially in the sixteenth century. Although *corporations de métiers* are frequently seen as quintessentially medieval institutions, the first great wave of royal letters patent granting approval for guild statutes only came in the fifteenth and early sixteenth centuries. Even though the number of guilds continued to expand steadily throughout the subsequent centuries, largely with the encouragement of the monarchy, which saw in them a source of fiscal exploitation (guildsmen paid a fee to the crown on being received as masters) as well as economic quality control, guilds never became numerous in certain provinces, such as Provence.[41] Furthermore, by the sixteenth century, certain guilds had already become closed castes in which the masters utilized their control of guild institutions to protect their particular interests, an extreme example being the Paris butcher's guild, which did not admit to mastership any individual who was not himself the son of a master and maintained so strict a monopoly over the stalls in the Paris *boucheries* that many members of the guilds could make a fine living simply renting these stalls to so-called 'étaliers' who did the actual job of butchering.[42] In other trades, only a relatively small fraction of all apprentices ever acceded to the status of guild master; most remained journeymen all their lives. By the sixteenth century, the journeymen of certain of these trades had organized to defend their interests, and the secret journeymen's brotherhoods known as *compagnonnages* had begun their long underground history.[43] Meanwhile, unskilled workers at the lower end of the social spectrum and merchants towards the top were seldom organized into formal occupational associations. The lawyers and subaltern court personnel of many towns, on the other hand, were grouped into the *basoche*, part guild and part festive association, while the various corporate judicial bodies formed a powerful force of loyalty for their members. For many, although not all, male town dwellers, social identity was intimately bound up with membership in a guild, corporation, or journeymen's association.

17

Religious confraternities formed another important set of formal institutions that had emerged toward the close of the Middle Ages. Some confraternities were linked to specific occupations and complemented or even acted in lieu of the occupation's guilds. Others drew members from a variety of trades. Whatever their social composition, the dominant concern of the sorts of confraternities that were most numerous around 1500 appears to have been to create a spirit of fraternity and mutual charity among their members through the performance of shared religious duties, not infrequently followed with banquets or dances, and through the enforcement of mutual obligations. When a member of the association of Notre Dame la Joyeuse of Limoges fell sick, for instance, his fellow *confrères* – there were 126 of them in 1525 – were all expected to provide him with 2 sous, 6 deniers each to help support his family. When a member of the group died, they were expected to attend the funeral bearing lighted candles, and the confraternity commissioned a special mass for the departed's soul.[44] Bordeaux contained about sixty such confraternities around 1500; Vienne had thirty.[45]

Closely related in character to these confraternities were a variety of other associations which at once promoted fellowship among their members, contributed to the festive calendar of the city and played a role in defending the city and maintaining order. The privileged militia units found in many towns to assist in their defense not only met regularly to drill, but also required that their members attend mass collectively and refrain from quarrelling with one another. These associations, or special 'compagnies de Papegaut', also staged annual shooting contests in many cities, where amid great pageantry the first person to hit a wooden parakeet (*papegaut*) atop a tall pole was crowned king and awarded special privileges for a year, usually the right to import a certain amount of wine tax-free.[46] In a different way, the associations of young men found bedecked with a variety of names in many cities (youth abbeys, kingdoms of Maugouvert, Mère Folle and her infantry in Dijon, Conards in Rouen) performed similar functions. Often supported by subsidies granted them by the municipal government, these associations staged charivaris or, more prosaically, levied fines against those who offended the moral order of the community, while also playing a central role in the festive life of the city, especially at carnival time. The feast of Corpus Christi, with its lavish procession of the consecrated host through the tapestry-bedecked streets of the city, followed by neighborhood banquets in the towns of Champagne, raised confraternal rituals of fellowship to the level of the entire city. Out of the flowering of these institutions grew those theatrical forms which, although occasionally dated vaguely as being simply 'medieval' in character, in fact reached their peak of popularity in the years between approximately 1430 and 1540: the *sottie*, farces staged by the youth abbeys or *basoche* subjecting to carnivalesque mockery those members of the different estates of society who failed to live up to the ideals appropriate to their station, and the mystery play, a more solemn enactment of scenes drawn from biblical history and the lives of the saints, often subsidized by the city government and staged as a result of a communal vow.[47]

A complex web of associational, residential, occupational, and family solidarities thus bound town dwellers together, but the force of each of these ties was naturally not equally strong for every resident of a given city. On the contrary, Claire Dolan's highly original contribution to this book shows how much their strength might vary from occupation to occupation among the artisans of a single city. In revealing the variety of life courses and social experiences found among Aix's *gens de métier*, her article also underscores a fundamental point about urban society that the work of Maurice Garden, Robert Darnton, Michael Sonenscher and others has already begun to point toward. This is that different trades within urban society varied significantly from one another in such matters as their patterns of labor recruitment, their ratio of journeymen to masters and consequently the possibility for journeymen to accede to the status of master, their relations between masters and journeymen, and their specific argot and traditions.[48] The only fully adequate sociology of urban society must consequently be a micro-sociology sensitive to these variations. Dolan's article offers new tools for constructing such a micro-sociology and marks an important step toward its elaboration. When we have fully constructed a picture of urban society finely grained enough to capture these differences between trades, we will not only know a great deal more about the lives of town dwellers of all ranks and occupations; we may also be able better to explain certain still partially unresolved issues of early modern French history, such as why it was that the members of certain trades were far more attracted to the cause of the Reformation than others.

Since institutions such as the civic militia or youth abbeys grouped residents together to contribute to the defense and good order of the community, they may also be placed among the formal institutions of political authority. By the beginning of the sixteenth century, most cities of any significance had obtained a municipal charter and the right to exercise a degree of self-government, which they generally exercised through councils that went under a variety of names – *échevinage* in northern France, *consulat* throughout much of the Midi, *jurade* in the Southwest, *capitoulat* in Toulouse, etc. The autonomy and power of these bodies was often limited, however. Not only did all power in a monarchical system ultimately stem from royal grant; rival judicial and administrative bodies, either seigneurial or royal, also vied for power.

As several scholars have recently stressed, it is misleading to think of sixteenth-century municipal governments as the direct heirs of medieval communes, exercising a political independence that they had heroically wrested away from a local overlord, be he bishop or seigneur. Perhaps no more than half of the larger medieval French towns had ever witnessed the establishment of a commune, whose authority often only extended to a fraction of the city. Furthermore, little direct continuity existed in most towns

19

between the institutions of self-government established during the era of the communes and those that prevailed at the end of the Middle Ages. The latter, found in many more cities than had ever established communes, were typically royal concessions.[49] Rights of municipal government were still being extended in the late fifteenth and early sixteenth century – to Angers in 1475, for instance, as Louis XI sought to gain the loyalty of this great stronghold within what had formerly been an independent apanage, or to Etampes in 1514, in return for a cash payment, or to Langres on several occasions in the sixteenth century in order to encourage the commitment of this border town's inhabitants to its defense and the upkeep of its walls.[50] The motivations that inspired these grants suggest the sources of municipal political power at the close of the Middle Ages. The cities' wealth and considerable strategic value impelled the crown to grant them a degree of self-government, both to maintain a loyalty which the crown lacked the military force to compel and to ensure more effective compliance with the king's will than could otherwise be obtained. The privileges of which cities were so proud nonetheless remained royal grants, and city councillors saw their own authority as a reflection of the king's.[51]

The extent of urban self-government varied a great deal from town to town and was typically a function both of the concessions the city had been able to obtain and the strength of rival governing institutions located within it. Municipal councils were just one institution among several engaged in an ongoing contest to define each one's sphere of influence. In Langres, the power of the municipal council never extended significantly beyond overseeing the city's defense and its fortifications. The various duties classified by contemporaries under the general rubric of 'la police' – public health, the regulation of commerce and the marketplaces, provisioning, etc. – remained primarily within the seigneurial jurisdiction of the city's bishop, a duke and peer of the realm. When a *bailliage* court was established in Langres in 1561, its officials also sought to claim a degree of influence over police matters. The municipal council of Langres was weaker than most, but the example nonetheless demonstrates the division of political authority among seigneurial officials, the officers of the local *bailliage* or *sénéchausée* court, and the municipal council typical of most cities – a division that became even more complicated and fraught with contention in those cities that also housed provincial parlements or were home to a resident governor or lieutenant-general, who, as the king's chief military representative in the localities, also played an important role in city politics. Where the municipal authorities were more powerful than those of Langres, they often retained considerable authority over the broad variety of police matters, occasionally possessed the right to judge specified categories of crimes, and controlled the disbursement of revenues obtained from duties on goods entering and leaving the city, although this fiscal autonomy had its limits because the granting of these *octrois* generally remained a royal prerogative. Along with such powers went privileges, ranging from exemption from the chief direct royal tax, the *taille* (frequent 'free gifts' and *soldes pour les gens de guerre* nonetheless ensured that cities by no means escaped royal taxation altogether), to, most glorious of all, the right of having election to the municipal council confer nobility on those so chosen. Not surprisingly, municipal autonomy tended to be particularly strong in regions that had been hotly contested during the Hundred Years' War and where the crown had consequently been obliged to reward loyalty generously. Eight of the sixteen cities in which election to the municipal council conferred the privilege of *noblesse de cloche* were located in the Southwest.

In their lush profusion of local variants, the forms taken by municipal governments offer a caricature of that fundamental characteristic of the Ancien Régime, the absence of uniform institutions. Most commonly, an inner council of officials, often led by a mayor, handled routine administrative business; a larger council would assemble to decide more important issues; while for matters of truly exceptional import, an 'assemblée générale' of the city might be convened, although the variations on these basic themes were endless. Only in some small towns were the general assemblies truly general; most commonly, participation was limited to an ill-defined group of notables who seem generally to have attained the prestige necessary to participate through some combination of wealth, occupational status, age, length of time resident in the city, and proper moral behavior.[52] The members of the more restricted bodies were chosen through election, co-optation, or some combination of the two. In certain cities, especially in the southeast, seats within the various governmental councils were allotted to different groups by formula. Thus, one *consul* of Romans was always to come from within the ranks of the *laboureurs*, one from the city's artisans, one from its merchants, and one from either the nobility, the medical or legal professions, or the bourgeoisie *vivant de ses rentes*. In Chartres, the lieutenant-general of the *bailliage* was perpetual mayor, while two seats in the fourteen-member council were reserved for the king's advocates of the city's royal courts and another two for elected delegates of the cathedral chapter, an indication of how both royal and ecclesiastical authorities could be integrated into the structure of municipal government. Even in towns such as Romans where places were reserved for representatives of the artisans and *laboureurs*, however, the *consuls* from these groups came from their wealthiest members.[53] Most city governments were more oligarchic yet. Wealthy merchants and *gens de loi* dominated the great majority of city councils, with the precise proportions of each of these two large groups varying according to the character of the city in question; men of the law dominated the city councils of Poitiers and Paris during the sixteenth century, while merchants and bourgeois filled the majority of seats in commercial Lyon.[54] The tendency to oligarchy was not accepted everywhere without opposition. Where those in power abused their authority too flagrantly, agitation could develop in favor of more broadly inclusive participation in city government, as in Agen in 1514 or La Rochelle in the 1520s.[55]

Open conflict such as that found in these cities over municipal institutional arrangements appears to have been relatively rare – certainly far more rare than in the cities of the Holy Roman Empire during this era – but it must be confessed that few aspects of the Ancien Régime city are as poorly understood as the dynamics of local politics. As Robert Schneider shows, a clearly formulated ideal of civic virtue existed in sixteenth-century cities, stressing that public office required those entrusted with a charge to set aside their personal interests in order to serve the *res publica*.[56] How frequently those in power lived up to this ideal is much harder to say – for one reason because the records of many municipal governments provide no tally of the votes cast for different candidates for office and no indication of the positions taken by individual councillors on specific issues, thereby obscuring whatever factional or party divisions might have existed. The fact that, with very few exceptions, Rouen's *conseillers-échevins* ascended steadily upward to their position through a regular sequence of lesser offices suggests that election to municipal office was not generally subject to violent swings of political opinion or partisan conflict, but instead involved the selection of men widely recognized to have the qualities requisite for office. But the more abundant administrative correspondence of the seventeenth century speaks recurringly of leading families entering into 'cabals and intrigues' in order to gain access to municipal office and then, once in power, using it for personal advantage.[57] Other documents, too, occasionally lift the veil of obscurity cast over the dynamics of local political life by uncommunicative records. Marmande's consular elections in the 1660s, we know from a letter from the city's curé to the bishop, were the occasion for both litigation and violence of such intensity that certain inhabitants abstained from communion for years rather than participating alongside their enemies, 'even though all the preachers informed about this have publicly proclaimed the indispensable law of charity to one's neighbor'.[58] The list of grievances drawn up in 1514 by Agen's insurgents – who identified themselves as 'la commune' – accused those who monopolized consular positions of a series of acts of malfeasance ranging from using civic funds for their own profit to taking women from the town's prisons 'to know them carnally'.[59]

On occasion, clear divisions of economic interest led to urban political conflict. Between 1598 and 1612, Marseille found itself divided over whether or not the city ought to repay in full the large debts contracted during the last phase of the League. Those who had advanced money to the city, notably the wealthier merchants, were pitted against those who stood to lose by having to repay the debts, primarily landholders and smaller artisan producers. The conflict not only dominated municipal elections, but also provoked a number of violent demonstrations before the party of repayment finally won the day thanks to the intervention of the provincial governor, who temporarily suspended free municipal elections.[60] Much more research capable of penetrating the facade of unanimity so often conveyed by the local records is needed before we can identify whether such conflicts were the norm of local politics or were relatively infrequent interruptions of a responsible, broad-based oligarchic consensus. How and how consistently municipal politics might have served the economic interests of specific groups within cities, and the possible influence of regional or national clientage networks on city decision-making, especially in times of national political crisis, also deserve detailed exploration.[61]

If the political forces that shaped the actions of municipal government and the degree of probity city fathers displayed in carrying out their administrative responsibilities remain largely opaque, the concerns with which they had to deal and the measures they took in response are reflected clearly enough in the impressive series of municipal deliberations which survive in many municipal archives. Between 1553 and 1556, Rouen's *conseillers-échevins* – among other actions – reiterated a requirement that the city's innkeepers provide the *bailli* with lists of those staying in their establishments every two days, sought to obtain more advantageous terms for the city's merchants trafficking in pastel in response to a royal measure granting a special tax exemption to Toulouse's pastel merchants, ordered the city's dyers and cloth finishers to be sure that all cloth hung out to dry across the town's streets be placed high enough so that a man on horseback could pass underneath it, ordered repairs on the bridge across the Seine and an inspection of the gaps in the city's walls, and, after deliberations provoked by the scarcity of 'bon vin vieil' said to be necessary for the health of the well-to-do, barred the city's artisans and laborers from drinking in the city's taverns and cabarets, which were supposed to be reserved for non-residents passing through the city. During the same years, after calling in the *conseillers-échevins* for a special assembly in the Palais de Justice, the parlement issued an extended *arrêt* that sought to improve public safety by reorganizing the night watch, requiring the owners of every six houses to provide a lantern to hang over the street in front of their doors, and forbidding gambling in public.[62] As can be seen, the governing authorities of a larger city sought to monitor closely what happened in town, to ensure at least a rudimentary level of sanitation and public safety, to supervise the production and sale of basic commodities, and to voice local interests to the crown. Three recurring concerns were the subject of particularly anxious and protracted deliberations whenever events brought them to the fore: ensuring an adequate supply of grain in times of dearth, which might require measures ranging from decrees that all city dwellers with private reserves of grain put them on sale immediately to subsidizing the importation of wheat from abroad; providing relief for the poor, usually done prior to the establishment during the sixteenth century of regular Bureaux des Pauvres through contributions to the city's charity hospitals, public works projects and the distribution of subsidized bread; and combatting the recurring visitations of the plague, against which the battery of measures ranged from communal vows and mandated prayer to attempts to isolate the sick and disinfect their houses to, in the cities of the Midi, requirements that those entering the city present certificates testifying that the locality from which they were coming was not infected.[63]

II

Although certain of the institutions and social patterns characteristic of France's cities endured throughout the early modern centuries, the history of the kingdom's towns was no *histoire immobile*. Changes in the country's economy, governmental structure, and culture all transformed its cities and their role within the larger society. The altered character of the cities may in turn have exercised its influence in transforming the larger society.

An initial context for understanding these changes is provided by evidence about the demographic evolution of different cities. Table 1.2 assembles population figures for those towns for which reliable information is available over a span of at least two of the three centuries in question here. This information provides a demographic framework on which to hang a broader

Table 1.2 Urban Population Trends, 1500–1790. (Figures in parentheses are those for cities acquired by the king of France over the course of this period for dates prior to their attachment to the kingdom. Square brackets are utilized in cases of new towns and denote the period prior to their foundation.)

1. Towns of 10,000 or more inhabitants in the 16th century and major new towns of later vintage

	c. 1500	c. 1550	c. 1600	c. 1650	c. 1700	c. 1750	c. 1790
Paris		250,000	250,000	450,000	510,000	570,000	660,000
Versailles	[			]	28,500		51,000
Rouen	40,000	75,000	60,000	82,000	64,000	67,500	73,000
Lyon	37,500	58,000	32,500	67,500	97,000	120,000	146,000
Toulouse		50,000			43,000	48,000	53,000
Orléans		47,000	37,500	52,500	50,000		48,500
Troyes	23,500		25,000		19,500	22,500	28,000
Bordeaux	20,000	33,000	35,000	40,000	45,000	60,000	111,000
Marseille[1]		30,000	45,000	65,000	75,000	88,000	110,000
Lille	(17,500)	(40,000)	(32,000)	(45,000)	57,500	61,000	62,500
Amiens		28,000			35,000		44,000
Strasbourg		(22,000)	(23,000)	(19,000)	26,500		50,000
Tours	16,000				32,000	22,000	22,000
Nantes	(14,000)	17,000	25,000	35,000	42,500		80,000
Rennes	(13,000)	13,000	17,500	36,000	45,000		35,000
Angers	12,500	17,500	25,000	30,000	27,000	25,500	32,000
Reims	12,500		22,500	35,000	31,000		32,000

	c. 1500	c. 1550	c. 1600	c. 1650	c. 1700	c. 1750	c. 1790
La Rochelle			20,000	17,500	21,500	19,000	21,500
Metz			19,000		22,000	32,000	36,500
Montauban			17,000	17,000	17,000		28,500
Blois			16,500	18,000	14,500		13,500
Bourges		16,000	14,000		17,000		18,500
Poitiers		15,000	18,000	23,500	20,000	18,000	21,500
Aix-en-Provence		15,000			28,500	26,500	28,500
Perpignan		(13,000)	(12,500)	(11,500)	17,000		13,000
Chartres		12,500	12,500	14,000	14,000	13,000	13,000
Dijon		12,500	14,000	18,500	21,500	19,000	22,000
Montpellier		12,500	15,500		22,500		32,000
Besançon	(8,000)		(11,000)	(11,000)	15,000		32,000
Auxerre	7,500		10,500		10,000		10,500
Nîmes	6,000		13,000	14,000	17,000	28,500	50,000
St-Omer			(12,000)	(13,000)	14,000		20,000
St-Malo	(3,000)	5,500	10,500	16,000	23,500	19,000	18,000
Grenoble		6,000	10,000	14,000	20,500		24,000
Toulon			10,000	19,000	35,000	17,000	26,000
Rochefort	[				] 15,500		20,500
Lorient	[				] 4,000		16,000

2. Smaller towns

	c. 1500	c. 1550	c. 1600	c. 1650	c. 1700	c. 1750	c. 1790
Albi	6,000	7,000			7,500		9,000
Alençon			8,500	11,000	11,000		13,500
Auch			4,000	3,500	4,500		8,500
Bayonne			9,000	11,000	12,000		13,000
Bourg-St-Andéol			3,000	2,500	2,500	3,000	4,500
Brest				1,000	15,000		30,000
Châlons-sur-Marne	9,000				12,500		12,000
Châteaudun		7,500	8,000	7,500	6,000		6,000
Cherbourg		3,000	4,500	3,000	4,000	6,000	10,000
Clermont-l'Hérault			4,500		4,500		5,000
Corbeil			2,500	2,500	2,500		3,500
Coulommiers		5,500	4,500	4,000	3,000		3,000
Coutances			5,000	6,000	6,000		8,000
Dreux		7,500	5,500	5,500	5,500		6,000
Joigny		5,500	5,000	5,500	4,500		5,000
Le Havre	[	]	3,000		6,000	14,000	18,000
Lisieux			9,000	9,000	9,000	9,000	11,000
Mayenne			3,000	5,000	6,000		7,000
Meulan			1,500	1,500	1,000	1,500	2,000
Morlaix		5,500	7,500	10,000	10,000		10,000
Niort		8,000	8,000	12,000	12,000		17,000
Privas			2,500	1,000	2,000	2,000	2,500
Roanne			3,000	5,000	6,000		7,000
Romans	4,000	8,000			7,500		9,000
St-Denis			3,000	5,000	4,000		4,000
Saumur			9,500		10,000	10,000	11,000
Tarbes			2,500	2,500	2,500		6,500
Valence		6,500			7,500		9,500

[1]Including surrounding *terroir*.
For sources for population estimates, see Appendix, p. 60.

analysis of changing rates of urbanization and the processes that stimulated or retarded the growth of cities. For the purposes of this analysis, it makes sense to divide the centuries between 1500 and 1789 into the three periods defined by the course of France's broader economic and demographic history: the era of buoyant nationwide growth that ran from the late fifteenth century to the outbreak of the Wars of Religion in 1562; the subsequent century and a half of intermittent domestic strife and costly international warfare lasting to the death of Louis XIV; and finally the renewed demographic and economic upturn of the eighteenth century.

We are particularly poorly informed about the first of these periods. If this was an era of general demographic and economic expansion, Table 1.2 suggests that it was an era of expansion for most cities as well. But the sample of cities for which population evidence is available is too small and our knowledge of the general movement of the kingdom's population is too uncertain to permit any estimate of how the growth of the kingdom's cities compared to that of the total population.

Certain socio-economic changes, many of them trends that would become still more marked in subsequent centuries, can be discerned in this period. The general expansion of commerce stimulated the emergence of increasingly wealthy merchants in many towns, most spectacularly Lyon, which emerged as a major European banking and commercial center – although Frederick Irvine's study of Montpellier in this volume reminds us that other cities found themselves bypassed by changing trade routes.[64] In those towns that housed a parlement, the first beginnings can also be discerned in the expansion in the number of royal offices that would become so dramatic after 1560, with Bordeaux's court for instance growing from 25 to 62 members between 1515 and 1543; little expansion, however, occurred on the level of *bailliage* and *sénéchaussée* courts, where a growing number of increasingly educated lawyers fought over a volume of business that grew less rapidly, and sought solace for the relative closure of opportunity in the cultivation of literary pursuits or the quest for municipal office.[65] James Farr's pioneering survey in this volume of one town's social structure during three centuries shows the consequences of these developments: the wealth of Dijon's merchants and legists came to overshadow that of the rest of the population.[66] Such changes could also have political ramifications. Artisans were formally excluded from sitting on the municipal councils of Nevers in 1512 and of Sens in 1530.[67]

At the other end of the social spectrum, a serious increase in the incidence of poverty appears to have affected many cities, as population growth outstripped the rural economy's capacity to provide employment from the 1520s onward, and the cities increasingly found themselves overrun by beggary. Faced with growing poverty, the largest of them began to organize institutionalized forms of public charity.[68] If these developments bespeak a growing tendency towards the polarization of wealth, the fate of the great mass of urban artisans of middling wealth is far less clear. In Dijon and Rouen, the first signs of a second trend that was to intensify in subsequent centuries can be seen: the emigration of textile production to the surrounding countryside. On the other hand, Amiens' textile industry experienced healthy growth.[69] Real wages unquestionably declined in the face of inflation, but recent work on the eighteenth century has provided reason to be wary of the neat curves of real wages that can be constructed from institutional account books. The eighteenth century was also an age of declining real wages, yet, as we shall see, studies based on marriage contracts or probate records consistently suggest that private wealth increased among urban workers in this period.[70] No study has yet utilized such records for the first half of the sixteenth century, although Frederick Irvine's piece in this volume reveals a modest increase in the average dowries of *laboureurs* and artisans in Montpellier between 1550 and 1610, an era during which the 'price revolution' continued to erode real wages.

Some of the clearest changes in urban life between 1500 and 1560 were in the domain of culture. Certain of these changes furthered the separation of an emerging elite from the rest of urban society. During this period, the judges of the sovereign courts articulated a corporate ethos which urged court members to emphasize the dignity of their office by maintaining an outward mien of gravity in public and refraining from mixing promiscuously in the festive life of the city.[71] Aspects of that festive life also came under fire. With the spread of the early evangelical movement and the Renaissance's exaltation of ancient literary forms, mystery plays, which both violated the classical rules of drama and frequently incorporated apochryphal elements in their plot lines, fell into discredit and ceased to be performed in many towns.[72] As the growth of poverty made all forms of disorder appear increasingly threatening, the parlements also sought to forbid the charivaris of youth abbeys, which they had been willing to bless just fifty years previously.[73] Although traditional religious confraternities did not disappear, many experienced a significant decline of membership as the century progressed.[74] Above all else, the rise of Protestantism divided many cities into increasingly polarized confessional groups and turned rituals such as the feast of Corpus Christi, which had once been ceremonies of civic solidarity, into the occasion for violent confrontations.

III

During the 150 years between the outbreak of the Wars of Religion and the death of Louis XIV, France alternated between periods of prolonged crisis and eras of recovery and expansion. The civil wars quickly disrupted much of the country, although certain regions were largely spared until the 1580s. Reconstruction followed the end of the wars, with population levels rising well beyond their sixteenth century peaks in Britanny but failing to regain them in wide areas of the Paris Basin. France's entry into the Thirty Years' War and the internal upheavals of the Fronde brought a new period of difficulties, followed by a Colbertian period of relative prosperity and then another prolonged period of warfare and disruption from the outbreak of the War of the League of Augsburg until the Peace of Utrecht (1688–1714). Demographic trends in the early part of this period remain very poorly understood, but it is possible that, excluding the growth that resulted from the annexation of new territories, the kingdom's population registered no overall increase between 1560 and 1715. The most recent estimate for the period 1600–1700 (i.e. in the wake of whatever population decline the Wars of Religion may have provoked) suggests modest growth from 18–20 million to 21.5 million within fixed boundaries.[75]

As the population estimates assembled in Table 1.2 demonstrate, many cities felt the impact of the events just described. A majority of the cities for which figures are available around both 1550 and 1700 either declined or stagnated, with the most consistent losers being the smaller towns in the vicinity of Paris, a group of cities whose growth was consistently stunted throughout the early modern period by the expansion of the capital. But the lack of dynamism displayed by many towns was counterbalanced by the vigorous growth of a sizeable minority. Paris's population more than doubled during the seventeenth century, reaching 530,000 by 1680 before declining slightly in the last decades of the century. The Wars of Religion brought an end to Lyon's most glorious era as a banking and commercial center, but the fabulous expansion of its silk industry in the seventeenth century more than compensated, carrying its population above the 100,000 level before another end-of-the-century decline. Most provincial administrative capitals containing sovereign courts also grew substantially (e.g. Rennes, Aix-en-Provence, Dijon, Montpellier, Grenoble), although neither Toulouse, whose great era as a center of the pastel trade came to an end with the Wars of Religion, nor Rouen, which lost part of its port functions to Le Havre and some of its industry to the surrounding countryside, expanded particularly. Equally buoyant were many ports, notably Marseille, Nantes, and Saint-Malo, all of which more than doubled in size between 1550 and 1700. This period also saw the creation of several new towns that grew rapidly into substantial cities – Versailles most notably, but also Rochefort – as well as the installation of major centers of the royal navy in Brest and Toulon, which carried the population of those cities well above their modest previous levels. Added together, the 28 provincial cities that were part of the kingdom throughout this period and for which population figures are available in both 1550 and 1700 show an overall growth of 44 per cent. The larger sample of 46 such cities available for the period 1600–1700 reveals a 42 per cent increase. These figures, furthermore, exclude the new towns as well as Paris; to include them in these calculations would have unduly exaggerated the degree of overall growth. During this 150-year period, then, France's cities as a whole grew substantially more rapidly than its total population. As other students of European urbanization have already discerned, this 'age of crisis' was also France's period of most rapid net urbanization during the early modern era.[76] The urban growth concentrated particularly in the administrative capitals, ports, new towns, and industrial cities specializing in the production of luxury goods.

This pattern of urbanization was the product of five broad trends that transformed French society between 1560 and 1715. The first was the growth of the state, which can in turn be divided into two overlapping phases, each with distinct consequences for cities. Phase one involved the dramatic expansion of what French historians have labelled the *'Etat d'offices'*, that is, a state characterized by a great number of patrimonial office holders. The classic remark about the sale of offices, that each time His Majesty created an office, God created a fool to buy it, dates from the reign of Louis XIV. During earlier reigns, no great nobleman would have joked so complacently about the phenomenon. Frederick Irvine's essay in this volume contains the best attempt yet made to measure the precise growth of the number and remuneration of royal officers within a single locality, and it highlights just how dramatic this process was in Montpellier during the second half of the sixteenth century. Although Irvine does not carry this aspect of his investigation beyond 1600, the reign of Louis XIII was another period in which a fiscally hard-pressed crown turned to the multiplication of offices for sale. The *bureau des élus* of Valognes increased in size from four members in 1540 to twenty-one in 1640, and where the remuneration of these officials skimmed off 1.8 per cent of the taxes raised within the jurisdiction in 1540 and 4.1 per cent in 1600, that figure was up to 7.1 per cent in 1631.[77] Overall, the number of judicial and financial officials throughout the kingdom quadrupled or more between 1515 and 1665.[78] The economic significance for towns of this multiplication of venal offices was such that even during the troubled era of the Wars of Religion, the cities that were uniquely administrative capitals uniformly expanded in size.

Phase two of the growth of the state was the maturation under Louis XIV of the *'Etat d'administration'*, i.e. a state of considerably greater administrative capacity able effectively to implement centrally determined policies and marshal the kingdom's resources for war. The chief bureaucratic agents of this new order, the intendants, had only small personal staffs and typically recruited their *subdélégués* from the ranks of those who already owned other offices. This development consequently bred no great increase in the numbers of administrators. Its chief consequences for urban society lay in the considerably augmented outlay for military and naval purposes that resulted. The growth of the vast naval arsenals at Brest, Rochefort and Toulon offers perhaps the best symbol of this; equally important, although dispersed among a greater number of towns, was the considerable outlay for new military fortifications around many cities and the growing presence of soldiers within them. The billeting of unruly troops had long been a burden dreaded by cities, but with the imposition of increasingly effective discipline, the excesses of soldierly extortion and theft were reduced, while as the lodging of troops became regularized toward the end of the seventeenth century, a few towns pioneered the construction of permanent barracks. Furthermore, the troops, who were provisioned at the government's expense and increasingly came to be paid their salaries with some regularity, did pump into cities money which had been raised through a tax system that fell disproportionately on the countryside. René Favier's demonstration in Chapter 7 that by the eighteenth century smaller towns positively solicited the presence of a garrison testifies to a remarkable change in the attitude of city officials toward the presence of soldiers in their town. While his study also warns against exaggerating the importance of military spending as a stimulus to urban economies, it should perhaps be observed as well that Dauphiné's undynamic new garrison towns were located in particularly inhospitable mountain settings. By contrast, Belfort, newly fortified between 1687 and 1703 to protect Franche-Comté, grew steadily during the subsequent century and housed 4300 civilians by 1774. The total pay of the 11,000 soldiers lodged in mid eighteenth-century Metz amounted to two million livres, or ten times the *gages* paid to the city's parlement.[79]

The second development stimulating urban growth was the movement to the city of a fraction of the old nobility of the sword and the elaboration of new cultural practices that were at once aristocratic and urban. Paris's growth was particularly linked to this trend. With an increasingly sedentary court, the appearance of the salon, and the articulation of the ideal of the *honnête homme*, the capital emerged as a center of high noble residence and entertainment and as the kingdom's central aristocratic marriage and money market even before Louis XIV imposed residence in the orbit of the court on any nobleman who harbored the slightest military ambition. In the early sixteenth century, certain great noble families already possessed Parisian *hôtels*, usually rather stern constructions on which they might suddenly descend for a brief while when their affairs brought them to Paris, rousting out those to whom they rented these residences in their absences on a daily or weekly basis. But the seventeenth century brought considerably more of the high nobility to Paris for longer sojourns, which they passed in increasingly elegant *hôtels* that now often became their chief residences.[80] On a smaller scale, certain provincial towns also emerged as centers of noble residence and entertainment. Nearly 400 families of sword nobles lived alongside the 193 members of the robe in Aix-en-Provence in 1695, while even little Auray, in Brittany, had become the principal residence of some twenty noble families, where two hundred years earlier, true to the picture painted by Noël du Fail, all of the noblemen of this region had lived on their *terres*.[81] The growing aristocratic presence in towns also derived from the adoption of increasingly aristocratic forms of behavior by members of the more prestigious sovereign courts and their successful assertion of their claim to constitute a branch of the nobility, as well as from the increased presence of army officers commanding the troops now garrisoned in cities.

The third trend was the extension of bourgeois control over the land. As the population growth of the sixteenth century forced a diminution of the average size of peasant holdings and the depredations of soldiers and higher taxation further aggravated the situation of the rural population, a fraction of the peasantry found itself forced into debt and finally obliged to sell part of its land to outsiders to the village community. Numerous studies have shown how town dwellers increased their ownership of rural property in the vicinity of the larger cities.[82] The result was the diversion of a growing percentage of the profit of agriculture into the cities, as well as the sort of expansion in the number of bourgeois rentiers suggested by Farr's essay (Chapter 4).

Fourth, commerce grew, and with it the wealth of cities. Although the volume of trade may not have expanded as dramatically between 1560 and 1700 as it did in either the early sixteenth or the eighteenth centuries, the available evidence nonetheless suggests a healthier growth in the volume of French commerce than pessimistic labels often applied to this period such as 'age of crisis' or (to use the language of François Simiand that was once influential among French historians) 'phase B' would suggest. Certain ports unquestionably suffered, notably La Rochelle, which found slaving and trade with Canada and the West Indies only partial compensation for the virtual decimation of its population and loss of its special tax exemptions as a result of the siege of 1628–29, the gradual decline of its long-standing staple, the salt trade, and the departure of many of its leading merchant families following the Revocation of the Edict of Nantes.[83] Statistical evidence concerning the volume of Bordeaux's wine trade, the total activity of the port at Marseille, and traffic along both the Loire and Rhône nonetheless shows considerable growth in every case, while this period witnessed the remarkable saga of Saint-Malo's maturation into a major international port trading directly with the Indian Ocean.[84]

Although these four developments all stimulated urbanization, alterations in the structure of manufacturing, the fifth set of changes affecting urban growth in this period, had more ambiguous consequences for urban economies. The most significant change here was the increasing tendency for industry to locate in the countryside. Although the expansion of rural industry is hard to trace prior to the establishment of royal inspectors of manufactures in the eighteenth century, it seems clear that the migration of industry from city to countryside was particularly marked during the difficult middle decades of the seventeenth century. By the end of the century, Pierre Goubert has estimated, two-thirds of the woolen cloth woven in the major textile region of Picardy and the adjoining Beauvaisis was produced in the country-side, while by 1737 three-quarters of the fine linens sold in Valenciennes that had once been the speciality of that city's *mulquiniers* were now fabricated in nearby villages.[85] The movement of industry between city and countryside was not unidirectional; urban weavers could be more closely supervised and worked without the interruptions for agricultural work that marked labor in the countryside, so periods of high demand often produced a reconcentration of production in the cities.[86] The result of the broad trend was nonetheless to reduce urban employment. While undercutting the livelihood of urban workers, however, the growth of rural industry enriched the urban merchants who controlled it. There is evidence of a clear increase in the wealth and commercial sophistication of Amiens' merchants and *marchands-saieteurs* in the course of the seventeenth century. Where early in the century these men had no better way to collect the debts owed them by distant creditors than to saddle up their mule and set off with their pistol and strongbox, by the end of the century they had mastered such techniques as the use of bills of exchange and the maintenance of regular account books and had expanded considerably the geographic range of their dealings.[87] Meanwhile, despite the trend toward the location of industry outside the towns, many products remained strictly urban specialities, and certain of these experienced considerable growth in the demand for them. This was especially true of luxury products, which profited from the new concentration of elite wealth in cities and the growing prestige of French taste and fashions abroad. By perfecting their technical skills and developing a flexible system of production that enabled them to respond rapidly to, and even to help to create, constantly changing tastes, the silk producers of Lyon and Tours wrested control of this market away from the Italians who had previously controlled it and fuelled the dramatic growth of those cities' silk industries.[88] The Parisian luxury trades remain woefully underexplored, but they too may have experienced a critical period of maturation in this era; by the end of the seventeenth century, Parisian luxury goods comprised an important element of trade at the Leipzig fairs, the most important in central and eastern Europe.[89] Changing patterns of manufacturing thus stimulated the growth of certain cities while limiting that of others.

In sum, the period from the outbreak of the Wars of Religion to the death of Louis XIV witnessed at once the expansion of aristocratic and rentier elements within urban society, some growth of commercial capitalism, and the continuing migration of certain basic manufacturing industries to the countryside. The implications of these changes for urban social and occupational structures are searchingly illuminated in the contributions of Irvine and Farr. Not only did the privileged grow in numbers and wealth; a clear shift is discernible within Dijon's artisan population from 1650 onward towards the production of luxury goods and services, while even between 1550 and 1650 artisan wealth increased significantly. Comparable studies for other sorts of towns will be needed before we can determine how typical these towns were; administrative capitals such as Montpellier and Dijon may in fact have been precisely the kind of city that profited most from the trends of the era. It nonetheless seems probable that the kingdom's wealth was increasingly being concentrated in the cities and shared there, albeit unequally, among much of the urban population.

Municipal political arrangements were also transformed between 1560 and 1715, with the crown significantly increasing the tutelage that it exercised over the kingdom's cities. This development is traced in detail for Toulouse in Schneider's contribution to this volume (Chapter 6). The timing and extent of the changes in urban government were not everywhere the same as in Toulouse, but everywhere the process of change was also a protracted one, which can only be properly understood when examined, as Schneider does, over the *longue durée*. The extended period of unrest which began with the Wars of Religion and continued through the Fronde first led to increasing crown intervention in urban affairs, not out of any desire to remake urban government systematically, but simply to keep the peace within cities and to ensure their loyalty to the crown in a troubled era. In certain towns, the concern for maintaining order led to constant experiments with the form and composition of the civic militia, often with the chief positions of command being reserved for local royal officials.[90] In others, the crown took control of the selection of municipal officials through modifications to the city constitution that permitted the king or his representative to choose the new mayor or city councillors from a list of candidates presented to him by the city.[91] Traditional rituals that on occasion led to rowdiness or criticism of the governing authorities also appeared increasingly dangerous, and between 1560 and 1660 urban kingdoms of Maugouvert were reined in and finally abolished.[92] The extent of royal tutelage then took a great leap forward throughout the kingdom with the establishment of the intendants and the gradual extension of their powers of oversight over municipal finances. This culminated in a royal edict of 1683, which declared all communities throughout the kingdom to have the legal status of minors and placed their finances under the *tutelle* of the intendancy. For each city a schedule of ordinary expenditures was ordered, drawn up on the basis of municipal budgets of the preceding ten years. All extraordinary expenditures not specifically listed in this schedule were required henceforward to obtain the approval of the intendant.[93]

As the kingdom's capital and largest city, Paris was the object of particularly thoroughgoing changes designed to ensure its security and proper administration. In 1667 Nicolas La Reynie was installed as the first lieutenant general of police, with extensive authority over the full range of police matters. In that same year, the crown more than tripled in size the previously small corps of paid, permanent night watchmen charged with keeping the peace. With time, this *guet* and its companion, the royal guards, effectively replaced the old citizen militia, giving the capital something approximating a modern police force. Seven years later the many surviving seigneurial jurisdictions within the city were abolished, although a few of the most powerful ecclesiastical establishments were subsequently able to regain their judicial authority.[94]

In the final analysis, the erosion of the effective independence of most cities probably resulted at least as much from the simple growth of royal military power as it did from the administrative changes just detailed. The events of the Wars of Religion demonstrated with particular clarity the serious difficulties that rebellious cities could still cause for the crown and thus the need to retain their loyalty. It is no accident that occasions can be found when the monarchs of this period felt it prudent to extend certain urban privileges, and that their dealings with many cities involved the sort of prolonged negotiations found in the tale Descimon relates of the free gift of 1571 (see Chapter 2). Similarly, the frequent riots provoked by new taxation during the period of Louis XIII and Richelieu often succeeded in obtaining a reduction or annulment of the contested levy. The cities remained a political and military force to be bargained with. In the wake of the Fronde, however, Louis XIV moved forcefully to require those towns that had participated in the revolt to turn over their artillery to the crown and frequently ordered the demolition of their walls. His subsequent wars provided him with the occasion to requisition the artillery of all of the cities in the kingdom, thereby depriving them of one of the great symbols of their military importance.[95] The creation of a large standing army meanwhile gave the monarch the ability to repress disorder quickly and without mercy. Henceforward, soldiers were regularly stationed in most larger cities. The era in which cities could extract significant concessions from the crown because of their military importance was at an end.

Once the ability of cities to command a degree of respect because of their potential for independent political action was eliminated, it was an easy step for the monarchy to regard city governments as institutions that could be altered at will and exploited for fiscal purposes. Kings had had recourse to the expedient of threatening to make positions in municipal government venal royal offices and placing them up for sale since at least as far back as 1581, but amid the costly wars of the later part of Louis XIV's reign the temptation to try this on a hitherto unprecedented scale proved irresistible. In 1690 the fullest attack yet on traditional municipal forms of governance began when offices of king's solicitor and town scribe were established and placed up for bids in every city of the kingdom. During the next nineteen years, positions of mayor, tax assessor, lieutenant general of police, lieutenant mayor, more tax assessors, some city councillorships, alternate mayor, alternate lieutenant mayor, and alternate scribe were likewise created. This did not spell the death knell for municipal elections or for the rich variegation of urban governmental forms, since many cities were able to retain their traditional procedures by buying the new offices back as a collectivity. Furthermore, the crown's appetite for maximum profit was tempered by an unwillingness to upset local balances of power too greatly.

Since the establishment in every city of new offices of lieutenant general of police on the Parisian model threatened at one stroke to overturn the traditional division of police functions that rival administrative bodies had worked out among themselves through a long process of conflict and negotiation, the intendants commonly intervened to guarantee that, even if other bidders offered more, the office was sold to the institution that was most powerful locally – the municipality in Gray, the presidial court in Troyes, the episcopal or archiepiscopal officials in Beauvais and Reims, and so forth.[96] But many of the new offices did pass into private hands. The incongruities that could arise were epitomized in Saint-Quentin, where the municipality only had the funds to buy back one of the two alternate mayorships and the office consequently alternated annually between an elected mayor and one who owned the office.[97] The new venal offices were ultimately suppressed in 1717, but a precedent of wholesale exploitation of municipal government for fiscal purposes had been set, which the crown would subsequently find impossible to resist repeating.

Although the significant changes in city government between 1560 and 1715 thus reshaped municipal institutions in many cities and increased the degree of royal control exercised over all, they did not abolish the authority of municipal governments entirely or alter that basic characteristic of urban administration: the presence within cities of a variety of rival institutions uneasily sharing local police and judicial power. The creation of the office of intendant added to the local scene a new administrator of considerable power. Energetic intendants with a strong interest in urban government could leave a significant imprint on the cities of their *généralité*, as is attested by the numerous late seventeenth- and eighteenth-century town squares or promenades named after the intendants who oversaw their development and completion. In many cases, however, important initiatives continued to originate from the *échevinages*.[98] In Gray, successive eighteenth-century intendants closely oversaw municipal finances and the repartition of taxes but otherwise played little active role in the administration of the city.[99] Similarly, the establishment of the office of lieutenant general of police did not put an end to all local conflicts about rights of jurisdiction over different aspects of municipal policing; typically, it merely represented little more than the inauguration of a new stage in the centuries-old tug-of-war between rival institutions for authority in municipal affairs. And while local governments emerged from this period with their fiscal autonomy curtailed, they had also been obliged to take on new responsibilities as a result of the changes in the period of Louis XIV, for, under the supervision of the intendant, they determined where soldiers billeted in a city would be lodged and drew up the rolls for the new taxes imposed on all communities, the *capitation* and the *dixième*. The fate of municipal government thus illustrates a central point about the rise of the absolutist state. This was not forged through the systematic elimination of all institutions or individuals that were potential

35

rivals to the crown. It was forged by respecting pre-existing institutions so long as they could be induced to cooperate with the king, modifying those that proved too recalcitrant in an effort to make them more pliable, and only occasionally constructing new institutions for circumventing, although rarely replacing outright, those that proved particularly obdurate or inefficient. As Schneider stresses, city governments retained an element of power throughout this period, both because they performed useful functions and because they could be exploited for fiscal purposes.

The kinds of people chosen to fill these still consequential offices changed surprisingly little over this period. Irvine's contribution (Chapter 3) shows how the growth in the numbers and wealth of the *gens de loi* in Montpellier led in turn to their greater representation within that city's *consulat*. In other cities, too, men with legal training fought to limit or bar those engaged in commerce or manufacturing from seats within the city council. These trends found a counterweight, however, in an increasingly mercantilist state, which sought to enhance the dignity of commerce and guarantee effective administration of its increasingly detailed industrial regulations and consequently intervened to ensure that merchants remained significantly represented within city governments.[100] Consequently, we find merchants still filling 55 to 60 per cent of the places in Lyon's city council in the eighteenth century, where merchants and bourgeois together had filled 79 per cent between 1520 and 1579.[101] Tighter restrictions on participation in municipal elections further reinforced the oligarchic character of city government in certain cities, but again the extent of the change was limited.[102]

The social and political changes just described left a clear imprint on the physical face of French cities. The Paris of 1571 described by Descimon was already beginning to be transformed by the construction of town houses by court-linked elites. Still more dramatic changes would follow in the seventeenth century. Successive monarchs built the first of the centrally planned royal squares flanked by buildings of uniform appearance that would become the staple of so much subsequent French monumental city planning. Private investors developed new and fashionable quarters, dotted with the *hôtels* of great noblemen, parlementaires, and financiers, first on the Ile Saint-Louis and around Marie de Medici's Luxembourg palace, then, once the construction of the Palais Royal and Versailles drew the center of fashionable Paris inexorably to the west, in the faubourgs Saint-Germain and Montmartre and around the Louvre and Palais Royal. 'Here the Palaces and Convents have eat up the Peoples Dwellings, and crouded them excessively together, and possessed themselves of far the greatest part of the Ground', the English visitor Martin Lister wrote at the end of the century.[103] The appearance of certain provincial capitals changed scarcely less. Between 1583 and 1646, Aix-en-Provence witnessed the development of three new quarters that more than doubled that city's size. The last expansion also permitted the construction through the center of town of a broad avenue (today's Cours Mirabeau) lined with aristocratic *hôtels* and wide enough for the city's leading residents to drive up and down it in that new means of conveyance, the carriage.[104] The spread of the carriage also stimulated the construction of broad *allées* and promenades on the edges of many towns for the fashionable to see and be seen – arenas for display whose influence in spreading fashion-conscious consumer behavior should not be underestimated. In some cases, the land on which these were built had become available because of the demolition of the city's walls, for with the extension of French frontiers to the east and the construction of stronger border fortifications, the monarchy felt sufficiently secure about the defense of the interior to permit town walls to be torn down or left to decay. The pace of the architectural changes just described was anything but uniform, but few towns of any significance did not see at least the construction of a few fashionable *hôtels* and such gradual modifications as the advance of stone houses at the expense of wood and of tile roofs at the expense of thatch.[105]

With the growing aristocratic presence in urban life, the contours of urban culture also changed. The emergence of the salon in the early seventeenth century created a new forum for private sociability and stimulated the elaboration of codes of conduct whose self-conscious refinement set those who moved within these circles – essentially the wealthiest financiers, noblemen of the robe, a growing number of great sword noblemen, and of course their wives – still more distinctively apart from the rest of urban society.[106] Another new cultural development was the rise of the commercial theatre, whose maturation can be dated to the definitive establishment of two permanent companies in Paris in 1629, although travelling troupes of actors had been circulating through the kingdom from the 1570s onward. This too was tied to the growing aristocratic presence in towns. Many early troupes were patronized by great noblemen or scheduled their visits to provincial towns to coincide with occasions that assembled many of the locally prominent, such as meetings of the provincial estates in Languedoc, while Paris theatre audiences appear to have grown more and more overwhelmingly elite in composition.[107] What the Parisian stage or salons pioneered, the provinces were able to follow through the circulation of printed copies of the latest theatrical successes, engravings of fashions in the capital, and, after 1672, the weekly *Mercure Galant*, which reported extensively on literary events and changing modes. Little salons formed in many towns, and the second half of the century saw academies modelled on the Académie Française established in several provincial cities.[108]

Throughout the kingdom, the manners and literary tastes of the urban elites thus increasingly came to be modelled on those of the Parisian *beau monde* and to distinguish themselves from those of the rest of the population. At the same time this sharpened in certain ways the sense of cultural difference between different strata within cities, however, the powerful religious changes conventionally subsumed under the label of the Counter-

Reformation ensured that urban society would still be characterized by a considerable degree of social interaction between people of different social strata, for many aspects of the Counter-Reformation involved an active paternalism that led the rich to visit the homes of the poor or to join the same confraternities.

Under the impulse of the Counter-Reformation, urban confraternal life was reinvigorated and restructured. Numerous new devotional confraternities sprang up, the most celebrated (or at least the most intensively studied by recent historians) being the associations of Penitents, which began their spread throughout the Midi in the beginning of the sixteenth century but multiplied especially rapidly between 1560 and 1630. Instead of being linked to specific occupational groups, these devotional confraternities brought together people of any social status willing to accept the regulations of the group and to participate in certain common devotions. Studies of their membership suggest that they did indeed cut across the social spectrum in their recruitment.[109] At the same time that these new devotional confraternities spread, the ecclesiastical authorities also reshaped the older guild and journeymen's confraternities, banning banquets and revelry from the roster of confraternal activities and replacing them with such elements of Counter-Reformation spiritual discipline as frequent communion or daily examination of conscience.[110]

The reformation of confraternities was just one concern of the circles of devout activists that took shape in virtually every city of any importance in the seventeenth century. New religious houses, often dedicated to teaching or other forms of active service, multiplied. New charitable institutions were founded to succor repentant prostitutes, provide dowries or apprenticeships for the poor, offer shelter to women turned out by their family, or deliver alms to the *pauvres honteux*, those whose high birth prevented them from openly acknowledging their need to depend on public charity. Perhaps the most energetic and effective promoter of a variety of good works was the company of the Holy Sacrament, that secret association of *dévots* founded in Paris in 1627, which ultimately came to have branches in more than fifty cities. Its members worked actively – in conjunction with the local authorities wherever possible – to counter indecency in dress and action, increase respect for Lent, reclaim prostitutes, and stamp out *compagnonnage*, whose rites they considered blasphemous. Above all, they became the driving force that carried through to implementation in many cities ideas already advanced by early mercantilist thinkers, urging the forced internment of the poor in workhouses. Manifestations of a harsh paternalism, these measures nonetheless arose from an active, missionary charity that brought its practitioners into personal contact with those whom they sought to redeem.[111] Schneider suggests elsewhere that these activities must be related to the social and political changes of the early seventeenth century, arguing that the *dévot* movement offered a combination of spiritual heroism and social activism through which local elites could assert their claim to being the proper governors of society in the face of the growing encroachments of the absolutist state.[112] Early support for the Counter-Reformation indeed appears to have come primarily from the *officiers* and lawyers, although the movement ultimately altered the behavior of all classes of town dwellers. A recent study of Grenoble wills reveals the language and gestures of Counter-Reformation piety showing up first among the high robe and men of the law but spreading by the 1670s to artisans and day laborers as well.[113] If other studies corroborate these findings, it will be clear that even the religious changes of this period were influenced by those two forces shaping urban society so powerfully in this period, the multiplication of the ranks of *officiers* and lawyers and the growth of state power.

IV

The configuration of forces shaping urban society from the beginning of the eighteenth century to the outbreak of the Revolution changed markedly in comparison with the preceding century and a half. The considerably more abundant demographic information available for this period suggests that most cities slowed the pace of their expansion slightly, while France's total population quickened its growth. In consequence, René Favier's piece in this volume, which assembles population figures for all of Dauphiné's cities, finds urban growth matching the general expansion of the province's population almost exactly. A comparable study for Brittany shows that urban growth there lagged somewhat behind overall population trends.[114] Meanwhile, the population figures assembled in Table 1.2 reveal 63 provincial cities growing by 32 per cent and Paris by 29 per cent, percentages which frame neatly the best recent estimate of the kingdom's overall population growth – 31 per cent between 1700 and 1790.[115] In sum, the eighteenth century in France witnessed neither the net urbanization visible in the British Isles at the same time nor the positive de-urbanization that characterized Belgium and the Netherlands in these years.[116] Telling differences can be discerned between the rate of growth of different categories of cities. The thirteen ports represented in Table 1.2 increased their total population by 47 per cent, while the eight cities that were primarily provincial administrative capitals augmented in size by only 21 per cent.

As the modest expansion of the administrative capitals would suggest, the growth of the state was no longer as powerful a stimulus to urban expansion as during the preceding century and a half. The last great period for the creation of new offices in the royal courts occurred during the years 1690–1709. Thereafter, not only did the monarchy no longer resort to this expedient in times of financial difficulty, it actually cut back the size of certain royal courts.[117] Informed contemporary estimates place the number of royal offices at 45,780 in 1664 and 50,969 in 1778, and the modest increase between these two dates must be attributed to the annexation of several border provinces in the intervening years and the new creations of the later years of Louis XIV's reign.[118] Not only did the size of the courts cease to grow, but certain of them also witnessed a decline in the volume of their business, although this did not stop an expanding number of young men from pursuing legal studies.[119] The per capita tax burden, which had increased rapidly in the seventeenth century, grew only slightly in real terms during the course of the eighteenth.[120] With a rising population and a stable or declining number of legal officials, this level of taxation could support increasing peacetime military expenditures; the growth of cities such as Cherbourg and Brest in this period was fuelled by their large naval installations, and the impact of military spending on towns such as Belfort or Metz has already been suggested. Still, the great age of the growth of the state was over.

The expansion of aristocratic and rentier elements within France's cities did not entirely cease as a result. Bourgeois expropriation of the peasantry has been far less of a theme for rural historians of the eighteenth century than for those of preceding eras, but although this process reversed itself in the Beauce, where a counter-offensive of peasant property has been detected between 1761 and 1790, it continued, if perhaps at a slower rate, in Burgundy and around Toulouse.[121] The urbanization of the nobility also continued, as the pleasures and behavior patterns of the city cast their spell over a growing percentage of the Second Estate and rising revenues from land permitted more of its members to bear the costs associated with a residence in town. Where tax rolls from the *élection* of Saint-Maixent in the later seventeenth century list ten of approximately fifty nobles as having their chief residence in the town, 31 of 41 families paid their capitation in Saint-Maixent by 1765.[122] Jonathan Dewald's excellent recent study of the barons of Pont-St-Pierre shows that changes in attitudes toward property and consumption accompanied this shift. Where previously this family of the upper provincial nobility had pursued an ideal of autarchy and purchased only few of the luxury goods that urban markets had to offer, now during its infrequent visits to its estate it dispatched its servants to Neufchâtel for cheese, Gournay for poultry, and Rouen for oysters, asparagus and marzipan, while summoning from the city cabinetmakers and upholsterers to furnish the château and a master gardener to trim the *orangerie*.[123]

Above all, the eighteenth century was an era in which commerce and industry expanded with new vigor. Foreign trade increased particularly rapidly, paced by the dramatic growth of the colonial trade. Total imports and exports grew in constant value from 190 to 452 million livres between 1726 and 1775.[124] The most prosperous colonial ports, Bordeaux, Nantes, and Marseille, dazzled visitors with the animation of their quays and the elegance of their newly constructed quarters.[125] The growth of foreign trade also stimulated certain new industries, although the regional impact of this was very uneven. Nîmes provided perhaps the greatest urban success story of the century, tripling in size owing to the development of a silk stocking industry catering primarily for the South American market. The colonial trade also generated such growth industries as flour milling in Toulouse, Montauban and Castelnaudary, soap manufacturing in Marseille, and sugar refining in Orléans.[126]

Improved roads and transportation facilities meanwhile stimulated internal trade. Although this is notoriously hard to quantify, receipts of the *cloison* of Angers, a tax by unit on all goods sold within the town, reveal an increase from 7,100 livres in 1660 to 28,289 livres a year in the mid-eighteenth century and 44,372 livres a year throughout the 1780s.[127] Of course, improvements in transportation, while stimulating the prosperity of some towns, could undercut those that found themselves bypassed by the new road systems of the era or were losing custom to more important retail markets nearby. The merchants of Sens complained in 1742 that their trade had suffered ever since the wealthy of that town had begun to use the efficient thrice-weekly water coach service to Paris to shop for luxury foods, silks and other fine cloths there.[128]

Expansion in manufacturing could be equally selective in its consequences for urban growth. Within the centrally important textile sector, a recent estimate places the increase in the volume of woolens produced throughout the kingdom at 76.4 per cent over the course of the century. New forms of textile manufacturing, notably of printed cotton fabrics, spread still more rapidly.[129] Once again, however, much of this growth occurred in the countryside, and textile production continued to hemorrhage out of towns such as Rouen, Valenciennes, Caen, Reims, and Aumale. Buoyant demand did, however, encourage the concentration of large numbers of workers under a single roof, and cities such as Amiens, Louviers, and Sedan saw the number of active looms increase substantially, while proto-factories grouping large numbers of weavers in a single establishment began to multiply.[130] The impact of the century's industrial and commercial growth thus varied from place to place, but it brought the towns as a whole new commercial prosperity, concentrated especially in the leading ports, while encouraging the expansion of some urban as well as rural manufactures.

The pattern of change just sketched altered the configuration of wealth within France's cities as well as shaping the broad contours of urban growth. In Farr's Dijon, growth in numbers and wealth among the elite was now concentrated primarily among the nobility on the one hand and merchants on the other, while the legal and official classes fared less well. In Toulouse, too, merchants and rentiers assembled wealth more rapidly than lawyers.[131] In booming Bordeaux, the expansion of trade and industry bred the accumulation of mercantile fortunes on a scale previously unparallelled, with such giants among *négociants* as the Gradis and Bonaffé families even amassing fortunes comparable in size to those of leading members of the nobility of the robe. In most towns, however, the wealthiest individuals at the end of the Ancien Régime were noble. In Lyon, in the 1780s, large noble fortunes were still three times the size of important mercantile ones, while in a sample of 234 probate inventories from Châlons-sur-Marne, the fifteen inventories concerning noblemen account for nearly 60 per cent of the total value of the inheritances recorded.[132] But it was not simply the wealthiest elements of urban society who prospered in this era. The evidence of both dowries and inventories after death from cities as diverse as Paris, Toulouse, Lyon, Chartres, and Angers is unanimous in demonstrating that fortunes increased in real terms among virtually all social groups.[133] The growth was, however, unevenly distributed. In both Chartres and Lyon, the largest fortunes represented a substantially greater percentage of the total wealth on the eve of the Revolution than they did at the beginning of the century. The poorest quintile of Lyon's population registered no increase at all in its real wealth.[134]

The augmented wealth of the majority of the urban population was accompanied by changes in patterns of consumption. The concern of recent social historians to write the annals of the humble means that we are actually better informed about this development among the poorer town folk than among the rich. Daniel Roche's remarkable study of inventories after death of the '*peuple de Paris*' underscores a series of 'micro-ameliorations' ranging from fuller wardrobes to the diffusion of porcelain, mirrors, and soap.[135] Such phenomena as the growth of a fine furniture industry characterized by rapidly changing styles, the spreading availability of a wide range of culinary delicacies, the emergence of the café, and the diffusion of wigs and hair-powdering all bespeak even more significant changes in spending habits among those of higher and middling station – changes that began as early as the mid- and later-seventeenth century but accelerated in this period.[136] By the 1730s, observers were remarking on the important role of luxury spending in the economy and the phenomenon of industries dependent upon constantly changing styles. 'As soon as people stopped wearing ribbons', wrote Jean-François Melon in 1734, 'furbelows were introduced, then *pretintailles*, and finally hoop-petticoats, which will soon have their successors. . . . The goods sold in the stalls of the Palais-Royal only become an object of trade because of their continuous modification.'[137] The range and numbers of specialized retail merchants and artisans grew in consequence; the single most dramatic change consistently revealed by studies of the occupational structure of eighteenth-century cities, in fact, is the rise of the *perruquiers*, those 'light-fingered, lying, intriguing, impudent, corrupt barbers, Provençals and Gascons for the most part', whose proliferation Sebastien Mercier deplored as a sign of the frivolity of the age.[138] Luxury craftsmen and specialized retail merchants even appeared in small towns. Aumale was a declining textile town that slipped below 2,000 inhabitants during the course of the century, yet despite a drop of nearly one-third in the total number of people appearing on its tax rolls between 1670 and 1789, the range of non-textile-related artisan occupations actually widened slightly, and for the first time the city came to house seven *perruquiers*, a sculptor, a clock-maker, a jeweller and a mattress-maker.[139] Historians of France have yet to follow the lead of the English and explore the extent to which one can speak of the 'birth of a consumer society' in the eighteenth century.[140] In comparison with England, French steps in this direction were indeed probably limited and concentrated more heavily on upscale consumer goods, for English visitors still found Parisian shops 'the poorest gloomy Dungeons you can possibly conceive, however rich their Contents may be' late in the eighteenth century, while per capita consumption of such new consumer items as tobacco attained barely half the level they did across the Channel.[141] That movement in this direction nonetheless occurred is unmistakeable. The history of elite consumption and of the luxury trades is clearly a topic of central importance for France's economic and social history that deserves considerably more investigation.[142]

The growing range of commercial entertainments found in eighteenth-century cities also testifies to the diffusion of new patterns of consumption and culture. By the latter part of the century, waxworks, animal combats, mechanical shows, and *spectacles pyriques* combining dance, music, and fireworks vied for the custom of the crowds that strolled the Parisian boulevards. So too did six *théâtres de boulevard*, while masked balls took place at glittering outdoor music halls such as the Waux-hall or La Redoute Chinoise. Again, these pleasures were within reach of a widening audience. An increasing number of people from the middling ranks of urban society could be found attending the theatre as the century progressed, while the recent historian of the other forms of popular entertainment, Robert Isherwood, has stressed their appeal to people of all social strata.[143] In the course of the century, most leading provincial cities also built new theatres and developed a regular theatrical season. The opening of Paris's Vauxhall was soon followed by imitations in Dijon and Beaune.[144]

'Games, luxury, spectacles and pleasures of all kinds absorb all of the money', the curé of Nantes's St Nicholas parish confided to his parish register in 1787. 'This sort of epidemic is spreading among all classes of citizens and is turning everything topsy-turvy as it corrupts morals.'[145] Modern interpreters might be less inclined to judge the spread of such activities so censoriously, but there can be no doubt that this coincided with declining enthusiasm for the institutions and rituals of the church. As the century advanced, confraternities entered another phase of decline even more marked than that of the earlier sixteenth century, and those that survived seem to have recruited their shrinking membership more and more from similar social strata.[146] Wills reveal a decline in pious bequests and mass endowments in cities such as Marseille, Grenoble, and Salon-de-Provence from the 1740s onward that was more marked among the merchants, lawyers, and laboring population than among the aristocracy or shopkeepers. The small towns of the mountains of Haute-Provence, however, remained faithful to the church.[147]

At the same time, the tenor of social relations within urban society changed significantly. David Garrioch has recently discerned that a growing number of retail merchants and master artisans adopted the models of social behavior typical of 'men of quality', withdrawing from the promiscuous sociability of the street and the tavern to the bosom of an increasingly sentimentalized and psychologically charged family life or the company of men of comparable station in voluntary associations.[148] For the members of these and higher social strata, a variety of such associations multiplied: dining clubs, reading societies, Masonic lodges (830 are known to have been founded between 1725 and 1790), and, for the most distinguished, academies (23 in the provinces by 1789). The extent to which these associations promoted the fusion of noblemen and *roturiers* into a unified elite sharing a common commitment to the values of the Enlightenment remains a matter of controversy among historians. Studies of the academies and Masonic lodges demonstrate that these associations brought together both noblemen and commoners, who alike proclaimed such enlightened sentiments as the value of useful labor and the equality of men of virtue. The question remains of the extent to which the full universe of urbanized noblemen participated in such associations and embraced such values.[149] In any case, the equality embodied by such institutions was unquestionably an equality among men who possessed certain qualities of education and refinement. 'I do not see why a man even of a middling estate ... who can display nobility of conduct, *honnêteté* in his behavior and suavity in his relations with his equals should not be worthy of being welcomed among the Masons', wrote one Masonic official expressing the character of the social inclusiveness that ultimately took hold within this group.[150]

Between those who did and did not possess these qualities, relations took on a new distance and formality. A variety of trends testify to the weakening of ties between people of substantially unequal status: the diminishing frequency with which members of Toulouse's governing elites stood as godparents for children of the *menu peuple*, the declining percentage of illegitimate births in Nantes, Aix-en-Provence and Grenoble that grew out of cross-class liaisons, the withdrawal of the elites from religious confraternities, the new distance and formality characteristic of relations between the officials in charge of poor relief and their wards.[151] Perhaps the clearest example of all is the change in relations between masters and servants. Well into the eighteenth century, this relationship was one of close physical proximity and a strong element of paternalism. From mid-century onward, however, employers began to keep their servants at a greater distance; paternalistic economic relationships in which masters often held back much of their servants' pay to help them save for a dowry or other major expenditure gave way to the punctual payment of wages; and servants changed masters more frequently.[152] The percentage of journeymen living with their employer also declined significantly in Paris in the course of the century.[153] A series of broader transformations lie behind these changes: the spread of market relationships, the increasing cultivation of domestic intimacy, the weakening hold of traditional Catholicism, and the diffusion of egalitarian sentiments, which injected a new awkwardness into relationships with people of manifestly less wealth.

In the sphere of urban government and politics, the combination of fitful reformism with a constant concern to reduce recurring budget deficits that characterized so much of the activity of eighteenth-century French government also shaped the crown's relationship with its cities. The monarchy's fiscal difficulties prompted it to repeat Louis XIV's maneuver of creating new municipal offices to be put up for sale in 1722 (to help liquidate the debts left in the aftermath of the failure of Law's system), in 1733 (to raise funds for the War of the Polish Succession), and in 1742 (to help pay for the War of the Austrian Succession). As in earlier times, these offices were frequently repurchased by the towns themselves, which thereby preserved their traditional systems of choosing their own officials – albeit at a cost that amounted in Angers for the full period 1690–1771 to 730,000 livres, or as much as the city disbursed for all extraordinary building projects during the same period.[154] As earlier, a fraction of offices did pass into private hands, with unfortunate consequences for the quality of local administration.[155] It may have been in part the recognition of these problems and of the consequences for civic spirit of two generations of cynical financial exploitation of municipal office, which led the controller-general Laverdy to attempt his wholesale reform of municipal government in 1764–5.[156] His decree that a uniform system of elective municipal governments with modestly increased powers be established throughout the kingdom initiated a cycle of reforms begun and then reversed that lasted until the Revolution. The measure had only been implemented in parts of the kingdom before Terray came to power in 1771; he not only annulled the reforms but instituted a new round of creations of venal municipal offices. New efforts at reform followed in the decade immediately preceding the Revolution. By the time the National Assembly came into being, whatever sense of legitimacy France's different forms of municipal government had once derived from being time-honored institutions had been destroyed by the constant changes. The ground was cleared for the new experiments of the Revolution.

Despite the need to defend themselves constantly against threats to their traditional structure, Jacques Maillard's careful study of Angers suggests that municipal governments may actually have experienced a modest revival in their authority and autonomy in this period. Angers's *échevins* regularly exaggerated civic expenditures and underestimated revenues in the reports they sent to the intendants in order to create a reserve they could spend themselves. Furthermore, as we have already seen, revenue from the city's basic source of funds for ordinary expenditures, the *cloison*, increased dramatically. The city councillors thus presided over a growing treasury, and in 1745, over the protests of the intendant, they were able to reassert their ability to authorize certain expenditures without the intendant's approval. In 1729 the city's residents had also regained the ability to participate in the selection of their mayor and *échevins*, a privilege that they had lost in 1656 as punishment for their participation in a revolt against new taxes. Venality increasingly corroded the system. Under the terms granted by Louis XV, municipal electoral assemblies only had the right to nominate three candidates for each position. The king's local representative, either the governor or the *prince apanagiste*, then chose the new officials from among the nominees. With time, he came to expect payments from those selected, and offices started to go to the highest bidder. Still, within the limitations provided by the continuing oversight of the intendants and the spread of different forms of venality, the *échevinage* made most of the critical decisions governing the embellishment of the city during this period.[157]

The economic growth registered during the century also appears to have guaranteed that many cities were like Angers in having revenue to invest in urban improvements, even despite the large sums diverted to repurchase venal offices. Some of Angers's extraordinary expenditures still went for purposes such as importing grain in times of scarcity, but the city was also able to undertake new projects: a municipal lighting system, the creation of a special fire brigade equipped with water pumps (an invention of 1699), a covered market, a riding academy, and a new building to house the collège d'Anjou.[158] The eighteenth century was an important period of both public and private construction in many other provincial cities as well. Promenades and gardens were constructed, streets were widened and straightened, and barracks were built in many towns. The most rapidly growing cities such as Bordeaux or Nîmes witnessed the construction of entire new quarters built around the broad avenues and geometric plazas favored by the prevailing theories of urban design.[159]

Cities had always housed inventive souls eager to peddle their bright ideas to those in power – Rouen's *conseillers-échevins* had, for instance, been approached in 1567 by a man offering a submarine-like '*engin*' designed to permit underwater repairs to their recently collapsed bridge[160] – but the eighteenth century's concern for the amelioration of mankind through the application of reason to practical problems made it an era of special ingenuity devoted to urban improvement. In Paris, police guardposts were equipped in 1775 with first-aid kits, and where previously the law had decreed that a fee be paid to those who fished corpses from the Seine, a measure that was felt to provide a certain disincentive for people to come to the aid of those who were drowning, this was now changed to provide rewards to those who pulled people from the river while they were still alive. New *machines fumigatoires*, designed to revive those brought out unconscious by pumping

46

tobacco smoke into their rear end, were even added to the equipment of riverside guardposts.[161] At the same time, the spread of house numbering and uniform street signs brought a new legibility and rationality to the organization of urban space, and the adoption of mirrored oil lamps known as *réverbères* (following a public competition in 1763) improved the quality of street lighting.[162]

Slowly, the night life characteristic of modern cities began to develop. Parisian cabarets, which had been required to close at 8pm under Louis XIV, were allowed to remain open until 9pm under Louis XV and 10pm under Louis XVI.[163] The spread of improved street lighting, the reinforcement of the municipal police force, and even more important the broader cultural and political changes that had led to the disciplining of French society also made cities considerably safer. Where Boileau wrote in 1660 that Paris made the darkest and most deserted wood appear safe by comparison, Mercier asserted in 1781 that 'the streets of Paris are safe both night and day'.[164] Urban life was assuming a tenor and a set of temporal rhythms very different from those that had prevailed two centuries previously.

By the eve of the Revolution, French cities were thus different in many ways from what they had been as the Middle Ages drew to a close. Urban social structures had been stretched upwards by the growth of both rentier-aristocratic and wealthy mercantile elements, and this in turn had provoked some reorientation of occupational structures toward the provision of luxury goods and services. The urban elites had also elaborated new codes of conduct that condemned to oblivion certain of the associations and cultural forms typical of cities around 1500 while generating new patterns of associational life and culture, ones that increasingly accentuated the differences between *gens de qualité* and the *menu peuple*. In many towns, the old walls had been demolished by 1789 and the city lay open to traffic arriving from all directions. This development may be taken as a metaphor for the growing economic interaction between city and countryside. It stemmed quite tangibly from the growing power of the state and the decline of such municipal independence as the cities were earlier able to enjoy because of their strategic importance and the king's need to retain their loyalty.

At the same time, the changes experienced by France's cities during this period should not mask the substantial element of continuity that also characterized the patterns and institutions of urban life in these three centuries. For the poorer elements of the urban population, the material conditions of life changed little, and the basic patterns of sociability remained those of the neighborhood, tavern, guild, and confraternity. Equally little changed was the physical face of large parts of many cities, whose still medieval appearance would enchant romantic sensibilities in the nineteenth century and spawn the ubiquitous *rues piétonnes* of the twentieth. In the face of all of the political and institutional changes of the early modern era, the forms of municipal government also demonstrated a tenacious capacity for survival.

Above all, the extent of the changes varied from locality to locality. For every Paris, Bordeaux, Brest, or Grenoble that witnessed particularly dramatic growth and transformation, there was a Chartres, Blois, or Vannes, whose size and outward appearance changed little. Considerably more research remains to be done before we understand just how powerful were the forces of continuity and of change among the full range of cities of different size and character during all three early modern centuries. The essays that follow all contribute in different ways to the exploration of this subject. As this introduction has tried to show, it is one of central importance to the history of early modern France, because the changes experienced by urban society were shaped by and serve to reveal so many of the broader economic, political, and cultural transformations occurring in French life during these centuries. As this introduction has also tried to suggest, if more obliquely, these changes in urban society may also themselves have contributed to the process of economic change, as the emergence among urban elites of new cultural forms of self-conscious refinement and distinction stimulated luxury consumption and rapidly changing styles that subsequently spread downward to a growing fraction of the urban population, generating new manufactures and services while drawing increasing numbers of noblemen into the cities and their commercial networks in a self-reinforcing process.

NOTES: CHAPTER 1

An earlier version of this essay was presented to the History Department Research Seminar of Brown University. I profited greatly from the generous observations offered by the seminar members, for which I am extremely grateful. Special thanks are due to Judith Benedict, Anthony Molho, Louise Newman, James Patterson, Nancy Roelker, and Robert Schneider for their editorial and critical comments on earlier drafts.

1 The first precise nationwide information about the number of people living in communities of different sizes comes from the censuses of 1806–9. These reveal that 18.8 per cent of the population resided in communities of 2,000 or more inhabitants. The cities seem, however, to have declined in population during the course of the Revolution and early Napoleonic years relative to the population as a whole. A percentage of city dwellers for 1789 in the vicinity of 20 per cent thus seems reasonable. Jacques Dupâquier, *La population française aux XVIIe et XVIIIe siècles* (Paris: Presses Universitaires de France, 1979), p. 91.

2 Neveux, 'Les discours sur la ville', in Georges Duby (ed.) *Histoire de la France urbaine*, Vol. 3. *La ville classique: de la Renaissance aux Révolutions* (Paris: Seuil, 1981), p. 17.

3 The evolution of the urban population in the course of the period covered in this essay is discussed at greater length below, pp. 24–5, 28, 39. My estimate of the percentage of the population living in towns in 1550 derives from a back projection based on the data provided there.

4 Jan de Vries, *European Urbanization 1500–1800* (Cambridge, Mass.: Harvard University Press, 1984), p. 39.

5 *Ordonnances des Rois de France, règne de François Ier*, Vol. 9 (Paris: Imprimerie Nationale, 1973), pp. 74–81. The information in this document is presented cartographically in Richard Gascon, 'La France du mouvement: les commerces et les villes', in Braudel and Labrousse, Vol. 1, Part 1, p. 407; and Bernard Chevalier, *Les bonnes villes de France du XIVe au XVIe siècle* (Paris: Aubier–Montaigne, 1982), p. 40.

6 Alain Croix, *La Bretagne aux 16e et 17e siècles: Les hommes, la mort, la foi* (Paris: Maloine, 1981), p. 130.

7 Calculated on the basis of René Le Mée, 'Population agglomérée, population éparse au début du XIXe siècle', *Annales de Démographie Historique*, 1971, pp. 467–94.

8 See Marcel Lachiver, *La population de Meulan du XVIIe au XIXe siècle. Etude de démographie historique* (Paris: S.E.V.P.E.N., 1969); Nicole Lemaître, *Un horizon bloqué: Ussel et la montagne limousine aux XVIIe et XVIIIe siècles* (Ussel: Musée du pays d'Ussel, 1978); Christine Tainturier-Lamarre, 'Professions et pouvoir économique des petites villes bourguignonnes à la fin du XVIIIe siècle', in Georges Livet and Bernard Vogler (eds), *Pouvoir, ville et société en Europe 1650–1750* (Paris: Ophrys, [1983]), pp. 607–14; and especially Michel Vovelle, 'Villes, bourgs, villages: le réseau urbain-villageois en Provence (1750–1850)', in his *De la cave au grenier. Un itinéraire en Provence au XVIIIe siècle: De l'histoire sociale à l'histoire des mentalités* (Québec: Serge Fleury, 1980), pp. 19–38. René Favier's ongoing research on Dauphiné's small towns, fruits of which are contained in this volume, is parallelled by similar investigations by Christine Lamarre on small towns in Burgundy and by Claude Nières on Brittany's urban network.

9 Raymond Quenedey, *L'Habitation rouennaise: Etude d'histoire, de géographie et d'archéologie urbaines* (Rouen: Lestringant, 1926), pp. 77–81; Jean-Pierre Bardet, *Rouen aux XVIIe et XVIIIe siècles. Les mutations d'un espace social* (Paris: S.E.D.E.S., 1983), pp. 172–4; Vital Chomel *et al.*, *Histoire de Grenoble* (Toulouse: Privat, 1976), p. 137.

10 Roger Mols, *Introduction à la démographie historique des villes d'Europe du XIVe au XVIIIe siècle*, Vol. 1 (Louvain: J. Duculot, 1954), pp. 89–96.

11 Quoted in Lucien Romier, *Le Royaume de Cathérine de Médicis* (Paris: Librairie Académique, 1922), p. 161.

12 As late as 1696 just four sword nobles lived in Beauvais, while Agen, a city of roughly comparable size in Guyenne, housed 34 in 1640. Gregory Hanlon, 'Culture et comportements des élites urbaines en Agenais-Condomois au XVIIe siècle', thèse de 3e cycle, Université de Bordeaux III, 1983, p. 31.

13 *Histoire de Nîmes* (Aix-en-Provence: Edisud, 1982), p. 202.

14 Emmanuel Le Roy Ladurie, *Les paysans de Languedoc* (Paris: S.E.V.P.E.N., 1960), pp. 337–8, 342; Farr, Chapter 4 in this volume, p. 139; A. G. Manry, *Histoire de Clermont-Ferrand* (Clermont-Ferrand: Editions Volcans, 1975), pp. 186–8; Favier, Chapter 7 in this volume, p. 236; Vovelle, 'Villes, bourgs, villages', pp. 34–5.

15 Cissie Fairchilds, *Domestic Enemies: Servants and Their Masters in Old Regime France* (Baltimore, Md: Johns Hopkins University Press, 1984), p. 2; Sarah Maza, *Servants and Masters in Eighteenth-Century France: The Uses of Loyalty* (Princeton, NJ: Princeton University Press, 1983), pp. 26–7.

16 Philip Benedict, *Rouen during the Wars of Religion* (Cambridge: Cambridge University Press, 1981), p. 5; Bardet, *Rouen*, p. 187; Jean-Pierre Marque, *Institution municipale et groupes sociaux: Gray, petite ville de province*

(1690–1790) (Paris: Les Belles Lettres, 1979), p. 80.

17 John McManners, *French Ecclesiastical Society under the Ancien Régime: A Study of Angers in the Eighteenth Century* (Manchester: Manchester University Press, 1960), ch. 4; Philip T. Hoffman, *Church and Community in the Diocese of Lyon, 1500–1789* (New Haven, Conn.: Yale University Press, 1984), pp. 11–15; Georges Viard, 'Les chanoines de Langres au XVIIe siècle: recrutement, origines, fortunes', *Annales de l'Est*, 5th ser., vol. 28 (1976), pp. 111–17; Philippe Loupès, *Chapitres et chanoines de Guyenne aux XVIIe et XVIIIe siècles* (Paris: Ecole des Hautes Etudes en Sciences Sociales, 1985), pp. 237–43.

18 A. D. Seine-Maritime, 35 H, Liber Professorum des Cordeliers; McManners, *French Ecclesiastical Society*, p. 134; Hoffman, *Church and Community*, p. 14.

19 Richard Gascon, *Grand commerce et vie urbaine au XVIe siècle. Lyon et ses marchands* (Paris: Mouton, 1971), pp. 435–50; Olivier Zeller, *Les recensements lyonnais de 1597 et 1636: démographie historique et géographie urbaine* (Lyon: Presses Universitaires de Lyon, 1983), pp. 181–7; Benedict, *Rouen*, pp. 26–31; Bardet, *Rouen*, pp. 238–41.

20 See Gascon, *Grand commerce et vie urbaine*, pp. 435–50; Zeller, *Les recensements lyonnais*, pp. 181–7; Hugues Neveux, 'Structurations sociales de l'espace caennais (XVIe-XVIIIe siècles)', in Jean Chennebenoist *et al.*, *Villes et sociétés urbaines: Basse-Normandie XVIe–XXe siècles* (Caen: Cahiers des Annales de Normandie, 1985), pp. 1–78.

21 Jean-Pierre Goubert and Bernard Lepetit, 'Les niveaux de médicalisation des villes françaises à la fin de l'Ancien Régime', *Historical Reflections/Réflexions Historiques*, vol. 9 (1982), pp. 45–67.

22 T. J. A. Le Goff, *Vannes and Its Region: A Study of Town and Country in Eighteenth-Century France* (Oxford: Clarendon Press, 1981), p. 49.

23 Evidence on immigration is most abundant for the late seventeenth and eighteenth centuries, whose well-maintained parish registers regularly list the place of birth of both parties entering into a marriage. Useful tables summarizing immigration in a number of cities in this period may be found in Bardet, *Rouen*, p. 211, and Alain Cabantous, 'Rodez et sa population dans la première moitié du XVIIIe siècle: évolution d'ensemble et attraction migratoire', *Annales du Midi*, vol. 96 (1984), p. 160.

24 Sharlin, 'Natural decrease in early modern cities: a reconsideration', *Past & Present*, no. 79 (1978), pp. 126–38.

25 Perrenoud, 'Croissance ou déclin? Les mécanismes du non-renouvellement des populations urbaines', *Histoire, Economie, Société*, vol. 1 (1982), pp. 581–601.

26 Perrenoud, *La Population de Genève du XVIe au début du XIXe siècle: étude démographique* (Geneva: A. Jullien, 1979), p. 59.

27 Bardet, 'Esquisse d'un bilan urbain: L'exemple de Rouen', *Bulletin de la Société d'Histoire Moderne*, 6th ser., no. 11 (1981), p. 27.

28 On the prevalence of the recourse to wet nurses, see Bardet, *Rouen*, pp. 288–302, esp. p. 300; Abel Poitrineau, 'Un type de document et une paroisse urbaine: Saint-Jean-du-Passet, à Thiers, d'après une information ecclésiastique de 1785' in *Démographie urbaine, XVe–XXe siècle* (Lyon: Publications du Centre d'histoire économique et sociale de la région lyonnaise, [1977]), pp. 181–2. *Livres de raison* such as B. M. Rouen, Ms Y 128 and Henri Labrosse (ed.), 'Le livre de raison de la famille Le Court de Rouen (XVIe–XVIIe siècle)', *Bulletin de la Société Libre d'Emulation du Commerce et de l'Industrie de la Seine-Inférieure* (1937), pp. 121–54, suggest that the practice was well established by the sixteenth century.

29 Bardet, *Rouen*, pp. 371–3; Perrenoud, 'L'inégalité sociale devant la mort à Genève au XVIIe siècle', *Population*, vol. 30 (1975), pp. 221–44.

30 André Lespagnol *et al.*, *Histoire de Saint–Malo* (Toulouse: Privat, 1984), p. 143; Pierre Desportes *et al.*, *Histoire de Reims* (Toulouse: Privat, 1983); Pierre Deyon, *Amiens, capitale provinciale. Etude sur la société urbaine au XVIIe siècle* (Paris: Mouton, 1967), p. 36; Bardet, *Rouen*, p. 255; Maurice Garden, *Lyon et les lyonnais au XVIIIe siècle* (Paris: Les Belles Lettres, 1970), p. 91; Jean-Claude Perrot, *Genèse d'une ville moderne, Caen au 18ᵉ siècle* (Paris: Mouton, 1975), p. 820. Age at marriage was lower in small towns than among the rural population. Jacques Dupâquier, *La population rurale du Bassin parisien à l'époque de Louis XIV* (Paris: Ecole des Hautes Etudes en Sciences Sociales, 1979), p. 307.

31 Mols, *Introduction à la démographie historiques des villes*, Vol. 3, pp. 184–5; Philippe Guignet, *Mines, manufactures et ouvriers du Valenciennois au XVIIIe siècle* (New York: Arno Press, 1977), pp. 271, 353–4; Garden, *Lyon*, pp. 149–51; Bardet, *Rouen*, p. 232; Perrenoud, *Population de Genève*, p. 23.

32 Perrenoud, 'Variables sociales en démographie urbaine. L'exemple de Genève au XVIIIe siècle', in *Démographie urbaine*, pp. 153–65; Bardet, *Rouen*, pp. 269–71; Garden, *Lyon*, pp. 96–107; idem, 'La fécondité des familles consulaires lyonnaises du XVIIIe siècle', in *La France d'Ancien Régime: Etudes réunies en l'honneur de Pierre Goubert* (Toulouse: Privat, 1984), pp. 279–87; Benoît Garnot, 'La fécondité des classes populaires à Chartres au XVIIIe siècle', *Annales de Démographie Historique* (1986), pp. 195–214.

33 Bardet, *Rouen*, pp. 214–17.

34 Zeller, *Les recensements lyonnais*, p. 235.

35 Abel Poitrineau, *Remues d'hommes: Essai sur les migrations montagnardes en France aux XVIIe et XVIIIe siècles* (Paris: Aubier-Montaigne, 1983), passim.

36 For examples of rupture migration among the well-to-do: A. D. Seine-Maritime, G 3427 (reference to 'mon nepveu vaccabont' in the will of a canon); A. D. Tarn-et-Garonne, 6 E 149/9 (reference to the son of a Protestant pastor who has severed all ties with the family and moved to Spain); among the poor: Alain Collomp, *La Maison du père: Famille et village en Haute-Provence aux XVIIe et XVIIIe siècles* (Paris: Presses Universitaires de France, 1983), pp. 233–6.

37 Jean-Pierre Poussou, *Bordeaux et le Sud-Ouest au XVIIIe siècle: croissance économique et attraction urbaine* (Paris: École des Hautes Etudes en Sciences Sociales, 1983), ch. 4; Daniel Roche, *Le Peuple de Paris: Essai sur la culture populaire* (Paris: Aubier-Montaigne, 1981), pp. 30–1; Michel Vovelle, *Ville et campagne au 18e siècle (Chartres et la Beauce)* (Paris: Editions Sociales, 1980), pp. 32–3; Collomp, *Maison du père*, pp. 225–33; Jean-Pierre Gutton, *Domestiques et serviteurs dans la France de l'ancien régime* (Paris: Aubier-Montaigne, 1981), p. 79; Michael Sonenscher, 'Journeymen's migrations and workshop organization in eighteenth-century France', in S. L. Kaplan and C. J. Koepp (eds) *Work in France: Representations, Meaning, Organization, and Practices* (Ithaca, NY: Cornell University Press, 1986), p. 89.

38 Jean-Pierre Babelon, *Demeures parisiennes sous Henri IV et Louis XIII* (Paris: Editions du Temps, 1965), p. 43; Bardet, *Rouen*, pp. 174–5.

39 Recent works stressing the bonds of neighborhood include Roderick Phillips, *Family Breakdown in Late Eighteenth-Century France: Divorce in Rouen 1792–1803* (Oxford: Oxford University Press, 1980), pp. 180–7; Kathryn Norberg, *Rich and Poor in Grenoble, 1600–1814* (Berkeley, Calif.: University of California Press, 1985), p. 47; James R. Farr, 'Popular religious solidarity in sixteenth-century Dijon', *French Historical Studies*, vol. 14 (1985), p. 208; idem, 'Crimine nel vicinato: ingiurie, matrimonio e onore nella Digione del XVI e XVII secolo', *Quaderni storici*, no. 66 (1987), pp. 839–54; Hanlon, 'Culture et comportements des élites urbaines', p. 108; David Garrioch, *Neighbourhood*

and Community in Paris, 1740–1790 (Cambridge: Cambridge University Press, 1986), ch. 1.

40 Natalie Zemon Davis, 'Charivari, honneur et communauté à Lyon et à Genève au XVIIe siècle', in Jacques Le Goff and Jean-Claude Schmitt (eds), *Le Charivari* (Paris: Mouton, 1981), p. 212.

41 Emile Coornaert, *Les corporations en France avant 1789* (Paris: Editions Ouvrières, 1966); William H. Sewell, Jr., *Work and Revolution in France: The Language of Labor from the Old Regime to 1848* (Cambridge: Cambridge University Press, 1980), pp. 25–39; Gabriel Désert *et al., Histoire de Caen* (Toulouse: Privat, 1981), p. 159.

42 Henri Hauser, *Ouvriers du temps passé, XVe–XVIe siècles* (Paris: Alcan, 1909), p. 74.

43 Etienne Martin Saint-Léon, *Le Compagnonnage* (Paris: A. Colin, 1901); Emile Coornaert, *Les Compagnonnages en France du moyen age à nos jours* (Paris: Editions Ouvrières, 1966); Sewell, *Work and Revolution*, ch. 3.

44 A. Leroux (ed.), 'Statuts de la Confrérie de Notre-Dame la Joyeuse ou des Pastoureaux à Limoges', *Revue des Langues Romanes*, vol. 35 (1891), pp. 421–2. See also Michel Cassan, 'Les multiples visages des confréries de dévotion: l'exemple de Limoges au XVIe siècle', *Annales du Midi*, vol. 99 (1987), pp. 35–52.

45 Duby (ed.), *Histoire de la France urbaine*, Vol. 2, pp. 524–9; Marc Venard, 'Confréries et charités en Haute-Normandie du Moyen-Age à nos jours', in *La sociabilité en Normandie* (Rouen: Musées départementaux de la Seine-Maritime, 1983), pp. 17–18, 39–40.

46 B.N., MS Français 5340, statutes of the Arquebusiers of Rouen; Charles Laronze, *Essai sur le régime municipal en Bretagne pendant les guerres de religion* (Paris: Hachette, 1890), pp. 189–93; Albert Babeau, *La ville sous l'ancien régime*, Vol. 2 (Paris: Didier, 1884), pp. 54–77.

47 Natalie Zemon Davis, 'The reasons of misrule', in *Society and Culture in Early Modern France* (Stanford, Calif.: Stanford University Press, 1975), pp. 109–17; Jacques Rossiaud, 'Fraternités de jeunesse et niveaux de culture dans les villes du Sud-Est à la fin du Moyen Age', *Cahiers d'Histoire*, vol. 21 (1976), pp. 67–102; Duby (ed.), *Histoire de la France urbaine*, Vol. 2, pp. 529–32; A. N. Galpern, *The Religions of the People in Sixteenth-Century Champagne* (Cambridge, Mass.: Harvard University Press, 1976), pp. 71–82; Chevalier, *Bonnes villes*, ch. 12; Heather Arden, *Fools' Plays: A study of satire in the sottie* (Cambridge: Cambridge University Press, 1980).

48 Garden, *Lyon*, Part 2, chs 4, 5; Sonenscher, 'Journeymen's migrations', passim; idem, 'Journeymen, the courts and the French trades 1781–1791', *Past & Present*, no. 114 (1987), pp. 77–109; Garrioch, *Neighbourhood and Community*, ch. 3; Robert Darnton, 'A printing shop across the border', in *The Literary Underground of the Old Regime* (Cambridge, Mass.: Harvard University Press, 1982); idem, *The Great Cat Massacre and Other Episodes in French Cultural History* (New York: Basic Books, 1984), ch. 2.

49 Bernard Chevalier, *La ville de Tours et la société tourangelle 1356–1520* (Lille: Service de Reproduction des Thèses, 1974), pp. 79–84; idem, *Bonnes villes*, ch. 9; William Beik, *Absolutism and Society in Seventeenth-Century France: State Power and Provincial Aristocracy in Languedoc* (Cambridge: Cambridge University Press, 1985), p. 66.

50 François Lebrun *et al.*, *Histoire d'Angers* (Toulouse: Privat, 1975), pp. 39–40; Zeller, *Institutions de la France*, p. 43; Georges Viard, 'L'emprise sur la ville: seigneurs ecclésiastiques et serviteurs du roi à Langres de 1650 à 1750', in Livet and Vogler (eds), *Pouvoir, ville et société*, pp. 599–606.

51 Arlette Jouanna, 'La première domination des réformés à Montpellier (1561–

1563)', in Bernard Chevalier and Robert Sauzet (eds), *Les Réformes, enracinement socio-culturel* (Paris: La Maisnie, 1985), p. 152.

52 Zeller, *Institutions de la France*, pp. 38–47; Maurice Bordes, *L'administration provinciale et municipale en France au XVIIIe siècle* (Paris: S.E.D.E.S., 1972), ch. 9; Jean-Marie Constant, *Nobles et paysans en Beauce aux XVIème et XVIIème siècles* (Lille: Service de Reproduction des Thèses, 1981), p. 518.

53 Emmanuel Le Roy Ladurie, *Le Carnaval de Romans* (Paris: Gallimard, 1979), pp. 34–7; André Sanfaçon, 'Organisation municipale, mobilité et tensions sociales à Chartres dans la seconde moitié du XVIIe siècle', *Historical Reflections*, vol. 8 (1981), p. 48.

54 René Favreau, *La ville de Poitiers à la fin du Moyen Age. Une capitale régionale*, Vol. 2 (Poitiers: Société des Antiquaires de l'Ouest, 1978), p. 494; Barbara Diefendorf, *Paris City Councillors in the Sixteenth Century: The Politics of Patrimony* (Princeton, NJ: Princeton University Press, 1983), p. 44; Gascon, *Grand commerce et vie urbaine*, p. 412.

55 Giuliano Procacci, *Classi sociali e monarchia assoluta nella Francia della prima metà del secolo XVI* (Turin: Einaudi, 1955), pp. 171–8; Vladimir I. Raytses, 'Le programme de l'insurrection d'Agen en 1514', *Annales du Midi*, vol. 93 (1981), pp. 255–77; Judith Chandler Pugh Meyer, 'Reformation in La Rochelle: religious change, social stability, and political crisis, 1500–1568', PhD thesis, University of Iowa, 1977, pp. 178–84; David Parker, *La Rochelle and the French Monarchy: Conflict and Order in Seventeenth-Century France* (Royal Historical Society, 1980), pp. 39–47.

56 Schneider, Chapter 6 in this volume, p. 202. See also Benedict, *Rouen*, pp. 35–6.

57 G. B. Depping (ed.), *Correpondance administrative sous le règne de Louis XIV*, Vol. 1 (Paris: Imprimerie Nationale, 1850), part 2.

58 Hanlon, 'Culture et comportements des élites urbaines', p. 76.

59 Raytses, 'Programme de l'insurrection', pp. 265, 271–2.

60 René Pillorget, *Les mouvements insurrectionnels de Provence entre 1596 et 1715* (Paris: Pedone, 1975), pp. 206–36.

61 In addition to the works already cited in this paragraph, some preliminary exploration of these issues may be found in William H. Beik, 'Urban factions and the social order during the minority of Louis XIV', *French Historical Studies*, vol. 15 (1987), pp. 36–67. Sharon Kettering, *Patrons, Brokers, and Clients in Seventeenth-Century France* (Oxford: Oxford University Press, 1986), pp. 74–85, asserts that regional and national power-brokers often manipulated municipal elections to ensure the selection of men who would guarantee the city's loyalty to them in times of political conflict, but it is not clear just how these brokers exercised their influence. Such intervention may also have been a phenomenon largely of the 1630s and 1640s.

62 A. C. Rouen, A 16–17; B. M. Rouen, MS Y 214 (4), fos. 411–15.

63 G. Panel, *Documents concernant les pauvres de Rouen*, Vol. 1 (Rouen: Lestringant, 1917); Chevalier, *Bonnes villes*, pp. 236–8; Jean-Noël Biraben, *Les hommes et la peste en France et dans les pays européens et méditerranéens*, Vol. 2 (Paris: Mouton, 1975); Croix, *La Bretagne*, pp. 443–8, 472–534.

64 Gascon, *Grand commerce et vie urbaine*, passim; Gilles Caster, *Le commerce du pastel et de l'épicerie à Toulouse de 1450 à 1560* (Toulouse: Privat, 1963), passim; Farr, Chapter 4 in this volume, pp. 151–2; Irvine, Chapter 3 in this volume, p. 107.

65 Robert Boutruche *et al.*, *Bordeaux de 1453 à 1715* (Bordeaux: Fédérations Historique du Sud-Ouest, 1966), p. 289; Benedict, *Rouen*, p. 6; Farr, Chapter 4 in this volume, p. 141; Bernard Guenée, *Tribunaux et gens de justice dans le bailliage de Senlis à la fin du moyen âge* (Paris: Les Belles Lettres, 1963), bk 3,

ch. 3; Irvine, Chapter 3 in this volume, p. 112.

66 Farr, Chapter 4, pp. 151–2; Henry Heller, *The Conquest of Poverty: The Calvinist Revolt in Sixteenth-Century France* (Leiden: Brill, 1986), pp. 83–4, provides evidence of a similar trend toward the concentration of wealth in the hands of the richest citizens in Agen.

67 Hauser, *Ouvriers du temps passé*, pp. xl–xli.

68 Le Roy Ladurie, *Paysans de Languedoc*, part 2, ch. 5; Natalie Zemon Davis, 'Humanism, heresy, and poor relief', in *Society and Culture in Early Modern France*, pp. 17–64.

69 Benedict, *Rouen*, pp. 14–15; Farr, Chapter 4, pp. 145–6; Pierre Deyon, 'Variations de la production textile aux XVIe et XVIIe siècles: Sources et premiers résultats', *Annales: E.S.C.*, vol. 18 (1963), pp. 948–9.

70 The evidence on this question is cited below, p. 42. For sixteenth-century wage trends, see Gascon, *Grand commerce*, pp. 752–4; and Micheline Baulant, 'Le salaire des ouvriers du bâtiment à Paris de 1400 à 1726', *Annales: E.S.C.*, vol. 26 (1971), pp. 463–83. Michael Sonenscher's important 'Work and wages in Paris in the eighteenth century', in Maxine Berg *et al.* (eds), *Manufacture in Town and Country before the Factory* (Cambridge: Cambridge University Press, 1983), pp. 147–72, shows that for many workers money wages were just one part of their total compensation.

71 Jonathan Dewald, *The Formation of a Provincial Nobility: The Magistrates of the Parlement of Rouen, 1499–1610* (Princeton, NJ: Princeton University Press, 1980), pp. 54–7; Colin Kaiser, 'Les cours souveraines au XVIe siècle: morale et Contre-Réforme', *Annales: E.S.C.*, vol. 37 (1982), pp. 15–31.

72 Petit de Julleville, *Les Mystères* (reprinted edn, Geneva: Slatkine, 1968), ch. 13.

73 Michel Cassan, 'Basoches et basochiens à Toulouse à l'époque moderne', *Annales du Midi*, vol. 94 (1982), pp. 270–2.

74 Galpern, *Religions of the People*, pp. 102–6; Cassan, 'Les multiples visages des confréries', p. 38.

75 Dupâquier, *Population française*, pp. 11, 34; idem, *Population rurale du Bassin parisien*, pp. 191–2; Emmanuel Le Roy Ladurie, 'Les masses profondes: la paysannerie', in Braudel and Labrousse, Vol. 1, pp. 691–3, 727–30; Croix, *La Bretagne*, ch. 3.

76 De Vries, *European Urbanization*, p. 39; Paul Bairoch, *De Jéricho à Mexico. Villes et économie dans l'histoire* (Paris: Gallimard, 1985), ch. 11. A recent study reveals the same pattern in still-independent ducal Lorraine, where the percentage of the population living in communities of more than 600 hearths increased from 9–10 per cent in 1585 to 14.5 per cent in 1708. Marie-José Laperche-Fournel, *La population du Duché de Lorraine de 1580 à 1720* (Nancy: Presses Universitaires de Nancy, 1985), pp. 94, 176.

77 Alain Lefebvre and Françoise Tribouillard, 'Fiscalité et population dans l'élection de Valognes de 1540 à 1660', *Annales de Normandie*, vol. 21 (1971), pp. 211–12.

78 Roland Mousnier *et al.*, *Le Conseil du Roi de Louis XII à la Révolution* (Paris: Presses Universitaires de Fance, 1970), pp. 18–20.

79 Yvette Baradel, 'Belfort au XVIIIe siècle: les problèmes financiers d'une ville de garnison', *Actes du 103e Congrès National des Sociétés Savantes: Section d'histoire moderne et contemporaine* (Paris, 1979), Vol. 1, pp. 522–4; François-Yves Le Moigne, 'Le rôle économique des garnisons évêchoises au XVIIIe siècle d'après les exemples de Metz, Sarrelouis et Verdun', in Hans-Walter Herrmann and Franz Irsigler (eds), *Beiträge zur Geschichte der frühneuzeitlichen Garnisons- und Festungsstadt* (Saarbrücken: Minerva-Verlag Thinnes & Nolte, 1983), p. 210. See also the useful synthesis of André Corvisier, 'Le pouvoir

militaire et les villes', in Livet and Vogler (eds), *Pouvoir, ville et société*, pp. 17–18.

80 David Thomson, *Renaissance Paris: Architecture and Growth 1475–1600* (Berkeley, Calif.: University of California Press, 1984), chs 2 and 4, esp. p. 50; Robert R. Harding, *Anatomy of a Power Elite: The Provincial Governors of Early Modern France* (New Haven, Conn.: Yale University Press, 1978), pp. 171–9.

81 Sharon Kettering, *Judicial Politics and Urban Revolt in Seventeenth-Century France: The Parlement of Aix, 1629–1659* (Princeton, NJ: Princeton University Press, 1978), p. 28; Jean Gallet, *La Seigneurie bretonne 1450–1680: L'exemple du Vannetais* (Paris: Publications de la Sorbonne, 1983), pp. 145, 562.

82 Gascon, *Grand commerce et vie urbaine*, Part 3, ch. 3; Jean Jacquart, *La crise rurale en Ile-de-France, 1550–1670* (Paris: A. Colin, 1974), pp. 723–40; Emmanuel Le Roy Ladurie, 'Sur Montpellier et sa campagne aux XVIe et XVIIe siècles', *Annales: E.S.C.*, vol. 12 (1957), pp. 223–30; Roupnel, *La ville et la campagne*, Part 3; E. Gruter, *La naissance d'un grand vignoble: Les seigneuries de Pizay et Tanay en Beaujolais aux XVIe et XVIIe siècles* (Lyon: Presses Universitaires de Lyon, 1977), ch. 9.

83 Marcel Delafosse *et al.*, *Histoire de la Rochelle* (Toulouse: Privat, 1985), ch. 6.

84 Michel Morineau, 'Flottes de commerce et trafics français en Méditerranée au XVIIe siècle (jusqu'en 1669)', *XVIIe Siècle*, no. 86–87 (1970), pp. 150–1, 159; P. Mantellier, *Histoire de la communauté des marchands fréquentant la rivière de Loire*, Vol. 1 (Orléans: G. Jacob, 1867), pp. 326–8; Duby (ed.), *Histoire de la France urbaine*, Vol. 3, p. 81; Lespagnol *et al.*, *Histoire de Saint-Malo*, ch. 4.

85 Goubert, *Beauvais et le Beauvaisis de 1600 à 1730. Contribution à l'histoire sociale de la France du XVIIe siècle* (Paris: S.E.V.P.E.N., 1960), p. 128; Guignet, *Mines, manufactures et ouvriers du Valenciennois*, p. 204.

86 Deyon, *Amiens*, pp. 212–15; J. K. J. Thomson, *Clermont-de-Lodève 1633–1789: Fluctuations in the prosperity of a Languedocian cloth-making town* (Cambridge: Cambridge University Press, 1982), p. 121 and passim; Bardet, *Rouen*, p. 200.

87 Deyon, *Amiens*, pp. 98–103, 145–63, 261.

88 Salvatore Ciriacono, 'Silk manufacturing in France and Italy in the XVIIth century: two models compared', *Journal of European Economic History*, vol. 10 (1981), pp. 167–99; Bernard Chevalier *et al.*, *Histoire de Tours* (Toulouse: Privat, 1985), pp. 192, 199–200.

89 Karin Newman, 'Hamburg in the European economy, 1660–1750', *Journal of European Economic History*, vol. 14 (1985), p. 63.

90 Benedict, *Rouen*, p. 44; Jean Chagniot, *Paris et l'armée au XVIIIe siècle* (Paris: Economica, 1985), p. 77.

91 Such changes were made, for instance, in Orléans in 1568, Amiens in 1598, Metz in 1640 and Angers in 1656. François Bonnardot, 'Essai historique sur le régime municipal à Orléans d'après les documents conservés aux archives de la ville (1389–1790)', *Mémoires de la Société Archéologique et Historique de l'Orléanais*, vol. 18 (1884), p. 136; Deyon, *Amiens*, ch. 30; Yves Le Moigne, '"Hommes du roi" et pouvoir municipal à Metz (1641–1789)', in Livet and Vogler (eds), *Pouvoir, ville et société*, p. 571; Jacques Maillard, *Le Pouvoir municipal à Angers de 1657 à 1789*, Vol. 1 (Angers: Presses Universitaires d'Angers, 1984), p. 105.

92 Rossiaud, 'Fraternités de jeunesse', p. 102; Davis, 'Reasons of misrule', p. 119.

93 Richard Bonney, *Political Change in France under Richelieu and Mazarin* (Oxford: Oxford University Press, 1978), ch. 14; Nora Temple, 'The control and exploitation of French towns during the Ancien Régime', *History*, vol. 51 (1966), pp. 16–34.

94 J. Saint Germain, *La Reynie et la police au Grand Siècle* (Paris: Hachette, 1962);

Leon Bernard, *The Emerging City: Paris in the Age of Louis XIV* (Durham, NC: Duke University Press, 1970), chs 2, 7.

95 Corvisier, 'Le pouvoir militaire et les villes', p. 14; Babeau, *La ville sous l'Ancien Régime*, Vol. 1, p. 13.

96 Temple, 'Control and exploitation', p. 25; Marque, *Institution municipale*, p. 49; Lynn Hunt, *Revolution and Urban Politics in Provincial France: Troyes and Reims, 1786–1790* (Stanford, Calif.: Stanford University Press, 1978), p. 24; Goubert, *Beauvais*, p. 271. In Angers the office passed between a private individual, the *bailliage*, and the municipality. Maillard, *Pouvoir municipal à Angers*, Vol. 2, pp. 59–60.

97 Charles Petit-Dutaillis, *Les communes françaises. Caractères et évolution des origines au XVIIIe siècle* (Paris: Albin Michel, 1947), p. 250.

98 Bernard Lepetit, 'Pouvoir municipal et urbanisme (1650–1750): Sources et problematique', in Livet and Vogler (eds), *Pouvoir, ville et société*, p. 40.

99 Marque, *Institution municipale*, pp. 293–9.

100 Depping (ed.), *Correspondance administrative*, pp. xxxvii–viii, 815, 866; Juliette Turlan, *La commune et le corps de ville de Sens (1146–1789)* (Paris: Sirey, 1942), p. 113; Sanfaçon, 'Organisation municipale', p. 48; Deyon, *Amiens*, p. 464.

101 Gascon, *Grand commerce*, p. 412; Garden, *Lyon*, p. 502. For additional information on the social composition of city councils, see Maillard, *Pouvoir municipal à Angers*, Vol. 1, p. 229; François Lebrun *et al.*, *Histoire d'Angers* (Toulouse: Privat, 1975), p. 42; Philippe Guignet, 'Permanence et renouvellement des oligarchies municipales à Lille et à Valenciennes (de Louis XIV à la Révolution)', in Livet and Vogler (eds), *Pouvoir, ville et société*, pp. 203–16; Maurice Gresset, *Gens de justice à Besançon 1674–1789* (Paris: Bibliothèque Nationale, 1978), pp. 612–13; Marque, *Institution municipale*, pp. 101, 109–13; Jacques Godechot, 'Aux origines du régime représentatif en France: Des conseils politiques languedociens aux conseils municipaux de l'époque révolutionnaire', in Ernst Hinrichs, Eberhard Schmitt and Rudolf Vierhaus (eds), *Vom Ancien Régime zur Französischen Revolution: Forschungen und Perspektiven* (Göttingen: Vandenhoeck and Ruprecht, 1978), pp. 11–23.

102 Roupnel, *La ville et la campagne*, p. 166; Maillard, *Pouvoir municipal à Angers*, Vol. 1, pp. 76–86; Bordes, *L'Administration provinciale et municipale*, pp. 198–207.

103 Martin Lister, *A Journey to Paris in the Year 1698*, ed. R. P. Stearns (Urbana, Ill.: University of Illinois Press, 1967), p. 7; Louis Hautecoeur, 'L'Urbanisme à Paris de la Renaissance à la Monarchie de Juillet', in *Paris, croissance d'une capitale* (Paris: Hachette, 1961), pp. 101–8; Pierre Lavedan, *Histoire de l'urbanisme à Paris* (Paris: Hachette, 1975); Orest Ranum, *Paris in the Age of Absolutism: An Essay* (New York: Wiley, 1968), pp. 83–105, 282–7.

104 *Histoire d'Aix-en-Provence* (Aix-en-Provence: Edisud, 1977), p. 137.

105 Pierre Lavedan *et al.*, *L'urbanisme à l'époque moderne, XVIe–XVIIIe siècles* (Geneva: Droz, 1982), pp. 138–76; Delafosse *et al.*, *Histoire de la Rochelle*, p. 81; Roupnel, *La ville et la campagne*, p. 115.

106 L. Clark Keating, *Studies on the Literary Salon in France, 1550–1615* (Cambridge, Mass.: Harvard University Press, 1941); David Maland, *Culture and Society in Seventeenth-Century France* (New York: Scribner's, 1970), chs 2, 5; Carolyn C. Lougee, *Le Paradis des Femmes: Women, Salons, and Social Stratification in Seventeenth-Century France* (Princeton, NJ: Princeton University Press, 1976), esp. part 3.

107 W. L. Wiley, *The Early Public Theatre in France* (Cambridge, Mass.: Harvard University Press, 1960); Jean Robert, 'La clientèle aristocratique des comédiens et des musiciens dans le Midi méditerranéen (1610–1720)', in Jean Jacquot (ed.),

Dramaturgie et société: Rapports entre l'oeuvre théâtrale, son interprétation et son public aux XVIe et XVIIe siècles Vol. 1 (Paris: Editions du C.N.R.S., 1968), pp. 267–85; John Lough, *Writer and Public in France: From the Middle Ages to the Present Day* (Oxford, Clarendon Press, 1978), pp. 147–63.

108 Maland, *Culture and Society*, ch. 10; Henri-Jean Martin and M. Lecocq, *Livres et lecteurs à Grenoble: les registres du libraire Nicolas (1645–1668)* Vol. 1 (Geneva: Droz, 1977), pp. 91–3; Robert Schneider, 'Urban sociability in the Old Regime: religion and culture in early modern Toulouse', PhD thesis, University of Michigan, 1982, ch. 9.

109 Maurice Agulhon, *Pénitents et Francs-Maçons dans l'ancienne Provence* (Paris: Fayard, 1968), p. 144; Schneider, 'Urban sociability', p. 185; Benedict, *Rouen*, pp. 83–5.

110 Few good studies of such confraternities exist, but see Marc Venard, 'Le milieu spirituel rouennais à l'époque de Corneille', in Alain Niderst (ed.), *Pierre Corneille: Actes du colloque tenu à Rouen (2–6 octobre 1984)* (Paris: Presses Universitaires de France, 1985), pp. 163–70.

111 Raoul Allier, *La Cabale des Dévots 1627–1666* (Paris: A. Colin, 1902); Jean-Pierre Gutton, *La société et les pauvres: L'exemple de la généralité de Lyon 1534–1789* (Paris: Les Belles Lettres, 1971), pp. 295–326; Norberg, *Rich and Poor in Grenoble*, chs 2, 3; Schneider, 'Urban sociability', ch. 8.

112 Schneider, 'Urban sociability', pp. 404–5.

113 Norberg, *Rich and Poor in Grenoble*, pp. 126–32.

114 Nières, 'Une province et ses villes', pp. 509–10.

115 Dupâquier, *Population française*, pp. 34, 81.

116 Both Bairoch, *De Jéricho à Mexico*, p. 280, and de Vries, *European Urbanization*, p. 39, arrive at essentially similar conclusions. De Vries's figures actually show a slight decline in the percentage of the French population living in cities during the eighteenth century, but it should be noted that he relies on the 1806–09 censuses as his terminus ad quem, i.e. after the de-urbanization that accompanied the revolutionary period. A discordant note is sounded by Emmanuel Le Roy Ladurie, who discerns on the basis of a smaller sample of urban population figures considerably more rapid population growth in the cities than in the kingdom as a whole from 1725 to 1790. Duby (ed.), *Histoire de la France urbaine*, Vol. 3, pp. 295–7.

117 Gresset, *Gens de justice à Besançon*, pp. 47–8; Olwen H. Hufton, *Bayeux in the Late Eighteenth Century: A Social Study* (Oxford: Clarendon Press, 1967), pp. 7–8; Monique Cubells, *La Provence des Lumières. Les parlementaires d'Aix au 18e siècle* (Paris: Maloine, 1984), p. 13.

118 Mousnier *et al.*, *Conseil du Roi*, p. 19; William Doyle, 'The price of offices in pre-revolutionary France', *The Historical Journal*, vol. 27 (1984), p. 832.

119 Colin Kaiser, 'The deflation in the volume of litigation in Paris in the eighteenth century and the waning of the old judicial order', *European Studies Review*, Vol. 10 (1980), pp. 309–36; Hufton, *Bayeux*, p. 8. But cf. Nicole Castan, *Justice et répression en Languedoc à l'époque des lumières* (Paris: Flammarion, 1980), pp. 133–4. Richard L. Kagan, 'Law students and legal careers in eighteenth-century France', *Past & Present*, no. 68 (1975), pp. 62–8, traces the rising enrollments in the law faculties.

120 Alain Guéry, 'Les finances de la monarchie française sous l'Ancien Régime', *Annales: E.S.C.*, vol. 33 (1978), p. 227; James C. Riley, 'French finances, 1727–1768', *Journal of Modern History*, vol. 59 (1987), pp. 236–7.

121 Gérard Béaur, *Le marché foncier à la veille de la Révolution. Les mouvements de propriété beaucerons dans les régions de Maintenon et de Janville de 1761 à 1790* (Paris: Ecole des Hautes Etudes en Sciences Sociales, 1984), pp. 186–204;

Pierre de Saint Jacob, *Les paysans de la Bourgogne du Nord au dernier siècle de l'Ancien Régime* (Paris: Les Belles Lettres, 1960), pp. 186–7, 306–7, 437; Georges Frêche, *Toulouse et la région Midi-Pyrénées au siècle des lumières (vers 1670 – vers 1789)* (Paris: Cujas, 1974), pp. 464–76.

122   André Benoist, 'Les populations rurales du "Moyen-Poitou Protestant" de 1640 à 1789', thèse de troisième cycle, Université de Poitiers, 1983, pp. 365–70. Evidence of a growing noble presence can also be found for Dijon, Amiens, and Bayeux. The number of resident noblemen declined in Rouen, although not as rapidly as the total size of the nobility in the surrounding region. Farr, Chapter 4, p. 150; Mohammed El-Kordi, *Bayeux aux XVIIe et XVIIIe siècles. Contribution à l'histoire urbaine de la France* (Paris: Mouton, 1970), pp. 46–7; Robert Fossier *et al.*, *Histoire de la Picardie* (Toulouse: Privat, 1974), p. 277; Jonathan Dewald, *Pont-St-Pierre 1398–1789: Lordship, Community and Capitalism in Early Modern France* (Berkeley, Calif.: University of California Press, 1987), pp. 113–14.

123   ibid., pp. 193–9.

124   James C. Riley, *The Seven Years War and the Old Regime in France: The Economic and Financial Toll* (Princeton, NJ: Princeton University Press, 1986), pp. 109–10.

125   François-Georges Pariset *et al., Bordeaux au XVIIIe siècle* (Bordeaux: Fédération Historique du Sud-Ouest, 1968), Bks. 2, 4; Paul Butel, *Les négociants bordelais, l'Europe et les Iles au XVIIIe siècle* (Paris: Aubier-Montaigne, 1974); Gaston Rambert *et al.*, *Histoire du commerce de Marseille*, Vols 4–7 (Paris: Plon, 1954–66); Charles Carrière, *Négociants marseillais au XVIIIe siècle. Contribution à l'histoire des économies maritimes* (Marseille: Institut Historique de Provence, 1973); John Lough, *France on the Eve of Revolution: British Travellers' Observations 1763–1788* (Chicago: Dorsey Press, 1987), pp. 87–97.

126   *Histoire de Nîmes*, pp. 190, 198–201; Poussou, *Bordeaux et le Sud-Ouest*, pp. 243 ff.; J. Peyrot, M. Cordurié and C. Carrière, 'Capitalisme commercial et fabriques dans la France du Sud-Est au XVIIIe siècle', in *Négoce et industrie en France et en Irlande aux XVIIIe et XIXe siècles* (Paris: Editions du C.N.R.S., 1980), pp. 87–9; Georges Lefebvre, *Etudes orléanaises* Vol. 1 (Paris: Commission d'histoire économique et sociale de la Révolution, 1962), pp. 111–12.

127   Maillard, *Pouvoir municipal à Angers*, Vol. 2, p. 19.

128   Turlan, *Sens*, p. 15; see also Favier, Chapter 7, pp. 231–2.

129   Tihomir J. Markovitch, *Les industries lainières de Colbert à la Révolution* (Geneva: Droz, 1976), p. 458. On the general expansion of manufacturing, see Pierre Léon, 'La réponse de l'industrie', in Braudel and Labrousse, Vol. 2, pp. 217–66.

130   Jean François Belhoste, Gérard Gayot, *et al.*, *La manufacture du Dijonval et la draperie sedanaise 1650–1850* (Charleville-Mézières: Ministère de la Culture, Inventaire Général des Monuments et des Richesses Artistiques de la France, région de Champagne–Ardennes, 1984), pp. 20–21, 36–8, 43; Jean-Michel Chaplain, *La chambre des tisseurs. Louviers: cité drapière 1680–1840* (Seyssel: Editions du Champ Vallon, 1984), p. 110; Ronald Hubscher *et al.*, *Histoire d'Amiens* (Toulouse: Privat, 1986), p. 147; Bardet, *Rouen*, p. 200; Desportes *et al.*, *Histoire de Reims*, pp. 206–11; Guignet, *Mines, manufactures et ouvriers du Valenciennois*, p. 204; Perrot, *Genèse d'une ville moderne*, p. 395; Joan Wesselmann Reinhardt, 'A French town under the Old Regime: Aumale in the seventeenth and eighteenth centuries', PhD thesis, University of Wisconsin, 1983, pp. 100–2.

131   Lenard R. Berlanstein, *The Barristers of Toulouse in the Eighteenth Century (1740–1793)* (Baltimore, Md: Johns Hopkins University Press, 1975), p. 68; Norberg, *Rich and Poor in Grenoble*, p. 244, finds both merchants and lawyers prospering.

132 Daniel Roche, *Le siècle des lumières en province: Académies et académiciens provinciaux, 1680–1789* (Paris: Mouton, 1978), pp. 224–6; Garden, *Lyon*, pp. 380–98.

133 Roche, *Le peuple de Paris*, p. 76; J. Godechot and S. Moncassin, 'Structures et relations sociales à Toulouse (1749, 1785)', *Annales Historiques de la Révolution Française*, vol. 37 (1965), pp. 159–60; Garden, *Lyon*, pp. 150, 196; Vovelle, *Ville et campagne*, p. 61; Maillard, *Pouvoir municipal à Angers*, Vol. 1, p. 286; also Norberg, *Rich and Poor in Grenoble*, p. 244. Per capita wealth may have declined in Vannes, although the evidence presented by Le Goff, *Vannes*, pp. 42–8, is inconclusive.

134 Garden, *Lyon*, p. 150; Vovelle, *Ville et campagne*, p. 60.

135 Roche, *Peuple de Paris*, Part 2. See also Perrot, *Genèse d'une ville moderne*, pp. 916–17.

136 Pierre Verlet, *L'art du meuble à Paris au XVIIIe siècle* (Paris: Presses Universitaires de France, 1958); John Woodforde, *The Strange Story of False Hair* (Routledge and Kegan Paul, 1971); Jean-François Revel, *Un festin en paroles: Histoire littéraire de la sensibilité gastronomique de l'Antiquité à nos jours* (Paris: Pauvert, 1979); Aileen Ribeiro, *Dress in Eighteenth-Century Europe* (New York: Holmes and Meier, 1985).

137 Melon, 'Essai politique sur le commerce (1728)', in M. Daire (ed.), *Economistes-financiers du XVIIIe siècle* (Paris: Guillaumin, 1843), p. 738; André Morize, *L'apologie du luxe au XVIIIe siècle et 'Le Mondain' de Voltaire* (Paris: Didier, 1909).

138 Louis Sebastien Mercier, *Tableau de Paris* (Amsterdam, 1782–83), Bk. 1, p. 101. Poussou, *Bordeaux et le Sud-Ouest*, pp. 26–8, reveals that where just six *perruquiers* married in Bordeaux between 1668 and 1677, 190 did so between 1782 and 1791. See also Perrot, *Genèse d'une ville moderne*, pp. 269–71; Guignet, *Mines, manufactures et ouvriers du Valenciennois*, p. 383.

139 Reinhardt, 'Aumale', pp. 86, 118–26, 421. See also Favier, Chapter 7, p. 238.

140 Joan Thirsk, *Economic Policy and Projects: The Development of a Consumer Society in Early Modern England* (Oxford: Oxford University Press, 1978); Neil McKendrick, John Brewer and J. H. Plumb, *The Birth of a Consumer Society: The Commercialization of Eighteenth-Century England* (Bloomington, Ind.: Indiana University Press, 1982).

141 Lough, *France on the Eve of Revolution*, p. 76; Jacob M. Price, *France and the Chesapeake: A History of the French Tobacco Monopoly 1674–1791 and of Its Relationship to the British and American Tobacco Trades* (Ann Arbor, Mich.: University of Michigan Press, 1973), pp. 376–7.

142 The potential significance of this neglected topic is also underscored by Josef W. Konvitz, 'Does the century 1650–1750 constitute a period in urban history? The French evidence reviewed', *The Journal of Urban History*, Vol. 14 (1988), pp. 419–54, a stimulating set of suggestions for further research on this period. I am grateful to Professor Konvitz for letting me see a copy of this article prior to publication.

143 Isherwood, *Farce and Fantasy: Popular Entertainment in Eighteenth-Century Paris* (Oxford: Oxford University Press, 1986), passim; Lough, *Writer and Public*, pp. 259–70.

144 Jean Quéniart, *Culture et société urbaines dans la France de l'Ouest au XVIIIe siècle* (Paris: Klincksieck, 1978), pp. 485–514; Babeau, *Ville sous l'ancien régime*, Vol. 2, p. 154.

145 Quéniart, *Culture et société urbaines*, p. 488.

146 Agulhon, *Pénitents et Francs-Maçons*, pp. 145–6, 154–9; Schneider, 'Urban sociability', p. 235.

147   Michel Vovelle, *Piété baroque et déchristianisation en Provence au XVIIIe siècle* (Paris: Plon, 1973), Part 2, chs 1, 2; Norberg, *Rich and Poor in Grenoble*, pp. 240–57.
148   Garrioch, *Neighbourhood and Community in Paris*, pp. 72–7, 177–80, 202–4, 207–8.
149   The extent to which the upper nobility had come to embrace the values of the Enlightenment is stressed by Roche, *Siècle des Lumières en province*, and Guy Chaussinand-Nogaret, *La noblesse au XVIIIème siècle: De la Féodalité aux Lumières* (Paris: Hachette, 1976), chs 4, 7, 8. Michel Vovelle, 'L'élite ou la mensonge des mots', *Annales: E.S.C.*, vol. 29 (1984), pp. 49–72, argues for the continued existence of differences in behavior between the nobility and the rest of the population.
150   Roche, *Siècle des Lumières en province*, pp. 270–71.
151   Schneider, 'Urban sociability', p. 258; Jacques Depauw, 'Naissances illégitimes et société à Nantes au XVIIIe siècle', *Annales: E.S.C.*, vol. 27 (1972), pp. 1155–82; Cissie Fairchilds, 'Female sexual attitudes and the rise of illegitimacy: a case study', *Journal of Interdisciplinary History*, vol. 8 (1978), pp. 635, 649; Norberg, *Rich and Poor in Grenoble*, pp. 192, 208.
152   Fairchilds, *Domestic Enemies*; Maza, *Servants and Masters*.
153   Garrioch, *Neighbourhood and Community in Paris*, p. 111. See also Bardet, *Rouen*, p. 239.
154   Maillard, *Pouvoir municipal à Angers*, Vol. 2, p. 31.
155   Marque, *Institution municipale*, passim.
156   Despite Maurice Bordes, *La réforme municipale du contrôleur général Laverdy et son application (1764–1771)* (Toulouse: Association des Publications de la Faculté des Lettres, 1968) and *L'administration provinciale et municipale*, chs 11–14, Laverdy's motives or any broader debate on the appropriate character of municipal government that might have shaped his reforms remain obscure.
157   Maillard, *Pouvoir municipal à Angers*, passim.
158   ibid., Vol. 2, Part 3.
159   Duby (ed.), *Histoire de la France urbaine*, Vol. 3, pp. 439–81; Pariset *et al.*, *Bordeaux au XVIIIe siècle*, Bk. 4, ch. 2; Daniel Ligou and Christine Tavernier, 'Les problèmes d'urbanisme dans le Dijon du XVIIIe siècle', in *Les Villes: Contribution à l'étude de leur développement en fonction de l'évolution économique* (Reims: Publications de l'Université de Reims, 1972), pp. 109–32; Line Teisseyre-Sallmann, 'Urbanisme et société: L'exemple de Nîmes aux XVIIe et XVIIIe siècles', *Annales: E.S.C.*, vol. 35 (1980), pp. 965–86; Bardet, *Rouen*, ch. 3; Perrot, *Genèse d'une ville moderne*, ch. 10.
160   A. C. Rouen, A 19, deliberation of 5 July 1567.
161   Williams, *Police of Paris*, pp. 260–1.
162   Lavedan, *Histoire de l'urbanisme à Paris*, p. 282; Roche, *Peuple de Paris*, p. 235.
163   ibid., p. 262.
164   Williams, *Police of Paris*, p. 237. There is abundant evidence that such a trend indeed occurred. See Chagniot, *Paris et l'armée*, pp. 145–50; Norberg, *Rich and Poor in Grenoble*, pp. 44–8, 94, 227–30.

APPENDIX: SOURCES FOR TABLES 1.1 AND 1.2

Tables 1.1 and 1.2 present the most reliable information I have been able to compile about the size of France's cities at roughly fifty-year intervals between 1500 and 1789.

Wherever possible, extrapolations based on information from parish registers, censuses, or tax rolls have been used, but estimates derived according to other procedures have also been retained for the sixteenth century when these are provided by scholars well acquainted with the city in question. Unless an authority on a given city provides a reason for accepting other procedures, estimates based on parish registration information assume urban birth rates of forty births per thousand people in the sixteenth and seventeenth century, declining to thirty-three per thousand by 1789, while those based on tax rolls assume 4.5 people per hearth. Where it has been necessary to rely for late eighteenth-century data on the 1806–09 census figures in René Le Mée, 'Population agglomérée, population éparse au début du XIXe siècle', *Annales de Démographie Historique*, 1971, pp. 466–93, these have been increased by 5 per cent to compensate for the decline that occurred in the size of most cities between 1789 and 1806.

I am extremely grateful to Jean-Noël Biraben of the Institut National des Etudes Démographiques for kindly providing me with baptismal figures concerning thirty cities that he assembled in the course of his ongoing research on the movement of the French population prior to 1670. Cases where I have relied upon his figures are indicated by the notation 'Biraben'. Short titles only have been provided for works listed in the Select Bibliography below.

Agen: Henry Heller, *The Conquest of Poverty: The Calvinist Revolt in Sixteenth Century France* (Leiden: Brill, 1986), p. 82.

Aix-en-Provence: *Histoire d'Aix-en-Provence* (Aix-en-Provence: Edisud, 1977), pp. 113, 209.

Albi: Jean-Louis Biget *et al.*, *Histoire d'Albi* (Toulouse: Privat, 1983), pp. 93–4, 200–1.

Alençon: A. C. Alençon, 11 E 1–2, 12 E 1–8, 21, 26–39; A. D. Orne, registres paroissiaux, Alençon; Le Mée, 'Population agglomérée,' p. 483.

Amiens: Edouard Maugis, *Recherches sur les transformations du régime politique et social de la ville d'Amiens des origines de la commune à la fin du XVIe siècle* (Paris: Picard, 1906), Appendix 4; Robert Fossier *et al.*, *Histoire de la Picardie* (Toulouse: Privat, 1974), pp. 275–6.

Angers: Biraben; François Lebrun *et al.*, *Histoire d'Angers* (Toulouse: Privat, 1975), p. 91; idem (ed.), *Paroisses et communes de France: Dictionnaire d'histoire administrative et démographique – Maine-et-Loire* (Paris: Editions du C.N.R.S., 1974), p. 36.

Arles: Edouard Baratier, *La démographie provençale du XIIIe au XVIe siècle* (Paris: S.E.V.P.E.N., 1961), p. 144; Le Mée, 'Population agglomérée', p. 470.

Auch: Biraben; *Histoire de Tarbes* (Pau: Marrimpouey, 1975), p. 153 n.

Aurillac: Biraben; Grimmer, *Vivre à Aurillac*, p. 19.

Auxerre: Jean-Pierre Rocher *et al.*, *Histoire d'Auxerre* (Roanne: Horvath, 1984), pp. 238–40.

Bayonne: Biraben; Le Mée, 'Population agglomérée', p. 485.

Besançon: Claude Fohlen *et al., Histoire de Besançon* (Paris: Nouvelle Librairie de France, 1964–5), Vol. 1, pp. 567–8, Vol. 2, pp. 86, 156.

Blois: Biraben; Le Mée, 'Population agglomérée,' p. 477.

Bordeaux: Robert Boutruche *et al.*, *Bordeaux de 1453 à 1715* (Bordeaux: Fédération Historique du Sud-Ouest, 1966), p. 69; Biraben; Poussou, *Bordeaux et le Sud-Ouest*, p. 20.

Bourges: Francis R. Hodges, 'War, population and the structure of wealth in sixteenth-century Bourges, 1557–1586', PhD Thesis, University of Tennessee, 1983, p. 133; Jacques Dupâquier, *Statistiques démographiques du Bassin Parisien, 1636–1720* (Paris: Gauthier-Villars, 1977), p. 219; Le Mée, 'Population agglomérée', p. 471.

Bourg-St-Andéol: Alain Molinier, *Stagnations et croissance: Le Vivarais aux XVIIe–XVIIIe siècles* (Paris: Ecole des Hautes Etudes en Sciences Sociales, 1985), pp. 140, 236.

Brest: Yves Le Gallo *et al.*, *Histoire de Brest* (Toulouse: Privat, 1976), pp. 67, 102.

Châlons-sur-Marne: Georges Clause and Jean-Pierre Ravaux *et al.*, *Histoire de Châlons-sur-Marne* (Roanne: Horvath, 1983), p. 129; Dupâquier, *Statistiques démographiques du Bassin Parisien*, p. 219; Hélène Boucher (ed.), *Paroisses et communes de France: Dictionnaire d'histoire administrative et démographique – Marne* (Paris: Editions du C.N.R.S., 1984), p. 189.

Chartres: Biraben; Vovelle, *Ville et campagne au 18e siècle*, pp. 108–9.

Châteaudun: Biraben; Le Mée, 'Population agglomérée', p. 474.

Cherbourg: Biraben; Georges Lefebvre, *Cherbourg à la fin de l'Ancien Régime et au début de la Révolution* (Caen: Cahier des Annales de Normandie, 1965), p. 13; Le Mée, 'Population agglomérée', p. 479.

Clermont-l'Hérault: Thomson, *Clermont-de-Lodève*, p. 47.

Corbeil: Biraben; Le Mée, 'Population agglomérée', p. 488.

Coulommiers: Biraben; Le Mée, 'Population agglomérée', p. 488.

Coutances: Biraben; Le Mée, 'Population agglomérée', p. 480.

Dijon: James R. Farr, 'The rise of a middle class: artisans in Dijon, 1550–1650', PhD Thesis, Northwestern University, 1983, p. 95; G. Bouchard, 'Dijon au XVIIIe siècle: Les dénombrements d'habitants', *Annales de Bourgogne*, vol. 25 (1953), pp. 46, 54.

Dreux: Biraben; Le Mée, 'Population agglomérée', p. 474.

Grenoble: Vital Chomel *et al.*, *Histoire de Grenoble* (Toulouse: Privat, 1976), p. 96; Norberg, *Rich and Poor in Grenoble*, p. 14; Favier, Chapter 7, p. 224.

Joigny: Biraben; Le Mée, 'Population agglomérée', p. 493.

La Rochelle: Marcel Delafosse *et al.*, *Histoire de la Rochelle* (Toulouse: Privat, 1985), pp. 185–7.

Le Havre: André Corvisier *et al.*, *Histoire du Havre* (Toulouse: Privat, 1983), p. 80.

Lille: Alain Lottin, *Lille, citadelle de la Contre-Réforme? (1598–1668)* (Dunkerque: Westhoek, 1984), p. 19; Pierre Deyon, 'Dénombrements et structures urbaines', *Revue du Nord*, no. 210 (1971), p. 498; Michel Morineau, *Les faux-semblants d'un démarrage économique: agriculture et démographie en France au XVIIIe siècle* (Paris: A. Colin, 1970), p. 317.

Lisieux: Biraben; Le Mée, 'Population agglomérée', p. 470.

Lorient: Josef W. Konvitz, *Cities and the Sea: Port City Planning in Early Modern Europe* (Baltimore: Johns Hopkins University Press, 1978), p. 138; Le Mée, 'Population agglomérée', p. 481.

Lyon: Gascon, *Grand commerce et vie urbaine*, p. 347; Benedict, *Rouen*, p. 3; Zeller, *Les recensements lyonnais*, pp. 224, 231; Garden, *Lyon et les lyonnais*, p. 34.

Marseille: Edouard Baratier *et al.*, *Histoire de Marseille* (Toulouse: Privat, 1973), pp. 138, 166–7; Jean-Pierre Bardet, review of Michel Terrisse 'La population de Marseille et de son terroir de 1694 à 1830', *Annales de Démographie Historique*, 1973, pp. 357–9, 366.

Mayenne: Biraben; Le Mée, 'Population agglomérée', p. 480.

Metz: Jean Rigault, 'La population de Metz au XVIIe siècle: quelques problèmes de démographie', *Annales de l'Est*, 5th ser., vol. 11 (1951), p. 308; François-Yves Le-Moigne *et al.*, *Histoire de Metz* (Toulouse: Privat, 1986), p. 178.

Meulan: Marcel Lachiver, *La population de Meulan du XVIIe au XIXe siècle (vers 1600–1870): Etude de démographie historique* (Paris: S.E.V.P.E.N., 1969), pp. 38–42, 73–80, 209.

Montivilliers: Jacques Bottin, *Seigneurs et paysans dans l'Ouest du Pays de Caux 1540–1640* (Paris: Le Sycomore, 1983), p. 351.

Montauban: A. D. Tarn-et-Garonne, 1 GG 2, 2 GG 1, 12 GG 8–10, 22–24; Daniel Ligou *et al.*, *Histoire de Montauban* (Toulouse: Privat, 1984), p. 168.

Montpellier: Irvine, Chapter 3, p. 105; A. C. Montpellier, CC 1043–9, GG 3–6, 320–4; Duby (ed.), *Histoire de la France urbaine*, Vol. 3, p. 297; Le Mée, 'Population agglomérée', p. 475; Gérard Cholvy *et al.*, *Histoire de Montpellier* (Toulouse: Privat, 1985), p. 205.

Morlaix: Biraben; Le Mée, 'Population agglomérée', p. 474.

Nantes: Biraben; Le Mée, 'Population agglomérée', p. 478.

Nevers: Jean-Bernard Charrier *et al.*, *Histoire de Nevers* (Roanne: Horvath, 1984), Vol. 1, p. 188.

Nîmes: *Histoire de Nîmes* (Aix-en-Provence: Edisud, 1982), pp. 176, 187, 201; Line Teisseyre-Sallmann, 'Urbanisme et société: L'exemple de Nîmes aux XVIIe et XVIIIe siècles', *Annales: E.S.C.*, vol. 35 (1980), p. 967.

Niort: Biraben; André Benoist, 'Les populations rurales du "Moyen-Poitou Protestant" de 1640 à 1789', thèse de troisème cycle, Université de Poitiers, 1983, p. 911.

Orléans: Biraben; Christian Poitou (ed.), *Paroisses et communes de France: Dictionnaire d'histoire administrative et démographique – Loiret* (Paris: Editions du C.N.R.S., 1982), p. 387.

Paris: Biraben; Marcel Lachiver, 'L'approvisionnement de Paris en viande au XVIIIe siècle', in *La France d'Ancien Régime: Etudes réunies en l'honneur de Pierre Goubert* (Toulouse: Privat, 1984), p. 352.

Périgueux: Arlette Higounet-Nadal, *Périgueux aux XIVe et XVe siècles: Etude de démographie historique* (Bordeaux, Fédération Historique du Sud-Ouest, 1978), p. 191.

Perpignan: Biraben; Le Mée, 'Population agglomérée', p. 485.

Poitiers: Robert Favreau *et al.*, *Histoire de Poitiers* (Toulouse: Privat, 1985), pp. 178, 210, 237.

Privas: Molinier, *Stagnations et croissance*, pp. 140, 247–9.

Reims: Galpern, *Religions of the People in Sixteenth-Century Champagne*, p. 15; Biraben; Pierre Desportes *et al.*, *Histoire de Reims* (Toulouse: Privat, 1983), p. 165.

Rennes: Biraben; Jean Meyer *et al.*, *Histoire de Rennes* (Toulouse: Privat, 1972), p. 246.

Roanne: Biraben; Le Mée, 'Population agglomérée', p. 478.

Rochefort: Konvitz, *Cities and the Sea*, p. 137; Philippe Hercule (ed.), *Paroisses et communes de France: Dictionnaire d'histoire administrative et démographique – Charente–Maritime* (Paris: Editions du C.N.R.S., 1986), p. 411.

Romans: Le Roy Ladurie, *Carnaval de Romans*, pp. 10–11; Favier, Chapter 7, p. 224.

Rouen: Michel Mollat, *Le commerce maritime normand à la fin du Moyen Age* (Paris: Plon, 1952), p. 529; Philip Benedict, 'Catholics and Huguenots in sixteenth-century Rouen: the demographic effects of the Religious Wars', *French Historical Studies*, vol. 9 (1975), pp. 209–33; Bardet, *Rouen*, Vol. 2, p. 34.

St-Denis: Biraben; Le Mée, 'Population agglomérée', p. 489.

St-Malo: Biraben; André Lespagnol *et al.*, *Histoire de Saint-Malo* (Toulouse: Privat, 1984), p. 140.

St-Omer: Biraben; Alain Derville *et al.*, *Histoire de Saint-Omer* (Lille: Presses Universitaires de Lille, 1981), p. 150.

Sarlat: Biraben; Le Mée, 'Population agglomérée', p. 473.

Saumur: François Lebrun, *Les hommes et la mort en Anjou aux 17e et 18e siècles: Essai de démographie et de psychologie historiques* (Paris: Mouton, 1971), p. 159; idem (ed.), *Paroisses et communes de France: Dictionnaire d'histoire administrative et démographique – Maine-et-Loire* (Paris: Editions du C.N.R.S., 1974), p. 389.

Strasbourg: Jean-Pierre Kintz, *La société strasbourgeoise du milieu du XVIe siècle à la fin de la Guerre de Trente Ans 1560–1650: Essai d'histoire démographique, économique et sociale* (Paris: Ophrys, 1984), p. 235; Franklin Ford, *Strasbourg in Transition, 1648–1789* (New York: Norton, 1966), pp. 115–6.

Tarbes: *Histoire de Tarbes*, pp. 133, 153–4.

Toulon: René Baehrel, *Une croissance: la Basse-Provence rurale (fin XVIe siècle– 1789)* (Paris: S.E.V.P.E.N., 1961), pp. 235–6; Michel Vovelle, 'Entre la peste de 1720 et le siège de 1793: Les aventures de la démographie toulonnaise au XVIIIe siècle', in *La France d'Ancien Régime: Etudes réunies en l'honneur de Pierre Goubert*, pp. 705–6.

Toulouse: Jean Coppolani, *Toulouse: étude de géographie urbaine* (Toulouse: Privat, 1954), pp. 97, 102–3.

Tours: Bernard Chevalier, *La ville de Tours et la société tourangelle 1356–1520* (Lille: Service de Reproduction des Thèses, 1974), p. 347; idem *et al.*, *Histoire de Tours* (Toulouse: Privat, 1985), pp. 193–4.

Troyes; Galpern, *Religions of the People*, p. 15; Jean-Louis Bourgeon, *Les Colbert avant Colbert: Destin d'une famille marchande* (Paris: Presses Universitaires de France, 1973), p. 107; Thalia Cosmos, 'The textile industry of Troyes: a study of urban society in late seventeenth century France', PhD Thesis, New York University, 1977, pp. 15–16; Hunt, *Revolution and Urban Politics*, p. 44.

Ussel: Biraben; Nicole Lemaitre, *Un horizon bloqué: Ussel et la montagne limousine aux XVIIe et XVIIIe siècles* (Ussel: Musée du pays d'Ussel, 1978), pp. 38–9.

Valence: Heller, *Conquest of Poverty*, p. 209; Favier, Chapter 7, p. 224.

Versailles: Bernard Lepetit, 'Une création urbaine: Versailles de 1661 à 1722', *Revue d'Histoire Moderne et Contemporaine*, vol. 25 (1978), pp. 611, 618.

Select Bibliography

This bibliography seeks to indicate only the most important secondary works pertaining to the urban history of Ancien Régime France. Philippe Dollinger and Philippe Wolff, *Bibliographie de l'histoire des villes de France* (Paris: Klincksieck, 1967), offers a full bibliography of works published before 1967. The more recent books of Duby (ed.) and Meyer cited below also contain useful bibliographies. Mention should be made as well of the general histories of individual cities that have appeared at an accelerating rate in recent years from a growing number of French regional publishing houses. Although I have not listed these works below lest I overload the bibliography, those interested in exploring further the history of French cities should not neglect these works. They often contain valuable information not easily available elsewhere.

Agulhon, Maurice, *Pénitents et Francs-Maçons dans l'ancienne Provence* (Paris: Fayard, 1968).

Babeau, Albert, *La ville sous l'Ancien Régime*, 2 vols (Paris: Didier, 1884).

Babelon, Jean-Pierre, *Demeures parisiennes sous Henri IV et Louis XIII* (Paris: Le Temps, 1965).

Babelon, Jean-Pierre, *Paris au XVIe siècle* (Paris: Hachette, 1986).

Bairoch, Paul, *De Jéricho à Mexico: Villes et économie dans l'histoire* (Paris: Gallimard, 1985).

Bardet, Jean-Pierre, *Rouen aux XVIIe et XVIIIe siècles. Les mutations d'un espace social* (Paris: S.E.D.E.S., 1983).

Baulant, Micheline, 'Le salaire des ouvriers du bâtiment à Paris de 1400 à 1726', *Annales: E.S.C.*, vol. 26 (1971), pp. 463–83.

Belhoste, Jean-François, Gayot, Gérard, *et al.*, *La manufacture du Dijonval et la draperie sedanaise 1650–1850* (Charleville-Mézières: Ministère de la Culture, 1984).

Benedict, Philip, *Rouen during the Wars of Religion* (Cambridge: Cambridge University Press, 1981).

Berg, Maxine, Hudson, Pat, and Sonenscher, Michael (eds), *Manufacture in Town and Country before the Factory* (Cambridge: Cambridge University Press, 1983).

Bordes, Maurice, *L'administration provinciale et municipale en France au XVIIIe siècle* (Paris: S.E.D.E.S., 1972).

Bossenga, Gail, 'City and state: an urban perspective on the origins of the French Revolution', in Keith Baker (ed.), *The Political Culture of the Old Regime* (Oxford: Pergamon Press, 1987).

Boudon, Françoise, Chastel, André, *et al.*, *Système de l'architecture urbaine. Le quartier des Halles à Paris* (Paris, Editions du C.N.R.S., 1977).

Braudel, Fernand, and Labrousse, Ernest (eds), *Histoire économique et sociale de la France*, 3 vols (Paris: Presses Universitaires de France, 1970–77).

Chevalier, Bernard, *Les bonnes villes de France du XIVe au XVIe siècle* (Paris: Aubier-Montaigne, 1982).

Coornaert, Emile, *Les corporations en France avant 1789* (Paris: Editions Ouvrières, 1966).

Coornaert, Emile, *Les compagnonnages en France du Moyen Age à nos jours* (Paris: Editions Ouvrières, 1966).

Couturier, Marcel, *Recherches sur les structures sociales de Châteaudun, 1525–1789* (Paris: S.E.V.P.E.N., 1969).

Daumard, Adeline, and Furet, François, *Structures et rélations sociales à Paris au milieu du XVIIIe siècle* (Paris: A. Colin, 1961).

Davis, Natalie Zemon, *Society and Culture in Early Modern France* (Stanford, Calif.: Stanford University Press, 1975).

de Vries, Jan, *European Urbanization 1500–1800* (Cambridge, Mass.: Harvard University Press, 1984).

Deyon, Pierre, *Amiens, capitale provinciale. Etude sur la société urbaine au XVIIe siècle* (Paris: Mouton, 1967).

Diefendorf, Barbara, *Paris City Councillors in the Sixteenth Century: The Politics of Patrimony* (Princeton, NJ: Princeton University Press, 1983).

Duby, Georges (ed.), *Histoire de la France urbaine*, 5 vols (Paris: Seuil, 1980–85).

Fairchilds, Cissie, *Domestic Enemies: Servants and their Masters in Old Regime France* (Baltimore, Md: Johns Hopkins University Press, 1984).

Farge, Arlette, *La vie fragile. Violence, pouvoirs et solidarités à Paris au XVIIIe siècle* (Paris: Hachette, 1986).

Farr, James, *Hands of Honor: Artisans and Their World in Early Modern France (Dijon, 1550–1650)* (Ithaca, NY: Cornell University Press, 1988).

Galpern, A. N., *The Religions of the People in Sixteenth-Century Champagne* (Cambridge, Mass.: Harvard University Press, 1976).

Garden, Maurice, *Lyon et les lyonnais au XVIIIe siècle* (Paris: Les Belles Lettres, 1970).

Garrioch, David, *Neighbourhood and Community in Paris, 1740–1790* (Cambridge: Cambridge University Press, 1986).

Gascon, Richard, *Grand commerce et vie urbaine au XVIe siècle. Lyon et ses marchands*, 2 vols (Paris: Mouton, 1971).

Goubert, Pierre, *Familles marchandes sous l'Ancien Régime: les Danse et les Motte, de Beauvais* (Paris: S.E.V.P.E.N., 1959).

Goubert, Pierre, *Beauvais et le Beauvaisis de 1600 à 1730. Contribution à l'histoire sociale de la France au XVIIe siècle* (Paris: S.E.V.P.E.N., 1960).

Goubert, Pierre, *L'Ancien Régime*, 2 vols (Paris: A. Colin, 1969–73). English translation of Vol. 1: *The Ancien Regime* (New York: Harper & Row, 1973).

Grimmer, Claude, *Vivre à Aurillac au XVIIIe siècle* (Aurillac: PUF, 1983).

Guignet, Philippe, *Mines, manufactures et ouvriers du Valenciennois au XVIIIe siècle* (New York: Arno Press, 1977).

Hanlon, Gregory, 'Culture et Comportements des élites urbaines en Agenais-Condomois au XVIIe siècle', thèse de 3e cycle, Université de Bordeaux III, 1982.

Hauser, Henri, *Ouvriers du temps passé, XVe–XVIe siècles* (Paris: Alcan, 1927).

Hohenberg, Paul M., and Lees, Lynn Hollen, *The Making of Urban Europe 1000–1950* (Cambridge, Mass.: Harvard University Press, 1985).

Hufton, Olwen H., *Bayeux in the Late Eighteenth Century: A Social Study* (Oxford, Clarendon Press, 1967).

Hufton, Olwen H., *The Poor of Eighteenth-Century France 1750–1789* (Oxford: Oxford University Press, 1974).

Hunt, Lynn, *Revolution and Urban Politics in Provincial France: Troyes and Reims, 1786–1790* (Stanford, Calif.: Stanford University Press, 1978).

Isherwood, Robert M., *Farce and Fantasy: Popular Entertainment in Eighteenth-Century Paris* (Oxford: Oxford University Press, 1986).

Kaplan, Steven Laurence, *Provisioning Paris: Merchants and Millers in the Grain and*

Flour Trade during the Eighteenth Century (Ithaca, NY: Cornell University Press, 1984).

Kaplan, Steven Laurence, and Koepp, C. J. (eds), *Work in France: Representations, Meaning, Organization and Practice* (Ithaca, NY: Cornell University Press, 1986).

La France d'Ancien Régime: Etudes réunies en l'honneur de Pierre Goubert (Toulouse: Privat, 1984).

Lavedan, Pierre, *Histoire de l'urbanisme à Paris* (Paris: Hachette, 1975).

Lavedan, Pierre, *et al.*, *L'urbanisme à l'époque moderne, XVIe–XVIIIe siècles* (Geneva: Droz, 1982).

LeGoff, T. J. A., *Vannes and its Region: A Study of Town and Country in Eighteenth-Century France* (Oxford: Clarendon Press, 1981).

Le Roy Ladurie, Emmanuel, *Le Carnaval de Romans* (Paris: Gallimard, 1979), English translation: *Carnival in Romans* (New York: Braziller, 1979).

Livet, Georges, and Vogler, Bernard (eds), *Pouvoir, ville et société en Europe 1650–1750* (Paris: Ophrys, [1983]).

Lottin, Alain, *Vie et mentalité d'un lillois sous Louis XIV* (Lille: Raoust, 1968), reprinted as *Chavatte, ouvrier lillois. Un contemporain de Louis XIV* (Paris: Flammarion, 1979).

Maillard, Jacques, *Le pouvoir municipale à Angers de 1657 à 1789*, 2 vols (Angers: Presses Universitaires d'Angers, 1984).

Marque, Jean-Pierre, *Institution municipale et groupes sociaux: Gray, petite ville de province (1690–1790)* (Paris: Les Belles Lettres, 1979).

Meyer, Jean, *Etudes sur les villes en Europe occidentale (milieu du XVIIe siècle à la veille de la Révolution française)*, Vol. 1 *Généralités – France* (Paris: S.E.D.E.S., 1983).

Mols, Roger, *Introduction à la démographie historique des villes d'Europe du XIVe au XVIIIe siècle*, 3 vols (Louvain: J. Duculot, 1954–6).

Mousnier, Roland, *Recherches sur la stratification sociale à Paris aux XVIIe et XVIIIe siècles: L'échantillon de 1634, 1635, 1636* (Paris: Pedone, 1976).

Norberg, Kathryn, *Rich and Poor in Grenoble, 1600–1814* (Berkeley, Calif.: University of California Press, 1985).

Parker, David, *La Rochelle and the French Monarchy: Conflict and Order in Seventeenth-Century France* (London: Royal Historical Society, 1980).

Perrenoud, Alfred, 'L'inégalité sociale devant la mort à Genève au XVIIe siècle', *Population*, numéro spécial (1975), pp. 221–43.

Perrenoud, Alfred, 'Variables sociales en démographie urbaine. L'exemple de Genève au XVIIIe siècle', in *Démographie urbaine, XVe–XXe siècles* (Lyon: Centre d'histoire économique et sociale de la région lyonnaise, 1977).

Perrenoud, Alfred, *La population de Genève du XVIe au début du XIXe siècle: étude démographique* (Geneva: A. Jullien, 1979).

Perrenoud, Alfred, 'Croissance ou déclin: Les mécanismes du non-renouvellement des populations urbaines', *Histoire, Economie, Société*, vol. 1 (1982), pp. 581–601.

Perrot, Jean-Claude, *Genèse d'une ville moderne. Caen au XVIIIe siècle* (Paris: Mouton, 1975).

Piasenza, Paolo, 'Rapimenti, polizia e rivolta: un conflitto sull'ordine pubblico a Parigi nel 1750', *Quaderni Storici*, no. 64 (1987), pp. 129–52.

Pillorget, René, *Les mouvements insurrectionnels de Provence entre 1596 et 1715* (Paris: Pedone, 1975).

Porchnev, Boris, *Les soulèvements populaires en France de 1623 à 1648* (Paris: S.E.V.P.E.N., 1963).

Poussou, Jean-Pierre, 'Les mouvements migratoires en France et à partir de la France de la fin du XVe siècle au début du XIXe siècle: Approches pour une synthèse', *Annales de Démographie Historique* (1970), pp. 11–78.

67

Poussou, Jean-Pierre, *Bordeaux et le Sud-Ouest au XVIIIe siècle: croissance économique et attraction urbaine* (Paris: Ecole des Hautes Etudes en Sciences Sociales, 1983).

Quéniart, Jean, *Culture et sociétés urbaines dans la France de l'Ouest au XVIIIe siècle* (Paris: Klinksieck, 1978).

Ranum, Orest, *Paris in the Age of Absolutism: An Essay* (New York: Wiley, 1968).

Roche, Daniel, *Le siècle des Lumières en province. Académies et académiciens provinciaux, 1680–1789*, 2 vols (Paris: Mouton, 1978).

Roche, Daniel, *Le Peuple de Paris: essai sur la culture populaire au XVIIIe siècle* (Paris: Aubier-Montaigne, 1981). English translation: *The People of Paris: An Essay on Popular Culture in the Eighteenth Century* (Berkeley, Calif.: University of California Press, 1987).

Roche, Daniel (ed.), *Journal de ma vie. Jacques-Louis Ménétra, compagnon vitrier au 18e siècle* (Paris: Montalba, 1982). English translation: *Journal of My Life* (New York: Columbia University Press, 1986).

Roupnel, Gaston, *La ville et la campagne au XVIIe siècle. Etude sur les populations du pays dijonnais* (Paris: A. Colin, 1955).

Sanfaçon, André, 'Organisation municipale, mobilité et tensions sociales à Chartres dans la seconde moitié du XVIIe siècle', *Historical Reflections*, vol. 8 (1981), pp. 43–67.

Sewell, William H., Jr., *Work and Revolution in France: The Language of Labor from the Old Regime to 1848* (Cambridge: Cambridge University Press, 1980).

Sonenscher, Michael, 'Journeymen, the courts and the French trades 1781–1791', *Past & Present*, no. 114 (1987), pp. 76–109.

Temple, Nora, 'The control and exploitation of French towns during the Ancien Régime', *History*, vol. 51 (1966), pp. 16–34.

Temple, Nora, 'Municipal elections and municipal oligarchies in eighteenth-century France', in J. F. Bosher (ed.), *French Government and Society 1500–1800: Essays in Memory of Alfred Cobban* (London: Athlone Press, 1973).

Thomson, J. K. J., *Clermont-de-Lodève 1633–1789: Fluctuations in the Prosperity of a Languedocian Cloth-Making Town* (Cambridge: Cambridge University Press, 1982).

Vovelle, Michel, *Ville et campagne au 18e siècle (Chartres et la Beauce)* (Paris: Editions Sociales, 1980).

Williams, Alan, *The Police of Paris 1718–1789* (Baton Rouge: Louisiana State University Press, 1979).

Zeller, Olivier, *Les recensements lyonnais de 1597 et 1636: démographie historique et géographie sociale* (Lyon: Presses Universitaires de Lyon, 1983).

Additional works of importance, all of which appeared too late to be utilized in the preparation of the preceding essay, are:

Brennan, Thomas, *Public Drinking and Popular Culture in Eighteenth-Century Paris* (Princeton, NJ: Princeton University Press, 1988).

Bulst, Neithard, and Genet, J.-P. (eds), *La ville, la bourgeoisie et la genèse de l'état moderne (XIIe–XVIIIe siècles)* (Paris: Editions du C.N.R.S., 1988).

Pardailhé-Galabrun, Annik, *La naissance de l'intime: 3000 foyers parisiens, XVIIe–XVIIIe siècles* (Paris: Presses Universitaires de France, 1988).

2

Paris on the eve of Saint Bartholomew: taxation, privilege, and social geography

ROBERT DESCIMON

With a population that the most recent estimate places at 300,000 people in 1565, Paris was sixteenth-century Christendom's largest city – *'non urbs, sed orbis'* ('not a city but a world'), to repeat the over-used phrase of the day.[1] So vast a product of human industry appeared disconcerting, even precarious, to contemporaries. In the spring of 1563, in an atmosphere darkened by the recent outbreak of civil war, a captain of the bourgeois militia reported that a common laborer had brought him a letter addressed to a member of the parlement suspected of Protestantism. On the surface, the letter discussed nothing more than ordinary judicial matters, but when held up to the fire, the laborer claimed, another message appeared instructing the judge to hide as many of his valuables as possible because the Huguenots planned soon to turn Paris back into a pasture (*'rendre Paris champêtre'*).[2] Such fears that the earlier sack of Rome by Imperial forces might now be re-enacted in Paris by the Huguenots stemmed partially from the atmosphere of eschatalogical fear building up in France around this time,[3] but they also reveal a perception of the city as the continuing creation of urban ingenuity, prey to obscure forces threatening a return to primitive rusticity. Frequently compared to Jerusalem, Paris seemed extraordinary and almost miraculous even to its own inhabitants, exuding a charisma rivalled only by Rome.

This city/world naturally deserved to have its 'true and natural portrait', and from the beginning of the sixteenth century onward an image of 'Paris without peer' had begun to develop, embodied in encomia, accounts of its antiquities, and maps, and most notably in Gilles Corrozet's two volumes published respectively in 1532 and 1550, describing the city's churches, major private residences, and streets.[4] A geographic view of the city was thus beginning to develop, but it was one in which physical space was often anthropomorphized. The quarters into which the city was divided were each designated by the name of the official responsible for them, the *quartenier*. Typically, they were not clearly delineated blocks derived from a cartographic representation of the city, but a collection of adjoining streets or sections of streets that formed a lived reality. The one consistent marker that could be used to identify them was the power of their notable inhabitants.[5] The city 'lies in the body of its citizens' wrote Jean Bodin in 1576, reiterating a commonplace of the day. His *Six Books of the Republic* glosses the stock phrase used in contemporary references to Paris, the '*ville, cité et université de Paris*', not as referring to the three-fold division of the city into right bank, Ile de la Cité, and left bank, but thus: 'The *ville* contains the circuit of the walls and suburbs, . . . the *université* is the community of all bourgeois of Paris; the *cité* the entire Provostship and Viscounty utilizing the same customary law.'[6] Even the equation here of *ville* with a walled circuit, echoed constantly in contemporary definitions of the word, reflects not merely a geographic vision but a perception of the social and political realities of urban life. The enclosure of cities within walls helped to engender the movement of 'fraternization' that underlay the rise of the medieval commune and imposed on all inhabitants common responsibility for the maintenance and guard of the walls. It is highly probable that the renovation of Paris's walls, begun in 1553, and the restructuring of the city militia after 1562 reinforced the sense of community among the city's inhabitants and their desire for municipal autonomy. In short, sixteenth-century conceptions of Paris did not distinguish between the city as a physical and geographic entity and the city as a socio-political organism. Its spatial organization at once structured and displayed its social and political makeup.

How is the modern historian to begin to reconstruct Paris's social geography? One exceptional source is provided by the copy of the 'account of the gift of 300,000 livres tournois granted by the city of Paris in the year 1571 to the late king Charles', surviving by a unique stroke of good fortune in the Bibliothèque Nationale.[7] This is the only complete Parisian tax roll to survive for the early modern period; until 1520 the city's municipal officials regularly burned all such documents as soon as they had finished with them, and even after that date they do not appear to have been very concerned to ensure their preservation. The document is well known to historians of Paris, but it is at once so massive – containing 16,640 entries – and so laconic – no indication of profession accompanies most names on the list, and not infrequently the streets on which people lived are omitted as well – that none has previously attempted to exploit it systematically.[8] A collective effort to do so has now been under way for some time under the direction of Denis Richet at the Centre de Recherches Historiques in Paris. This study, presenting the first results of this investigation, will begin by exploring the sequence of events that gave rise to this document and determined its character. This, it turns out, is not only an exercise in historical criticism necessary for interpreting properly the information contained in the record of the free gift; it also sheds a great deal of light on the politics of municipal taxation and town–crown relations in the sixteenth century. The information contained in the document, supplemented by additional data, will then be utilized to explore the broad outlines of the distribution of wealth and social geography of Paris on the eve of the Saint Bartholomew's Massacre.[9]

THE STRUGGLE OVER THE AMOUNT AND CHARACTER OF THE FREE GIFT

The king's demand for a 'free gift' in 1571 fell on a city whose character was in the midst of transformation. To utilize Weberian typologies, Paris was at once a 'princely city' of rentiers, nobles, and state servants living off income from land and office, and a city of merchants and artisans living from production and exchange. Francis I's pronouncement of 24 March 1528 that he intended henceforward to make Paris his chief residence combined with the growth in the number of royal officials visible throughout the fifteenth and sixteenth centuries to tilt the balance between these two foundations of the city's splendor toward the 'princely city'. The city's trade prospered in the sixteenth century. Its leading merchants had European-wide horizons and were actively engaged in long-distance trade; its drapers underwrote cloth production throughout much of the kingdom; the printing, dying, construction and, to a lesser extent, leather and woolen industries all expanded handsomely; the rich surrounding countryside of the Ile-de-France at once supplied the city's wants, engendering considerable wealth for those engaged in the provisioning trades, and supported important rural industries. Yet this commercial and industrial activity was increasingly outpaced by the growth of the '*Etat d'offices*'. The sale of offices and government borrowing absorbed more and more of the city's wealth, especially during the reigns of Henry II and Charles IX, which were particularly fertile in the creation of new offices in the sovereign courts. Power was increasingly concentrated in the hands of the king's men, and the relative autonomy which the crown had granted to the best of its '*bonnes villes*' came to rest less and less on the social independence of their citizens.

Under Henry II, the balance between royal and municipal taxation, which Bernard Chevalier has described as 'slowly ripening between 1400 and 1550 and highly favorable to the *bonnes villes*', shattered.[10] Paris had established its right of exemption from the chief royal tax, the *taille*, by 1449. During the second half of the fifteenth and first half of the sixteenth centuries, the chief levies paid by the capital were small impositions assessed by the Bureau de la Ville to provide municipal services, such as the *taxe des boues et lanternes* or, from 1553 onward, the fortifications' tax. Around the middle of the sixteenth century, however, increasing royal demands for direct fiscal assistance rained down upon the privileged cities. The subventions that successive kings sought to impose were distinguished from *tailles*. Habituated to justifying 'extraordinary finances' by appeal to 'necessity' and 'the common good' ('*le bien universel*'), the chancellery asked for them in formulae whose contradictory language – 'we pray and at the same time order you . . .' – shows them to have been part of a system of temperate, rather than absolute, monarchy in which it was accepted that a degree of negotiation and consent accompanied the levying of taxes on privileged groups or localities.[11] The multiplication of such demands nonetheless shows that the equilibrium of the preceding period had been gradually sapped from within.

The extension of 'extraordinary' subventions had begun when the crown had managed to establish the principle that the recognition of subjects' privileges implied a reciprocal financial obligation on their part. From 1484 onward, the *joyeux avènement* ceremonies with which privileged cities welcomed their new king on his first visit to them became linked to the provision of a monetary 'gift' to the crown. Similarly, it became habitual during the sixteenth century for the king to require a *droit de confirmation* from his officials in return for confirming them in their positions upon his accession. These innovations became traditions in the treatises of such theoreticians of temperate monarchy as Claude de Seyssel and René Choppin, both of whom described the *don du joyeux avènement* as 'customary since all antiquity' in support of their vision of monarchical authority as a pact in which subjects and officials pledged their loyalty in return for certain privileges.[12] Then, under Francis I and Henry II, the kings turned to the *bonnes villes* for free gfts and *soldes* to support troops in periods of warfare or to meet other extraordinary needs. The first such contribution was demanded of Paris in 1528 to help Francis I pay his ransom following his capture at Pavia. The city was obliged to raise subsequent contributions through direct taxes in 1544, 1545, 1548, 1556 and 1568.

In requesting extraordinary levies with greater frequency and expecting privileged cities such as Paris to collect them, the crown also implicitly accepted and used for its purposes the broadly inclusive logic of municipal taxation. Participation in the privileges associated with the right of bourgeoisie implied obligations as well, and the municipal levies such as the fortifications' tax fell on all established residents of a city without exception. In 1576, the Auvergnat magistrate Jean Combes drew inspiration from Baldus in defining what he called the 'privilege of *deniers communs*'. 'A good citizen who merits being honored with that glorious title must not refuse any service which his place of birth or residence requires of him . . . Should he not perform this service, he merits being stripped of the title and honor of citizen and deprived of all of the privileges and benefits belonging to his city.' Even kings, exclaimed Combes, had accepted this principle and consented to pay taxes in cities in which they resided.[13] The only legitimate reason for exemption was poverty.

Charles IX first requested the free gift of 1571 in a set of letters addressed on 3 January to fifteen leading figures in both the municipal and royal government. The levy was part of a more general subsidy imposed on all walled towns and intended to pay off the German mercenaries who had been billeted in Lorraine ever since the August 1570 peace of Saint-Germain brought to an end the third and (to date) longest of the civil wars that racked France throughout this period. But it was also set against the background of plans for Charles to stage his solemn entry into Paris. Although he had been king since 1560 and had been legally declared of age to rule since the 1563 *lit de justice* that, to the great dismay of the Parisians, had taken place before the parlement of Rouen, he still had not yet made his formal entry into the city. In deciding to make his entry into the city now, after both the conclusion of the peace of Saint-Germain and his marriage to Elizabeth of Austria in November, Charles may well have been seeking to symbolize a new beginning to his reign and to revive the hopes for a general renewal of state and society that were always felt so strongly on the accession of a new king. Was he also calculating that at such a moment the Parisians might be especially likely to consent to a free gift without undue protest? Whatever the case, the link between the request for the free gift and the plans for the royal entry is suggested by the fact that the same *échevin* charged with supervising the organization of the royal entry, the financier and poet Simon Bouquet, also presided over the negotiations that quickly surrounded the free gift.

Had the Parisians been more favorably disposed toward the peace of Saint-Germain, they might have looked upon the king's request for the free gift favorably. The spirit of civil war, however, had entrenched itself deeply in a capital whose ardor for the Catholic cause burned all the more fiercely because the city had largely escaped the direct impact of the fighting. In these same years, the preacher Simon Vigor, curé of Saint-Paul, was warning Parisians of the divine chastisement that the toleration of heresy could not fail to bring down upon the kingdom.[14] A widow thought it prudent in January 1571 to insert a provision in a rental contract for a house she was leasing covering the eventuality that the house be 'ruined or demolished by the troubles which might arise'.[15] The climate of fear was exacerbated by high prices and unnatural weather. High water and strong currents impeded the supply of wood from up-river, bringing to crisis proportions the always difficult problem of providing fuel for the city. And agitation over the question of tolerating heresy had received a symbolic flashpoint in the form of the Cross of Gastines, a commemorative cross erected on the former site of the house of three Huguenots executed for holding illicit Protestant services, which a special article of the peace of Saint-Germain now ordered be torn down. Throughout 1571, the Parisians would defend the cross against all efforts to put this provision of the peace into effect.

Even in better times, however, the Parisians were reluctant to pay taxes levied on all heads of household. Even though the city had been forced to pay certain previous royal demands for assistance in this manner, it still considered all taxes by head to be *tailles*. A 1556 appeal against a capitation from the chief spokesman of the city government, the Prévôt des marchands, urged to the king 'not to suffer this wound to be inflicted on his city of Paris, the capital of his kingdom ... which from time immemorial has been exempt from the *taille* and yet would be subject to such a tax by the means of the aforesaid tax by head'.[16] The Parisians preferred another method for raising taxes, one which they were able to convince the crown to allow them to use to pay their share of the *solde* levied by Henry II on all '*villes closes*' to support 50,000 '*hommes de pied*'. This was issuing municipal bonds (*rentes*), to be repaid with revenue raised by creating or augmenting indirect taxes (*aides*) levied on goods entering or leaving the city. The Hôtel de Ville tried whenever possible to press this method of raising revenue on the king and his Council. It offered the city councillors the triple advantage of diluting the immediate impact of a new impost, creating an instrument that brought revenue to bourgeois with capital to invest, and inserting the city into France's burgeoning system of extraordinary finances as a sort of collective financier of the crown. Nothing shows more clearly the financial cooperation between the crown and the *bonnes villes* than the enormous expansion of *rentes sur les Hôtels de Ville* following their introduction in 1522. On certain occasions, the proliferation of *rentes*, which even came to be secured by the *taille*, reached such a point that the Parisian municipality expressed fears that the multiplication of new *rentes* might endanger the repayment of old ones. The remonstrances stimulated by such levies never, however, awakened anything like the protests against taxes by head.[17]

Furthermore, the city still had not finished paying off an earlier request for a free gift. Even though in March 1568 Charles IX had created *rentes* with a capital value of 14.4 million livres, requiring 120,000 livres in annual repayments, his financial straits were such that he had also had to demand a free gift of 300,000 livres in September of the same year. The duke of Anjou, the king's brother and future Henry III, had come personally to the Hôtel de Ville to assure the city of the king's and his own gratitude for such a gift, 'begging them not to refuse this first request which he made of the city'. Despite this display of royal solicitude and the apparent willingness of the Hôtel de Ville to cooperate, the initial assessment of this levy yielded forty to fifty thousand livres less than the 300,000 requested by the king. Resistance from inhabitants of Paris made it impossible to make up the difference, and finally the crown consented to allow the most heavily assessed individuals to transform their payments into purchases of *rentes* with a capital value of three times the sums they had been assessed.[18] The full sums still had not been turned over to the crown by the beginning of 1571.

The request for another free gift in 1571 touched off protracted negotiations.[19] Initially, as it had done in 1568, the Council demanded that the city pay 600,000 livres as its share of the free gift. The municipality responded with three successive remonstrances, claiming that it was incapable of paying more than 200,000 livres. Finally, on 13 March, agreement was reached setting the gift at 300,000 livres. The manner in which the tax would be assessed was also a subject of negotiation. Royal letters patent of 22 February stated that nobody was to be exempt from the gift, not even the clergy, the nobility, or those of the royal suite 'such as our household officials and our notaries and secretaries of the House and Crown of France', but they also specified that the clergy, courtiers and leading financiers said to be in the suite of the court were to be assessed no more compared with the rest of the population than they were in the fortifications' tax. A general assembly held on 26 February pointed out to the king that 'it would seem that the largest part of this very large sum, or whatever the city is able to provide, would remain if *messieurs* of his clergy and *messieurs* of his suite were assessed so little, and would fall upon the rest of the citizens of this city'.[20] Finally, letters patent of 2 April specified that the leading figures of the king's entourage might be assessed up to eight times what their households paid for the fortifications' tax, but no more. Furthermore, the ward officials who participated in determining each person's assessment, the *cinquanteniers* and *dizeniers*, were excluded from having any voice in setting their assessments. Artisans and lesser shopkeepers predominated overwhelmingly among these officials, and the King's Council clearly feared that they would attempt to soak the members of the royal entourage.

Even while these negotiations continued, the Bureau de la Ville began to take the steps necessary to collect the tax. On 20 March the city's *quarteniers* were ordered to draw up in duplicate rolls of 'every bourgeois, citizen, *manant*, and inhabitant' living in their quarter. It was clearly expected that they could work from already established documents and knew the inhabitants of their quarter well, as barely two weeks later the Bureau de la Ville was urging them to turn in their completed censuses of householders. It appears that the *quarteniers* went from house to house to update whatever earlier lists they possessed, for the final tax roll includes such traces of a house-to-house investigation as entries for individuals who refused to identify themselves.

The actual assessment of the tax was carried out by a committee composed of four representatives each from the Parlement, the Chambre des Comptes, and the Cour des Aides, two *conseillers* of the city, two designates each from the ranks of the 'bourgeoisie' (in the event, two leading *marchands merciers* still active in commerce) and the 'merchants' (a mercer and a draper), plus, for every territorial circumscription assessed, the *quartenier, cinquantenier, dizenier* and two leading inhabitants elected from among twelve 'notable persons' of the *dizaine*. The free gift was not assessed, as typically were other taxes such as the *taille*, by dividing the total amount among smaller territorial units and expecting each one to provide a certain fraction of the whole. Instead, each household was assessed according to its ability to pay. Instructions sent to each city with the initial notification of the establishment of the free gift recommended that all forms of income, including those from land, salaries, *rentes*, and 'man's industry', be taken into consideration.[21] These instructions also included some rather unclear guidelines for determining the precise assessment, guidelines that the Parisian committee for assessing the tax seems to have judged of little utility, since it drew up its own tax table, widening the range of possible assessments at the bottom end of the scale in a manner that allowed it to tax residents of middling or lesser wealth at a lower rate than the original scale provided by the King's Council would have permitted. The final range of assessments ran from 2 to 300 livres. The committee was enjoined to carry out its functions 'with loyalty and according to conscience'.

Just how the committee determined which of the city's residents would be retained on the final assessment roll of the gift is uncertain, but it is evident that only certain inhabitants were assessed, since the 16,000 names on the roll could not possibly represent more than 40 per cent of all households in a city of about 300,000 people, even making the most generous estimations for average household size for a town whose population included many families with large retinues of servants or retainers. Most probably, only those who enjoyed the formal status of 'bourgeois' were included, i.e. those *'chefs de maison'* occupying the main body of a house who had lived in the city for at least a year and contributed to such common charges as the *taxe des boues et lanternes*.[22] If this hypothesis is correct, it reveals that the city government was balking at accepting new principles governing taxation that the crown had sought to impose upon it as early as 1545, requiring that *'caméristes'* – that is, *manants* and inhabitants living in rented rooms – be subject to assessment as well as bourgeois.[23] The rights and privileges associated with bourgeois status were not inconsiderable, and the city government, in the face of a long jurisprudential tradition that linked the acquisition of this status with participation in taxation, apparently wanted to ensure that they were not too easily usurped, the surprisingly 'democratizing' directives emanating from the crown notwithstanding.

In determining what each household had to pay, the assessment committee appears to have relied above all upon its members' impression of each family's wealth. The frequent interaction among neighbors typical of urban life unquestionably meant that members of the committee may well have had clues about this, but it is equally evident that such a procedure guaranteed that the assessments would be linked above all to the extent to which a given family appeared well-established and prosperous to the outside world, not to its actual fortune. The assessments established for the 1568 free gift and the most recent fortifications' tax (1570) probably provided a model of how to carry out the process, but comparison of the final assessments with those found in a surviving fragment of a 1579 fortifications' tax roll shows no consistent correlation between the two documents.[24] Similarly, comparison of the 1571 assessments with a hundred house rental contracts taken from Paris's notarial archives reveals no consistent correlation between what families paid in rent and what they were asked to pay in taxes. We know from their inventories after death that the widows of two secretaries of state, Robertet d'Alluye and Robertet de Fresnes, lived under a crushing burden of debt that would make their estates virtually worthless.[25] They nonetheless were assessed the maximum amount of 300 livres, a sign of how the assessments reflected assumptions about their wealth. More generally, it appears that widows were consistently taxed more than comparable male heads of household. Conversely, recently married couples were often assessed modest sums; the same people who appear on this document with small figures against their name can often be found in notarial documents ten or twenty years later prospering in commerce or the law or filling one of the royal offices that placed them among the city's elites.[26]

The tax assessors began their work in May and, despite considerable royal impatience to see the job finished, did not complete it until June. It appears that all those assessed were then given printed sheets with the sum they owed filled in – it is known that such a form was used for the fortifications' tax of 1584 – indicating where they were to turn in this sum. By June, these had been distributed and the money was beginning to come in to the coffers of François de Vigny the younger, agent for his father for the collection of the free gift. Those who failed to pay promptly were put on notice by the municipality and the King's Council alike that they were subject to the full rigors of the law.

Then, on 15 June, a thunderbolt arrived from the king. Royal letters ordered that the noblemen and financiers in his suite be excused from the share of the levy they had been ordered to pay. The total sum demanded remained unchanged, so, the king announced, a new assessment would have to be drawn up. He added that measures would also have to be taken to see that those who still had not paid the sums levied in 1568 did so. Immediately the collection process ground to a halt. From June until November, while town and crown waged a battle of negotiations and the most exaggerated rumors concerning the tax circulated through the city, virtually the only inhabitants to pay the tax were the officers of the sovereign courts, threatened with the loss of their *gages* if they did not do so. Sergeants attempting to seize the property of others who were delinquent were prevented by force from doing so. Some inhabitants left their homes rather than pay. The King's Council had the original rolls established for the tax brought before it at the beginning of August, and then, after much resistance, a second set of tax rolls established in 1570 for the fortifications' tax. Finally, the Council itself decreed a new repartition of the tax, with a total assessment of 344,500 livres where the city's original repartition had totalled 279,912. The Prévôt des marchands and the *échevins* were meanwhile pressed to borrow as private individuals 100 to 120 thousand livres and to provide that as a loan to the king until the full sum of the free gift was raised. When the Bureau de la Ville presented the revised rolls to a general assembly of the city's inhabitants on 21 November, vigorous protest arose, and an appeal was drafted to the king to consider the new rolls null and void and preserve the city's liberties and privileges in matters of taxation. Then, in December, the tension provoked by the Cross of

Gastines affair broke out into full-scale rioting when efforts were made to implement a compromise reached with the city to have the Cross moved to a different site. The matter of the free gift was temporarily eclipsed.

As the king and city council worked to restore calm in the wake of the Cross of Gastines affair, the occasion arose to unblock the standstill which had set in on the question of the free gift. Some of the proceeds of the tax had begun to come in once again, and on 24 January 1572 the Hôtel de Ville presented a memorandum to the king, urging that, since 200,000 of the 300,000 livres requested by the king had now been remitted, the city be excused from half of the remaining 100,000 livres and allowed to pay the other half in the form of *rentes*. The king responded with letters patent accepting this compromise. These were registered by the Parlement on 1 March on condition that the Hôtel de Ville cease all connivance with those who still refused to pay their share of the free gift and work to speed up its collection.[27] Several court cases were soon initiated against delinquent individuals – cases which we know lasted in some instances for ten years, without it being certain that they ever succeeded in extracting any money from these people.

But the story of the free gift still was not finished. Charles, it turned out, had not abandoned his original goal of extracting 600,000 livres from the city. He had merely postponed the timetable. On 22 April he informed the city that he expected a second installment of 200,000 livres in 1572 and a third installment of 100,000 livres in 1573. The municipality protested and stalled, even as it may have proceeded to begin revising the 1571 rolls.[28] Matters were still at a deadlock when the gathering of the great nobility in Paris for the wedding of Henry of Navarre and Marguerite of Valois precipitated the series of events which culminated in the Saint Bartholomew's Massacre. On 18 October, two months after the Massacre, the king finally consented to accept 150,000 livres from the city levied in the form of *rentes* backed by new duties on woolens, silks and gold-thread cloth.[29] This would be the last of the sums demanded in consequence of the letters issued on 3 January 1571.

This highly compressed account of the king's demand for a free gift in 1571 and the long negotiations to which it gave rise illustrates several important points about municipal politics and privilege in the sixteenth century. First, the contribution that the conflict about taxation might have made to the atmosphere of contention leading up to the Saint Bartholomew's Massacre has not been sufficiently recognized. The royal letters patent of 8 October 1571, in which Charles IX both congratulated the municipality on its decision to quadruple penalties against those who refused to pay the free gift and in the same letter ordered the demolition of the Cross of Gastines, suggest a striking lack of political finesse on the part of the King's Council. Second, the tenacity with which both parties clung to their positions in this conflict is telling. The city replied to the royal demands time and again with the claim that it could pay no more than 200,000 livres and was equally dogged in requesting that the sums demanded be raised in the form of *rentes*, not a head tax. In so doing, it was faithful to the 'policy of temporization' that Jean Favier has defined as typical of the attitude of medieval taxpayers and which continued to characterize cities' responses to royal tax demands throughout the sixteenth century.[30] The zeal with which the Hôtel de Ville defended the city's interests is particularly noteworthy since the Bureau de la Ville contained several of Catherine de Medici's clients, notably the Prévôt des marchands Claude Marcel, who was also the Queen Mother's personal treasurer.[31] Apparently these links did not prevent the city council from pressing the city's case strongly – a case which must not be regarded as expressing anti-monarchical sentiment, but simply a traditional strategy of defense of the taxpayers' purses. The king was no less determined to have his way, stating several times his 'anger' and 'very great dissatisfaction', taxing the Parisians with 'always putting things off until tomorrow', and pointing out to them that no other city was as recalcitrant as they in paying the free gift. Charles and his council were aware that the costs of the civil wars had fallen overwhelmingly on the countryside and unprivileged towns. They were little inclined to grant the justice of the Parisians' appeals.

Were the Hôtel de Ville and the Parisian populace correct in thinking that the King's Council aimed at nothing less than the *de facto* abolition of the city's fiscal privileges? Did the peace, royal marriage, and royal entry provide the crown with an apparently perfect pretext for establishing an 'exceptional' tax, which it could then try to make permanent if circumstances allowed? The attempt to renew the tax in 1572 certainly suggests as much. In the course of pursuing this ambitious goal a second assault on the city's privileges also developed, aimed at the city's right to control assessment procedures for subventions raised on its inhabitants. In order to achieve its ends, the Council sought to undermine the unified commitment of the Bureau de la Ville and the city's inhabitants to the maintenance of their privileges. Hence, the stratagem of forcing the Prévôt des marchands and the *échevins* to borrow on their own names the money that remained to be remitted to the king, a stratagem designed to put them in a position where their personal interest would incite them to make sure the tax was successfully collected, so that they would be repaid. In the event, the stratagem failed, for collectively the members of the Bureau de la Ville borrowed no more than 72,000 livres, a figure well in line with what standard mechanisms for recovering unpaid taxes might be expected to yield. Furthermore, if the Council failed in its efforts to make the Bureau de la Ville a cooperative ally, its assault on Parisian privileges was also weakened by its respect for the privileges of the first two orders. While it was willing to accept in an early phase of negotiation the fundamental principle of urban government that all citizens were obliged to contribute to the common good, it appears to have been incapable of resisting for long pressure from the leading courtiers and financiers to have their share of the tax reduced. The sudden about-face of 15 June reveals either that the initial decision to accept the city's idea of how the tax ought to be assessed was simply a negotiating ploy designed to get the collection process moving or the extent of the crown's dependence on the most powerful of its nominal vassals and servants. In either case, how could the Parisians be convinced to accept the violation of their privileges in the name of the principle that all should contribute to the needs of the state, when that principle would not be extended to those in the king's entourage?

The free gift of 1571 would not be the last such gift demanded of the capital. Henry III imposed two such levies on Paris, in 1576 and 1585. Tellingly, however, the sums he requested on both occasions were smaller than that demanded by Charles IX. Even these sums contributed to the resentment of his rule, which finally burst forth in the League. Henry IV's reign then inaugurated a long hiatus in requests for direct taxes from the capital accompanied by a shift toward indirect taxes such as the notorious 'pancarte' of 1596. Even the municipal *taxe des boues et lanternes* came to be financed by an *aide* on wine from 1609 onward. Direct royal taxation of the capital did not reappear again until 1636, when the advance of Habsburg forces to within a hundred miles of Paris, following their victory at Corbie, incited an atmosphere of alarm within which such imposts would be accepted. In 1637 the *taxe des boues et lanternes* reverted to being levied through a capitation. During the decade that followed, the superintendant of finances Particelli d'Hémery ignored the advice attributed to Richelieu 'that one had better not awaken that great beast' and multiplied new exactions on Paris – providing in the process one of the major sparks of the Fronde. If the resistance to the free gift of 1571 thus was not a turning point in the history of royal attempts to tax Paris, it was a demonstration of the difficulties that would consistently be involved in doing so and of the sharp reaction in defense of privilege that attempts to levy such a tax provoked, both within the capital as a whole and in the immediate entourage of the king.

THE GEOGRAPHY OF PARISIAN WEALTH

The story of the conflicts surrounding the king's request for a free gift also helps us to interpret the quality of the information contained in the surviving roll of the levy. The document in the Bibliothèque Nationale is a copy, apparently dating from the later 1570s and destined for the Chambre des Comptes, of the 'particular account' of receipts and expenditures that François de Vigny the younger appears to have drawn up with considerable care on the basis of the individual lists of names and assessments established for each quarter. It is followed by a series of shorter accounts, listing those excused from the original assessment, those delinquent in their payments, and the costs involved in collecting the tax. Thus, the original source for this copy dates from prior to the king's intervention to shield those in his entourage from the burden of the tax. The document includes even the most well connected and highly privileged inhabitants of the capital.

As a guide to the wealth of Paris's inhabitants, the roll of the free gift certainly has its limitations. As we have already seen, the assessments recorded in the document were supposed to reflect the overall wealth of each household, but they were established according to a social process of judgement that unquestionably allowed inequities to creep in. Furthermore, the city's less securely established inhabitants do not appear at all; given the vast numbers of residents omitted, the 3,000 households that do show up with the notation '*néant*' against their name could hardly be used to map the geography of Parisian poverty.[32] Finally, five of the document's 350 folios are missing.[33] Despite these limitations, however, the document stands up under close examination much better than a superficial reading of it might lead one to fear. The accounting is scrupulous; where the document's addition can be checked, the few errors discovered are trivial. The fact that the assessments resulted from a social process of judgement can be seen as a strength as well as a weakness. They partook of the same logic as that governing the discernment of those critical sixteenth-century markers of status, 'honorability', 'notability', 'dignity', and 'honor', so the document embodies a logic of social analysis that may not be our own but is that of the era itself. It offers an unusually comprehensive view of the city's better established and more prosperous households, assessed in a manner that was supposed to take all of their forms of wealth into account and did not spare the privileged and the well connected. If the distribution of the tax burden which it reveals is compared with that of a series of other levies from the same era, for which we know the repartition by quarter from the published records of the Bureau de la Ville (see Table 2.1), the wealthiest quarters such as Saint-Séverin stand out as more heavily taxed than usual, while the most populous, poorer quarters such as Saint-Germain and Sainte-Geneviève escaped more lightly than usual.

The Paris described in the roll of the free gift was a city that, despite efforts to forbid new construction outside the walls, had long since spilled out beyond the ramparts, while within the walls population growth had steadily fostered the development of once unbuilt spaces on the fringes of town and the cramming of houses ever more tightly together in the city core. Although some protected spaces, such as the Temple close and the property of the Abbey of Saint-Martin des Champs remained undeveloped, new parcels were opened up for construction on both the eastern and western side of the city from the reign of Francis I onward. In the heart of Paris, 33 new houses were squeezed into the quarter of Saint-Germain l'Auxerrois between 1525 and 1553, increasing the total number of houses by nearly 10 per cent.[34] Houses also stretched ever higher upward, regularly attaining four to six storeys in the central parts of town.[35] Even though the integration of the *faubourgs* into the circumscriptions of municipal government was opposed by the seigneurs possessing rights of high justice over these areas, by the city's guildsmen

Table 2.1 Distribution by quarter of the free gift of 1571 compared with other Parisian levies. (The figures indicate each quarter's percentage of the citywide total.)

quarter	1545[1]	1556[2]	1564[3]	1567[4]	**1571[5]**	**1571[6]**	1575[7]	1576[8]
St Jacques de l'Hôpital	6.09	4.56	5	5.83	**5.68**	**5.30**	4.78	5.95
St Germain l'Auxerrois	5.02	4.43	4	4.17	**3.35**	**3.76**	4.35	4.29
St Sépulcre	6.56	6.16	6	5.83	**4.95**	**5.12**	5.22	4.76
St Honoré	4.03	4.87	5	5.00	**5.24**	**5.13**	4.78	4.76
St Jacques de la Boucherie	6.04	6.18	5.5	5.00	**4.53**	**5.24**	4.35	4.76
Sts Innocents	2.98	3.26	3.5	4.17	**3.85**	**3.24**	4.35	4.29
St Eustache	5.16	6.11	n.a.	8.33	**5.97**	**7.80**	5.95	5.50
St Gervais	1.97	3.26	4	2.50	**3.00**	**3.22**	3.48	2.86
St Esprit	2.19	3.09	3	2.50	**1.78**	**2.96**	2.61	2.86
St Martin	10.80	7.85	8	8.33	**7.31**	**9.11**	7.83	8.33
Temple	7.65	8.75	9	10.00	**13.45**	**7.10**	11.74	13.10
St Jean en Grève	3.94	3.42	3.5	3.33	**3.16**	**3.47**	3.91	3.57
St Antoine	2.24	4.36	4.5	4.17	**5.78**	**3.19**	3.48	5.95
Notre Dame	10.99	8.33	n.a.	8.33	**8.95**	**9.61**	9.13	7.14
Ste Geneviève	9.71	11.52	13	10.00	**6.79**	**13.33**	10.87	8.33
St Séverin	14.59	13.85	12	12.50	**16.21**	**12.43**	11.30	13.10

[1]Tax of 120,000 livres for *l'entretien des hommes de pied* (assessments tied to house rents). Source: *R.D.B.V.*, Vol. 3, p. 60.
[2]Fortifications tax (assessments linked to 'la grandeur des maisons, qualités et facultés des personnes'). Source: *R.D.B.V.*, Vol. 4, p. 441.
[3]Fortifications tax. Source: B.N., MS Français 11733, fos. 74v–76v.
[4]*Levée de 1200 pionniers.* Source: *R.D.B.V.*, Vol. 5, pp. 612–13.
[5]Free gift, amount assessed by quarter.
[6]Free gift, number of households assessed.
[7]*Levée de 2400 hommes de pied.* Source: *R.D.B.V.*, Vol. 7, pp. 288–9.
[8]Tax of 133,333 livres, 6 sous, 8 deniers *pour le solde de 2000 Suisses.* Source: *R.D.B.V.*, Vol. 7, pp. 343–5.

(who feared competition from suburbanites now brought into their ranks), and by many of the craftsmen of the *faubourgs* themselves (whose guild statutes were often less restrictive than those of the city), the areas built up on the fringe of town were regularly incorporated into the city, so the lesson in bourgeois ecology provided by our document covers many parts of the suburbs. Overall, according to the *quarteniers*, the city contained 10,000 houses in 1549. A census of 1553 reveals approximately 11,700 in the city and *faubourgs* combined (figures are lacking for one quarter). The *conseiller d'état* Morvilliers estimated the number at 14,000 in 1568.[36]

This mass of buildings was divided into sixteen quarters, whose boundaries are indicated in Map 2.1. The left bank contained just two quarters: Sainte-Geneviève, to the east of the Rue Saint-Jacques, housing numerous convents and the colleges attached to the university of Paris and spilling out

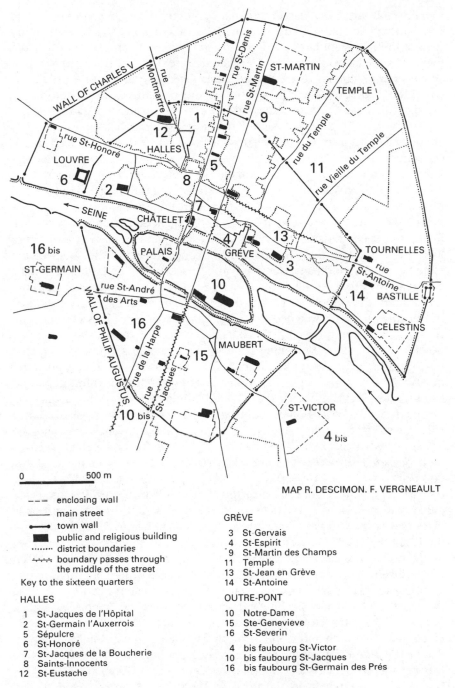

0   500 m

MAP R. DESCIMON. F. VERGNEAULT

- - - enclosing wall
—— main street
•—• town wall
■ public and religious building
········ district boundaries
⌐⌐⌐ boundary passes through
the middle of the street

Key to the sixteen quarters

HALLES

1 St-Jacques de l'Hôpital
2 St-Germain l'Auxerrois
5 Sépulcre
6 St-Honoré
7 St-Jacques de la Boucherie
8 Saints-Innocents
12 St-Eustache

GRÈVE

3 St-Gervais
4 St-Espirit
9 St-Martin des Champs
11 Temple
13 St-Jean en Grève
14 St-Antoine

OUTRE-PONT

10 Notre-Dame
15 Ste-Genevieve
16 St-Severin

4 bis faubourg St-Victor
10 bis faubourg St-Jacques
16 bis faubourg St-Germain des Prés

Map 2.1   Paris in 1571.

into the faubourg Saint-Marcel, a traditional center of tanning and cloth dying concentrated around the little stream of the Bièvre; and Saint-Séverin, to the west of the Rue Saint-Jacques, home to the Franciscans and Dominicans and flanked by the faubourg of Saint-Germain des Prés and its celebrated Abbey. A single quarter encompassed the Ile de la Cité, where, in close proximity, stood the Cathedral, the Palais (housing the parlement, the Chambre des Comptes, and the Cour des Aides), the Conciergerie, and the Marché Neuf – truly new in 1571, as it had been completed just three years peviously. The antiquity and density of construction of this part of town was such that it contained no less than fifteen parishes. The thirteen remaining quarters formed an intricate jigsaw puzzle on the populous right bank, with certain of them having developed along a central street in an elongated fashion, and others being arranged more compactly around a single central open space or radiating outward along several axes. Saint-Jacques de la Boucherie stood at the center, encompassing the Châtelet and the Grande Boucherie. Adjacent to it to the west were the Saints-Innocents, concentrated to the south of the famed cemetery, and Saint-Germain l'Auxerrois, extending farther westward along the river to the walls of the Louvre. Saint-Honoré's quarter covered the area dotted with imposing *hôtels* to the east and north of the Louvre, while to the northwest of it stretched the large quarter of Saint-Eustache, encompassing both recently developed residential sections of great cachet (the Hôtel de la Reine, just in the planning stages in 1571, would soon be constructed here) and the famous Cour des Miracles, reputed as the haunt of rogues and beggars. The central wedge of the right bank beyond the Saints-Innocents and Saint-Jacques de la Boucherie contained three quarters: Saint-Jacques de l'Hôpital, around the Halles; Saint-Sépulcre, a narrow strip of a quarter running along the Rue Saint-Denis, with its numerous hospitals and the houses of what the Prévot des marchands Claude Guyot called in 1550 '*la fleur des anciens bourgeois*'; and Saint-Martin, the largest of the quarters, covering a wider area to both sides of the parallel Rue Saint-Martin. The eastern edge of the right bank near the river was likewise divided into three parts: compact Saint-Esprit, between the Rue des Arcis and the waterside Place de Grève, a hub of mercantile activity tied to river traffic and the site of the Hôtel de Ville; Saint-Gervais, stretching to the west of the Place de Grève along the river as far as the old walls of Philip Augustus; and Saint-Jean en Grève, just inland to the north. To the north and east of these last two quarters were the two large and still relatively sparsely populated quarters covering the area that would later become known as the Marais: the Temple, extending northward from the cloister of Saint-Merry as far as the substantial Temple close with its church and castle formerly belonging to the Knights Templar; and Saint-Antoine, site of the royal *hôtels* of Saint-Paul and of the Tournelles, this last the crown's favored Parisian residence until Henry II received his fatal wound jousting in its tiltyard. Like the quarters of Saint-Honoré and Saint-Eustache, these two quarters had witnessed a great deal of new development in the decades prior to 1571 as old seigneurial or ecclesiastical properties such as the *couture* Sainte-Catherine were subdivided and opened up for construction.

The city's sixteen quarters were in turn divided into a variable number of *dizaines* of equally variable size. A *dizaine* such as that of Jean de Compans, an important *marchand drapier* (and future *échevin* during the period of the League) from an old and honorable Parisian family, formed the heart of the quarter of Notre-Dame and encompassed within its boundaries the Palais de Justice, half of the Pont Saint-Michel, portions of several other streets, and 200 taxable households. That of Jean Crestol in the quarter of Saint-Jacques de la Boucherie, on the other hand, covered merely a fraction of the Rue des Lombards and included just 26 taxed households. The intramural boundaries of the quarters had been largely fixed since the beginning of the fifteenth century, but the *faubourgs* were only integrated into the system from the 1520s onward, while the *dizaines* were regularly modified as the city changed and new sections of town were built up. In 1571 itself, three new *dizaines* were added to Saint-Germain des Prés.[37]

In order to provide the most detailed picture possible of the distribution of wealth, the tax assessments contained in the roll of the free gift have been analyzed by *dizaine*. Map 2.2 displays the mean tax in each of these 154 units. The pattern revealed is extremely complex. Although it is a commonplace that wealth tended to cluster in the center of traditional European cities, Jean-Claude Perrot's observation that 'the centers of cities are almost always conservatories of earlier eras' must also be recalled.[38] The *dizaine* boasting the highest average tax assessment turns out to have been Pierre Larzy's on the northeastern fringe of the city in the quarter of the Temple. It was followed in the ranking of most heavily taxed *dizaines* by six others located in peripheral sections of town. The dense, petrified world of central Paris no longer was the most attractive part of town for the wealthiest inhabitants of a city increasingly dedicated to the theatrical display of power. But while the regions of greatest wealth were found toward the periphery, so too were some of the poorest sections of town, while the center still retained evident concentrations of wealth as well. Rather than by a simple opposition between center and periphery, Paris was characterized by a multi-nuclear pattern of wealth and poverty. The differences between regions of town, it should be observed, derive above all else from the uneven distribution of the very wealthiest Parisians. The 80 per cent of those who appear in the document paying 20 livres or less were distributed relatively evenly across the sixteen quarters of the city. The taxpaying population was thus composed of a fairly uniform substratum of modest contributors, out of which arose a small group of 'fiscal notables' distributed unevenly from neighborhood to neighborhood.

The wealth contrasts between neighborhoods were particularly marked around the periphery of Paris, especially on the right bank. Here, within the

Legend

□ 1–10
▦ 11–20
▤ 21–40
▩ 41+

Map 2.2 Mean tax assessment by *dizaine*.

sector of the city between the wall of Charles V and the emplacement of the old wall of Philip Augustus, the western portion around the Louvre formed an area of middling average assessments; the central portion, running from the Rue Montmartre to the Rue du Temple, formed the poorest part of the city proper; while the eastern portion encompassed many of the wealthiest *dizaines*. On the left bank, the walls of Philip Augustus still defined the periphery of the city proper. Outside them, the *faubourgs* were for the most part regions of poverty, as also were the smaller *faubourgs* of the right bank, although the '*ville Saint-Marcel*', one of the first *faubourgs* to be integrated into the Parisian administrative system, formed something of an exception to this rule because of the presence of the Gobelins and other wealthy dyers of fine cloth, while Saint-Germain des Prés, which was nearly elevated to the status of seventeenth quarter in the 1550s, was characterized by genuine social diversity. Its historic center around the Abbey was marked by extremely low average assessments, while its more sparsely built fringes already had elite residences springing up amid the dwellings of market-gardeners and artisans, producing regions of both higher average assessments and an unusually broad range of individual values.

Intramural Paris was neatly cut down the middle by the chief north–south routes through town, the '*maitresse voie*' linking the Rues Saint-Martin and Saint-Jacques and the parallel axis of the Rues Saint-Denis and de la Harpe. The opposition between the two halves of the city thus created was always a basic element of Parisian geography.[39] A clear division appears on the left bank between the wealthier *dizaines* to the west of the rue Saint-Jacques and the poorer ones to the east, whose convents and colleges secreted a population of poor intellectuals and *basochiens*. Since the nineteenth century, a cliché of Parisian geography has opposed the posh western side to the poor eastern side of town, but this pattern did not yet exist in the sixteenth century on the Ile de la Cité and the right bank. Average tax assessments were below the city mean in all of the western *dizaines* of the Ile de la Cité except that of Laurent Lechassier, which encompassed many of the wealthy goldsmiths' shops on the Pont au Change, and assessments were above average in the Ile's two eastern *dizaines*. On the right bank, the importance of the Hôtel des Tournelles and the numerous new *lotissements* near it had helped to make the eastern fringes of the built-up sections of the city into the most exclusive sections of all, while in the western half of the right bank average tax assessments did not exceed 50 livres in any *dizaine* except possibly that of Etienne du Vaissel along the Rue Saint-Denis, where one of the lacunae appears in the records; the five *dizaines* in this half of town where the average exceeds 40 livres are scattered, with two located along the Rue Saint-Denis, a thoroughfare emblematic as the residence of wealthy merchants, two in islands of recently constructed aristocratic *hôtels* around the Rue des Bourdonnais and the Rue des Poulies, and one located along the Rue des Prouvaires near the church of Saint-Eustache.

Paris's social geography was structured not merely by the division between the halves of the city located on either side of the chief north–south streets, but also by the distance between different quarters and the river. The Seine played a fundamental role in the city's economic life. Its water was essential for the work of the dyers of the Rue de la Vieille Pelleterie on the Ile de la

Cité, the tanners of the Place de la Grève, the leather-dressers (*mégissiers*) of the quarter of Saint-Germain l'Auxerrois, and the millers whose mills captured the river's current from a special bridge of their own stretching across the river between the right bank and the Ile de la Cité. Wood, wine, and grain brought down-river to Paris was unloaded along the right bank at the Place de la Grève and on the left bank at the Pavé de la Tournelle, while downstream from the bridges the Ecole Saint-Germain served as the port for goods heading to or coming from the lower Seine. But the river's attraction was also increasingly felt as a place to live, especially after the construction of stone embankments between 1540 and 1560 reduced the danger to riverside houses of flooding. By 1571, the Port Saint-Landry facing the right bank on the Ile de la Cité, the Quai des Bernardins facing Notre Dame from the left bank, the eastern edge of the right bank near the Célestins, and both sides of the river near the Louvre were all fashionable residential addresses. The pace of renovation nonetheless remained slow in these old quarters along the river. The chief land route across the city from east to west had moved from what is presumed to be the original axis of the Rues Saint-Germain l'Auxerrois and de la Mortellerie, near the river, to the route formed by the Rues Saint-Honoré, des Lombards, de la Verrerie, and Saint-Antoine, farther inland. Three bands can consequently be distinguished on the right bank: that between the river and the Rues Saint-Germain l'Auxerrois–de la Mortellerie, relatively poor and ill considered despite the presence of the Châtelet and the Hôtel de Ville and some pockets of renovation; that between these streets and the Saint-Honoré–Saint-Antoine axis, better-to-do on the average and yet with many poorer artisans and shopkeepers cheek by jowl with rich merchants and tradesmen; and that between these last streets and the emplacement of the old walls of Philip Augustus, divided between the genuine wealth found to the east around Saint-Merry and the more westerly region of the Halles, where average assessments clustered around the mean.

Focusing the microscope still more sharply, it emerges that the forms of social segregation characteristic of the medieval city, where wealthier inhabitants tended to live along the main streets while the poor were relegated to the side streets and rear courtyards, still characterized many parts of town.[40] Map 2.3 sets out the pattern of assessments along the Rue Saint-Denis and nearby streets in the heart of the right bank. Overall, average assessments on the chief cross streets were just half that found on the Rue Saint-Denis; on the smaller side streets assessments averaged just one-third the level of the Rue Saint-Denis. Along the Rue Saint-Denis itself, the assessments mounted as one moved inland from the Seine, peaking just inside the old wall of Philip Augustus before declining brutally as one passed into a noticeably poorer section of town. The occupations found along the street reflected the same gradient of wealth and economic domination. Gold and silver wire-drawers lived toward its upper end. The *merciers passe-mentiers* who wove the wire they produced into fancy silks and laces lived

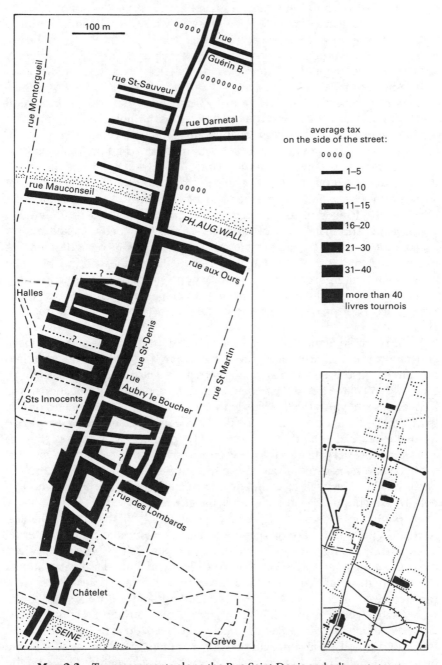

Map 2.3 Tax assessments along the Rue Saint-Denis and adjacent streets.

down the street around the Rues des Lombards and Vieille-Monnaie, while the great silk merchants and *merciers grossiers* who controlled the commercialization of luxury cloths lived at the very center of the Rue Saint-Denis. Patterns of economic domination were not displayed as clearly in every section of town, but the example is nonetheless evocative of the logic governing local residential patterns.

Numerous notarial contracts from the era show that rooms on several different floors of a house were often rented out as a single dwelling unit. The vertical pattern of social segregation found in eighteenth-century Paris, where the well-to-do occupied the lower floors of multi-storeyed buildings and the poor the garrets, had not yet emerged. (It would only do so around the end of the seventeenth century.[41]) A step in the direction of a horizontal form of such micro-segregation can nonetheless be seen in the less densely built areas on the fringes of town, where *hôtels particuliers* had recently been constructed. The main body of these *hôtels* was frequently flanked by low shops, rented out by the aristocratic proprietor to artisans or tradesmen.[42] A fundamental division of Parisian urban space lay in the contrast between those long-built-up sections of town where property was divided into minuscule lots and those more recently developed residential areas whose larger parcels of property permitted different patterns of construction and land use.[43]

As the example of the Rue Saint-Denis suggests, the analysis of Paris's social geography proves particularly revealing when it is possible to take into account not just levels of wealth and prestige, but also occupational identity. Since the roll of the free gift is very uneven in its notation of occupations – the frequency with which this is recorded varies from 0 to 60 per cent according to *dizaine* – the information it provides has been supplemented by evidence from the notarial records and *censiers*. To date, it has been possible to determine for every quarter the occupational status of 65 per cent or more of those taxpayers assessed a rate above the citywide mean, labelled here the 'fiscal notables', as well as a significant (albeit smaller) fraction of the less heavily taxed population in each part of the city.

Although this examination will focus primarily on the fiscal notables, residential patterns for artisans cannot be entirely neglected, as the clustering of members of certain trades in one or several parts of town created pockets throughout the heart of the city that were clearly identified as the traditional preserve of the craft in question and consequently formed poles of repulsion for elite residence. Streets or neighborhoods dominated by a single trade were relatively rare on the left bank, where only the printers and booksellers, clustered along the Rues Saint-Jacques, Saint-Jean de Beauvais, and Clos-Bruneau, formed clear concentrations of members of a single trade. In the heart of the right bank, however, no pattern had a stronger influence on the character of different streets. The new Rue de la Friperie in the recently renovated Halles was the domain of the used clothes dealers. The wealthier goldsmiths lived on the Pont aux Changeurs and spilled from it around the Grand Châtelet and towards Saint-Germain l'Auxerrois as far as their guild chapel on the Rue des Deux-Portes. The Rue de la Heaumerie abounded in armorers. The pillars of the Halles protected the tinsmiths. The Rue Aubry-le-Boucher was dominated by coppersmiths. The Rue Maubué and its vicinity was the territory of the shoemakers, leather curriers, and belt-makers. Most grain, wine, and wood merchants lived near the river ports along the Seine, while the leather-dressers and dyers clustered along their quays or around the canals and streams flowing through the city.

Within those trades that displayed a strong tendency toward concentration, not all members lived in the regions of greatest density. The goldsmiths' guild, for example, included both a great number of wealthy and prestigious members concentrated overwhelmingly in the zone around the Pont aux Changeurs, and also many poorer workers, the majority of whom were scattered around the humbler fringes of town. Furthermore, the members of many other occupations dispersed themselves more broadly around the city. This was true of the construction trades, tallow chandlers, tailors, saddlers, spurriers, pastrychefs, and surgeons. To a certain extent, the distinction between concentrated and dispersed trades was that between trades that involved loud or noxious activities and those that did not. To a certain extent, it was the distinction between craftsmen producing items of common consumption, who scattered themselves around the city in search of customers, and those producing more costly or specialized items, which potential purchasers were willing to travel some distance to buy. Simple geographic constraints dictated the tendency of grain and wood merchants to live near the Seine or the concentration of leather-dressers and dyers around the Bièvre and near the Seine. But none of these explanations can account for all of the nuances of the situation. The localization of many trades was the product of rather arbitrary patterns of occupational implantation inherited from the past and reinforced by institutional solidarities and rivalries. In streets or neighborhoods where one trade predominated, members of the trade tended to monopolize local positions of authority in institutions such as the bourgeois militia, discouraging practitioners of other crafts from moving in. Contemporary wisdom furthermore emphasized the desirability of separation between different 'estates' within a well policed city. Bernard de La Roche Flavin drew on his experience in both Paris and Toulouse when he explained that 'locksmiths, blacksmiths, coppersmiths, and other artisans engaged in activities which make a great deal of noise may not lodge near noble magistrates: and should they be there, several *arrêts* oblige them to leave'. Such regulations, La Roche Flavin explained, did not apply, however, in cases where a magistrate might move into a quarter dominated by such activity, 'for it would not be reasonable to make all of the many artisans of a single street move because of a single newcomer'.[44] The street belonged to those who had been there first. Traditional patterns inherited from an earlier

91

age were thus maintained, impeding the uniform colonization of the central sections of town by the elites.

Table 2.2 sets forth the average tax paid by the members of each of the major corporate bodies or groups among the fiscal notables, as well as the extent of variation found in the tax assessments levied on all identified members of these groups. The fiscal hierarchy revealed by the document largely duplicates the image that the era – and especially the early seventeenth century – created of its own hierarchies, with the average assessments cascading downward from those surrounding the court, through the different ranks of officials in the sovereign courts, the barristers and doctors, and finally down to the notaries and solicitors. Within this hierarchy, the *secrétaires du roi*, out of whose ranks the secretaries of state had just begun to emerge, outshone the bulk of fiscal and judicial officers. Other lessons could also be drawn from the tax assessments, such as the fact that the *conseillers laics* in the parlement were wealthier than the *conseillers clercs* or that the financiers engaged in providing money to the court and the army were better off than those involved in collecting taxes (the *receveurs généraux* and *receveurs particuliers*), but the broad picture is clear enough. A large divide separated all those crowned with the halo of prestige attached to proximity to

Table 2.2 Tax assessments of the Parisian elite.

	number of cases	average tax (livres)	maximum assessed (livres)	minimum assessed (livres)
courtiers, great nobility and leading prelates*	136	185	300	(20)
présidents au parlement	23	177	300	40
conseillers au parlement	124	97	300	20
présidents au Chambre des Comptes	7	200	300	100
maîtres des comptes	31	122	240	25
auditeurs des comptes	31	49	100	20
présidents, Cour des Aides	8	88	200	25
conseillers, Cour des Aides	20	73.5	200	15
généraux aux Monnaies	18	49.5	150	15
conseillers au Châtelet	21	42.5	100	20
secrétaires du roi*	72	125	300	(20)
financiers*	177	101	300	(20)
medical doctors	57	39.5	300	2
barristers *(avocats)*	239	38.5	300	2
notaries	99	19	160	3
procureurs au parlement	145	19	200	2
procureurs au Châtelet	106	13.5	50	2
merchant drapers	252	31	250	4

*This category includes only those identified members of these groups who were assessed 20 livres or more.

royal power from those fiscal notables whose prominence was purely urban and local. As for the '*bons marchands*' upon whom notarial documents commonly bestowed the honorific '*honorable homme sire*', their wealth did not slip markedly below that attributed to those legal and professional men typically given the more exalted honorific '*noble homme*' (barristers, medical doctors, *conseillers au Châtelet*, auditors in the Chambre des Comptes, etc.). The Paris of the Wars of Religion was a city in which a number of avenues for success were open to people, and it is even possible to find large assessments bestowed upon artisans working for the court or prominent building contractors. In this respect, the free gift offers a quite different vision of society from that of the capitation of 1695, where the state imposed a single tax scale reflecting its own vision of the social hierachy and grouping people rigidly according to their occupational status.[45]

Different groups among the fiscal notables clustered primarily in different quarters, as can be seen from Map 2.4, which indicates the degree of concentration of members of these groups in Paris's sixteen administrative subdivisions. The great nobles, prelates, and financiers who moved in the orbit of the royal court lived preponderantly in the peripheral sections of the city that provided enough land for their *hôtels*. Nearly one quarter of them lived in the quarters of Saint-Honoré and Saint-Eustache near the Louvre, the region of choice for such favorites of Catherine de Medici and her sons as the Gondis and the Villequiers. Nearly another quarter lived in the future Marais, to which the great feudal magnates more independent of the court such as the Guises and the Montmorencys remained faithful. The purest concentration of such individuals was to be found in the faubourg of Saint-Germain des Prés, but this region earned its reputation as the 'noble faubourg' less because the *grands* linked to the court were exceptionally numerous there – 18 per cent of this category in fact resided here – than because more purely bourgeois notables were rare.

The magistrates of the sovereign courts clustered more consistently inside the city walls, but, except for the clerical members of their ranks who inhabited the courtyard of the Palais or the cloister of Notre Dame, they too had largely forsaken the high densities of the Ile de la Cité and the areas of the right and left banks immediately facing it. Their regions of choice were the quarters of Saint-Séverin, on the western side of the left bank, and the Temple, encompassing the north-eastern right bank. Twenty-nine per cent of the members of the parlement lived in Saint-Séverin and 24 per cent in the Temple. Among the members of the financial courts, slightly more dispersed around the city at large, the preferences were reversed, with 23 per cent inhabiting the Temple and 14 per cent Saint-Séverin. Sometimes magistrates pioneered the development of new areas, as Jacques de Ligneris did for the *couture* Sainte-Catherine in 1545. Noblemen and financiers soon followed behind, contesting judicial pre-eminence within these areas slated to become strongholds of the aristocracy.[46]

Map 2.4   Residential distribution by quarter of select groups of notables (index).

A. Index of concentration relative to the universe of fiscal notables

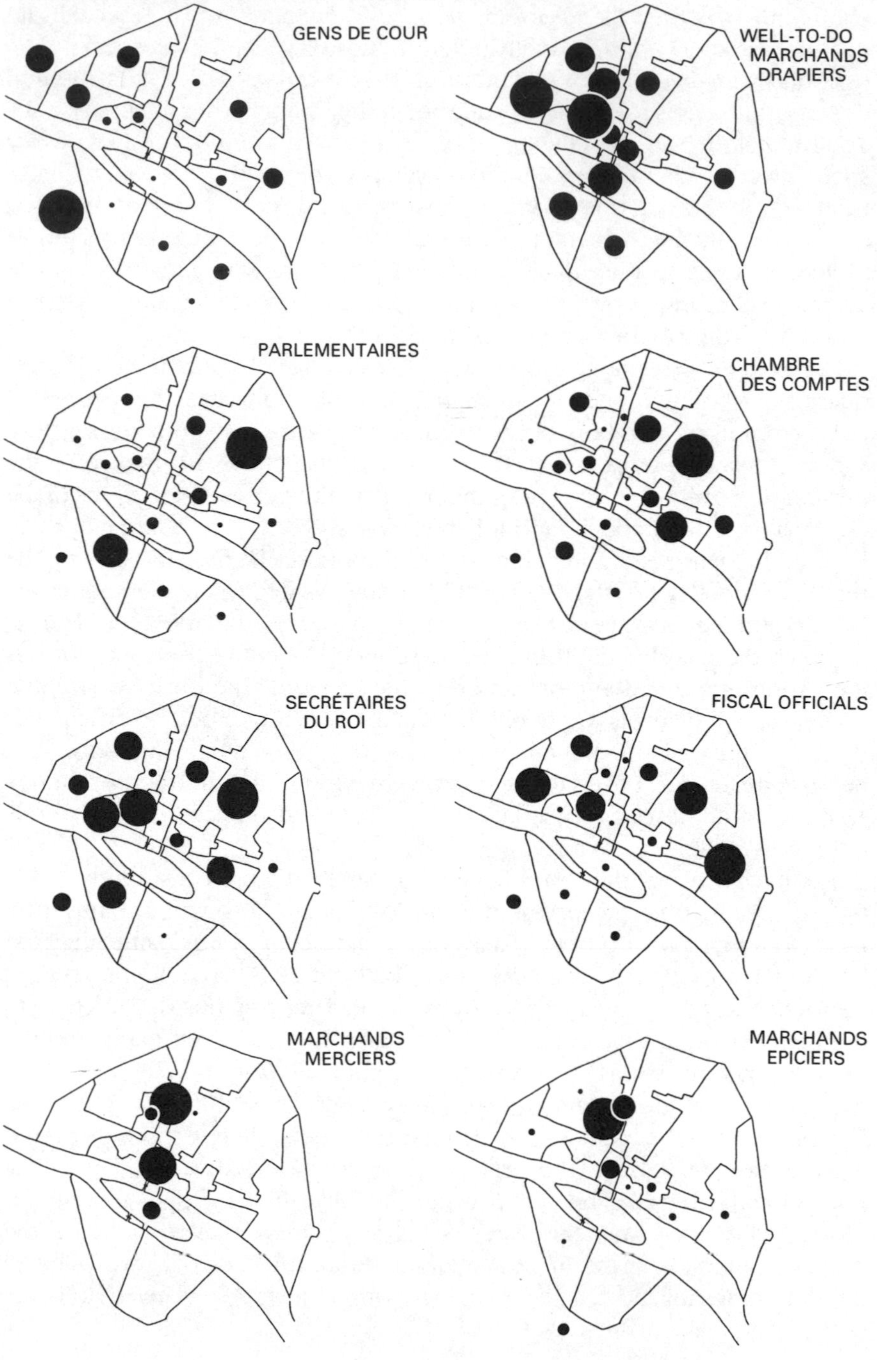

GENS DE COUR

WELL-TO-DO
MARCHANDS
DRAPIERS

PARLEMENTAIRES

CHAMBRE
DES COMPTES

SECRÉTAIRES
DU ROI

FISCAL OFFICIALS

MARCHANDS
MERCIERS

MARCHANDS
EPICIERS

B. Index of concentration relative to all taxpayers

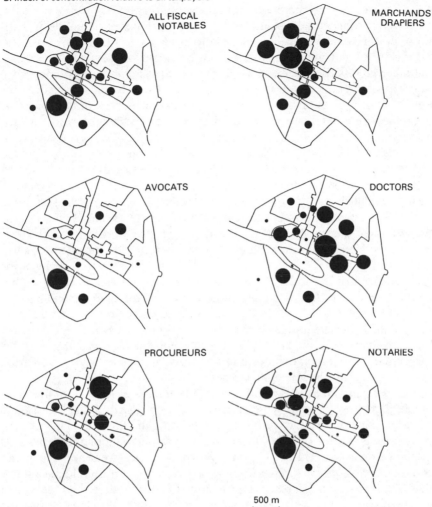

500 m

The index of concentration is calculated by using the formula :

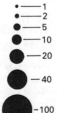

$$\frac{a^2}{n\,m}$$

a: number of people in a given category living within the quarter
n: total number of people within that category throughout the city
m: total population of the quarter

For each category the highest value obtained is then given an index value
of 100 and all other values are represented as a percentage of that value

The *secrétaires du roi* and financial officials showed a preference for the same quarters as the members of the sovereign courts, but they were less thoroughly concentrated in them. Among these men, the Temple was the most popular quarter, followed closely by Saint-Antoine, Saint-Eustache, Saint-Honoré and the Saints-Innocents. The degree of correlation between the financial officials and those magistrates in the Chambre des Comptes was lower than one might expect, amounting to just 0.69. Overall, however, it can be seen that the residential patterns of the lay magistrates of the sovereign courts and the chief financial officials overlapped substantially, expressing the considerable degree of similarity that existed among these groups in their relationship with the city and its other influential denizens.

The milieu of the lawyers and other liberal professionals demonstrated far less unity. The notaries, like many retail merchants, had an incentive to reside near potential clients, and they consequently distributed themselves across all of the city's quarters, with nevertheless a visible preference for Saint-Séverin, the wealthiest quarter of all. Within each quarter, they were particularly likely to be found on the busiest streets. Paris's doctors also spread themselves across the city. Conversely, the *avocats*, halfway between the world of the *basoche* and that of the high robe, imitated the magistrates in so far as they could. A quarter of them resided in the quarter of the Temple, and another forty per cent on the left bank, primarily in Saint-Séverin. Where their residential patterns show a degree of correlation of 0.8 with those of the magistrates, those of the *procureurs* reveal a correlation of just 0.59 with the magistrates. These men demonstrated a particular affection for Saint-Martin's quarter, especially the Rue Quincampoix.

The '*bons marchands*' favored very different parts of town from the other notables. Among the leading *merciers*, specialists primarily in the luxury cloth trade, 71 per cent lived in the two quarters along the Rue Saint-Denis or the neighboring quarter of Saint-Jacques de l'Hôpital and another 16.5 per cent on the Ile de la Cité. The same three right bank districts were home to 69 per cent of the rich *apothicaires-épiciers*. (The members of this guild paying less than 20 livres in tax, presumably mainly retailers rather than important wholesale importers, were by contrast far more widely dispersed around the city.) The region of the Halles and the Rue Saint-Denis was clearly still the hub of Paris's wholesale commerce.

Other parts of the city were home to the *marchands drapiers* who specialized in the sale and redistribution of woolens produced outside the city, primarily in Normandy, Berry, and the Brie. The drapers' guild was first in precedence and prestige among the six pre-eminent guilds known as the '*six corps*' and was exceeded in wealth only by its great rival, the mercers' guild. The 149 of its members who appear among the fiscal notables concentrated especially heavily around the Halle aux Draps and the guild bureau in the Hôtel des Carneaux on the right bank, but a significant minority of them lived in other quarters across the city. Like other occupational groups, when they were found on the right bank, they too were tightly clustered. Just about all 35 merchant drapers in the quarter of Saint-Eustache lived on the Rue de la Tonnellerie. Those in the quarters of Saint-Honoré and the Saints-Innocents were concentrated on the rue Saint-Honoré, near the guild's bureau. Still other, smaller hubs existed around the Porte Baudoyer and along the Rue Saint-Martin. The merchant drapers of the Ile de la Cité or the left bank lived, on the other hand, in far less proximity to one another. Although the forces governing this pattern are not readily obvious, it is striking that the quarters of choice of these men were clearly distinct from those of the mercers, even though they were located close by them. (The correlation between the residential patterns of the two groups was just 0.05.) The rivalry between these two groups appears to have given rise to a strategy of inhabiting different subdivisions of the municipal electoral machinery.

The breakdown of residential patterns according to occupation thus shows clearly the geographic – and social – distances that existed between certain of the constituent parts of the Parisian elites. In particular, the examination reveals the effort of the royal officials to distance themselves from the mercantile elites – and their own bourgeois origins. The coefficient of correlation between the quarters of residence of magistrates and mercers was −0.27. Between magistrates and merchant drapers, the figure was 0.09. Even in those quarters that housed members of both groups, the two often appear on closer inspection to have largely concentrated in different parts of the quarter, as in Saint-Jacques de l'Hôpital or in Saint-Séverin, divided between the *gens de justice* around the Rue Saint-André des Arts and the merchants of the Rues de la Harpe and de la Huchette. Conversely, the world of the *basoche* sought residential proximity to the upper magistracy, which would become its great enemy during the era of the League. The broad patterns of social segregation, it seems, followed lines of occupational function, not *qualité*.

By 1571, an element of distance was beginning to separate mercantile Paris from the Paris of the city's rentier and judicial elites. A glance backwards and forwards at other fiscal documents reveals that this was part of a broad process of change in Parisian residential patterns that had begun to transform the capital as early as the fifteenth century and would continue to do so through the seventeenth. To judge by the *taille* rolls for the late thirteenth and early fourteenth centuries, many of the patterns found in 1571 were already in place around 1300. The right bank was already characterized by a strong tendency for the members of certain occupations to cluster in clearly delimited areas, while the prevalence of clerics and scholars immunized the left bank against the colonization of individual streets by craft guilds.[47] Often, the patterns of concentration demonstrated remarkable endurance, as in the case of the butchers, who were dispersed from the vicinity of the Grande Boucherie following its closure in 1421 only to reconcentrate themselves within the quarter of Saint-Jacques de la Boucherie by 1571, even though the trade suffered a serious deterioration of its economic position between the two periods. The combined evidence of the *taille* roll of 1421 and the *taxe des aisés* of 1423 shows that the region of the Halles already housed the better part of the city's leading merchants. But these same documents show that this part of town also housed 48 per cent of the lay magistrates in the parlement. Another 21 per cent lived in the quarters around the Place de la Grève (just 10 per cent in the quarter of the Temple), 28 per cent on the left bank (17 per cent in the quarter of Sainte-Geneviève as opposed to just 10 per cent in Saint-Séverin), and 3 per cent on the Ile de la Cité.[48] Here are patterns very different from those that would emerge later.

Although in many medium-sized French cities the reconstruction following the dark days of the Hundred Years' War permitted a growing concentration of wealth in the heart of the city, it appears that it was precisely in this same period that the Parisian separation between mercantile and magisterial quarters began to manifest itself. By 1488, royal officials seem to have established their hegemony over Saint-Séverin, and a document from that date identifies the region of the Temple (still known as the quarter of Saint-Merry) as a '*grand quartier*' of '*officiers et praticiens*'.[49] With the continued multiplication of royal functionaries increasingly concerned to provide visible evidence of their distinctiveness from the rest of the population, this trend only intensified in the subsequent period, accelerated by the second broad trend that reshaped Paris's social geography: the renovation policies favored by the kings from Henry IV to Louis XIV. During the seventeenth century, the Ile Saint-Louis was formed out of two previously uninhabited islands in the Seine, the construction of the Pont Neuf and 'Ile du Palais' created a new pocket of elite residence on the western tip of the Cité, and the Place Royale (today's Place des Vosges) took shape in the Marais. Finally, and most important of all, the remodelling of the Louvre, the construction of the Palais Cardinal (later Palais Royal), and the erection of Versailles to the west of the city made the western fringes of town the most favored location of all for aristocratic residences, inaugurating the subsequent shift of the center of gravity of fashionable Paris toward this side of the city.[50] At the same time, continued growth also bred new *faubourgs populaires* such as the faubourgs Saint-Antoine and du Temple on the eastern edge of the city.

The *taxe des boues et lanternes* of 1637–43 has already been the object of a rapid analysis based on the simple but nonetheless revealing distinction between the Parisian 'working' population (merchants and artisans) and all other social categories. It shows the Marais, the eastern edge of the Ile de la Cité, and certain 'residential islands' such as the area around the Hôtel de Soissons all standing out as centers of judicial, financial, and aristocratic 'idleness', revealing a large measure of persistence, and in some cases accentuation, of the patterns already visible in 1571.[51] A certain decline in the economic fortunes of parts of the center of town is suggested by the replacement of drapers by *fripiers* along the Rue de la Tonnellerie, but other merchants catering to an aristocratic clientele showed great adaptibility, notably the goldsmiths (*orfèvres*), who, after the collapse of the Pont aux Changeurs, took over the quay on the right bank that still bears their name. Several sources permit a rough reconstruction of the residential patterns of the leading merchants, legal personnel and magistrates in the mid-seventeenth century. (See Table 2.3.) Taken together, these suggest that the magistrates continued to avoid the quarters around the Halles, increased their presence on the eastern fringes of the right bank, especially in Saint-Antoine and on the new Ile Saint-Louis, and began to desert the sections of Saint-Séverin inside the walls of the left bank in favor of either the newly developed sections of the right bank or the growing faubourg Saint-Germain. The financiers increasingly abandoned the left bank and continued their drift outward toward the more peripheral sections of town, while the *procureurs* clustered increasingly on the Ile de la Cité, the left bank, and certain right bank quarters such as Saint-Eustache and Saint-Jean en Grève. Meanwhile, the *juges-consuls* of the mercantile *juridiction consulaire*, a sample of prominent merchants, moved away from Saint-Eustache and neighboring Saint-Jacques de l'Hôpital toward the right bank quarters located closest to the Ile de la Cité. This appears to have been the one group that continued to prize centrality of location, although its members may also have been nudged in this direction by the proliferation of aristocratic *hôtels* in the western sections of the right bank around the Louvre and Saint-Eustache.

The later fifteenth and sixteenth century thus witnessed two significant changes in the social organization of France's capital. The first was the growing divergence in the residential choices of the city's mercantile and legal elites. The second was the colonization of certain peripheral quarters of the city by those moving in the entourage of a royal court that resided in Paris with increasing permanence. These people were the true innovators in elaborating a new manner of using urban space, offering a model of behavior that the leading magistrates increasingly emulated. By the sixteenth century, two cities had begun to coexist within the confines of the capital, as they would continue to do for centuries to come: the antiquated Paris of the central parts of town, where artisans and merchants squeezed tightly amid one another; and the newer Paris just inside and outside the walls, where the fashionable residential neighborhoods of the rentier classes alternated with working quarters and *faubourgs* dominated by an artisan and laboring population.[52] Both of these cities, however, appear to have been marked by similar patterns of social behavior, for in both the members of different corporate groups chose to live in locations near other members of their group, thereby reinforcing the associative links of the group.

This article began with the politics of municipal taxation that brought the 1571 roll of the free gift into being. By way of conclusion, I would like to advance the tentative hypothesis that the changes which that document helps

Table 2.3 Residential preferences within the Parisian elites, 1571 and c.1650. (Figures refer to the index of dispersion. A value of 100 would indicate that the number of members of a group living in a given quarter equalled the number one would expect were the members of the group distributed evenly among all sixteen quarters. Higher or lower figures are index values indicating greater or lesser numbers of group members living in the quarter in question.)

quarter	parlement			Chambre des Comptes		financiers		notaries of Châtelet		procureurs au parlement		juges-consuls des marchands	
	1571	1649[1]	1656[2]	1571	1649	1571	1st ½ 17th c.[3]	1571	1650[4]	1571	1641[5]	1564–88[6]	1615–53[6]
St Jacques de l'Hôpital	11	7	8	21	15	63	5	65	41	33	24	445	150
St Germain l'Auxerrois	54	14	42	62	73	45	43	97	68	99	27	0	32
St Sépulcre	0	0	8	41	29	36	11	32	68	22	12	253	222
St Honoré	43	43	17	21	44	181	92	129	150	0	9	48	63
St Jacques de la Boucherie	0	7	0	0	0	18	5	48	55	11	15	229	277
Sts Innocents	54	65	33	62	59	145	16	129	68	55	27	96	135
St Eustache	87	58	75	125	117	145	366	48	68	88	35	144	79
St Gervais	22	43	42	145	44	9	97	16	14	55	21	12	40
St Esprit	11	0	0	21	0	0	0	65	27	22	32	0	8
St Martin	151	94	92	187	132	127	226	129	137	331	234	48	63
Temple	421	340	360	374	279	271	361	97	150	77	50	36	32
St Jean en Grève	87	29	33	83	73	45	32	81	41	88	74	24	40
St Antoine	54	115	142	104	205	244	205	97	164	11	15	36	40
Notre Dame	97	137	109	83	44	54	5	145	137	154	231	144	261
fbg St Jacques	0	14	8	0	0	0	0	0	0	0	0	0	0
Ste Geneviève	87	80	126	62	132	63	11	113	96	231	393	0	40
Ile St Louis	—	130	92	—	103	—	65	—	14	231	3	—	0
St Séverin	357	282	243	166	220	90	27	307	164	254	372	84	79
fbg St Germain	54	137	159	41	29	63	32	66	137	66	30	0	0
Number of cases:	148	221	191	77	109	177	297	99	117	145	541	133	202

[1] Figures based on an extensive search in the records of the Minutier Central.
[2] Source: Bibliothèque Historique de la Ville de Paris, MS 132828 (provisional côte), 'liste des membres du Parlement de Paris'.
[3] Source: Françoise Bayard, *Le monde des financiers au XVIIe siècle* (Paris: Flammarion, 1988), pp. 445–8.
[4] Source: *Les Archives nationales: Etat général des fonds*, Vol. 4, *Fonds divers* (Paris: Archives Nationales, 1980), pp. 15–142.
[5] Source: B.N., 8⁰ Lf⁴² 13, 'Liste de la demeure des procureurs de la Cour de Parlement'.

us to observe in the city's residential geography may have been linked to the political strategies encouraged by the structure of local power. As the Bureau de la Ville underscored in 1615, election to the *échevinage* was 'effused through every quarter'.[53] A group's participation in the structures of local power passed through control of individual quarters. There is a strong correlation between the sociological character of individual quarters and the occupational status of those of their residents called to participate in general assemblies at the Hôtel de Ville, the so-called '*bourgeois mandés*', who held the strategic key to city politics.[54] From the fifteenth century onwards, the central tension within municipal politics was the unavowed competition between the mercantile and the judicial bourgeoisie. The diverging residential patterns of merchants and magistrates may well have stemmed in part from each group's efforts to guarantee that its voice would be heard by establishing its dominance within individual sections of town, just as the mercers and drapers appear to have pursued the strategy of establishing themselves in different quarters. As for the new elite residents linked to the court, cannot their preference for the peripheral sections of town be read not simply as the desire to establish a more comfortable mode of life in less crowded quarters, but also as a sign of their lack of involvement with the affairs of the civic community? The king's increasing residence in the capital, after all, now allowed the road to political influence to pass through court as well as through control of the Hôtel de Ville. The battle over the assessments for the free gift revealed this clearly enough.

NOTES: CHAPTER 2

The author wishes to express his gratitude to Denis Richet, who conceived this project, to Philip Benedict, whose editorial suggestions helped so much in its reconceptualization, and to Hugues Neveux, whose studies of Caen's social geography furnished a constant point of reference, comparison, and inspiration.

1   Jean Jacquart, 'Le poids démographique de Paris et de l'Ile-de-France au XVIe siècle', *Annales de Démographie Historique* (1980), pp. 87–96; Jean-Pierre Babelon, *Paris au XVIe siècle* (Paris: Hachette, 1986), pp. 159–66.

2   B.N., MS Français 11733, fo. 45, 6 March 1563.

3   Denis Crouzet, 'La représentation du temps à l'époque de la Ligue', *Revue Historique*, vol. 270 (1984), pp. 297–388, stresses the 'inflation of existential unease' in the 1560s.

4   Corrozet, *La fleur des antiquitez de la noble et triumphante ville et cité de Paris* (Paris, 1532); idem, *Les antiquitez, histoires et singularitez de Paris, ville capitale du royaume de France* (Paris, 1550).

5   Robert Descimon and Jean Nagle, 'Les quartiers de Paris du Moyen Age au XVIIIe siècle. Evolution d'un espace plurifonctionnel', *Annales: E.S.C.*, vol. 34 (1979), p. 961. For the sake of clarity, I shall refer to individual quarters throughout this article by the fixed names that emerged toward the end of the sixteenth century and during the seventeenth.

6   Bodin, *Six livres de la République*, Vol. 1 (Paris: Fayard, 1986), pp. 120–3. Changing conceptions of the city are analyzed in detail in Françoise Choay, *La règle et le modèle. Sur la théorie de l'architecture et de l'urbanisme* (Paris: Seuil, 1980).

7   B.N., MS Français 11692.

8   Jean-Pierre Babelon is the historian of Paris who has utilized this document most thoroughly. See his 'Le Paris de Coligny', *Actes du colloque l'amiral de Coligny et son temps (Paris, 24–28 octobre 1572)* (Paris: Société de l'Histoire du Protestantisme Français, 1974), pp. 549–76; and *Paris au XVIe siècle*, pp. 215–61, 508–16.

9   All of the collaborators on this project, and especially Béatrice Véniel, deserve a share of the credit for this essay. The author assumes full responsibility for any deficiencies.

10   Chevalier, *Les bonnes villes de France du XIVe au XVIe siècle* (Paris: Aubier Montaigne, 1982), p. 217. See also his 'Fiscalité municipale et fiscalité d'Etat en France du XIVe à la fin du XVIe siècle. Deux systèmes liés et concurrents', in Jean-Philippe Genet and Michel Le Mené (eds), *Genèse de l'Etat moderne. Prélèvement et redistribution* (Paris: Editions du C.N.R.S., 1987), pp. 137–51.

11   Alain Guery, 'Le roi dépensier. Le don, la contrainte, et l'origine du système financier de la monarchie française d'Ancien Régime', *Annales: E.S.C.*, vol. 39 (1984), pp. 1256–7.

12   Lawrence M. Bryant, *The King and the City in the Parisian Royal Entry Ceremony: Politics, Ritual and Art in the Renaissance* (Geneva: Droz, 1986), pp. 35–48.

13   Jean Combes, *Traité des tailles et aultres charges et subsides* (Paris, 1576), fos. 129–37. See also Jacques Revel, 'Les corps et communautés', in Keith M. Baker (ed.), *The French Revolution and the Creation of Modern Political Culture*, Vol. 1, *The Political Culture of the Old Regime* (Oxford: Pergamon Press, 1987), pp. 226–7.

14   Barbara B. Diefendorf, 'Simon Vigor: A Radical Preacher in Sixteenth-Century Paris', *Sixteenth-Century Journal*, vol. 18 (1987), pp. 399–410.

15   A.N., Minutier Central, XCVIII, 45, act of 17 January 1571.

16   *R.D.B.V.*, Vol. 4, p. 471.

17   Paul-Louis Cauwès, *Les commencements du crédit public en France: les rentes sur l'Hôtel de Ville au XVIe siècle* (Paris: Larose, 1895), pp. 107, 423.

18   *R.D.B.V.*, Vol. 4, pp. 53–5, 74.

19   The account of these negotiations that follows draws upon *R.D.B.V.*, Vol. 6, pp. 202–476, and A.N., H_2 1881, a *liasse* containing several letters sent back to Paris by Simon Bouquet and his fellow city officials from the Loire valley, where the court was residing at the time, reporting on the fate of missions with which they had been entrusted.

20   *R.D.B.V.*, Vol. 6, pp. 224–6.

21   *R.D.B.V.*, Vol. 6, pp. 202–5; B.N., MS Français 11692, fo. 3v.

22   For the rules governing the attribution of the status of bourgeois of Paris, see *R.D.B.V.*, Vol. 12, p. 79; René Choppin, *Oeuvres*, Vol. 3 (Paris, 1662), p. 290. Surviving letters of bourgeoisie confirm that these rules were applied in practice.

23   *R.D.B.V.*, Vol. 3, p. 54.

24   A.N., Q^1 1133[7].

25   Hélène Michaud, *La grande chancellerie et les écritures royales au XVIe siècle* (Paris: Presses Universitaires de France, 1967), pp. 200–2.

26   Robert Descimon, *Qui étaient les Seize? Mythes et réalités de la Ligue parisienne (1585–1594)* (Paris: Klincksieck, 1983), pp. 240–2; Barbara B. Diefendorf, 'Widowhood and remarriage in sixteenth-century Paris', *Journal of Family History*, Vol. 7 (1982), pp. 380–2. Widows account for 20 per cent of the assessments greater than 50 livres and just 10 per cent of those paying less than this sum.

27 *R.D.B.V.*, Vol. 6, p. 446.

28 See A.N., H$_2$ 1881.

29 A.N., H$_2$ 2153, entry of 18 October 1572, and KK 1013, fos. 24–6.

30 Jean Favier, *Les finances pontificales à l'époque du Grand Schisme d'Occident* (Paris: Publications de l'Ecole Française de Rome, 1966), pp. 378–89.

31 On Marcel and municipal politics, see Léo Mouton, *La vie municipale au XVIe siècle. Claude Marcel, Prévôt des marchands 1520–1590* (Paris: Perrin, 1930), p. 3; Claude Michaud, 'Claude Marcel, prévôt des marchands et receveur du clergé de France 1520–1590', in *Etudes européennes. Mélanges offerts à Victor-Lucien Tapié* (Paris: Publications de la Sorbonne, 1973), pp. 295–320.

32 All of the cases where individuals were assessed nothing have been eliminated from the analysis that follows. An undeterminable percentage of these cases refer to unbuilt properties owned by individuals who lived elsewhere in the city rather than people too poor to pay any tax.

33 The lacunae appear between folios 21 and 22 in the Saint-Jacques de l'Hôpital quarter, between folios 62 and 63 in the Sépulcre quarter, between folios 166 and 167 in the Notre Dame quarter, and between folios 253 and 254 and 263 and 264 in the Sainte-Geneviève quarter.

34 Calculations based on a comparison of B.N., MS Moreau 1055 and MS Français 11732, fo. 87v.

35 Babelon, *Paris au XVIe siècle*, p. 167.

36 Corrozet, *Les antiquitez de Paris*, p. 174; *R.D.B.V.*, Vol. 4, p. 113, and Vol. 6, p. 55.

37 Descimon and Nagle, 'Les quartiers de Paris', pp. 964–5.

38 Perrot, *Genèse d'une ville moderne. Caen au XVIIIe siècle* (Paris: Mouton, 1975), pp. 553–4.

39 Roger Dion, 'Le site de Paris dans ses rapports avec le développement de la ville', in *Paris, croissance d'une capitale* (Paris: Hachette, 1961), pp. 30–1.

40 On this pattern, see Jacques Rossiaud, 'Crises et consolidations, 1330–1530', in Georges Duby (ed.), *Histoire de la France urbaine*, Vol. 2 (Paris: Seuil, 1980), pp. 502–3.

41 Daniel Roche, *Le peuple de Paris. Essai sur la culture populaire au XVIIIe siècle* (Paris: Aubier-Montaigne, 1981), pp. 112–16.

42 André Chastel, 'L'Ilot de la rue du Roule et ses abords', *Mémoires de la Société de l'Histoire de Paris et de l'Ile-de-France*, vol. 16–17 (1967), pp. 77–129.

43 Françoise Boudon, André Chastel *et al.*, *Système de l'architecture urbaine. Le quartier des Halles à Paris* (Paris: Editions du C.N.R.S., 1977), pp. 183–91, 345–50.

44 Bernard de La Roche Flavin, *Treize livres des Parlemens de France* (Geneva, 1621), p. 800.

45 Alain Guery, 'Etat, classification sociale et compromis sous Louis XIV: la capitation de 1695', *Annales: E.S.C.*, vol. 41 (1986), pp. 1041–60.

46 Maurice Dumolin, *Etudes de topographie parisienne*, Vol. 3 (Paris: privately published, 1931), pp. 303–20.

47 Bronislaw Geremek, *Les marginaux parisiens aux XIVe et XVe siècles* (Paris: Flammarion, 1976), pp. 79–110.

48 Calculations of the author based on the figures provided in Jean Favier, *Les contribuables parisiens à la fin de la guerre de Cent Ans* (Geneva: Droz, 1970), pp. 61, 64.

49 A.N., X1A 8319, fo. 392, entry of 12 August 1488.

50 Maurice Halbwachs, 'Les plans d'extension et d'aménagement de Paris avant le XIXe siècle', in his *Classes sociales et morphologie* (Paris: Editions de Minuit, 1972), pp. 199–224; Pierre Francastel, *Une destinée de capitale, Paris* (Paris: Denoël, 1968).

51 Jean de Viguerie and Evelyne Saive-Lever, 'Essai pour une géographie socio-

professionnelle de Paris dans la première moitié du XVIIe siècle', *Revue d'Histoire Moderne et Contemporaine*, vol. 20 (1973), pp. 424–9.

52 Roche, *Peuple de Paris*, pp. 34–5.
53 *R.D.B.V.*, Vol. 16, p. 231.
54 The overall correlation between the residential distribution of the city's merchants and magistrates and their distribution by quarter among the *bourgeois mandés* is 0.75.

3

From renaissance city to ancien régime capital: Montpellier, c.1500–c.1600

FREDERICK M. IRVINE

During the course of the sixteenth century, Montpellier experienced in a particularly pure form a set of social changes that similarly transformed many provincial French towns which were the seats of major royal tribunals at that time. In the second half of the fifteenth century, the city's once flourishing commerce entered a phase of decline. At the same time, however, Montpellier began to emerge as a major centre of royal administration and, with Toulouse, as one of Languedoc's two administrative capitals. In the sixteenth century the number of courts and of royal officials within the city multiplied dramatically. The wealth of those staffing these courts also rose substantially, especially relative to other elements within the urban population. And at the same time, lawyers and the judicial officials associated with the royal courts (robe officers) extended their power within the municipal government. This study will explore these changes and trace the social contours of the robe class that increasingly came to dominate Montpellier in the sixteenth and early seventeenth centuries.

THE GEOGRAPHIC AND ECONOMIC CONTEXT

Montpellier is situated to the west of the alluvial delta of the Rhône on the edge of one of the narrowest portions of the coastal plain of Languedoc. The walled core of the city was situated on three low, interconnected hills from the summit of which there is a clear view to the north over the hills and low plateaux of the *garrigue* to the Cévennes, and a view of the Mediterranean to the south. The population within the city walls grew from roughly 12,500 in 1550 to 15,500 in 1600.[1] The streets within the walls tended to be extremely narrow and were lined with houses that were for the most part uninterrupted by gardens or other open spaces. The lack of open space reflected the fact that by the second half of the sixteenth century the city had long since outgrown its medieval walls. Perhaps by way of compensation, the houses within the city's walls were considered by foreign observers to be among the most beautiful in France.[2]

Beyond the city walls lay the *faubourgs* (suburbs) of Montpellier. During the first half of the sixteenth century they had contained buildings for roughly twenty-five religious or charitable establishments, certain schools including the Faculty of Law, and numerous private residences, but these were all razed to the ground in 1562 to make the city more defensible in the impending siege. At the end of the century the *faubourgs* were still largely devoid of structures and were planted with numerous vineyards, olive groves, orchards and gardens.[3]

The city of Montpellier was surrounded by its *terroir*, an area of land extending several kilometers in each direction from the city core. Property located within the *terroir* of Montpellier was subject to taxation to cover the city's share of the tax payable by the diocese of Montpellier. The land to the north of the city rises very gradually until the *garrigue* is reached within a distance of a few kilometers. The *garrigue* consists of low hills, whose poor, rocky soil made them unsuited to agriculture. In many places they were covered by scrub, herbs and weeds (many of which give off a beautiful fragrance) and were devoted to the grazing of sheep. The population pressures of the sixteenth century resulted in the enclosure of an increasing portion of the *garrigue* for cereal cultivation, but the yields were always marginal.[4]

The coastal plain to the south of the city is very fertile in places but is much narrower in the vicinity of Montpellier than it is to the west near Béziers or Narbonne. Land to the south of Montpellier was highly prized by urban investors because the better-drained land was well suited to cereal cultivation and the less well drained land closer to the sea coast or along the banks of the Lez and the Mosson made excellent natural pasture, a commodity in short supply in the diocese of Montpellier.[5] As a result, wealthy urban investors began to acquire land at Lattes as early as the fourteenth century.[6] In the words of Louise Guiraud, the historian of sixteenth-century Protestantism at Montpellier, 'il n'était pas de bourgeois ou de marchand montpelliérain qui n'ambitionnait un domaine, un champ, un pré à Lattes'.[7] Indeed, one of the first signs that a wealthy merchant or *bourgeois* had social aspirations for his family to enter the nobility was the purchase of a meadow or two at Lattes.[8]

During the fourteenth and fifteenth century Montpellier owed its commercial prosperity to its maritime commerce with the Levant. It was a major centre for the importation of spices and drugs from the Levant into France and at one point may have ranked second only to Venice in terms of the volume imported.[9] The city was also an important financial centre where wealthy money-changers carried on their operations.[10] This flourishing Levantine maritime commerce and the city's status as a major financial centre drew the famed international trader, Jacques Coeur, to Montpellier during the 1450s.[11]

This remarkable commercial prosperity did not last beyond the end of the fifteenth century. The city's maritime commerce with the Levant collapsed late in the fifteenth century, partly because Marseille became part of the kingdom in 1481 (depriving Montpellier of its royal monopoly on the import of spices), and partly because Montpellier's port of Lattes suffered from certain natural disadvantages that became more serious with time. Lattes was situated on the River Lez, several kilometers downstream from Montpellier, and owed its status as a port to the absence of good natural harbours on the Mediterranean coast. The Lez was a shallow river and during the summer dry season even ships of shallow draft sometimes could not penetrate to Lattes, so that it was necessary to unload cargo on to barges at the mouth of the river. The alternate, and more distant port of Aigues–Mortes, situated at the west end of the delta of the Rhône, had even less to recommend it because its access to the sea was periodically blocked by shifting sand-bars. Marseille had a tremendous competitive advantage as a maritime port because it had a deep, sheltered harbour. At the end of the fifteenth century Lattes and Aigues–Mortes ceased to enjoy even their reduced capacity as maritime ports when ships of deeper draft, already in use in the Atlantic, were introduced into the Mediterranean. These ships could not penetrate to Lattes even at the best of times, and this, along with the pre-eminence of Marseille as the leading French port on the Mediterranean, meant that Montpellier's merchants could no longer engage in maritime commerce with the Levant.[12]

The loss of the maritime trade with the Levant consigned Montpellier to the position of a centre of regional commerce. It was still possible to engage in the overland spice trade with Lyon, but it was neither as profitable (since the first and best profits were taken by middlemen and the market was regional rather than national) nor as exciting (since it did not involve ocean voyages and contact with foreign cultures) as was direct commerce with the Levant. Partly in response to this situation, prominent merchant families gradually withdrew from commerce and invested in seigneurial estates, robe offices, or both.

Families that remained in commerce still had a number of profitable economic opportunities open to them. They travelled to the fairs of Lyon to obtain spices from the Levant in exchange for woolen cloths, objects made from gold or silver, and perfumes or dyes distilled from the herbs of the *garrigue*. Some local herbs had medicinal properties which, with the dyes and perfumes from the *garrigue*, contributed to the reputation of the city's apothecaries.[13] The apothecary Jacques de Farges was so highly regarded that Charles IX made a point of visiting his boutique during his passage through the city in 1564.[14] Montpellier had only a modest cloth industry but enjoyed a reputation for the quality of its blankets and of its scarlet cloth, which was tinted with a dye derived from the oak trees that grew in the *garrigue*.[15] The cloth industry appears to have been fairly prosperous before 1560, owing to rapid population growth in the regional market area and a healthy export of cloth to Italy and the Levant.[16] The civil wars caused considerable damage to the commerce and industry of Montpellier, as was the case with other cities in Languedoc. The cloth industry went into decline after 1560[17] with the levelling-off of population growth, loss of export markets, and the disruption of regional markets and production that was caused by the fighting in the region during the civil wars, especially before 1585. The city suffered prolonged sieges in 1562 and 1577. Fulling mills on the River Lez were destroyed on each occasion, while both the sieges and the passage of a ravaging Protestant army through the region in 1570 caused a marked decline in demand for cloth as incomes were diverted to pay for scarce foodstuffs.[18] At Toulouse, the unfavorable trading conditions of the period helped to precipitate the liquidation of the commercial enterprises of the de Laran, a family of rich cloth merchants, and similar commercial failures probably occurred at Montpellier.[19] The cloth industry may have revived after 1582 with a partial return to peace in the region.[20]

The economy of Montpellier also benefitted from the presence of a university whose Faculty of Medicine enjoyed an international reputation during the sixteenth century. Students from all parts of Europe came to study at Montpellier, and among their number were the father and son, Felix and Thomas Platter, who left accounts of Montpellier and its student life in the 1550s and 1590s respectively.[21] Most of the students who came from elsewhere left after completing their studies, but their presence in the city gave Montpellier a cosmopolitan flavour.[22] The Faculty of Law did not enjoy an international reputation and most of its students were drawn from Montpellier or the other towns of Bas-Languedoc.[23] There was a precipitous drop in enrollment after 1560, no doubt as a result of the disruption caused by the civil wars.[24]

As commercial difficulties increased and Montpellier's prominent merchants withdrew from trade, the initial response of many families was to invest in rural estates and to seek to 'live nobly'. This caused a swelling of the ranks of a new, urban-based nobility, particularly during the first half of the sixteenth century when scions of wealthy merchant families invested in rural estates in numbers unmatched before or since. Living nobly meant that at least a portion of one's income came from a rural estate, but urban nobles also typically earned income from urban real estate, annuities (based on loans to private parties or the monarchy), and commodity speculation. Only commerce was off limits. Such individuals increasingly adopted the title of *écuyer*, in imitation of the old nobility or *noblesse de race*, which was not very well represented in the region of Montpellier.[25] In this manner, many individuals made a seamless transition during the early decades of the century from being bourgeois (a term which in theory designated a non-noble who lived off the revenues of his investments without pursuing any particular occupation) to being *écuyers*. After about 1560 it became harder to get accepted as noble on this basis. The purchase of robe offices gradually became the central route open to families intent on climbing out of the bourgeoisie.

GROWTH OF THE ROYAL ADMINISTRATION

The late fifteenth and sixteenth centuries were in many respects a period of economic difficulty for Montpellier, and yet, as we have already seen, the city's population actually increased during the turmoil of the second half of the sixteenth century. This underscores the significance for the city's economy of its elevation late in the fifteenth century to the status of a regional administrative capital and of the substantial expansion that occurred during the course of the next century, particularly the second half of the century, in the size of the royal administration. Increasingly, the wealthier members of the bourgeoisie responded to the loss of opportunities in the commercial sphere by investing a portion of their fortunes in royal offices, which offered status, a safe investment, and a generous rate of return on investment.

Montpellier's emergence as an administrative capital of province-wide significance can be traced to the establishment in the city in 1467 of the Cour des Aides. Before this time the town already housed a few courts whose jurisdiction encompassed the immediate region, but the Cour des Aides was a prestigious sovereign court whose jurisdiction over all matters concerning the imposition and collection of taxes, individual tax liability, and criminal acts relating to tax collection and administration extended to the entire *ressort* of the Parlement of Toulouse, that is, all of Languedoc and Rouergue and parts of the Quercy and Guyenne.[26] The creation of this court provoked considerable opposition from the Parlement of Toulouse and the provincial estates, both of whom wanted it abolished, as well as from Toulouse's municipal authorities, who wanted to see the court transferred to their city. In consequence, it enjoyed only an intermittent existence before 1490 and was frequently joined to the Parlement of Toulouse.[27] It is not clear why it was finally established on a permanent basis at Montpellier rather than Toulouse but the most likely explanation is that this was seen as a way of maintaining an interregional balance between Bas-Languedoc and Haut-Languedoc. Once permanently established, the court began to grow in size, increasing from eleven robe officers in 1500 to nineteen in 1600.

The Cour des Aides was soon followed by several other financial tribunals of province-wide significance, which cemented Montpellier's position as the centre of Languedocian financial administration. In 1523, a new Chambre des Comptes was established for Languedoc and located in Montpellier. Initially charged with auditing the accounts of all officers who received royal revenues except the *receveur-général des finances* and the *receveurs-ordinaires* of the royal domain (their accounts continued to be audited in Paris), the court extended its jurisdiction over these officials in 1589. It grew

109

even more dramatically in size than the Cour des Aides, increasing from seven members in 1523 to thirty-eight in 1600.[28] In 1542 further decentralization of the state's fiscal apparatus led to the creation of sixteen *recettes-générales*, or regional treasuries, one of which was located in Montpellier. Those charged with collecting the revenue from royal taxes (the *généraux des finances*) and the royal domain (the *trésoriers de France*) in the region quickly came to be gathered around the *recette-générale*. In 1552 the two offices were combined into a single office of *trésorier-général*.[29] The number of offices of *trésorier-général* soon multiplied, and in 1577 a final layer of bureaucracy was created with the establishment of a Bureau des Finances, composed of the various *trésoriers-généraux* meeting in regularly scheduled sessions. By 1600 the Bureau had eleven members. These men were robe officers and were entitled to attend sessions of the Cour des Aides and participate in its debates.[30]

Less prestigious than these sovereign courts of province-wide significance were Montpellier's more strictly local tribunals and administrative agencies, which also increased in size and number. Most civil and criminal law cases came before the *cour ordinaire*. Its decisions could be taken on appeal to the *siège présidial*, which also held exclusive jurisdiction in cases where one of the parties was noble, where the king's interests were at stake, where certain types of ecclesiastical foundations were involved, or, after 1552, where the amount at issue in a civil case was under 250 livres. Both of these courts dated back to the Middle Ages, and the *cour ordinaire* was one of the rare courts not to increase in size at all in the sixteenth century, unlike the *présidial*, which was greatly expanded in 1552 with the creation of seven offices of *conseiller-magistrat*. Additional offices were created in the subsequent years.[31]

Special taxes also begat special courts. Litigation arising in connection with the *équivalent des aides*, a tax on certain foodstuffs, came before the *sièges de l'équivalent*, while that engendered by the salt tax (*gabelle*) came before the *visitation-générale des gabelles*. To these was added around mid-century the *visitation-générale de la foraine* to deal with conflicts arising from the administration of customs duties and excise taxes. The *sièges de l'équivalent* fell largely into disuse after 1500, but these other two court systems provided the crown with ample opportunity to create new judicial offices for sale, and the reigns of the later Valois witnessed the invention of such novel positions as *contregarde des gabelles* and *visiteur-général de la foraine*.[32]

Tax collection and accounting engendered an even more luxuriant profusion of special offices. The basic royal system of tax collection involved a division of responsibilities between *receveurs-particuliers*, who took in the revenue from a specific tax within a given administrative subdivision, and *receveurs-payeurs*, who received a fraction of the sums collected by the *receveurs-particuliers* and then disbursed this money to those local inhabitants dependent upon royal revenue, such as military units or the members of the royal courts. Monies that were not turned over to the various *receveurs-payeurs* were sent on to the *receveur-général* of the *généralité*. At the close of the fifteenth century, royal *receveurs-particuliers* existed in Languedoc to collect the income from two sources: the king's domain (they were assisted here by subaltern officials known as *clavaires*), and the *gabelle*.[33] As for the chief royal tax, the *taille*, it was collected throughout the province by individuals appointed for each diocese by an assembly of the consuls of its major centres. In 1572, however, the monarchy began to create royal offices of *receveur-particulier des tailles*, and the sale of these offices proved such a fertile source of revenue for a financially strapped crown that by 1600 the eleven dioceses of the *généralité* of Montpellier had sixty-six *receveurs-particuliers* and *contrôleurs des tailles*, each of whom served only every third year. Special offices of *receveur-particulier* and *contrôleur* were also created in 1581 to collect customs and excise revenues (previously collected by the officials in charge of the royal domain), and these offices also were soon divided between several different individuals, who held them on a rotating basis.[34] Meanwhile, the system of collecting the *gabelle* was modified and new offices were created in connection with that tax, so that where 35 *grenetiers* and *contrôleurs* had sufficed to collect this impost between 1500 and 1570, 102 men were involved in 1600.[35] At the top of the system, the position of *receveur-général* was made into an office in 1542, became *alternatif* in 1553, and *triennal* in 1597. The associated office of *contrôleur* was created in 1554 and followed the same pattern of multiplication thereafter. Special offices of *receveur-général* and *contrôleur* followed in turn for the *taillon* (a surtax on the basic *taille* first granted in 1549) and the *gabelle*, and they too underwent the same process of mitosis.[36]

The dramatic overall growth of the royal administration is illustrated in Table 3.1, which lists the number of important offices throughout the généralité from 1500 to 1600.[37] The near quadrupling of the total number of royal offices which this table displays came primarily after 1550 and was largely a function of the monarchy's need to raise money to finance warfare with the Habsburgs in the 1550s and the subsequent fighting that took place during the civil wars. This explains why useless *alternatif* and *triennal* offices were created, leaving the incumbents with one or two years of paid holidays for every year they performed their functions of office, and why the monarchy substituted offices for positions that had been held on the basis of annual local appointments, such as that of *receveur-particulier des tailles*. It is hardly surprising that the multiplication of offices had a certain Cartesian logic to it, which suggests a desire to rationalize the royal administration, but if rationalization was a motive for the creation of new offices it was definitely a secondary motive. Indeed, in some areas, such as the creation of offices for payment of the armed forces, the monarchy proceeded without any concern for logic or simplification and left it to the

111

Table 3.1 Total number of royal officers: Généralité of Montpellier.

Institution	1500	1550	1575	1600
Cour des Aides	11	16	20	19
Chambre des Comptes	—	10	17	38
Bureau des Finances	1	1	4	11
Chancery of the Cour des Aides	—	—	4	4
Présidiaux: robe longue				
Béziers	—	—	17	16
Montpellier	5	5	16	20
Nîmes	5	5	21	25
Puy	—	—	9	9
Présidiaux: robe courte	3	3	8	8
Cour ordinaire: juge ordinaire	30	30	30	30
Sièges de l'Equivalent				
juge de l'équivalent	9	4	3	3
Visitation des Gabelles				
visiteur-général	1	1	2	2
lieutenant	5	5	5	7
contrôleur-provincial	—	—	—	2
contregarde-général	—	—	—	2
contregarde	—	—	—	6
Visitation de la Foraine				
maître des ports	—	—	2	4
lieutenant	—	—	—	7
visiteur-général	—	—	—	3
Recettes-générales				
finances	—	1	4	8
taillon	—	—	—	4
gabelles	—	—	—	4
foraine	—	—	—	4
Recettes-particulières				
tailles	—	—	11	66
gabelles	36	34	68	102
domain	4	6	6	12
foraine	—	—	—	2
Subaltern Chambre des Comptes				
receveur-général des restes	—	—	—	2
contrôleur-général des restes	—	—	—	2
garde des archives	—	—	—	1
court usher	—	—	—	2
Receveurs-payeurs				
Cour des Aides	1	1	2	3
Chambre des Comptes	—	1	1	3
Présidiaux	—	—	1	3
Colleges and universities	—	—	—	2
Mortes-payes	—	1	1	1
Extraordinaire des guerres				
trésorier-provincial	—	—	—	2
contrôleur-provincial	—	—	—	2
Totals	111	124	252	441

purchasers to work out the inconsistencies inherent in their overlapping functions.[38]

A large proportion of the growing body of officials lived and worked in Montpellier. It appears that in 1500 at least 30 of the 111 officers in the *généralité* (27.8 per cent) did so. The figures increased to 168 out of a total of 441 (38.1 per cent) in 1600. It is clear from notarial documents and the tax rolls that a significant number of Montpellier residents held offices of *receveur-particulier* or *contrôleur* for the *tailles* or *gabelles* in other centres in Languedoc as well.

Just as the number of officers increased dramatically, especially during the second half of the century, so too did the wages (*gages*) these men were paid. Table 3.2 sets out the total *gages* and *menus droits*, expressed in livres tournois, allocated to royal officials at four dates from 1500 to 1600.[39]

Table 3.2 Administrative and judicial salaries for the Généralité of Montpellier: 1500–1600 (in livres tournois).

Institution	1500	1550	1575	1600
Cour des Aides	1,100	4,040	10,200	15,745
Chambre des Comptes	—	3,480	6,300	53,525
Bureau des Finances	2,500	2,500	10,000	46,880
Présidiaux (robe longue)	1,200	1,200	9,500	10,300
Présidiaux (robe courte)	1,100	1,100	1,700	1,700
Sièges de l'Equivalent	225	100	75	75
Visitation des Gabelles	800	800	1,400	3,340
Visitation de la Foraine	—	—	1,200	4,837
Recettes-particulières				
tailles	4,900	15,130	16,705	68,600
domain	320	450	450	920
gabelles	2,640	2,580	2,840	21,584
Recettes-générales				
finances	—	1,200	5,600	10,800
taillon	—	—	—	3,615
gabelles	—	—	—	4,600
Subaltern Chambre des Comptes	—	50	50	1,100
Receveurs-payeurs	100	720	1,500	2,900
Extraordinaire des guerres	—	—	—	6,570
Total Remuneration	14,885	33,350	67,520	257,091

Of course the sixteenth century witnessed significant inflation, but the increase in the amount of compensation paid to royal officers during the last quarter of the sixteenth century is striking even when allowance is made for the increase in prices. Table 3.3 shows the magnitude of the increase with the above figures adjusted for inflation according to the index for grain prices developed by E. Le Roy Ladurie for Béziers and Montpellier.[40]

Table 3.3 Public sector compensation indexed to inflation.

Year	1500	1550	1575	1600
Relative wheat price	18	36	72	100
Nominal remuneration	14,885	33,350	67,520	257,091
Referenced to 1550	29,770	33,350	33,760	92,553

Despite the rapid increase in the number of royal offices after 1550 there was no shortage of purchasers, as royal offices offered a safe investment with a generous rate of return at a time when most other forms of investment did not.[41]

THE URBAN SOCIAL STRUCTURE

The rapid growth in the size and remuneration of the royal administration brought in its wake a striking redistribution of income and property among Montpellier's urban elites, especially as it was combined with the commercial malaise of the civil wars and a steep rise in agricultural rents, which had set in everywhere in Bas-Languedoc by 1600 and was evident on some estates as early as 1585.[42] Two sorts of documents enable us to chart these changes in the distribution of wealth: the tax rolls of the city and its *terroir*, and the numerous marriage contracts contained in its abundant notarial archives.[43]

The fiscal assessments for each taxpayer holding property in the *terroir* of Montpellier were entered in the *guidons de taille*. These registers were drawn up each year to provide the tax collector with a list of taxpayers and the amount each had to pay. The amount payable was derived from the assessed value of each individual's holdings of real property as set out in the more permanent registers known as *compoix*. The assessed value of these holdings can be most easily determined from the annual tax assessments in the *guidons*. *Guidons de taille* for five *sizains* from 1549 were combined with the *guidon* for the *sizain* of St Mathieu from 1543 (which is the last one available) to determine assessments for 1549. Four *guidons* from the year 1596 (Ste Anne, St Firmin, St Paul and Ste Foi) were combined with two from 1597 (Ste Croix and St Mathieu) to determine assessments for 1596. All six *guidons* have survived from the year 1640, which was chosen as representative of the period immediately before the Fronde.[44] Table 3.4 shows the factor by which the average assessed value of the holdings of individuals in a number of occupational or status categories exceeded the average individual assessment for 1549, 1596 and 1640 of 28.8, 19.7 and 20.6 livres, respectively.

The data in Table 3.4 are subject to some serious limitations. The tax rolls only disclose ownership of real property in the city and its surrounding *terroir*, which may not be a very good guide to urban wealth. Furthermore, they tend to understate the wealth of persons or classes of persons whose

Table 3.4 Fiscal assessments for Montpellier.

Social category	1549			1596			1640		
	R	N	P	R	N	P	R	N	P
'Noble'	5.82	21	1.3	4.47	49	2.2	3.89	63	2.7
Robe officer	4.94	24	1.5	3.85	65	2.9	5.18	102	4.4
Financial officer	2.42	7	0.4	2.79	32	1.4	1.95	57	2.4
Ecclesiastic	0.80	68	4.1	1.00	26	1.2	0.72	16	0.7
Law graduate	1.52	31	1.9	1.91	28	1.2	2.0	32	1.4
Physician	2.88	15	0.9	3.27	14	0.6	3.77	7	0.3
Surgeon	3.41	13	0.8	3.13	7	0.3	1.94	14	0.6
'Bourgeois'	7.33	12	0.7	4.06	17	0.7	2.74	46	2.0
'Sire'	2.50	45	2.7	2.54	41	1.8	2.48	9	0.4
'Merchant'	2.49	88	5.4	1.80	155	6.8	1.98	209	8.9
'Sire' or 'Merchant'	2.50	133	8.1	1.95	196	8.7	2.0	218	9.3
Notary/Procureur	1.38	41	2.5	1.21	67	3.0	1.44	77	3.3
Artisan	0.59	350	21.3	0.57	537	23.8	0.54	588	25.1
Farm workers	0.45	292	17.8	0.44	451	20.0	0.40	422	18.1

Key to Table
R: ratio of each category's mean assessment to the mean for the entire tax roll
N: number of individuals in the category
P: percentage of total taxpayers

holdings were concentrated outside the *terroir* of Montpellier (notably the robe and nobility). Finally, they omit individuals who lived in the city but owned no real property there. The *guidons* thus do not offer as complete a picture of the city's social structure as would tax rolls based on the *taille personnelle*.

What the *guidons* do show is that the ratio by which the average assessment of robe officers exceeded the overall average increased significantly after 1596 from 3.85 to 5.18, an increase that was not shared by the other urban elites to nearly the same extent, if at all. This suggests that after 1596 robe officers were becoming wealthier compared with the rest of the population. The data in Table 3.5 show how the robe increased its share of total assessment after 1549, while that of the bourgeoisie (*marchands, bourgeois* and individuals addressed as 'Sire') declined (though with a slight recovery after 1596) and that of the nobility, having increased somewhat by 1596, remained fairly constant after that date. The clear tendency was for property to concentrate in the hands of robe officers.

Table 3.5 Percentage share of total assessment for selected Montpellier elites.

Social category	1549 (%)	1596 (%)	1640 (%)
Nobility	7.32	9.44	9.37
The Robe	7.10	10.78	20.16
Bourgeoisie	25.14	19.46	21.40

Outside Montpellier there was an even greater tendency for property ownership to concentrate in the hands of robe officers. Notarial documents show a pattern of acquisition of estates by robe officers in the *terroirs* near Montpellier, starting with the case of fertile *terroirs* situated on the coastal plain near the city (Lattes, Mauguio, and Candillargues) during the first half of the sixteenth century and spreading from there outwards to less fertile or more distant *terroirs*. This pattern is confirmed by the *compoix* for the *terroirs* of Lattes and Clapiers (a village immediately to the north of the *terroir* of Montpellier).[45] At Lattes, the proportion of the land owned by robe officers increased from 15 per cent in 1547 to 35 per cent in 1677, with other royal officers increasing their share from 0.5 per cent to 13 per cent. The nobility's share increased from 18 per cent to 25 per cent, while that of the bourgeoisie fell from 17 per cent to 8 per cent. At Clapiers, none of the land was owned by robe officers in 1520, but by 1606 robe officers accounted for 24.3 per cent of the enclosed land surface, increasing to 42.6 per cent in 1700. The bourgeoisie never had more than a marginal position at Clapiers, with 6.0 per cent of the enclosed land in 1520, 8.7 per cent in 1606, and 5.5 per cent in 1700. The dynamism of royal officers, particularly officers of the robe, as investors in rural estates in the countryside around Montpellier is in marked contrast to the stagnation or outright regression in the position of the bourgeoisie.

Marriage contracts provide a more representative measure of the comparative wealth of the various occupational and status groups than do fiscal assessments, as the size of the dowry was related to the total fortune of the family of the bride and not just to its holdings of land. Most, but not all marriage contracts in sixteenth-century Montpellier state the monetary value of the dowry; even where the monetary value of the dowry is not stated there is usually a provision for payment of an *augmente de dot*,[46] a sum of money which, where the value of the dowry is stated in the contract, is typically equal to one-third of the stated value of the dowry. This *augmente de dot* had to be paid to the family of the bride, with the refund of her dowry, in the event of the bride's dying without having had children. Where the value of the dowry is not specified in a contract it has been estimated by multiplying the *augmente* by the median ratio between dowries and *augmentes* for a given occupational or status group, and for a given decade.[47]

Average and median values for the twenty-year periods centered on 1550 and 1610 are set out in Table 3.6. The values for 1610 have been deflated to be roughly equivalent in real terms to those for 1550, using the grain-price index for Béziers and Montpellier.[48]

Table 3.6 confirms the growing wealth of Montpellier's robe elites compared with the rest of the population. Dowry sizes increased in real terms for most groups within the city, but the increase was particularly dramatic for the robe officers, who received dowries that were two-and-a-half times as large around 1610 as they had been around 1550. Two groups witnessed a decline

Table 3.6 Dowries paid to selected social groups (in livres tournois).

Social group	Average in 1550	Median in 1550	Average in 1610	Median in 1610
Laboureurs	53.1	40.0	62.0	50.8
Artisans	72.6	40.0	96.3	72.8
Merchants	662.1	500.0	484.8	455.0
Bourgeoisie	737.2	550.0	549.9	481.3
Lawyers	740.0	500.0	1,491.7	1,400.0
Robe officers	1,945.7	1,800.0	4,952.6	4,550.0

in the real value of their dowries, the merchants and the bourgeois, a finding that is consistent with the exodus of the wealthiest merchants and bourgeois from commerce into royal offices and the thesis that the disruption of commerce during the civil wars did not favour the accumulation or preservation of large commercial fortunes. By 1610, the median dowries received by robe officers exceeded those received by merchants by a factor of 10 and those received by the bourgeoisie by a factor of 9, where the figures had been just 3.6 and 3.3 in 1550. The economic distance between the robe and the *bourgeoisie commerçante* had increased dramatically.

The comparatively large increase in the dowries paid to officers of the robe was at least in part the direct outcome of the rise in agricultural rents and in the rewards of office. In the period from 1550 to 1610, robe dowries increased in real terms by a factor of approximately 2.5. In the period from 1585 to 1620, grain-equivalent agricultural rents in the coastal region of Languedoc underwent a steady increase, so that they doubled on some estates and increased by 50 per cent on others.[49] During that same period, the profits of office may have increased even more rapidly. The combined value of the *gages, épices* and *menus droits* for the office of *maître des comptes* increased from 400 to about 1700 livres in the period from 1580 to 1620. The increase in *gages* paid to officers in the other royal courts was usually less, but the rate of increase in the *épices* paid by the private parties appearing before those courts is not known for this period.[50] Nor is anything known about the movement of profits from urban real estate and commodity speculation, two other sources of income for members of the robe. A complete reconstruction of the sources of robe wealth is thus impossible, as is detailed examination of the fate of individual families.[51]

The dowries paid to lawyers increased at a somewhat slower rate than those paid to robe officers, but they too grew quite significantly, doubling on the average in real terms.[52] A considerable social and economic gulf separated barristers (*avocats*) from notaries and *procureurs* (the *basoche*); the median dowry for barristers in the twenty-year period centered on 1570 was 1,100 livres, while for members of the *basoche* it was 450 livres. But both of these groups did equally well during the subsequent fifty-year period, increasing their nominal median dowries by factors of 4.36 and 4.22

117

respectively, where the comparable figure for merchants in the same period was just 2.0. All those associated with the judicial and administrative system appear to have profited during the late sixteenth and early seventeenth century.

THE ROBE AT MONTPELLIER

So far, we have witnessed a significant growth in the size and wealth of royal officialdom in Montpellier. What were the social origins of those who filled these offices, and what became of individual families once they entered the robe? As we shall see, Montpellier's emerging robe elite was a fluid class in the sixteenth century, but, increasingly, access to its ranks began to close.

The pattern of recruitment into robe offices for persons entering office between 1514 and 1625 can be established with some certainty, owing in large measure to the research of Pierre Burlats-Brun, and is set out in Table 3.7.[53] One-third (99 out of 296) of Montpellier's robe officers were themselves the sons of robe officers, with the proportion increasing from 20.7 per cent (23 out of 111) for the sixty-year period ending in 1575 to 41.1 per cent (76 out of 185) for the fifty-year period ending in 1625. Sons of merchants or bourgeois accounted for 27.4 per cent of the total (81 out of 296), with the proportion falling from 39.6 per cent (44 out of 111) for the sixty-year period

Table 3.7   Recruitment of robe officers at Montpellier: 1514–1625.

Profession or Qualité of:	Father		Grandfather	
	1514–1575	*1576–1625*	*1514–1575*	*1576–1625*
Robe officer	23(20.7%)	76(41.1%)	3(2.7%)	23(12.4%)
Merchant	35(31.5%)	31(16.8%)	36(32.4%)	50(27.0%)
Noble	20(18.0%)	23(12.4%)	25(11.5%)	29(15.7%)
Lawyer	9(8.1%)	14(7.6%)	8(7.2%)	15(8.1%)
Bourgeois	9(8.1%)	6(3.2%)	8(7.2%)	15(8.1%)
Financial officer	2(1.8%)	13(7.0%)	1(0.9%)	6(3.2%)
Notary	4(3.6%)	5(2.7%)	2(1.8%)	7(3.8%)
Physician	2(1.8%)	4(2.2%)	None	3(1.6%)
Military officer	4(3.6%)	2(1.1%)	1(0.9%)	2(1.1%)
Secrétaire du roi	None	3(1.6%)	None	1(0.5%)
Bookseller	None	3(1.6%)	None	4(2.2%)
Surgeon	None	1(0.5%)	None	2(1.1%)
Procureur	None	1(0.5%)	None	None
Court usher	None	1(0.5%)	None	None
Court clerk	None	1(0.5%)	None	None
Artisan	1(0.9%)	None	6(5.4%)	2(1.1%)
Rural proprietor	None	None	2(1.8%)	5(2.7%)
Unknown	2(1.8%)	1(0.5%)	19(17.1%)	21(11.4%)
Total	111	185	111	185

ending in 1575 to 20.0 per cent (37 out of 185) for the fifty-year period ending in 1625. The marked decline in recruitment from the ranks of the bourgeoisie would seem to relate not only to the effect of the civil wars on the incomes and fortunes of merchants (and thus on their ability to purchase offices) but also to the rapid increase in the price of offices after 1600. Before 1575 only 3 of 111 individuals entering robe offices were the grandsons of robe officers. The proportion of robe officers whose grandfathers belonged to the robe rose to 23 out of 185 for the fifty-year period ending in 1625, indicating that by the end of the sixteenth century robe dynasties were already in the process of formation at Montpellier.

A number of officers in the Chambre des Comptes or Bureau des Finances were former merchants. Before about 1575 it was not uncommon at Montpellier for a person to pass directly from commerce into a robe office and this occurred in the Chambre des Comptes on thirteen occasions. A similar situation prevailed during the fifteenth and sixteenth centuries at Dijon, where there was so little social distance between magistrates and rich merchants that, as Gaston Roupnel put it, 'on pourrait presque dire qu'il y a là des situations interchangeables'.[54] This seems also to have been the case at Montpellier, where the rich merchant, Jean de Cezelli, a manufacturer of silk cloth during the 1520s and *régent de marchandise* in 1533, was admitted later that same year into the office of *président* of the Chambre des Comptes in the presence of François I. In 1552, he married Catherine de la Croix de Castries, daughter of Henri de la Croix, baron de Castries, a member of the leading noble family in Montpellier in terms of fame and rank. Near the end of his career he was honoured by Charles IX, who received him in person on his visit to Montpellier in 1564.[55] Another example of the type of mobility that was possible during this period was the career of Pierre de la Volhe, son of Jean de la Volhe, first consul of Montpellier in 1554. Pierre was engaged in commerce until at least 1568, but by 1571 he was seigneur de la Leuze and *receveur-électif* for the diocese of Montpellier. The following year he was admitted into the office of *premier président des comptes*, which he had purchased from Jean de Cezelli.[56]

Such rapid progress from commerce into the robe became rare after 1600. There is no record of sons of merchants actually having been refused entry into the Chambre des Comptes or Bureau des Finances at Montpellier, as occurred as early as the 1620s at Amiens,[57] but there does appear to have been the same hardening of attitudes towards rapid upward social mobility, or to use the concept put forward by E. Le Roy Ladurie for seventeenth-century Languedoc, a feudalization of values.[58] The rapid increase in the price of offices in the decades after 1600 and the fact that the incomes of merchants were rising only gradually, if at all, during that period no doubt accounts for much, though not all, of the decline in mobility from commerce into the robe after 1600.

The nobility was also important as a source of recruitment into the robe. As with the bourgeoisie, the preferred offices were those in the Chambre des Comptes and Bureau des Finances, as they did not require a law degree. Of twenty individuals entering the office of *trésorier-général de France* between 1514 and 1625, eleven were the sons of *écuyers*, of whom at least four belonged to the authentic *noblesse de race*. Thirteen members of old noble families entered offices in the Chambre des Comptes before 1600, a number which matches that for former merchants. Again, the phenomenon of scions of old noble families serving in robe offices was not peculiar to Montpellier and has been noted for Dijon and Rouen.[59]

Despite their varied origins, officers of the robe maintained a considerable degree of social cohesiveness. This was partly a function of shared status, as shown by the position of each officer in ceremonial processions, where pride of place was determined by the court to which one belonged, one's position in that court, and the date one was admitted to that position, rather than by one's background.[60] It was also partly a function of a common relationship to the monarchy and a common administrative or judicial role. Group solidarity was also reinforced by marriage alliances between robe families. As Table 3.8 shows, the marriage choices of Montpellier's robe officers extended across local elites, but the greatest number of marriages that can be traced – more than one-third of the total – were to the daughters of other robe officers.[61]

It might be thought that the growing tendency for members of the royal courts to be recruited from the ranks of those families already represented in these courts was linked to the institution in 1604 of the *droit annuel* or *paulette*, by which members of the court were able to guarantee that they could bequeath their office to an heir on payment of an annual tax equal to

Table 3.8 Marriage pattern of robe officers: 1500–1630.

Bride's father	Number	Percentage
Robe officer	75	35.4
Lawyer	6	2.8
Noble: degree I	6	2.8
Noble: degree II	7	3.3
Noble: degree III+	33	15.6
Noble: degree unknown	17	8.0
Financial officer	12	5.7
Notary or procureur	5	2.4
Bourgeois	23	10.9
Merchant	13	6.1
Professor of Medicine	4	1.9
Other Physicians	1	0.5
Surgeon	1	0.5
Status unknown	9	4.3
Total	212	100.2

one-sixtieth of the value of the office. The importance of the *paulette* should not to be overstressed in this context, just as its importance should not be exaggerated with respect to the increase in office prices from the turn of the seventeenth century onward. Instead, both the tendency for the robe to become an increasingly self-recruiting caste and the rise in office prices seem to stem primarily from the combination of the attractiveness of robe offices for those who held them and the fact that, after increasing so dramatically in the late sixteenth century, the number of new positions levelled off after 1598, with no major creations of offices until the late 1620s.[62]

As in other cities, the price of offices increased rapidly in Montpellier after 1600. Figures 3.1 and 3.2 illustrate the trend, using the example of certain offices in the Cour des Aides and the Chambre des Comptes respectively.[63] Some increase in the price of these offices was to be expected, given the increases in *gages* and *menus droits* for the period from 1589 to 1603, but the increase reflected in these figures was far greater than the increase in the level of remuneration received by these officials. Whereas the median rate of return on twenty-three offices sold in the period from 1552 to 1601 was 12.2

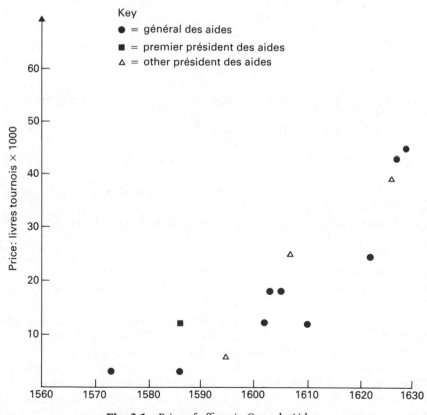

Fig. 3.1 Price of offices in Cour de Aides.

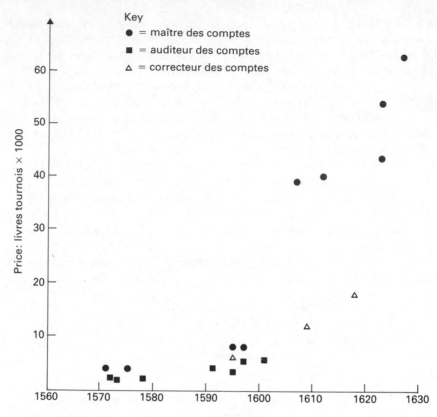

Fig. 3.2 Price of offices in Chambre des Comptes.

per cent, it was just 4.3 per cent for offices sold in the period from 1602 to 1629.

The increase in the price of offices after 1600 was sharp enough to attract considerable contemporary comment, and many commentators attributed the phenomenon to the institution of the *paulette*.[64] While it stands to reason that the elimination of the risk that an office would be lost through the unexpected death of its holder would increase its market value, it must also be observed that, as in Paris, the rise in the price of robe offices was already evident in the two or three years before 1604.[65] Furthermore, the institution of the *paulette* in 1604 does not seem to have had any immediate effect on the upward trend in the price of offices, as shown by prices for the office of *général des aides*, which, having sold for 12,000 livres in 1602 and 18,000 livres in 1603, subsequently sold for 18,000 livres in 1605 and 12,000 livres in 1610. The evolution of prices was similar at Rouen, where offices of *conseiller* in the Parlement sold for 18,000 livres in 1602, for 21,000 livres in late 1604 (after the *paulette* had been introduced), and for 17,000 livres in 1605.[66] The reason why the *paulette* did not have a major effect on the price of offices is that the frequency with which offices were forfeited to the monarchy on the death of the incumbent was not great even before 1604. Registers of the Bureau des Finances for Montpellier reveal that, between 1580 and early 1605, the resignations from office of eighty-one members of the Languedocian robe occurred at least forty days before their death, as was required prior to the *paulette* in order for the office to be passed on to the person of the incumbent's choice. Only twenty-seven resignations did not fulfil this condition.[67] Elimination of the risk that the capital value of an office would be lost owing to the sudden death of the incumbent could thus have been expected to increase the selling price of robe offices by no more than one-third, whereas, by way of example, the price of an office of *maître des comptes* increased by a factor of at least eight between the late 1590s and the early 1620s.

Rather than being a consequence of the *paulette*, the rise in office prices and the growing tendency for robe offices to remain within a restricted circle of families reflect the attractiveness and prestige with which these offices were increasingly adorned. Once families entered into the sovereign courts, their offspring tended either to stay there or to move into the landed nobility. Examination of the marriages of daughters of robe officers shows that the great majority married either other robe officers or nobles, with the percentage of marriages into the sword aristocracy increasing clearly after 1560 (see Table 3.9[68]). Conversely, alliances with the bourgeoisie, which were not all that common even before 1560, became progressively less

Table 3.9 Marriage pattern of daughters of robe officers.

Status of groom	1500–1559 (%)	1560–1599 (%)	1600–1640 (%)
Robe officer	54.5	29.7	40.6
Lawyer	9.1	9.4	3.1
Noble: degree I	4.5	3.1	0.0
Noble: degree II	0.0	9.8	3.1
Noble: degree III	9.1	20.3	17.7
Noble: degree unknown	4.5	7.8	13.5
Docteur en droit, noble of degree II	0.0	1.6	1.0
Docteur en droit, noble of degree III+	0.0	0.0	3.1
Docteur en droit, son of robe officer	0.0	0.0	1.0
Financial officer	0.0	10.9	12.5
Bourgeois	0.0	0.0	1.0
Merchant	9.1	4.7	2.1
Military officer	9.1	3.1	0.0
Physician	0.0	1.6	1.0
Number of alliances	22	64	96

common after that date. Whereas, for the entire period studied, 27 per cent of robe officers were the sons of merchants or bourgeois, only 4 per cent of their daughters married such men.

The sons of robe officers turned their backs even more resolutely on the commercial or bourgeois milieux from which a significant minority of their fathers had issued. As Table 3.10 shows, of 239 sons whose careers could be identified, only one became a merchant and two assumed the status and life-style of a bourgeois.[69] The career of choice was to remain within the royal courts, with 55 of the 117 individuals who became robe officers inheriting their father's office – 19 before 1600 and 36 after that date. More often than not it was the eldest son who inherited his father's office, but twenty-five individuals had two sons who entered the robe and three had three sons who did so. Among those who did not follow their father's footsteps and enter royal offices, the largest number, forty-seven, lived as noblemen. It is interesting that, of the thirty-four of these men who owned seigneurial or baronial estates, at least nineteen were younger sons. The Church attracted twenty-three individuals, of whom thirteen were first or second sons. Although an additional thirteen sons entered the army as commissioned officers, this does not appear to have been a very highly regarded career within this milieu. As in late seventeenth-century Amiens,[70] this career was reserved almost exclusively for younger sons; among the thirteen military officers, none was an eldest son, four were second sons, and the rest were either third or fourth sons. Virtually all of those entering the army did so after 1620. This was true for eleven of these individuals, while the remaining two

Table 3.10   Career pattern of sons of robe officers.

Career followed by son	Number	Percentage
Robe office	117	40.1
Unknown	53	18.2
Noble with a seigneurial estate	30	10.3
Noble with a baronial estate	4	1.4
Noble or *écuyer*	13	4.5
Church: canon, bishop, or member of a monastic order	23	7.9
Lawyer	16	5.5
Commissioned military officer	13	4.5
Profession of arms	1	0.3
Gouverneur of Montpellier	2	0.7
Viguier	2	0.7
Professor of medicine	2	0.7
Professor of Greek	1	0.3
Financial office	12	4.1
Merchant	1	0.3
Bourgeois	2	0.7
Total	292	100

entered the army between 1600 and 1620. In part, the apparent avoidance of military careers before 1600 may be an illusion of the sources; only around the beginning of the seventeenth century did something like a formal officer corps emerge in the French army, and only after that date might we find individuals with formal military titles.[71] Yet it is clear that sixteenth-century robe officers looked on military careers with some disfavour, partly because warfare tended to mean civil war.[72] One robe officer went so far as to forbid both of his sons from entering the army, on pain of disinheritance.[73] There was an apparent reversal of attitudes on the part of robe officers toward the middle of the seventeenth century, and the genealogies of such Montpellier robe families as the Baudan, Bornier, Grasset, Ranchin, Ratte, Rozel, and Trinquaire show an increasing number of family members entering the army as commissioned officers after 1640.[74] But throughout most of the period examined here, the clear pattern was for the sons of robe officers to seek to remain within the robe, while living nobly or a career in the church or in law provided the chief alternatives for those who were unwilling or unable to obtain a royal office.

THE POLITICAL STRUCTURE

One final consequence stemmed from the growth in the size and wealth of Montpellier's official and legal elites that has been traced here: a redistribution of political power in their favour. The tendency for merchants to be displaced by *gens de loi* within municipal government was not unique to Montpellier and has been documented for Amiens, Dijon, Lyon, Marseille and Poitiers, among others.[75] At Montpellier, however, this development appears to have occurred at an earlier date than at Lyon or Poitiers, a timing that tends to validate the thesis that changes in the regional economy led to a redistribution of political power at the municipal level. At Lyon and Poitiers, where commerce flourished until about 1560, merchants dominated municipal government until the last quarter of the sixteenth century,[76] whereas at Montpellier, where the scope and scale of commercial operations had contracted significantly by the end of the fifteenth century, the bourgeoisie had all but been displaced from the highest echelon of the consulate (city council) by the middle of the sixteenth century. Moreover, this shift is particularly striking in the case of Montpellier, which was one of those cities in which membership in the consulate was apportioned among the members of designated occupations, with royal officers and lawyers specifically excluded from the consulate until after 1500.

At the beginning of the sixteenth century, the six positions on the consulate were assigned to members of different trades on the basis of a system established in 1410. The first consul was to be a money-changer and the second consul an importer of spices, a manufacturer of Montpellier's famous scarlet cloth, or a bourgeois. The third consul was to be a merchant of cloth, fur, or silk and the fourth consul was to be a merchant of grain or linen or a retailer of spices or drugs. The fifth and sixth consuls were chosen from among the members of various artisan trades as well as, in the case of the sixth consul, the *laboureurs*.[77] That was the theoretical division of power, but as there were no money-changers at Montpellier at the beginning of the sixteenth century, and had been none for several decades owing to competition from cities in the Rhône valley,[78] the position of first consul was monopolized by an oligarchy of rich merchants and bourgeois.

The first and only overt challenge to the dominance of the consulate by the city's merchants and bourgeois came from the notaries and lawyers. They had attempted as early as 1470 to gain the right to be represented on the consulate, but were not successful until 1517 when they finally persuaded the monarchy that they should not be denied access to this council. Just why they managed to win over the monarchy at this date is not clear. Perhaps it was simply evident by 1517 that Montpellier was no longer a centre of maritime commerce; this made the argument that French commerce would suffer if the bourgeoisie were denied a monopoly over the position of first consul seem less plausible than it apparently had been fifty years earlier. In any case, the monarchy ruled that one of the three individuals nominated for the position of first consul each year was to be a lawyer and that one of three nominees to the position of third consul was to be a notary. From 1519 until 1541, eight lawyers were chosen to serve an annual term as first consul, and four notaries and four *bacheliers en droit* were chosen as third consul.[79]

A more significant change in the composition of the consulate took place with little controversy, that is, the appearance after 1500 of urban nobles in the position of first consul. In fact, until about 1550, urban nobles were elected to the position of first consul in some years but not in others, and this, combined with the fact that most of the incumbents came from merchant families whose members had served in the positions of first or second consul during the second half of the fifteenth century, may have contributed to a perception that their election was not a significant innovation. This would be consistent with the fact that until 1539 the electoral registers for the city referred to the urban nobles as *changeurs*, so that it is only by reference to outside documents that it is possible to discern a change in the composition of the consulate before that date.

An increasing number of first consuls belonged to families that had begun to move out of commerce around 1500, but until about 1550 it was still not uncommon for merchants or former merchants to be elected to the position of first consul. The last active merchant to serve as first consul was Guichard Sandre, who was elected to the position in 1537, but several former merchants were elected to the position during the following decade.[80]

No robe officers were nominated or elected to the position of first consul until the former merchant, Guillaume Boirargues, *maître des comptes*, was elected in 1547. Royal legislation passed later that year prohibited royal officers from serving in municipal offices[81] and forestalled the domination of the highest municipal offices by robe officers until the civil wars. The breakdown in order that took place after 1560 made it seem desirable to both Catholic and Protestant notables that robe officers, and in particular officers of the sovereign courts, should be placed in a position of leadership at the municipal level, as they would then have more leverage with the monarchy. The monarchy, for its part, was apparently of the view that officers in the sovereign courts would be less likely to side with Protestant insurgents and better able to maintain order in the city. The trend toward the elction of robe officers began in 1563 with the nomination of Michel Saint-Ravy, a *général* in the Cour des Aides. The following year, with the restoration of Catholic control, all three nominees to the position of first consul were officers of the robe, from whose number the military governor of Languedoc, Henri Montmorency de Damville, chose Pierre Convers, *maître des comptes*. In 1565, two urban nobles and one robe officer were nominated to the position of first consul and Charles IX, who intervened in the electoral process, chose Jean Lauzelergues, *général des aides*, as first consul.[82]

During the last third of the sixteenth century, the position of first consul was occupied by lawyers, robe officers, or urban nobles with seigneurial estates. Robe officers were elected to the position of first consul in fourteen of the thirty-four elections held during the period from 1566 to 1599. Nobles with seigneurial estates were chosen in fifteen elections, but they continued to be predominantly urban nobles of recent vintage – although on occasion a *noble de race* such as Michel de Pluvier, seigneur de Paulhan (first consul for 1566), or Jacques des Guillems, seigneur de Figaret (first consul for 1571), was elected.[83] By comparison, lawyers were under-represented during this period, being chosen on just five occasions. After 1597 there was a de facto exclusion of lawyers from the position of first consul, which continued despite a judgement of the Parlement of Toulouse in their favour in 1613.[84]

Lawyers and royal officers also began to penetrate the ranks of second consul after 1560. Although merchants or bourgeois gained election to the position of second consul in twenty of the thirty-four elections held during the period from 1566 to 1599, four lawyers, three nobles and three officers of the royal finances were also elected. In elections to the other positions on the consulate, no significant change from the pattern of the first two-thirds of the sixteenth century occurred.

CONCLUSIONS

The net effect of the disappearance of Montpellier's maritime trade with the Levant at the end of the fifteenth century and the accelerating creation of offices and institutions during the sixteenth century was the transformation of

Montpellier from a Renaissance city, with political control at the municipal level in the hands of a merchant oligarchy, into a provincial administrative capital of the type characteristic of the Ancien Régime.[85] The demise of the merchant oligarchy was basically complete by 1550 and, from the early 1560s onwards, the position of first consul was occupied in most years by officers of the Chambre des Comptes or Cour des Aides or by members of the nobility, usually but not always the new urban nobility as opposed to the *noblesse de race*. The wealth of these people compared with the bourgeoisie had increased substantially in the course of the sixteenth century and the transfer of political power from the bourgeoisie to the robe and nobility was simply a reflection of that fact.

Similarly, there was a tendency for ownership of rural estates to become concentrated in the hands of robe officers, a trend that would accelerate from 1600 onwards. Indeed, many of the trends discussed in this essay would continue until at least the middle of the seventeenth century, culminating with the transfer of the residence of the governor of Languedoc to Montpellier from Pézenas[86] and the establishment at Montpellier of the intendancy for all of Languedoc towards the middle of the seventeenth century.

NOTES: CHAPTER 3

1 Unpublished research by Philip Benedict shows that 2511 persons appear in the *guidon de taille* (tax roll) for 1607 and that between 1611 and 1619 an average of 656 baptisms were celebrated in the city each year. Assuming a birth rate of 40 per 1000, this suggests that the total population in that decade was roughly 16,300 and that a multiplier of 6 is perhaps the best one for determining the population from the number of persons who paid taxes on houses within the city walls. Extrapolation of this multiplier to earlier decades is problematic because wealthier individuals often owned several residences in addition to the one they lived in and the dispersal of residential property ownership could be expected to and did vary over time. Between 1549 and 1597 the number of individuals in the *guidon de taille* increased from 1613 to 2256, but this was accompanied by an increased dispersal of ownership, as shown by the 31.6 per cent decrease in average individual assessment. There was no increase in dispersal of ownership from 1600 to 1640. This suggests that 9 is probably a safer multiplier for the mid sixteenth century while 6 can safely be used for 1600. On that basis the city's population can be estimated at roughly 12,500 in 1550 and 15,500 in 1600.

2 Gerald Cholvy *et al.*, *Histoire de Montpellier* (Toulouse: Privat, 1984), pp. 143–4.

3 ibid., p. 150; Louise Guiraud 'Etudes sur la Réforme à Montpellier', *Mémoires de la Société Archéologique de Montpellier*, 2e série, vol. 6 (1918), p. 251.

4 Emmanuel Le Roy Ladurie, *Les paysans de Languedoc*, Vol. 1 (Paris: S.E.V.P.E.N., 1966), pp. 224–5; Raymond Dugrand, *La garrigue montpelliéraine* (Paris: Presses Universitaires de France, 1963).

5 I owe this observation to Marcel Gouron, in his lifetime municipal archivist for Montpellier, who noted that only at Frontignan was there an equally generous supply of natural pasture in the diocese of Montpellier.

6 See Jean Combes, 'Les investissements immobiliers à Montpellier au commence-

ment du XVe siècle', in *Recueil de mémoires et travaux publiés par la société histoire du droit et des institutions des anciens pays de droit écrit*, Vol. 2 (Montpellier, 1951), pp. 21–8. At Dijon, meadows yielded a far better rate of return on investment than did fields or vineyards: see Gaston Roupnel, *La ville et la campagne au XVIIe siècle: étude sur les populations du pays Dijonnais*, 2d edn (Paris: A. Colin, 1955), p. 178.

7   Guiraud, 'Réforme à Montpellier', p. 253.

8   Cholvy *et al.*, *Histoire de Montpellier*, p. 138. For examples of estates at Lattes owned by merchants or bourgeois, see Louise Guiraud, 'Etudes sur la Réforme à Montpellier: Preuves, chroniques et documents', *Mémoires de la Société Archéologique de Montpellier*, 2e série, vol. 7 (1919), pp. 475–81.

9   Louis Irrisou, *La pharmacie à Montpellier des origines aux statuts de 1572* (Paris: Editions Occitania, 1935), p. 2.

10 See Louis J. Thomas, *Montpellier, ville marchande: histoire économique et sociale des origines à 1870* (Montpellier: Valat et Coulet, 1936), pp. 107–8.

11 ibid., pp. 109–16.

12 ibid., pp. 84, 103 and 122–3; Michel and Mireille Lacave, *Bourgeois et marchands en Provence et en Languedoc* (Avignon: Aubanel, 1977), p. 86; Richard Gascon, *Grand commerce et vie urbaine au XVIe siècle: Lyon et ses marchands*, Vol. 1 (Paris: Mouton, 1971), pp. 82–6 and 91–2.

13 Thomas, *Montpellier, ville marchande*, pp. 59, 79 and 122–3; Raymond Dugrand, Robert Ferras and Philippe Joutard, *Bas-Languedoc, Causses, Cévennes* (Paris: Larousse, 1974), pp. 28–9.

14 Jean Philippi, 'Histoire des troubles de Languedoc', in Guiraud, 'Réforme à Montpellier: Preuves', p. 143.

15 Thomas, *Montpellier, ville marchande*, pp. 55–9; Cholvy *et al.*, *Histoire de Montpellier*, pp. 128–9.

16 Le Roy Ladurie, *Paysans de Languedoc*, Vol. 1, pp. 189–95 (population growth); Gascon, *Lyon et ses marchands*, Vol. 1, pp. 69–70 (cloth exports).

17 Guiraud, 'Réforme à Montpellier', p. 452.

18 Cholvy *et al.*, *Histoire de Montpellier*, p. 129; Guiraud, 'Réforme à Montpellier', pp. 245–73, 367–9 and 417–22 and 'Réforme à Montpellier: Preuves', pp. 76–89, 144–50 and 184–5.

19 Roger Doucet, 'Les de Laran, marchands drapiers à Toulouse au XVIe siècle', *Annales du Midi*, vol. 54 (1942), pp. 42–87.

20 Cholvy *et al.*, *Histoire de Montpellier*, p. 129.

21 Felix Platter, *Beloved Son Felix: The Journal of Felix Platter, a Medical Student in Montpellier in the Sixteenth Century*, trans. Jean Jennett (London: F. Muller, 1961); Thomas Platter, *Journal of a Younger Brother: The Life of Thomas Platter as a Medical Student in Montpellier at the Close of the Sixteenth Century*, trans. Jean Jennett (London: F. Muller, 1963).

22 Guiraud, 'Réforme à Montpellier', p. 23.

23 ibid., pp. 24–5.

24 See Frederick M. Irvine, 'Social structure, social mobility and social change in sixteenth-century Montpellier: from Renaissance city-state to *ancien–régime* capital', PhD thesis, University of Toronto, 1980, Appendix VIII: Table I, p. 504.

25 See Guiraud, 'Réforme à Montpellier', pp. 32–3.

26 For the legislation defining the jurisdiction of the court, see Anthoine Fontanon, *Les édits et ordonnances des rois de France depuis Saint Louis jusqu'à présent*, Vol. 2 (Paris: J. Dupuis, 1580), p. 1352 and A.D.H., B1:105–8v.

27 Jacques Michaud, 'Les cours souveraines des comptes et finances au pays de Languedoc du XVe au XVIIe siècle, 1437–1629', Vol. 1 *thèse droit*, University of Montpellier, 1970, pp. 33 and 40–61.

28 See A.D.H., B1:315v–17 and C6151:183v–86v.
29 See Fontanon, *Edits et ordonnances*, Vol. 2, pp. 885–98, 1278–82 and 1282–4.
30 ibid., Vol. 2, pp. 885–90; A.D.H., C6165:275–305v, and C6167:181–2.
31 ibid., Vol. 1, pp. 130–3, 261, 281–3 and 285–7.
32 Jacques Vidal, *L'équivalent des aides en Languedoc* (Montpellier: Imprimerie P. Déhan, 1963), pp. 1–18; A.D.H., C6165:141v–2v; Gaston Zeller, 'De quelques institutions mal connues du XVIe siècle', *Revue Historique*, vol. 197 (1944), p. 205, note 1: cf. Fontanon, *Edits et ordonnances*, Vol. 2, pp. 1189–94.
33 Dognon, *Les institutions politiques et administratives du pays de Languedoc*, p. 339; Fontanon, *Edits et ordonnances*, Vol. 2, p. 1317; A.D.H., C6155:227v, C6158:185 and C6166:201; and Irvine, thesis, pp. 26–8 and 36–9.
34 A.D.H., B2:83v–5, B51:309–12, B53:25, C6152:229–32 and C6158:200–4.
35 See Roger Doucet, *Les institutions de la France au XVIe siècle*, Vol. 2 (Paris: J. Picard, 1948), pp. 588–94; Fontanon, *Edits et ordonnances*, Vol. 2, pp. 1169, 1176, 1186, 1202–7, 1233–6 and 1526–7; A.D.H., B2:265–268; B21:53, 104v and 108v; C6149:70v–71 and 112; C6153:175; C6154:357v–8; C6155:39, 41v and 91; C6161:260; and C6162:220.
36 See, generally, Fontanon, *Edits et ordonnances*, Vol. 2, pp. 1308, 1361–3 and 1366–8; A.D.H., B2:265, B18:45v, B52:37, C6158:68v. On the *taillon* and its administration, see Fontanon, *Edits et ordonnances*, Vol. 2, pp. 1387–90, 1676–82 and 1690–1; A.D.H., B17081 and C6158:208; Doucet, *Les institutions de la France*, Vol. 2, p. 575. On the creation and suppression of offices, see Fontanon, *Edits et ordonnances*, Vol. 2, pp. 242–4, 1321–4 and 1403–4; A.D.H., B15:29 and 138; B51:179 and 245; C6149:147v–50 and 278–9v.
37 This table excludes from consideration the offices of lesser importance (e.g. *clavaire*, court clerk, court usher, *procureur du roi* in a court below the level of a *présidial*, *lieutenant* in a *cour ordinaire*) as well as those ceremonial offices of some prestige but little real significance for the functioning of the institution (e.g. *viguier*). Full sources for this table may be found in Irvine, thesis, pp. 6–40 and notes thereto, and include, specifically, Michaud, 'Les cours souveraines des comptes et finances'; Fontanon, *Edits et ordonnances*; A.D.H., B1–3 (registers of the Cour des Aides for 1490–1629); A.D.H. B45–53 (registers of the Chambre des Comptes for 1523–1582); and C6149–68 (registers of the Bureau des Finances for 1584–1610).
38 See Irvine, thesis, pp. 36–9.
39 Officers in the sovereign courts and the Bureau des Finances were entitled to *menus droits*, monetary payments which notionally went to cover the cost of items such as robes, ink, paper and firewood. This table also includes the *taxations* paid to certain *comptables* in lieu of *gages*. The table does not include *gages* paid to certain minor officials such as *clavaires*. Nor does it include *gages* paid to officers of the *robe courte* for the *cours ordinaires* (usually a *viguier* but sometimes a *châtelain* or *bailli*). The difficulty in determining their *gages* accounts for that omission. The sources for this table are those listed in note 37.
40 Le Roy Ladurie, *Paysans de Languedoc*, Vol. 2, p. 981.
41 See analysis of the rates of return on investments in agriculture, industry and commerce in Irvine, thesis, pp. 115–53.
42 On agricultural rents, see Irvine, thesis, p. 122; Le Roy Ladurie, *Paysans de Languedoc*, Vol. 2, pp. 860–4; on the political and military situation at Montpellier, see Guiraud, 'Réforme à Montpellier', pp. 449–50 and 464.
43 Unfortunately, there were very few *inventaires après décès* for this period; they tend to be incomplete (chattels but not real property, or vice versa); and they usually do not contain estimates of the value of the estate. For examples, see A.D.H., IIE56:40:31–8, IIE56:40:38–9, and IIE56:130:849v–52. A large number of

inventaires are to be found in IIE95:1448, and others covering the period from 1598 to 1634 are referred to in Le Roy Ladurie, *Paysans de Languedoc*, Vol. 1, pp. 340 and 455–6.

44 At the time the research for this study was carried out the *guidons de taille* were kept with the A.D.H. but were unclassified.

45 For Clapiers, see A.D.H., B10897 and A.C. Clapiers, CC1 and CC2 and the more extensive analysis in Irvine, thesis, pp. 208–15. For Lattes, see Emmanuel Le Roy Ladurie, 'Sur Montpellier et sa campagne aux XVIe et XVIIe siècles', *Annales: E.S.C.*, vol. 12 (1957), pp. 223–30. The percentages in the text are derived from bar graphs of holdings at Lattes. For other villages in the vicinity of Montpellier, see Irvine, thesis, Appendix III, pp. 461–84.

46 See Henry Cholvy, 'L'augmente de dot dans l'ancienne France et plus particulièrement en Languedoc, tel qu'il apparaît à travers des arrêts du Parlement de Toulouse', *thèse droit*, University of Montpellier, 1950.

47 The ratio of stated to estimated dowries in the sample of marriage contracts increases with the wealth and status of the group under consideration. For the sample of marriage contracts for the period from 1550 to 1629 the ratio is 1.6 for *laboureurs*, 2.5 for artisans, and 3.7 for merchants. The effect of the inclusion of estimated dowries was to reduce the average values for the twenty-year intervals for the period from 1550 to 1629 by 2.0 per cent for artisans and by 3.2 per cent for merchants. In the case of the *laboureurs* the effect was to increase the average ratio by 0.4 per cent.

48 See Le Roy Ladurie, *Paysans de Languedoc*, Vol. 2, p. 981. The figures in Table 3.6 are derived from an analysis of 1354 marriage contracts covering the period from 1540 to 1629. Except in the case of *laboureurs* and artisans, whose marriage contracts were sampled on a random basis, all of the marriage contracts from notarial registers that have indexes were examined. The relevant notarial registers for this period are classified under A.D.H., IIE55–8, 61–2, and 95.

49 ibid., Vol. 1, p. 465.

50 See discussion in Irvine, thesis, pp. 78–81 and sources there cited, notably A.D.H. B17057, 17069, 17073, 17089, 17097, 17106, 17116, C6152:362–6v; and Michaud, 'Les cours souveraines des comptes et finances', Vol. 2, pp. 102–3, 119, 125, and 168.

51 At Montpellier, the problem lies with the dearth of relevant documentation in the Série IE (family papers). Figures appear in Jonathan Dewald, *The Formation of a Provincial Nobility: The Magistrates of the Parlement of Rouen, 1499–1610* (Princeton, NJ: Princeton University Press, 1980), pp. 323–32, that relate to the incomes of robe officers in Normandy, but the documentation relied on is silent as to the profits from office and commodity speculation.

52 Two dowries had to be estimated. Excluding them would increase the average dowry for 1550 from 740 to 865.7 livres and the median dowry from 500 to 700 livres. The real increase in average and median dowries would then become 1.7 and 2.0.

53 In addition to the notarial archives and the Protestant birth and marriage registers, the author relied on information provided by Pierre Burlats-Brun, taken from his unpublished manuscript, 'Gens de robe à Montpellier du XVe au XVIIIe siècle', as well as the following published works: Louis de La Roque, *Armorial de la noblesse de Languedoc, Généralité de Montpellier* (Montpellier: F. Séguin, 1860); François-Alexandre Aubert de La Chesnaye Des Bois, *Dictionaire de la noblesse, contenant les généalogies, l'histoire et la chronologie des familles nobles de France* (Paris: Schlesinger, 1863–76); idem, *Une famille de l'ancienne France: les Baudan à Nîmes et à Montpellier pendant quatre siècles* (Cavaillon: Imprimerie Mistral, 1926); idem, *La maison d'Autheville* (Bergerac: Imprimerie

de J. Castanet, 1902); idem, *Un nîmois célèbre, Jean de Varanda et sa famille d'après les documents originaux inédits* (Nîmes: Imprimerie de A. Chastanier, 1899); idem, *Notice sur la famille de Bornier* (Paris: Revue Heraldica, 1912); Alexandre Germain, *Charles de Grefeuille et sa famille* (Montpellier: Boehm et fils, 1860); Louis de La Roque, *Premiers présidents des cours souveraines (1603–1867)* (Montpellier: J. Martel, 1878).

54   Roupnel, *La ville et la campagne au XVIIe siècle*, p. 178.

55   Pierre Burlats-Brun, 'Histoire de la famille Cezelli et Bourcier de Cezelli d'après des documents inédits', series of articles appearing in the *Croix de l'Hérault* and *Croix de l'Aude*, December 1966 to July 1967.

56   A.D.H., B52:31v–3 and 214v–16v, B17041, IIE62:1:74v, IIE62:1:247; A.C. Montpellier, CC 619:64v, GG 315:78v.

57   Pierre Deyon, *Amiens, capitale provinciale: étude sur la société urbaine au 17e siècle* (Paris: A. Colin, 1967), pp. 273–5.

58   Le Roy Ladurie, *Paysans de Languedoc*, Vol. 1, p. 641. See also Dewald, *The Magistrates of the Parlement of Rouen*, pp. 28–9, where he alludes to a similar phenomenon that was evident at Rouen by the 1590s.

59   Dewald, *The Magistrates of the Parlement of Rouen*, pp. 78–9; Roupnel, *La ville et la campagne au XVIIe siècle*, pp. 166–77.

60   See Michaud 'Les cours souveraines des comptes et finances', Vol. 1, pp. 206–11; A.D.H., B1:7v and B3:8.

61   The sources for Table 3.8 include marriage contracts and other documents from the notarial archives, the *compoix* for Montpellier, the Catholic birth registers (A.C. Montpellier, GG1–3), the Protestant birth or marriage registers (A.C. Montpellier, GG314–21 and GG364–6), information taken from the published genealogies listed above in note 53 and information provided by Pierre Burlats-Brun.

62   See Irvine, thesis, pp. 102–3.

63   The sources for the prices of offices sold by the monarchy were certain registers of the Chambre des Comptes (A.D.H., B45, 49, 50–3); the Bureau des Finances (A.D.H., C6149–52, 6154–6, 6161–2, 6165 and 6167); and to a lesser extent, the Cour des Aides (A.D.H., B3, 27 and 33). These sources were supplemented by contracts for the private sale of office from the notarial archives.

64   See Mark Cummings, 'The social impact of the Paulette: the case of Paris', *Canadian Journal of History*, vol. 15 (1980), pp. 332–4; Roland Mousnier, *La vénalité des offices sous Henri IV et Louis XIII* (Rouen: Maugard, 1945), p. 339.

65   For Montpellier, see Figures 3.1 and 3.2 above. For Paris, see Cummings, 'The social impact of the Paulette', p. 341.

66   Dewald, *The Magistrates of the Parlement of Rouen*, p. 336.

67   A.D.H., B53 and C6149–63.

68   The sources for this table are the same as those for Table 3.8. See note 61 above.

69   The sources for Table 3.10 include the published genealogies and information provided by Pierre Burlats-Brun, the wills of robe officers, the *guidons de taille* and *compoix* for Montpellier, the registers of the Chambre des Comptes (A.D.H., B45–53), Cour des Aides (A.D.H., B1–13, 16, 18, 21–2, 27, 38 and 55) and the Bureau des Finances (A.D.H., C6149–68), the Protestant marriage and birth registers, the Catholic birth registers, and the analytical inventory to the Série G.

70   Deyon, *Amiens, capitale provinciale*, pp. 36–9.

71   Davis Bitton, *The French Nobility in Crisis: 1560–1640* (Stanford, Calif.: Stanford University Press, 1969), p. 40.

72   ibid., pp. 11–13; George Huppert, *Les Bourgeois Gentilshommes* (Chicago: University of Chicago Press, 1977), pp. 36–43.

73 Will of Jean de Bousquet, *président des comptes*, January 27, 1597, A.D.H. IIE56:176:396.
74 Burlats-Brun 'Gens de robe' (Grasset and Ranchin); Falgairolle, *Baudan*; Falgairolle, *Bornier*; de La Roque, *Armorial de la noblesse*, Vol. 1, p. 416 (Ratte), p. 444 (Rozel) and p. 509 (Trinquaire). The same trend can be detected for seventeenth-century Amiens: see Deyon, *Amiens, capitale provinciale*, p. 277.
75 Doucet, *Les institutions de la France*, Vol. 1, p. 363 (Amiens and Dijon); Gascon, *Lyons et ses marchands*, Vol. 1, p. 412; Edouard Baratier *et al.*, *Histoire de Marseille* (Toulouse: Privat, 1973), p. 141; Paul Raveau, *Essai sur la situation économique et l'état social en Poitou au XVIe siècle* (Paris: M. Rivière, 1931), p. 6 (Poitiers).
76 Gascon, *Lyon et ses marchands*, Vol. 1, p. 412; Raveau, *Essai*, p. 6.
77 Thomas, *Montpellier, ville marchande*, p. 105; A.C. Montpellier, BB 1.
78 ibid., pp. 107–8.
79 A.C. Montpellier, BB 1; *Archives de la ville de Montpellier: Inventaires et documents*, Vol. 7, pp. 3–6; Thomas, *Montpellier, ville marchande*, pp. 123–4.
80 See Irvine, thesis, pp. 170–2 for a more detailed account of the displacement of the bourgeoisie from the highest echelon of the consulate.
81 Fontanon, *Edits et ordonnances*, Vol. 1, p. 595.
82 Guiraud, 'Réforme à Montpellier', pp. 148–9, 223, 247, 305 and 387–8; A.C. Montpellier, BB 2.
83 For the Guillems, see La Chesnaye Des Bois, *Dictionaire de la noblesse*, Vol. 10, pp. 94–9. For the Pelets, see J. Despetits, *Le chevalier d'Assas et les familles des seigneurs d'Assas du XIIe au XVIIIe siècle* (Montpellier: Imprimerie de la Manufacture de la Charité, 1908). For the consular elections for this period, see A.C. Montpellier, BB2.
84 *Archives de la ville de Montpellier: Inventaires et documents*, Vol. 7, p. 6.
85 See Deyon, *Amiens, capitale provinciale*; Roupnel, *La ville et la campagne au XVIIe siècle*; and Sharon Kettering, *Judicial Politics and Urban Revolt in Seventeenth-Century France: The Parlement of Aix, 1629–1659* (Princeton, NJ: Princeton University Press, 1978). For an overview, see Pierre Goubert, *L'ancien régime*, 2 vols (Paris: A. Colin, 1969).
86 Anne Blanchard, 'De Pézenas à Montpellier: transfert d'une ville de souveraineté (XVIIe siècle)', *Revue d'Histoire Moderne et Contemporaine*, vol. 12 (1965), pp. 35–49.

4

Consumers, commerce, and the craftsmen of Dijon:
The changing social and economic structure of a provincial capital, 1450–1750

JAMES R. FARR

Between the fifteenth and the eighteenth centuries France experienced a series of significant social changes: intermittent population growth; the acceleration of commercial exchange; industrial growth, often centered in the countryside; expansion of the state apparatus, notably in the number of government officials and an attendant army of lawyers; and the extension of bourgeois control over rural property. The great outpouring of research that has transformed and enriched our understanding of the social and economic history of early modern France during the past two generations has cast a good deal of light on all of these phenomena. Amid this upsurge of research, however, surprisingly little attention has been devoted to the question of how these developments might have altered the social makeup of the kingdom's cities. A few studies have sought with varying degrees of success to trace changes in the social and occupational structure of an Ancien Régime city during the course of a single century, most commonly the eighteenth.[1] Only one work, Marcel Couturier's pioneering quantitative study of Châteaudun, has sought to follow changes over a longer period of time. However, its utility in illuminating more broadly representative trends is limited by the fact that Châteaudun was an idiosyncratic, decaying city whose population shrank by half in a period when most French towns were growing in size; there is also a scarcity of relevant source materials prior to the seventeenth century.[2]

Much of the neglect of this topic unquestionably stems from the state of the sources, for tax rolls, the best guide to a locality's social structure before the establishment of regular census-taking, are extremely rare for most French cities before the eighteenth century. This is not true, however, of Burgundy's principal town, Dijon. Where most of France's larger cities were exempt from the Ancien Régime's chief direct tax, the *taille*, Dijon was not. And in contrast to the situation in many of those cities which did pay the *taille*, this tax was *personnelle*, not *réelle*, meaning that it was assessed on the full range of people's wealth, not merely, or primarily, their real property. Better still, numerous registers listing the taxes owed by Dijon's inhabitants survive today in the city's exceptionally rich municipal archives.

Dijon's experience in this period also makes it an excellent candidate for a case study to investigate the transformation of urban social structures over the *longue durée* of the early modern era. During these years, its population followed a course which was fairly typical of cities of its size. At the same time, Dijon solidified its position as a provincial administrative capital and was transformed into a more important commercial hub than many historians have previously recognized. It therefore offers an excellent vantage point for observing the consequences of commercial expansion and the growth of the royal bureaucracy in relation to urban society.

This study will utilize the complete rolls of the *taille* and its associated *taillon* for four years – 1464, 1556, 1643, and 1750 – to determine the changing mixture of occupations and of wealth found within the city's walls.[3] As we shall see, the economic and political changes involved in Dijon's emergence as a provincial administrative capital and commercial hub made it a magnet for capital and people. One consequence was an improvement in the economic fortunes of Dijon's burgeoning elite classes – royal officials, lawyers, merchants, and bourgeois *rentiers* – who multiplied at a greater rate than the rest of the population. As elite wealth grew, it in turn became possible for more well-born women to remain single. Together with demographic changes which, by the eighteenth century, made it more difficult for women to marry or remarry, this led to a dramatic increase in the number of women heading households in Dijon. A further repercussion of the political and economic changes was shown in the altered habits of consumption, which would in turn have two profound and related consequences for the rest of the urban population and especially for the city's craftsmen. First, the demand created by the elite consumer classes contributed to a restructuring of the occupational makeup of the city, a development quickened by an apparent migration of textile production to the surrounding countryside. Increasingly, shoes, tailored clothing, furniture, and a panoply of luxury goods issued from Dijon's workshops, replacing the bolts of finished cloth that once had been the town's prize product. Second, once occupationally restructured, the *artisanat* was favorably positioned to receive a transfer of wealth from the elite classes in return for their desired products and services. A combination of elite spending and the pursuit of a strategy by the master artisans to curtail guild membership during the middle of this period channeled some of the new wealth from the coffers of the upper classes into artisan pockets. The focus of this essay will be on the fate and fortune of the urban craftsmen (and women), but since their destiny was inextricably bound up with larger demographic and economic developments, the angle of analysis must also be wide enough to view the city within the region as well as all of the social classes that populated it.

I

Since the tax records are unusually complete in their notation of the occupations of those listed, the *taille* rolls offer an excellent source for tracing the changing size and makeup of the city's population. However, they are not without certain limitations. The rolls from the fifteenth to the seventeenth century omit virtually all of the tax-exempt members of the First Estate, although an occasional cleric or monastic house does appear, perhaps simply to provide a geographic reference point for the tax collectors. The 1750 tax register includes considerably more clerics, but even this listing is largely incomplete, judging from a census of clerical, official and military personnel made in 1753. Also, it seems probable that mobile elements such as migrant journeymen and vagrants would have escaped being recorded in these documents, as would have the hospitalized sick and servants, apprentices, and journeymen who lived with their masters and were considered part of the master's household.[4] Some tax-exempt laymen may also have been omitted, although one striking feature of Dijon's tax records, which make them particularly valuable as a guide to the city's social structure, is that they do list many of those who enjoyed exemptions from taxation because of noble status or the offices they held. Some 59 parlementaires, for instance, appear on the 1643 *taille* roll, but it is also known that the court contained 79 members in 1636,[5] suggesting that the remaining 20 members of the court may have been omitted from the rolls, or may simply have resided on country estates. A century later the correspondence was closer: the 1753 census lists 60 royal councillors at the Parlement and 28 at the Chambre des Comptes, while the tax rolls of 1750 count 54 and 25 respectively.[6] At the other end of the social spectrum, each tax roll lists a handful of individuals with the notation that they were too poor to pay a tax at all, but the number of such cases is so small – never more than 22 on any one year's register – that undercounting of the city's very poorest elements also must be suspected. The *taille* rolls thus certainly omit the bulk of the First Estate and probably fail to record the more mobile elements found within the city at any given moment, some of the poor, and perhaps a few of the wealthiest residents as well. These omissions aside, the records offer a comprehensive and regularly revised survey of the town's more sedentary inhabitants.

As is commonly the case with tax rolls from this era, some individuals appear without any notation of their occupation. No indication of status or trade is provided for just under 30 per cent of the lay heads of households in both 1464 and 1556. Such cases rise to 38.1 per cent in 1643, while the 1750 tax roll is considerably more complete in its listing of occupations, omitting these for just 11.1 per cent of family heads. Aside from a sizeable fraction of widows, most of those for whom occupations are not provided appear to have been relatively humble workers, for the tax assessments of men listed without any occupation are typically quite low. Many may have been employed in agriculture, since comparison of the tax rolls utilized here with others from nearby dates reveals agricultural designations for some of those for whom no occupation appears on the rolls used for this study.[7] Others were clearly unskilled workers, for the decline in 1750 in the number of individuals listed without occupation is accompanied by a marked increase in the number of people identified as laborers and loaders (*manouvriers, chargeurs*). Still, the increase in such people accounts for less than half of the decline in the 'Occupation Unknown' category, suggesting that many of those in this category in earlier years also earned their living in other ways.[8]

II

What do the tax rolls show us? First of all, they suggest that Dijon's population increased substantially in the course of the period examined here. In 1464, the roll lists 2365 lay *chefs de famille*, a figure which, utilizing the conventional assumption of 4.5 people per hearth, may be taken to indicate a total population for the city of approximately 10,500 inhabitants. By 1556, the number of lay heads of household had increased to 2820, and by 1643 to 4080. Slower growth marked the late seventeenth and early eighteenth century, bringing the figure to 4647 in 1750. It is very difficult to say just what Dijon's total population was by this time, for a substantial range of figures from which population figures can be extrapolated by standard demographic methods exists for the eighteenth century – all pointing toward different conclusions. I would put the city's population at about 24,000 souls in 1750.[9] Whatever the precise figure, the pace and magnitude of Dijon's demographic growth during these three centuries placed it close to the norm for European cities of middling size.[10]

This growth in size was parallelled by an even more dramatic diversification of the range of occupations and *qualités* found on the tax rolls. The 1700 lay *chefs de famille* for whom occupations or personal descriptions are provided in 1464 distributed themselves among 151 *qualités*. By 1750, the range of occupational and status indicators had exploded to 450.[11] Some of this increase, of course, resulted from the slightly improved quality of occupational recording just noted, but the greatest part of it is attributable to an incredible proliferation of specific administrative positions. Where just 6 different offices are mentioned in the 1464 records, 109 are listed in 1750. Differentiation also appears clearly in the commercial sector of the economy, where specialized *marchands de bétail, vendeurs de volaille* and the like gradually appear alongside the unspecialized merchants and pedlars of 1464. Similar developments within the artisan sector will be analyzed at greater length below. These changes highlight an important transformation in Dijon's social structure during these years: a significant increase in occupational differentiation and specialization, as well as an expansion of the range of goods and services offered for sale in the city.

Table 4.1 Numerical representation on tax rolls, by *qualité* and occupational group, both sexes, lay population.

Qualité or Occupational Group	1464 Male	1464 Female 1	1464 Female 2	1464 Female 3	1464 Total	1464 % of total lay population	1464 % Change	1556 Male	1556 Female 1	1556 Female 2	1556 Female 3	1556 Total	1556 % of total lay population	1556 % Change
High Officials	7	0	0	0	7	0.3	n.a.	73	6	1	0	80	2.8	1042.8
Lesser Officials	26*	0	0	0	26	1.1	n.a.	23	2	0	0	25	0.9	−4.0
Employees of Duke** or Town														
Civil	44	0	0	0	44	1.9	n.a.	90	3	0	4	97	3.4	120.5
Military	7	0	0	0	7	0.3	n.a.	21	0	0	0	21	0.7	200.0
Professions														
Legal	40	3	0	0	43	1.8	n.a.	82	23	0	0	105	3.7	144.2
Other	16	0	0	0	16	0.7	n.a.	39	1	0	1	41	1.5	156.3
Bourgeois, Rentiers	0	0	0	0	0	0.0	n.a.	0	0	0	0	0	0.0	n.a.
Monsieurs	1	0	0	0	1	0.1	n.a.	6	0	0	0	6	0.2	500.0
Madames, Dames	0	0	0	0	0	0.0	n.a.	0	5	0	0	5	0.2	n.a.
Mademoiselles, Demoiselles	0	0	0	0	0	0.0	n.a.	0	0	0	0	0	0.0	n.a.
Commerce	39	2	0	2	43	1.8	n.a.	116	2	0	5	123	4.4	186.0
Hôtellerie	7	0	0	0	7	0.3	n.a.	34	1	0	1	36	1.3	414.3
Transport	47	0	0	0	47	2.0	n.a.	34	2	0	0	36	1.3	−27.7
Agriculturalists	487	4	0	1	492	20.8	n.a.	379	5	0	0	384	13.6	−22.0
Urban Workers (unskilled)	26	0	0	0	26	1.1	n.a.	14	0	0	1	15	0.5	−42.3
Artisans	851	18	0	0	869	36.7	n.a.	910	36	0	4	950	33.7	9.3
Other	67	3	0	2	72	3.0	n.a.	25	0	0	8	33	1.2	−54.2
Unknown occupation	478	178	0	9	665	28.1	n.a.	617	227	2	17	863	30.6	29.6
Total	2143	208	0	14	2365			2463	313	3	41	2820		19.2

*includes 21 ducal retainers
**King after 1556
n.a. = not applicable
Female numbers: 1 = widows; 2 = wives; 3 = other females unaffiliated with any male.
For specific *qualités* of above categories, see Appendix 4A (p. 165).

Table 4.1 continued

Qualité or Occupational Group	1643							1750						
	Male	Number Female 1	2	3	Total	% of total lay population	% Change	Male	Number Female 1	2	3	Total	% of total lay population	% Change
High Officials	174	16	0	0	190	4.7	137.5	184	25	1	5	215	4.6	10.5
Lesser Officials	57	3	0	0	60	1.5	140.0	87	8	3	0	98	2.1	63.3
Employees of Duke** or Town														
Civil	127	11	0	0	138	3.4	42.3	131	26	0	1	158	3.4	14.5
Military	46	1	0	0	47	1.2	123.8	157	9	2	0	168	3.6	257.4
Professions														
Legal	289	35	0	0	324	7.9	208.6	148	35	0	0	183	3.9	-43.5
Other	39	5	0	1	45	1.1	9.8	69	16	0	10	95	2.0	111.1
Bourgeois, Rentiers	28	0	0	0	28	0.7	n.a.	62	13	0	45	120	2.6	328.6
Monsieurs	22	2	0	0	24	0.6	266.7	22	4	0	0	26	0.6	8.3
Madames, Dames	0	0	0	17	17	0.4	240.0	0	6	0	28	34	0.7	100.0
Mademoiselles, Demoiselles	0	0	0	50	50	1.2	n.a.	0	6	1	110	117	2.5	134.0
Commerce	136	12	0	7	155	3.8	26.0	173	84	8	36	301	6.5	94.2
Hôtellerie	44	2	0	0	46	1.1	27.8	107	22	2	2	133	2.9	189.1
Transport	23	0	0	0	23	0.6	-36.1	53	7	0	0	60	1.3	160.9
Agriculturalists	383	11	0	0	394	9.7	2.6	252	29	2	1	284	6.1	-34.2
Urban Workers (unskilled)	38	0	0	1	39	1.0	160.0	267	89	8	75	439	9.4	1025.6
Artisans	872	25	0	8	905	22.2	-4.7	1183	175	10	105	1473	31.7	62.8
Other	33	6	0	0	39	1.0	18.2	178	22	6	21	227	4.9	482.1
Unknown occupation	1055	439	11	51	1556	38.1	80.3	153	244	15	102	514	11.1	-66.9
Total	3366	568	11	135	4080		44.7	3226	820	60	541	4647		13.9

Other structural changes of considerable significance can be detected by arranging the vast multiplicity of specific *qualités* listed in the tax rolls into broad categories, as is done in Table 4.1. Appendix 4A spells out the specific occupations comprising each category (see pp. 165–9).

One change must have occurred between the fifteenth and eighteenth century but escapes inclusion in Table 4.1, since clergymen were so badly under-represented in the tax rolls: an expansion in the size of the First Estate. By the end of the seventeenth century Dijon contained, in addition to its seven parish churches, 27 religious establishments, and the 1753 census lists 1184 clerics within the city.[12] Since the bulk of the city's religious houses were founded during the seventeenth century amid the enthusiasm of the Catholic Reformation, this figure is probably considerably higher than that which comparable documents would reveal for the earlier periods of this study.

As Table 4.1 shows, a second group, the high secular officials (judges, royal councillors, and the like), also grew significantly in size. Dijon was the seat of several important jurisdictions. The oldest were the Bailliage of Dijon, the Chambre des Comptes, and, most prestigious of all, the Parlement of Burgundy, initially composed of a Grand' Chambre and Chancellery, but to which were added a new criminal chamber, the Tournelle, in 1537, a Chambre des Requêtes in 1575, and a Chambre des Enquêtes in 1630. With the growth of royal fiscal demands and the attendant venality of office, not only did the French kings increase the number of chambers in the Parlement, but they also created new courts – the Table de Marbre in 1554 and the Bureau des Finances in 1577. Since many officials within these courts enjoyed tax exemptions, the recorded increase in the number of their members is all the more striking. Where just seven high secular officials appear in the 1464 tax rolls, 73 such men, plus six widows of such officials, appear in 1556, following the incorporation of ducal Burgundy into the kingdom of France and the beginning of venality of office. In the next century, a still greater increase occurred in the absolute number of such officials; 174 men and 16 widows appear in the 1643 records. Thereafter, however, the kings stopped multiplying the offices in such courts, and over the next 100 years the enlargement of this class apparently slowed even below the generally sluggish overall rate of the city, expanding to 184 men and 25 widows for a slightly reduced percentage of the total number of lay heads of households listed.

An even more dramatic explosion occurred in the number of such subaltern officials as *receveurs*, *auditeurs* and *correcteurs* in the various royal courts, and in the ranks of minor administrative and military functionaries, both royal and municipal, such as tipstaffs (*huissiers*), bailiffs (*sergeants*), grain measurers, clerical secretaries, and military guards. Where 77 such individuals appear in 1464, there were 143 in 1556, 245 in 1643 and 424 in 1750. If, far from slowing its growth after 1643, this group continued to swell, this is primarily because of a sharp expansion in the number of military men appearing on the tax rolls, especially guards, militiamen, soldiers, and cavalrymen. An increase in the number of lesser venal offices, especially those associated with the royal tax farms, is also evident after 1643, as is an expansion of the number of administrative responsibilities carried out by permanent municipal functionaries. Between 1643 and 1750, the first firemen, municipal surveyors, and even traffic directors *(directeurs de circulation des caroisses)* all make their appearance on the tax rolls. On the other hand, the municipal brothelkeeper appears for the only time in the 1556 register.

The increase in the number of courts brought in its wake more judicial business and a mushrooming in the size of Dijon's legal establishment. Again, the first two centuries of our period, especially the years from 1550 to 1650, formed the great era of growth, with the number of practicing legal professionals increasing from 40 in 1464 to 82 in 1556 to 289 in 1643. During these same years, a noteworthy shift can also be detected in the pattern of specific occupations within this category. In 1464 notaries appear to have handled almost all the legal business, for 29 notaries appear on the rolls, as against just one solicitor *(procureur)* and no barristers *(avocats)* – although there were ten men called simply *maître*, probably indicating men of the law. By 1556 the judicial revolution was on. The number of barristers had jumped to 19 and of solicitors to 34, while the number of notaries had declined to 16. A century later 102 barristers, 96 solicitors, 64 *maîtres* and 27 notaries found work in Dijon. Between 1643 and 1750, the total number of legal professionals appearing on the tax rolls then declined sharply, from 289 to 148. It might be thought that this simply reflects the disappearance from the tax rolls of lawyers who were able to assert their nobility and gain tax exemption, but the records reveal no increase in the number of tax-exempt men of the law. Rather, the trend appears to reflect broader changes in the opportunities for legal careers. Not only did the size of the royal courts cease to grow from the reign of Louis XIV onward; during the same period, according to Roland Mousnier, 'large number[s] of cases [were] removed from the jurisdiction of the courts and transferred to the king's Council, many of these having to do with the activities of the provincial intendants, and to the many disputes that were settled by executive order from the ministerial bureaus'.[13] The consequence seems to have been a decline in legal business and a shrinkage in the number of men of the law. For other professionals, notably medical men, printer-booksellers (first appearing, of course, in 1556), and teachers and professors, growth characterized all three centuries. For medical men the periods 1464–1556 and 1643–1750 were the eras of most rapid expansion. Where only 4 surgeons and no doctors treated the sick in Dijon in 1464, a century later 8 and 5 did respectively, and by 1750 the 17 surgeons and 14 doctors were even joined by a dentist. For educators, the proliferation of schools and academies and the foundation of the University of Dijon in 1721 stimulated growth, especially in the seventeenth and eighteenth centuries. The handful of school masters and mistresses evident on the 1556 roll expanded in the next century, but unspectacularly compared with the years between 1643 and 1750, when their numbers bulged from 7 to 22, and they were joined by nearly a dozen grammar and latin teachers and university professors.

The growth of Dijon's administrative importance and royal fiscal policy, which relied heavily on the expansion of venal office, had direct consequences for Dijon's occupational structure, but this was not the only force at work transforming the city's social makeup. Although Dijon has not generally been known as a major commercial center, occupations of a commercial sort also expanded throughout this period, suggesting a quickening pace of exchanges.

Here, the timing of growth was rather different from within the legal and administrative sector. Between 1464 and 1556, the number of those involved in commerce increased from 43 to 123, while the *hôtellerie* sector, whose movement appears to have been closely linked to that of the commercial population, grew from 7 to 36 people. Over the next century, these sectors of the population then expanded less than the population as a whole, increasing to 155 and 46 people respectively. Dramatically renewed expansion marked the years 1643–1750, with the number of those involved in trade growing to 301 and those providing food and lodging to 133.

Dijon was a meeting place for merchant, courier and even tourist routes that became increasingly important in the early modern period. People and commodities from Paris en route to the south sailed down the Seine to Troyes and then trundled along the *grande voie* to Dijon and on to Auxonne or St Jean de Losne on the Saône. From there it was down that great river to Lyon and points farther south. Moving in the other direction human and material traffic from as far away as Italy followed the same route through Dijon to Troyes and then fanned out into Champagne or on to Paris or the Low Countries.[14] Dijon increasingly became a much-visited place. The notable woman of letters Lady Mary Wortley Montagu passed through Dijon from Paris on her way to Venice in August 1739, and wrote that 'France is so much improved it is not to be known to be the same country we passed through twenty year ago . . . The roads are all mended and the greatest part of them paved . . . and such good care taken against robbers that you may cross the country with your purse in your hand . . .'[15] The multiplication of routes of improved condition and the emergence of a true regional network after 1730 made possible what Pierre de Saint Jacob called a *revolution routière*. Burgundy's capital established itself as one of the most important *carrefours* in eastern France.[16]

Dividing the mercantile population between wholesale and retail traders (see Table 4.2) provides a finer picture of developments within this sector. The *qualité* 'merchant' described only those involved in wholesale trade; those who specialized entirely in local trade but not in production (a distinction that must be stressed, since many artisans also retailed the items they produced themselves) were usually designated as mercers or myriad types of retailers.

Between 1464 and 1556 local commerce expanded especially rapidly, while in the early seventeenth century growth was concentrated in wholesale

Table 4.2   Numerical representation of wholesale and local trade personnel.

		Wholesale			Local	
	Males	Females	Total	Males	Females	Total
1464	36	0	36	24	4	28
1556	43	0	43	73	7	80
1643	74	5	79	62	14	76
1750	79	46	125	94	82	176

trading, especially in wine and grain.[17] The next hundred years brought expansion in both wholesale and retail sectors, as well as a dizzying occupational diversification. The tax rolls of 1643 list only seven different occupations within the commercial sector, while those of 1750 contain fully 34, including 15 different types of wholesale merchants alone. Beyond numerous *négociants* in wine and grain, the city's wholesalers now included dealers in tobacco, iron, paper, wood, spices, and a variety of animals, while retailers specializing in fish, fowl, fruit, flowers, and many other specific products existed alongside the still numerous mercers, grocers, *fripiers*, and *revendeurs*.

As Dijon's commercial and administrative activity increased, the city became a magnet for capital. As was the case in so many other important provincial cities in France, investment often went into private loans or government bonds known as *rentes*, into secular offices and above all into land. The noted Burgundian historians Gaston Roupnel and Pierre de Saint Jacob have long since sketched the outline of the Dijonnais' conquest of the rich vineyards and farmlands surrounding the city; the apogee seems to have come in the late sixteenth and early seventeenth centuries, when the peasantry was heavily indebted as a consequence of the growing population pressure, heavy taxation, and wartime destruction, which was especially intense in Burgundy during the period of the Catholic League and the Thirty Years War.[18] The wealth of the countryside was increasingly sucked into the city, and so we find on the tax rolls of 1643 and even more so on those of 1750 burgeoning numbers of individuals described as merely *bourgeois* or *rentiers*, as well as single women of more than modest means (and no stated occupation) heading households when in the mid-sixteenth century none appeared at all. The provincial *rentier*, that classic figure of traditional French society, was above all a creation of the seventeenth and eighteenth centuries.

While all of the groups examined so far expanded their ranks, one sector of the population that was quite important at the beginning of our period, the agricultural workers living within Dijon's walls, experienced an absolute diminution in size. These men (and a few women), overwhelmingly *vignerons* at first, accounted for 21 per cent of all lay heads of household in 1464. By 1750, they formed just 6 per cent of all lay hearths. An initial decline in the number of *vignerons* living in Dijon can be observed during the late fifteenth and early sixteenth century, when the number of such people diminished from 486 to 370. The sharpest drop, however, occurred between 1643 and 1750, the result of a serious crisis experienced by the local wine industry during the reign of Louis XIV. Until then many *vignerons* had owned small vineyards around Dijon, or worked as sharecroppers for urban proprietors. The wine produced was of relatively low quality and, although it found a local market into the seventeenth century, a conjuncture of conditions soon put many of these producers out of business. By the last third of the seventeenth century, there is evidence that the land around Dijon was over-cultivated in vineyards, and when a depression in the wine trade struck between 1670 and 1685, many *vignerons*, already deeply indebted, were ruined. Viticulture was always a high-risk venture, requiring continual extension of credit to the grower, and with the collapse of the wine market many bourgeois proprietors withdrew their capital. Even when the market picked up again, the local *vignerons* did not benefit, for the improved transport routes of the eighteenth century now brought higher quality but inexpensive wine to the city, driving out the inferior local product.[19] Confronted with such grim prospects, the sons and grandsons of many *vignerons* may have turned from viticulture to market-gardening – with favorable economic consequences, as we shall see later on. Where 385 *vignerons* appear on the 1643 tax roll, just 165 are listed in 1750; between the same dates, the number of *jardiniers* increased from 7 to 102. To judge by the numbers alone, other descendants of *vignerons* might have become unskilled laborers or servants, for totals for both of these groups also increased dramatically between 1643 and 1750. But this change probably reflects above all else the improved quality of occupational notation in the 1750 tax roll. It would be unwise to draw any conclusions about real changes in Dijon's social structure from the modifications visible in the 'Urban Workers (unskilled)' and 'Other' categories in Table 4.1.

To recapitulate the changes observed so far, the growth in Dijon's law courts, the extension of bourgeois control over the surrounding countryside, and the acceleration of commercial exchanges all produced a remarkable expansion in the numbers of robe officials, professional men, *rentiers*, and merchants within the city between 1464 and 1750. If we classify as 'elite consumers' all noblemen, high and lesser officials, professionals, wholesale merchants, *rentiers*, and individuals indicated by the honorific *monsieur, madame, mademoiselle*, and *bourgeois*, we find this category growing from 6 per cent of all households in 1464, to 15 per cent in 1556, to 25 per cent in 1643, and finally to more than 30 per cent in 1750. During the same period the agricultural element within Dijon's population shrank from one in five of the city's hearths to barely one in twenty. This highly significant transformation in the city's makeup in turn provides the background for the analysis of the last major group within Dijon's population – indeed, the largest of all – its artisans.

As Table 4.1 shows, the size of Dijon's *artisanat* as a whole diminished in relation to the city's total population in the course of the early modern centuries, particularly between 1556 and 1643. One of the fundamental attributes of Ancien Régime craft guilds was that, by such devices as limiting the number of apprentices that master craftsmen could train or by increasing the fees required to become a guild master, they could control access to their trade and thereby defend and even enlarge the market for guild members' goods and services. The later sixteenth and early seventeenth century witnessed direct confrontation between Dijon's master artisans and its municipal authorities, who desired a more open guild system. In this confrontation, the masters pursued a deliberate strategy of solidarity that transcended differences between individual *métiers* and successfully maintained their ability to regulate their numbers, primarily by choking off the admission to mastership of all but a few hand-picked journeymen.[20] Where guilds continued to function effectively throughout the Ancien Régime, as in Dijon, it appears they were able to keep artisan ranks from swelling too rapidly, even in a growing city marked by a particularly notable expansion in the number of wealthy consumers. In 1464, individuals identified as artisans accounted for 36.7 per cent of all heads of households listed on the tax roll. By 1643, this figure was down to 22.2 per cent, although increase in the following century brought it back up to 31.7 per cent. The growth in the last period, it is worth noting, was concentrated particularly within the female workforce. The number of male artisans increased by 36 per cent between 1643 and 1750, while the number of women artisans listed separately on the rolls skyrocketed by 779 per cent.[21]

Broad changes within the *artisanat* can be discovered by dividing the artisans into craft groupings, as is done in Table 4.3. Although this table shows that the representation of many sectors remained remarkably stable over time, or experienced fluctuations that do not add up to any clear trend, a number of noteworthy changes emerge.

Most strikingly, a sharp decline is evident in the percentage of artisans employed in the city's textile industries between 1464 and 1643, with a slight recovery between 1643 and 1750 that was still not sufficient to restore the percentage of artisans active in this sector to half of the 1464 figure.[22] In the fifteenth century, the textile industry had been the backbone of Dijon's craft production, and textile workers numerically dominated the *artisanat*. A century

Table 4.3 Numerical representation of artisans by craft group as a percentage of all artisans (both sexes).

Craft group	1464	1556	1643	1750
Clothing	13.0	13.2	12.0	12.8
Construction	10.1	15.3	15.5	13.4
Food	11.2	15.8	13.9	9.5
Leather	18.0	15.1	21.3	19.7
Luxury	3.8	5.7	5.4	9.0
Metals/Weapons	9.2	10.0	7.5	5.6
Textiles	22.4	11.8	7.4	10.2
Wine-related	4.6	4.1	6.6	7.5
Woodworking	3.8	5.9	6.2	7.6

later, this was no longer the case, although the full range of textile-producing trades was still represented within Dijon's walls. By 1643 we search in vain on the tax rolls for fullers and carders (9 and 11 of these people, respectively, appear in the 1556 records, where there had been 16 and 22 in 1464).[23] Weavers, though still numerous, had seen their numbers dwindle to 41 from 69 in 1464 and 46 in 1556. While the ranks of these groups recovered somewhat by 1750, that recovery remained limited in scope.

Although the reasons for the decline and subsequent slight recovery of the city's textile manufacturing in the early modern period remain unclear, the most plausible hypothesis would seem to be the migration of textile production to the surrounding countryside. In many parts of Europe, rural industry emerged in the sixteenth century as part of a massive redeployment of capital and labor, which was contingent upon an emergent world economy and the attendant desire of merchants to escape rigid urban guild regulations and use cheaper labor. Production of certain commodities, textiles foremost among them, shifted to the countryside. Scattered pieces of evidence reveal the existence of rural industry in nearby regions of Burgundy in the seventeenth and eighteenth century. Roupnel discovered concentrations of woolen cloth-weavers in Is-sur-Tille and especially Marey-sur-Tille, where in 1657 one hundred craftsmen plied this trade, all but twelve of them dependent upon six Dijonnais merchants who provided them with their raw materials and marketed their finished product. Linenweavers also populated rural villages, sometimes densely as at Selongey, less than thirty kilometers from Dijon. In 1708 royal inspector Lambert observed that weavers in the villages around Dijon were producing many fabrics.[24]

The urban to rural migration of basic production continued in many regions in the next two centuries, but in some parts of Europe, perhaps Dijon among them, a tendency for industry to recolonize the cities in the eighteenth century has also been detected.[25] As mentioned, in Dijon the number of weavers more than stabilized after centuries of diminution, and the population of spinners soared between 1643 and 1750. Unfortunately, research into the economic history of early modern Burgundy is not yet far enough advanced for us to be certain that the cloth turned out in the countryside competed directly with that manufactured in the city and that an expansion in rural production coincided with the period of decline for Dijon's industry. Whatever the precise cause of the changes affecting the textile sector of the city's economy, it is clear that the percentage of Dijon's residents employed producing cloth declined markedly between the end of the Middle Ages and the seventeenth century.

While fewer Dijonnais made their living producing cloth, more and more were engaged in luxury production, catering to the growing number of elite consumers residing in the city. In 1464, thirty-three craftsmen produced luxury goods. Goldsmiths were the largest group within this category, but the city also offered wealthy consumers the skills of pewterers, painters, stained-glass makers (*peintres-verriers*), engravers, copper-potters, manuscript illuminators, sculptors and mirrormakers. By 1556, the numbers of luxury craftsmen had increased to 54, with embroiderers and glaziers making their appearance for the first time on the tax rolls, while the lone copper-potter and mirrormaker found in 1464 had disappeared. Rather surprisingly, the next century saw little expansion in this category of artisans, even though this was the period in which the number of robe *officiers* and lawyers expanded most dramatically. Just 49 luxury artisans appear on the 1643 roll spread out over only 7 trades. The years from 1643 to 1750, however, witnessed both explosive growth and diversification. The 1750 tax roll includes 133 luxury artisans, including faiencemakers, carriagemakers, gilders, jewelers, and wigmakers (all new trades), as well as considerably more painters and sculptors than had appeared on any of the earlier tax listings. Detailed investigation of the history of taste and consumption in early modern France remains seriously underdeveloped, but a number of synthetic works have spoken of an accelerating 'craze for fashion' in this period. Spending for the sake of appearance – a remodelled townhouse, a coach and pair, fine clothes, jewelry, fancy foods for entertaining – became practically compulsory. The taste for richness, for sumptuousness – what Forster called 'an almost psychopathic need for display' – was increasingly unbridled in the seventeenth century, and neither the preaching of moralists nor the abundant sumptuary legislation of the era could rein it in. In the eighteenth century, with the lapsing of the Catholic Reform, even these checks were removed. According to Chaunu, that plus the Lockean epistemological revolution and the consequent cult of sensibility ushered in a riot of artistic and decorative forms.[26] Dijon's tax rolls appear to confirm that the years from 1643 to 1750 witnessed a particular expansion of luxury consumption.

The growing concern for display benefited the construction trades as well. Examination of Dijon's history reveals a series of major building projects that must have provided employment for growing numbers of construction workers in these centuries. New bastions and repaired walls occupied dozens of masons in the mid-1550s. During the seventeenth century, municipally and royally sponsored public construction projects expanded, as did church-building. Late in the century, new streets and squares such as the city's *place royale* were carved out of the crowded texture of the medieval city, and, most grandiose of all, a new Palais des Etats was erected. In the private sector, Dijon's parlementaires increasingly poured capital into construction of stone *hôtels* to display their wealth and status. During the eighteenth century, reconstruction even came to be ordered by law; the municipality commanded the wealthy inhabitants of the city's major streets to restore the facades of their dwellings, stipulating that they must use cut stone. As the Dijonnais architect Joseph Taisand observed in 1684, if Dijon's construction continued at its present pace the town would shortly be 'one of the most agreeable cities in France'.[27] The most rapid expansion in the construction sector occurred between 1464 and 1556, when the total number of people involved in the building trades increased from 88 to 145. By 1750, the number stood at 166. As one might expect, growth was particularly marked among stoneworkers, while the number of carpenters remained roughly stable throughout the whole period.

The gradual rebuilding of Dijon's housing stock appears to have been accompanied by considerable refurnishing of house interiors, for another group of trades that expanded particularly rapidly was that involving wood-working. Furnituremakers, joiners, carvers, wainscotters, and panellers were all generally called *menuisiers* in Dijon. The number of such craftsmen moved in tandem with the luxury trades, increasing from 14 in 1464 to 39 in 1556, falling back to 34 by 1643, and then increasing again to 71 by 1750. One estimate claims that eighteenth-century rooms (increasingly panelled) held four times the amount of furniture, of a considerably wider variety, than did sixteenth– and seventeenth-century house interiors.[28] Whatever the accuracy of this statistic, it seems clear that demand for furniture and wood-panelled interiors increased substantially over time.

Demand also triggered expansion in the ranks of other woodworking trades. From the mid-fifteenth to the mid-seventeenth centuries twelve wheelwrights were all Dijon apparently needed, but with an increase in carters and the advent of carriage transport in the second half of the seventeenth century, the number of wheelwrights jumped to 23 by 1750.

Other developments are masked by the division of Dijon's artisans into broad categories but emerge under close scrutiny of individual trades. Thus, although the percentage of artisans involved in the clothing trades as a whole hardly changed over the course of the three centuries examined here, a significant increase in the number of tailors plying their needles in the city occurred during the later seventeenth and early eighteenth century, suggesting once again increased consumption. In 1464 Dijon housed 68 tailors. In the next two centuries, their numbers increased only slowly, to 73 and 80, but the 1750 tax roll reveals fully 144 tailors and seamstresses. If the percentage of artisans in the clothing trades as a whole did not expand over the early modern period, this is partly attributable to the disappearance of Dijon's hosiers from 1643 onward (22 hosiers had appeared on the tax roll in 1464 and 25 in 1556). This in turn is probably best explained by the collapse of local stocking production in the face of competition from more specialized centers of production elsewhere.

Similarly, Table 4.3 reveals first expansion, then contraction in the food trades. A look at the figures for specific occupations provided in Appendix 4B (p. 170) shows that the sharp increase between 1464 and 1556 in the percentage of artisans employed in this sector stems largely from a dramatic growth in the number of pastrycooks (from 3 to 36), a trade that catered above all for a growing wealthy clientele. Thereafter, the numbers of those identified on the tax rolls as pastrycooks declined but the number of those categorized as confectioners or café operators increased at the same time. Since it was common for pastrycooks to operate taverns on the side, it seems plausible to assume that more and more people in this line of work were operating more substantial establishments and coming to be classified by the tax collectors as caterers or tavernkeepers, in which case they would escape from the artisan category into the *hôtellerie* sector. If this was so, this is yet another manifestation of that central trend in the local economy during these years, the increasing orientation of the economy to the provision of relatively costly consumer goods and services.

This same trend also stimulated expansion in the number of different artisan occupations that Dijon could boast. Table 4.4 and Appendix 4B set out the full range of crafts practiced in Dijon. As can be seen, new trades appeared regularly on the tax rolls while old ones disappeared, with the years from 1643 to 1750 emerging as particularly fertile in novel craft specialties and the preceding period as one of surprising retrenchment. Stockingmaking and stages of textile production such as fulling were not the only dying industries of the period. Crossbow bolt-making, furskirt production, clog-making, and doublet production all fell prey to technological innovation and changing fashion. Their disappearance was more than counterbalanced by the establishment of new trades, especially after 1643. Tombstone-carvers, wigmakers, faiencemakers, and carriagemakers were among the new craftsmen who appeared in significant numbers in the late seventeenth and eighteenth centuries. The city now came to house specialized workers producing combs, umbrellas, chests, and chairs.

This incipient division of labor in the provisioning of local markets was parallelled by the rapid expansion of a specialized export industry built around the item perhaps most closely associated with Dijon's name down to the present day: mustard. The reputation for quality of Dijon's mustard dates back at least to the fourteenth century, when the French royal household purchased supplies of the condiment in dry form from the city's apothecaries, but a trade whose members specialized primarily in mustard-making did not appear until the sixteenth century, and the ranks of these *vinaigriers* swelled particularly rapidly in the later seventeenth and early eighteenth century, increasing from 11 in 1643 to fully 41 in 1750. This growth was linked at once to technological innovation, France's increasing culinary refinement, and the expansion of inter-regional commerce: the key changes that turned prepared mustard into an object shipped from Dijon throughout the kingdom were the replacement

Table 4.4 Appearing and disappearing trades.

Year	Number of trade descriptions	New	Lost
1464	81	—	—
1556	86*	20	14
1643	76	11	21
1750	102	36	10

*In 1556 linenweavers and woolenweavers were conflated on the tax roll as simply weavers.

of vinegar with verjus (juice from the grape before it is ripe), the blending of mustard with a variety of other different flavors to produce a range of prepared mustards, and the introduction of faience jars and pots, which permitted the transportation of these mustards in the now familiar containers.[29] The condiment yielded by these procedures appealed sufficiently to sophisticated palates throughout the country to make the *vinaigriers* Dijon's ninth largest *métier* in 1750. In the growth of new trades and the disappearance of old ones, as in so many other aspects, it is evident that changes in craft production in Dijon were related to, on the one hand, the demand exerted by the well-to-do consuming classes, and, on the other, by the increasing integration of the regional and even national economy.

III

If tax rolls have long been a favored source for social and economic historians, this is because they not only provide a window into the occupational structure of those communities for which they survive – at least when they note with regularity the occupations of those they list – but they also contain indications of the wealth of the community's inhabitants. So far, we have seen that between 1464 and 1750 Dijon experienced a substantial increase in the number of royal officials, *rentiers*, merchants, and lawyers living within its walls; a decline in its agricultural population; and a restructuring of local industry in response to increased local demand for luxury goods and the growing integration of the city's economy into larger commercial networks. The tax rolls can also tell us just how these changes affected the distribution of wealth within the city.

Of course, as a source for determining the distribution of wealth, these documents do have one great deficiency: a significant, and indeed significantly growing, fraction of the city's richest inhabitants enjoyed tax exemption because of their status. Table 4.5 shows the dramatic increase that occurred in the number of such people. In light of the large numbers of the tax exempt, certain of the highest status groups, notably the high robe officials, must be omitted from the analysis that follows.

In the groups liable for taxation, considerable care was taken by the authorities to ensure that the sums assessed conformed with reasonable accuracy to people's genuine ability to pay. From the fifteenth to the eighteenth

Table 4.5 Tax-exempt laymen and women on tax rolls.

People exempt	1464	1556	1643	1750
because of office	28	116	316	406
because of noble status	29	17	86	161
Total	57	133	402	567

century, the methods used to determine the repartition of the *taille* and, from the mid-sixteenth century on, the *taillon* changed little in Burgundy. Once a global amount was agreed upon between the ruler and the Estates of Burgundy, the tax was apportioned following the principle that 'the strong carry the weak'. This was supposed to guarantee a tax assessed according to individuals' ability to pay, and assessors were to take into account both mobile and immobile forms of wealth, including resources drawn from commerce or manufacturing. The *élus* of the Estates apportioned the burden by *généralité*, and, in the case of Dijon, left it to the Town Council to divide the burden by parish and individual. In ducal Dijon, this was done by the town's *receveur des finances ordinaires*, aided by two aldermen and several clerks and sergeants. In royal Dijon, the task was supervised prior to 1600 by an *asséeur* and after that date by the *collecteur*, both taxpayers chosen by the general assembly of inhabitants and subject to fine and imprisonment if they did not do the job properly and fairly. Significantly, under both regimes the assessor carried out a 'cerche des feux' and enlisted the help of neighbors, who knew better than anybody else what their neighbors possessed and, since parishes were assessed as a whole before individual partition, would find it in their interest to make sure that everybody declared their full liability. It would be foolish to pretend that these procedures guaranteed that the process of tax assessment excluded all caprice or corruption. Still, it seems reasonable to accept the tax rolls as a rough proxy for analyzing the relative wealth of different groups among the taxpaying population.[30]

Figure 4.1, which displays the median tax assessment for certain occupational groups in comparison with the median tax paid by all taxpayers in the

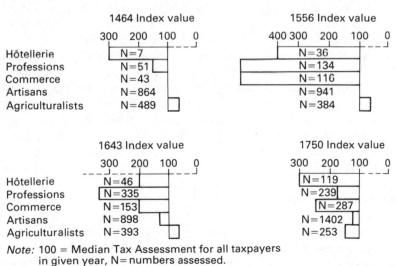

Note: 100 = Median Tax Assessment for all taxpayers in given year, N = numbers assessed.

Fig. 4.1. Median tax assessments for selected occupational groups relative to median for entire population.

151

given year, reveals some telling shifts in the relative wealth of different groups. Most notably, the disparity in wealth among the major occupational groups increased dramatically between the mid-fifteenth and mid-sixteenth century. In 1464 the median for all groups except for the small *hôtellerie* sector clustered around the overall median, but in 1556 the now much larger groups of commercial and professional people each paid a median tax five times as large as the overall median. In the next century, the tax burden shouldered by these two groups fell back somewhat in relation to the rest of Dijon's population, with the decline particularly marked among those involved in commerce. Then, between 1643 and 1750, a notable drop can be seen in the relative wealth of the professional group, a reflection of the decline of legal business, while merchants increased their relative wealth. This last period is also noteworthy for the significant increase in the taxes paid by the city's now reduced number of agriculturalists, a group whose median tax assessment had been below the overall median in all three previous periods. The changes of these last two centuries reduced somewhat the disparities between groups, but these were still markedly more significant in 1750 than in 1453 – and, of course, the city now also contained a substantial population of tax-exempt nobles and *officiers* of considerable wealth.

While medians can tell us much about the relative position of various groups within the city, they hide the range of tax assessment within these groups. This could be enormous. In 1464 assessments within the commercial sector ranged from 1 to 216 gros. In 1643 the master baker Antoine Leschenet paid a tax of 150 sous, ranking him in the 92nd percentile of wealth distribution. He was a wealthy man, holding *rentes* totalling 660 livres and capable of bidding for and obtaining the wine tax farm at the price of 3200 livres.[31] In that same year, a fellow guildsman paid a tax of only 5 sous (5th percentile). As wretched as his condition must have been, worse off yet were a tailor and a shoemaker who were classified as too poor to pay any tax at all, but who were fellow guildsmen of individuals assessed, respectively, 190 and 140 sous.

Despite the continued existence of wealthy artisans such as Leschenet, a fundamental change in wealth distribution nonetheless occurred between the fifteenth century and the early modern period. Where in the late medieval 'bonne ville' artisans of many trades were honorably represented among the wealthiest inhabitants, such men lost their pride of place during the early modern centuries. Of the 21 individuals of known occupation taxed in the top 2 per cent in 1464, 12 were artisans representing 10 different occupations. By 1556 the top 2 per cent (34 individuals from 15 different occupations) included only 7 artisans – three butchers, three tanners, and a widow of a cobbler who paid the highest tax in town. By 1643, even though the economic position of the *artisanat* as a whole had improved, there was no change at the very top of the scale. Now the top 2 per cent included 65 people from 20 occupations, numerically dominated by the legal professionals (there were 21 barristers in the group), but only 5 artisans, including 3 pastrycooks. A century later more craftsmen had rejoined the ranks of the wealthiest *roturiers*, but they still formed a small percentage of this group. Of the 79 people from 33 occupations in the top 2 per cent, 15 were artisans. Wholesale merchants now formed the single largest group within this category.

Figure 4.2 enables us to visualize the relative wealth distribution of the various occupational groups divided roughly into quartiles (because of the numbers of individuals in various tax brackets strictly equal quartiles are not attainable). As we can see, most of the professionals crowded into the top end of the wealth scale, at least until the eighteenth century when the decline of the caseload before the courts referred to earlier took its tolls on this group dominated numerically by men of the law. The decline hit the solicitors particularly hard; their median wealth standing dropped from the 87th

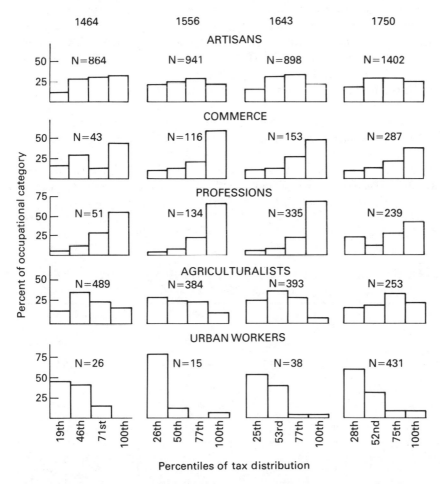

Percentiles of tax distribution

Fig. 4.2 Tax distribution by occupational category, male and female.

percentile in 1643 to the 75th a century later. The commercial classes comprised the other very wealthy taxpaying group, posting their greatest gains in the first early modern century. Their ranks were buoyed by the wholesale merchants, whose median assessment ranked in the 96th percentile in 1556 and the 87th in 1643. The growing number of retailers account for the slight flattening out of the group as a whole evident in 1643 and 1750, but the commercial classes were still clearly among the city's most affluent.

These figures demonstrate the notable trend we have discussed already: as Dijon became an administrative and commercial center, capital (land rent, legal fees, court costs, and commercial profits) was sucked within the walls and the privileged social classes fattened themselves on it. At the same time, as artisan production was increasingly restructured to cater for these individuals' growing demand for goods, changes also occurred in the relative wealth of different groups within the *artisanat*, although analysis of the median tax assessment of the major craft categories and of those individual trades practiced by the largest number of people also reveals considerable continuity in the relative wealth standing of different groups over time. Table 4.6 ranks each category of artisans by the median tax paid by its members at each of the four dates analyzed, while Table 4.7 provides a similar ranking for the largest individual trades.

As can be seen, the wealthiest group of artisans at each date comprised those involved in preparing and selling food, while the luxury and metal-working trades also stood consistently near the top of Table 4.6 across all four centuries. Similar continuities can be seen in Table 4.7. Butchers, tanners, goldsmiths, and pastrycooks (when enough people plied these trades for them to appear in this listing) seem consistently to have been among Dijon's wealthier artisans, while cobblers were among the poorest. One significant change does emerge from Table 4.6, however: the decline in the wealth standing of those involved in

Table 4.6 Tax scale by craft group, ranked by median; percentile in parentheses (males only 1464, 1556, 1643).

| 1464 | Assessment in gros | | 1556 | Assessment in sous | |
| | Number | | | Number | |
Group	taxed	Median	Group	taxed	Median
Food	96	11 (81st)	Food	146	9 (73rd)
Luxury	33	9 (69th)	Wine-related	39	5 (62nd)
Construction	85	8 (64th)	Miscellaneous	30	5 (62nd)
Metals/Weapons	76	6 (59th)	Metals/Weapons	84	4 (57th)
Textiles	189	6 (59th)	Luxury	48	4 (57th)
Clothing	108	6 (59th)	Clothing	120	4 (57th)
Woodworking	33	6 (59th)	Woodworking	51	4 (57th)
Leather	155	6 (59th)	Leather	137	4 (57th)
Wine-related	39	6 (59th)	Textiles	106	3 (49th)
Miscellaneous	33	6 (59th)	Construction	140	2.5 (42nd)

| 1643 | Assessment in sous | | 1750 | Assessment in livres | |
| | | Number | | | Number | |
Group	taxed	Median	Group	taxed	Median
Food	122	70 (80th)	Food	132	15 (80th)
Luxury	44	50 (70th)	M	111	16 (82nd)
Miscellaneous	35	50 (70th)	F	21	15 (80th)
Wine-related	58	43 (65th)	Metals/Weapons	78	12 (74th)
Metals/Weapons	66	40 (64th)	M	69	12 (74th)
Construction	136	30 (53rd)	F	9	14 (77th)
Clothing	98	30 (53rd)	Luxury	125	10 (69th)
Woodworking	52	30 (53rd)	M	102	10 (69th)
Leather	188	30 (53rd)	F	23	8 (61st)
Textiles	66	25 (43rd)	Wine-related	103	10 (69th)
			M	78	12 (74th)
			F	25	8 (61st)
			Woodworking	109	8 (61st)
			M	101	8 (61st)
			F	8	6 (52nd)
			Construction	193	6 (52nd)
			M	163	6 (52nd)
			F	30	3 (28th)
			Leather	275	6 (52nd)
			M	246	7 (56th)
			F	29	4 (36th)
			Miscellaneous	60	5 (42nd)
			M	52	5 (42nd)
			F	8	5 (42nd)
			Clothing	183	5 (42nd)
			M	76	7 (56th)
			F	107	4 (36th)
			Textiles	144	5 (42nd)
			M	115	6 (52nd)
			F	29	2.5 (17th)

the textile trades from a position comparable to most other artisans in 1464 to one which was clearly inferior by 1556 and which remained so for the remainder of the period. This decline, it might be noted, occurred despite the fact that the preliminary aspects of textile production, shearing, fulling, and carding, which involved the least skill and were the least remunerative, disappeared entirely from the urban scene between the fifteenth and seventeenth centuries. The diminution in the size of Dijon's textile trades over the early modern centuries was thus clearly accompanied by a deterioration in the wealth of those who continued to practice these crafts.

The consistently high ranking of the luxury trades also deserves to be underscored. The consequence of trends favoring these crafts was to shift a growing percentage of artisans into wealthier trades. Also among the most prosperous individual occupations in 1750 were several of the new trades that particularly expanded during these centuries, notably wig-making and the production of mustard and vinegar. Those sectors of the economy that grew particularly in size also seem to have been characterized by considerable prosperity for the individuals within them.

While this pattern holds true for the most rapidly expanding sectors of the *artisanat*, Tables 4.6 and 4.7 also suggest that within other sectors of the urban economy the relationship between the number of people active in a given craft or craft sector and its relative tax standing was an inverse one. Of course, there was no automatic correspondence between the numbers of producers, the numbers of elite consumers, and the relative wealth standing of artisans – too many possible variables affected the fortunes of different trades for a simple mathematical formula to account for this – but it is striking how often the median tax assessment of a fundamental element within the urban economy declined as its total size increased. The construction trades provide a clear example. In 1464, 85 artisans worked in construction, paying a median tax that ranked them third highest of the ten craft groups. By 1556 their numbers had nearly doubled, and they had plummeted to dead last in the rank of the ten groups. In the next century, they succeeded in reducing their ranks somewhat, and as they did so they passed four other craft groups in economic rank, a

Table 4.7 Tax rank, individual crafts (males), ranked by median; distribution percentile in parentheses.

1464: 21 most numerous crafts, assessment in gros			1556: 21 most numerous crafts, assessment in sous		
Craft	Number taxed	Median	Craft	Number taxed	Median
Butchers	17	22 (93rd)	Tanners	15	30 (94th)
Goldsmiths	13	12 (81st)	Butchers	37	17 (85th)
Tanners	14	12 (81st)	Goldsmiths	15	10 (77th)
Fourniers	31	10 (71st)	Candlemakers	16	10 (77th)
Blacksmiths	26	9 (69th)	Bakers	37	9 (73rd)
Roofers/Tilers	15	8 (64th)	Pastrycooks	36	6 (66th)
Carpenters	30	6 (59th)	Barrelcoopers	29	6 (66th)
Masons	33	6 (59th)	Hosiers	25	6 (66th)
Linen-weavers	53	6 (59th)	Blacksmiths	14	4 (57th)
Wool-weavers	16	6 (59th)	Tailors	70	4 (57th)
Clothworkers	54	6 (59th)	Furnituremakers	35	4 (57th)
Bakers	20	6 (59th)	Shoemakers	36	4 (57th)
Tailors	64	6 (59th)	Plasterers	18	3 (49th)
Hosiers	20	6 (59th)	Carpenters	35	3 (49th)
Barrelcoopers	39	6 (59th)	Masons	53	3 (49th)
Hatters	17	6 (59th)	Hatters	15	3 (49th)
Shoemakers	68	5 (46th)	Furriers	15	3 (49th)
Shearers	14	5 (46th)	Weavers	43	2.5 (42nd)
Carders	22	4 (45th)	Roofers/Tilers	17	2 (39th)
Furnituremakers	14	4 (45th)	Shearers	21	2 (39th)
Fullers	13	3 (36th)	Cobblers	32	2 (39th)

1643: 19 most numerous crafts, assessment in sous			1750: 20 most numerous crafts, assessment in livres		
Craft	Number taxed	Median	Craft	Number taxed	Median
Pastrycooks	24	120 (91st)	Vinegarmakers	24	23 (89th)
Butchers	15	110 (87th)	Bakers	51	20 (87th)
Tanners	15	100 (87th)	Wigmakers	29	13 (75th)
Carpenters	21	60 (77th)	Butchers	15	12 (74th)
Bakers	60	60 (77th)	Locksmiths	20	12 (74th)
Candlemakers	27	60 (77th)	Wheelwrights	21	11 (69th)
Goldsmiths	20	55 (71st)	Barrelcoopers	38	9 (64th)
Shoemakers	45	50 (70th)	Carpenters	31	7 (56th)
Barrelcoopers	46	45 (65th)	Basketmakers	16	7 (56th)
Locksmiths	13	40 (64th)	Shoemakers	149	7 (56th)
Wheelwrights	11	40 (64th)	Furnituremakers	63	7 (56th)
Roofers/Tilers	26	40 (64th)	Plasterers	36	7 (56th)
Plasterers	13	30 (53rd)	Tailors	54	7 (56th)
Tailors	71	30 (53rd)	Masons	17	6 (52nd)
Hatters	15	30 (53rd)	Stonecutters	36	6 (52nd)
Furnituremakers	32	30 (53rd)	Roofers/Tilers	19	6 (52nd)
Masons	56	25 (43rd)	Weavers	61	6 (52nd)
Weavers	41	25 (43rd)	Cardmakers	18	5 (42nd)
Cobblers	83	20 (37th)	Cobblers	56	5 (42nd)
			Wool and cotton spinners	25	4 (36th)
			Females		
			Wool and cotton spinners	12	2 (16th)
			Tailors/ seamstresses	86	5 (42nd)

position they were able to hold another hundred years. Within the industry, the carpenters were particularly able to improve their economic status between 1556 and 1643, jumping from the 49th to the 77th percentile while their numbers dropped from 35 to 21. The masons, on the other hand, expanded their numbers over the same period from 53 to 56 and saw their economic standing slide slightly.

Similar patterns appear among the shoemakers and cobblers. In 1464 no consistent distinction was made between these two trades, but by 1556 it was becoming clear that the former monopolized the making of new shoes and the latter the mending of old ones.[32] In 1556 there were 36 shoemakers and 32 cobblers, with the former paying a median tax almost twenty percentile points higher than the latter. By 1643, as the number of cobblers swelled to 83 and shoemakers increased to just 45, the gap between their economic fortunes widened still more; indeed, the cobblers were now Dijon's poorest craftsmen. The gap between the two groups narrowed again during the next hundred years, as the number of cobblers fell to 56 while the ranks of the shoemakers expanded to 149. Cases such as this suggest how significant it was for the economic standing of individual trades that they be able to control access to their ranks.

Tax rolls, of course, can reveal only the relative wealth of different groups within the urban population; they cannot demonstrate changes in absolute prosperity or impoverishment. Determining this requires the investigation of other sources, such as marriage contracts or probate records. The labor involved in recording the data contained in such documents is prodigious, and I have not undertaken a full examination of such records for the entire period covered by this study. I have, however, explored what such sources reveal about Dijon's artisans for the years between 1550 and 1650. During these years, the dowries that master craftsmen provided for the first marriage of their daughters rose by 150 per cent in real terms (adjusted to purchasing power in grain).[33] At the same time, master artisan investment in real estate rose by well over five-fold in real terms.[34] Together these findings suggest a significant increase in the absolute wealth of Dijon's master artisans in these years – years when, it will be recalled, the city's tax rolls suggest no significant rise in the position of the artisans in relation to the rest of the city's population. The artisans thus appear, in this period at least, to have been a cork borne upward by a rising tide of prosperity that affected the city as a whole.

IV

Thus far we have been discussing men and only incidentally women, since the entries on tax rolls are confined to heads of households, a traditional male preserve. However, even though this source has a male bias, some of the most interesting findings that emerge from our analysis concern the situation of women. Historical demographers have uncovered evidence of a declining percentage of widows who could expect to remarry and an increase in women who never married in the towns of France in the course of the early modern centuries.[35] Dijon's tax rolls suggest that these trends were of remarkable magnitude in Burgundy's capital. Where some 208 widows (8.8 per cent of all lay heads of households) appear on the 1464 register, 313 do so in 1556, 568 in 1643, and 820 (or 17.6 per cent of all lay heads of households) in 1750. The increase in never-married women listed separately on the rolls is even more marked. Just 14 and 41 such women, respectively, show up on the 1464 and 1556 documents, but in 1643 we find 135 such women and in 1750 there are .541. A far smaller but also growing number of women identified as married and yet listed under their own names also can be detected.[36]

Furthermore, some historians have spoken of a decline in the economic status of women during the early modern centuries.[37] But when we look at the economic profile of all of these women (see Table 4.8) we find a *rise* in the median percentile of their tax assessments from the 19th percentile in 1464 to

Table 4.8 Median tax percentile of women of selected *qualités* and occupational groups; number assessed in parentheses.

	1464		1556		1643		1750	
	Widows	*Single*	*Widows*	*Single*	*Widows*	*Single*	*Widows*	*Single*
	[All women: 19 (213)]		[All women: 39 (329)]		[All women: 37 (654)]		[All women: 36 (1299)]	
Qualité or Occupation								
Artisans	36 (18)	none	50 (36)	26 (4)	43 (25)	15 (8)	42 (174)	36 (105)
Commerce	8 (2)	8 (2)	49 (3)	22 (4)	77 (11)	15 (8)	69 (89)	57 (39)
Hôtellerie	none	none	none	none	65 (2)	none	82 (23)	83 (3)
Bourgeois	none	none	none	none	none	none	74 (13)	77 (43)
Madames	none	none	none	none	none	87 (15)	99 (1)	56 (6)
Mademoiselles	none	none	none	none	none	91 (29)	52 (3)	69 (97)
Agriculturalists	none	none	none	none	25 (11)	none	29 (29)	24 (1)
Urban Workers	none	none	none	none	none	15 (1)	16 (89)	28 (74)
Unknown Occu.	19 (172)	19 (2)	39 (223)	22 (15)	24 (420)	15 (51)	17 (238)	28 (100)

the 39th in 1556, after which date this figure essentially levels off at a plateau, which is, of course, still well below the average for all households.

It is difficult to determine the reasons for these developments on the basis of the tax rolls alone, for before 1750 this source is unfortunately uninformative about the specific status or occupation of the women it lists. Nearly all of the women appearing are simply described as widows, wives, or in 1643 and 1750, by some *qualité* (*madame*, *mademoiselle*, *demoiselle*, or *bourgeoise*). It is also important to recall that these documents tell us nothing about the substantial amounts of women's work performed within the context of the 'domestic work culture, hidden from the streets', and, we might add, hidden from the tax rolls as well.[38] Many of the widows who predominate among the women listed on the earlier tax rolls were probably widows of artisans, who carried on their husbands' trades after their death; in 1750, when the reporting of women's occupations becomes more complete, such cases form the largest single category among widows. Single women had no guild privileges in Dijon, and there were no purely female guilds in the city, but widows of master artisans could keep their husbands' shops open provided they had sufficient workers and did not remarry outside the guild.

Many of the widows in 1750 were also engaged in commerce, reflecting the integral place of women in the world of peddling and trading. Indeed, women comprised more than one-third of the wholesale merchants and more than one-half of the retail merchants appearing on the 1750 tax roll. Still another large group of widows, worlds away economically, was that of unskilled day laborers and washerwomen. Meanwhile, many of the never-married women who appear in 1750 worked in textile and clothing manufacture, as wool- and cotton-spinners, as lacemakers, and above all as seamstresses, while again others were active in commerce or as unskilled workers.

Perhaps, as Howell contends for Cologne and Leiden, the appearance of these single women heralds the disappearance of the pre-industrial family production unit, which increasingly found itself displaced from the 'developed urban market economies', of which, as we have seen, Dijon was one. Such economies provided opportunities for wage work, often piecework, which enabled single women to attain a degree of economic autonomy. However, this work also consigned its practitioners to low labor status and little control over the process of production and distribution.[39] Tellingly, the women involved in the needle trades and in spinning in Dijon had tax assessments significantly lower than men in these trades.[40] This discrepancy all but disappears among unskilled workers, where impoverishment was blind to gender distinction.

At the same time, it is clear that the expansion of work opportunities for women in the city must also be linked to the growth of commerce, especially retail commerce. The women involved in commercial activities also had tax assessments somewhat lower than men engaged in similar ventures, but their wealth nonetheless put them well above the median for the entire urban population, male and female alike. These women help to explain why, even with the expanding numbers of poorly paid artisan and unskilled women, the tax status of the women appearing on the *taille* rolls diminished only marginally in 1643 and 1750, after rising markedly in 1556. Another part of the explanation lies with those individuals described simply as *madames*, *demoiselles*, or *bourgeoises*, whose wealth again was well above average. In Dijon, as elsewhere in France in the seventeenth and eighteenth centuries, spinsters and widows of the middle classes and aristocracy were increasing, living on income from family property (made available by bourgeois acquisition of the surrounding countryside) without generating new wealth or draining existing patrimonies for dowries.[41] Any downward pressure on the wealth median of female heads of households exerted by changes in the forms of production was thus counteracted by growth in the number of relatively well-to-do women who never married and by expanding commercial opportunities that some of Dijon's women were able to seize.

Given the state of research on women in early modern Dijon, any generalizations must be speculative. Some of our findings in Dijon do appear to substantiate developments suggested elsewhere in France and northern Europe, and some offer information on city women that is new. The increased incidence of women as heads of households on Dijon's tax rolls in the seventeenth and especially eighteenth centuries and their economic profile points toward marriage at a later age (and the related increasing difficulty of remarrying or of marrying at all), the eclipsing of the pre-industrial family-based economy by the growing market economy, and perhaps the ebbing of a patriarchal culture. These may all be interrelated phenomena which, with more research, may be shown as developments of utmost importance.

V

This examination of tax rolls from four different centuries has served to lay bare a series of significant transformations in Dijon's social structure and wealth distribution between the waning Middle Ages and the eighteenth century. During the course of these years, the number of noblemen, royal officials, professional men, *rentiers*, and merchants living within the city increased dramatically, expanding no less than five-fold. Very quickly, these changes upset the wealth hierarchy typical of the late medieval city, yielding a sharp new disparity between the situation of Dijon's mercantile and professional classes on the one hand and the rest of the population on the other. More slowly, they increased demand for a wider range of consumer goods and services, especially as restraints on conspicuous consumption were loosened from the later seventeenth century onward, producing a shift in artisan production toward the provision of a widening range of luxury consumer items that was all the more marked in light of the decline of the traditional mainstay of the city's economy, textile production. As the growth of officialdom, the extension of bourgeois control over land in the surrounding countryside, and the increase in regional and long-distance trade all sucked additional wealth into the city, some of this in turn seems to have found its way into the purses of the city's artisans and agricultural workers, at least to judge by evidence of absolute artisan enrichment between 1550 and 1650 and a relative increase in the per capita wealth of the (now significantly smaller) agricultural population between 1643 and 1750. These, and perhaps other social changes, which still have not yet been clearly elucidated, also permitted a growing number of women to head households of their own and to pay taxes, which suggests that they were better off than their distant predecessors who appeared independently on the tax rolls at the beginning of our period. These were all fundamental changes, making the Dijon of 1750 a very different place from that of 1464. To what extent were these changes more broadly typical of France's cities as a whole? To what extent were they a product of Dijon's status as a provincial administrative capital and commercial hub, or of other, purely local circumstances? The answers to these questions must await further research.

NOTES: CHAPTER 4

I would like to thank John Bohstedt, Cathy Matson and Michael McDonald for their comments and criticisms on various drafts of this article. Research was made possible by financial support from Northwestern University, the University of Tennessee, and the Institut Français (Gilbert Chinard Scholarship for French Studies).

1 See, for example, Jean-Claude Perrot, *Genèse d'une ville moderne: Caen au XVIIIe siècle* (Paris: Mouton, 1975), ch. 6, and Jean-Pierre Poussou, *Bordeaux et le Sud-Ouest au XVIIIe siècle: Croissance économique et attraction urbaine* (Paris: Editions de l'Ecole des Hautes Etudes en Sciences Sociales, 1983), pp. 25–31.

2 Marcel Couturier, *Recherches sur les structures sociales de Châteaudun, 1525–1789* (Paris: S.E.V.P.E.N., 1969), esp. pp. 115–20.

3 The *taille* registers are preserved in the A.C. Dijon, series L. Those utilized here are registers 159 (1464), 170 (1556), 234 (1643), and 288 (1750). None of these years was a time of exceptional disruption or disaster.

4 102 clerics appear on the 1750 tax roll, whereas the census for 1753, A.C. Dijon, L32 (*liasse*), lists 1184 regular and secular clergy. It also counts the number of poor and sick at the various hospitals (608), as well as the number of servants (2033) engaged by the individuals recorded in great detail by clerical and judicial office as well as military rank. Unfortunately, this document simply lists a total number of 'chefs de famille taillables'. However, despite the implication that the individuals on the census were tax exempt, we cannot make this asssumpton because many offices and ranks listed on the census were filled by taxed individuals in 1750.

5 Pierre Gras *et al.*, *Histoire de Dijon* (Toulouse: Privat, 1980), p. 120.

6 The 1753 census does, however, count 100 'gentilshommes ou anoblis', where the 1750 tax roll lists 53 non-robe nobles and 26 men bearing the prestigious honorific 'Monsieur'.

7 I have undertaken such a comparison for Saint-Jean parish on the basis of A.C. Dijon, L195 (1560), 198 (1566), 200 (1571), 205 (1579), 230 (1630), 231 (1636), and 234 (1643). No other occupations were as consistently recorded only inter-

mittently by those charged with the responsibility of making up the tax rolls.

8   See Table 4.1, p. 139.

9   For the range of evidence available about Dijon's population in the seventeenth and eighteenth centuries, see Gaston Roupnel, *La Ville et la campagne au XVIIe siècle: Etude sur les populations du Pays Dijonnais* (Paris: A. Colin, 1955), pp. 109–12, 127; G. Bouchard, 'Dijon au XVIIIe siècle: Les dénombrements d'habitants', *Annales de Bourgogne*, vol. 25 (1953), pp. 30–65. In my book, *Hands of Honor: The World of the Artisans in Early Modern France (Dijon, 1550–1650)* (Ithaca, NY: Cornell University Press, 1988), I have estimated Dijon's population at 14,500 in 1556 and 21,000 in 1643. In light of subsequent trends, 24,000 seems a reasonable estimate for 1750.

10 Jan de Vries, *European Urbanization, 1500–1800* (Cambridge, Mass.: Harvard University Press, 1984), p. 35.

11 For 1556 and 1643 the figures are, respectively, 193 and 216.

12 Roupnel, *La Ville et la campagne*, p. 134; A.C. Dijon, L32.

13 Roland Mousnier, *The Institutions of France under the Absolute Monarchy, 1598–1789*, trans. Arthur Goldhammer, Vol. 2 (Chicago: University of Chicago Press, 1984), p. 344.

14 Richard Gascon, 'La France du mouvement: Les commerces et les villes', in Braudel and Labrousse, Vol. 1, pp. 384–5.

15 Robert Halsband (ed.), *The Selected Letters of Lady Mary Wortley Montagu* (New York: Viking Penguin, 1986), p. 169.

16 Roupnel, *La Ville et la campagne*, p. 112; Pierre de Saint Jacob, *Les Paysans de la Bourgogne du nord au dernier siècle de l'ancien régime* (Paris: Les Belles Lettres, 1960), pp. 257, 305.

17 During the fifteenth and sixteenth centuries the volume of wine entering Dijon remained roughly constant, most of it coming from the immediate environs and the Côte. Much of the wine was brought to market by small producers (nearby villagers as well as Dijonnais who owned and harvested small vineyards), but the larger volume imports and the higher quality *crus* were carried there by merchants. In the fifteenth century these wholesalers were 'foreigners', but by the sixteenth century they were native Dijonnais, mercantile families who would continue to hold prominent places in Dijon's wine trade. See C. Tournier, 'Le Vin à Dijon de 1430 à 1560: Ravitaillement et commerce', *Annales de Bourgogne*, vol. 22 (1950), pp. 7–32. Many historians have pointed to the first half of the seventeenth century as a period when regional economies rebounded from the disruption caused by war and became increasingly commercialized, especially in goods like wine and grain, and integrated around hub cities; see Jan de Vries, *The Economy of Europe in an Age of Crisis, 1600–1750* (Cambridge: Cambridge University Press, 1976), pp. 63–9; Hugues Neveux, 'Prélèvements et contrôles urbains', in G. Duby (ed.), *Histoire de la France Urbaine*, Vol. 3 (Paris: Seuil, 1981), p. 81. In Burgundy and Dijon the wine and grain trades were important commodities in this process; see E. Le Roy Ladurie, 'Les Masses profondes: la paysannerie', in Braudel and Labrousse, Vol. 1, pp. 762–3.

18 Roupnel, *La Ville et la campagne*, pt 3, ch. 1; Saint Jacob, 'Mutations économiques et sociales dans la campagne bourguignonne à la fin du XVIe siècle', *Etudes Rurales*, vol. 1 (1961), pp. 34–49, and idem, 'La Communauté villageoise', *Annales de Bourgogne*, vol. 12 (1941), pp. 169–202.

19 Roupnel, *La Ville et la campagne*, pp. 81–2; Saint Jacob, *Les Paysans de la Bourgogne*, pp. 153–5, 166, 257, 305, 315; Pierre Goubert, 'Les Campagnes françaises', in Braudel and Labrousse, vol. 2, pp. 114–16.

20 I detail these developments at length in my *Hands of Honor*.

21 How many of the artisans listed on the tax rolls were master craftsmen and how

many were journeymen? The *taille* records do not consistently distinguish master craftsmen from journeymen, but cross-referencing names drawn from sources sensitive to honorific epithets (notarized contracts, Town Council deliberations, and the like) with the names on the tax rolls reveals that 75 to 83 per cent of the artisans named on the tax rolls were masters in 1556, while 67 to 86 per cent were in 1643. From what is generally known about the evolution of the French guild system, it is likely that the percentage of masters was even higher in the fifteenth century and lower in the eighteenth. Farr, *Hands of Honor*, ch. 2; Maurice Garden, *Lyon et les lyonnais au 18e siècle* (Paris: Flammarion, 1970), pt 2, ch. 2 and pt 3, ch. 2; Emile Coornaert, *Les Corporations en France avant 1789*, 2nd edn (Paris: Editions Ouvrières, 1968).

22 We might wonder if the 'slight recovery' simply reflects more complete registration of women on the tax rolls. It is difficult to say, but other sources from the sixteenth and seventeenth centuries that I have examined, notably depositions of witnesses in court where a woman's vocation would be recorded, never reveal women involved in weaving and only rarely in spinning before the eighteenth century, largely confirming what the tax rolls tell us. In these documents craftswomen overwhelmingly called themselves *couturières*, or seamstresses, a sizeable workforce that was increasingly heading households by the eighteenth century and thus appearing on the tax rolls.

23 Appendix B itemizes the specific number of artisans listed under each trade designation on each of the tax rolls.

24 Roupnel, *La Ville et la campagne*, pp. 89, 151; Pierre Léon, 'La Réponse de l'industrie', in Braudel and Labrousse, Vol. 2, p. 250.

25 For useful and concise overviews of this process, see Peter Kriedte, *Peasants, Landlords and Merchant Capitalists: Europe and the World Economy, 1500–1800* (Cambridge: Cambridge University Press, 1983); de Vries, *Urbanization*, pp. 231–46; and J. K. J. Thomson, 'Variations in industrial structure in pre-industrial Languedoc', in Maxine Berg *et al.* (eds), *Manufacture in Town and Country Before the Factory* (Cambridge: Cambridge University Press, 1983), pp. 61–91.

26 Pierre Chaunu, *La Civilisation de l'Europe des lumières* (Paris: Flammarion, 1982), pp. 348, 402. See also Fernand Braudel, *Capitalism and Material Life, 1400–1800* (New York: Harper and Row, 1974), chs 3–4; Pierre Goubert, *The Ancien Regime* (New York: Harper and Row, 1973), pp. 136, 174; Carlo Cipolla, *Before the Industrial Revolution: European Society and Economy, 1000–1700*, 2nd edn (New York: Norton, 1980), pp. 34–7; André Corvisier, *Arts et sociétés dans l'Europe du XVIIIe siècle* (Paris: Presses Universitaires de France, 1978), pp. 31–3. Robert Forster's *The House of Saulx-Tavanes: Versailles and Burgundy, 1700–1830* (Baltimore, Md: Johns Hopkins University Press, 1971) is an excellent study of consumption patterns among the court aristocracy; see esp. p. 127.

27 Roupnel, *La Ville et la campagne*, pp. 118–19.

28 Chaunu, *Civilisation de l'Europe des lumières*, pp. 397, 401.

29 Joseph Garnier, *Essai sur l'histoire de la moutarde de Dijon* (Dijon: Jobard, 1854), pp. 11–27; *Dumas on Food: Selections from 'Le Grand Dictionnaire de Cuisine' by Alexandre Dumas*, trans. Alan and Jane Davidson (London: Michael Joseph, 1979), pp. 182–6. Thanks are due to Rebecca More for her knowledgeable assistance on this question.

30 For assessment procedures, see Françoise Humbert, *Les Finances municipales de Dijon du XIVe siècle à 1477* (Paris: Les Belles Lettres, 1961), ch. 4; Martin Wolfe, *The Fiscal System of Renaissance France* (New Haven, Conn.: Yale University Press, 1972), appendix G; Roger Doucet, *Les Institutions de la France au XVIe siècle*, Vol. 2 (Paris: Picard, 1948), pp. 562–77; Marcel Marion, *Les Impôts directs sous l'ancien régime* (Geneva: Slatkine, 1974), pp. 4–32.

31 A.C. Dijon, Series B, Register 278, fo. 259 (24 May 1641); A.D. Côte-d'Or, *Notaires* no. 1936 (5 October 1645).

32 A. Chapuis, *Les Anciennes corporations dijonnaises: règlements, statuts, et ordonnances* (Dijon: Nourry, 1906), pp. 286–92.

33 Farr, *Hands of Honor*, ch. 2. The figures are based on an evenly distributed random sample of 983 marriage contracts involving an artisan family as at least one of the parties. The 150 per cent increase reflects a comparison of the period 1551–1600 and 1601–1650, adjusted for inflation of 12.6 per cent in wholesale grain price recorded annually in Dijon's market.

34 ibid. These figures are based on an evenly distributed random sample of 524 real estate transactions involving artisans in some capacity; between 1550 and 1595, 118 masters invested 11,849 livres tournois in real estate, while from 1596 to 1650, 157 masters pumped 65,670 livres (adjusted to purchasing power in grain, 57,396) into real estate.

35 Olwen Hufton, 'Women without men: widows and spinsters in Britain and France in the eighteenth century', *Journal of Family History*, vol. 9 (Winter, 1984), p. 357, reporting Jacques Dupâquier's summary for France (*La Population française au XVIIe et XVIIIe siècles* (Paris: Presses Universitaires de France, 1979), pp. 60–1; G. Cabourdin, 'Le Remariage en France sous l'ancien régime (seizième–dix-huitième siècles)', in Dupâquier *et al.* (eds), *Marriage and Remarriage in Populations of the Past* (New York: Academic Press, 1981), pp. 273–85. But cf. Jean-Pierre Bardet, *Rouen aux XVIIe et XVIIIe siècles: les mutations d'un espace social* (Paris: S.E.D.E.S., 1983), p. 322.

36 See Table 4.1.

37 Natalie Z. Davis, 'Women in the crafts in sixteenth-century Lyon', in Barbara Hanawalt (ed.), *Women and Work in Preindustrial Europe* (Bloomington, Ind.: Indiana University Press, 1986), pp. 187–9; Martha C. Howell, 'Women, the family economy, and the structures of market production in cities of Northern Europe during the Late Middle Ages', in ibid., pp. 200–1.

38 Davis, 'Women in the crafts', p. 180.

39 Howell, 'Women, the family economy, and the structures of market production', pp. 202, 216.

40 Male tailors ranked in the 56th wealth percentile; female seamstresses in the 42nd. Male spinners ranked in the 36th percentile; women in this trade in the 16th.

41 Hufton, 'Women without men', pp. 357, 359, 367–9.

APPENDIX 4A   SPECIFIC *QUALITÉS* BY CATEGORIES USED IN TABLE 4.1

1464:

High Officials
Mayor, *Bailli, Maîtres des Comptes* and *Procureur de Duc.*

Lesser Officials
Auditeurs des Comptes and *Controlleur d'Audience.*

Employees of the Duke or Town
bailiffs (*sergeants*), tipstaffs (*huissiers*), mintmasters, *concierges*, secretaries, criers, buglers, drummers, archers, crossbowmen, and clerks of the Mayor, of the *Procureur*, and *des Comptes.*

Professions
solicitors (*procureurs*), *maîtres*, notaries, doctors (*médecins*), writers, and school-masters.

Commerce
merchants, apothecaries, mercers, and resellers.

Hôtellerie
innkeepers and *rôtisseurs*.

Transport
carters, couriers, and teamsters.

Agriculturalists
vignerons, gardeners, and shepherds.

Urban Workers, Unskilled
laborers (*manouvriers*) and loaders.

Other
barbers, cooks, servants, an almoner, a cellarer, and a priest.

1556:

High Officials
Mayor, *Syndic* of Dijon, municipal aldermen, presidents at the Parlement and *Chambre des Comptes*, *Elus*, *Bailli*, *Maîtres de Chambre des Comptes*, royal councillors at the Parlement, Guard of the Seal, Lieutenant Generals at the Bailliage and at the Chancellory, *Avocats du Roi* at the Parlement, at the Chambre des Comptes and at the Bailliage, *Procureurs* and *Soliciteurs du Roi* at the Parlement, at the Chambre des Comptes and at the Table de Marbre, *Trésoriers*, and royal mintmasters.

Lesser Officials
Greffiers at the Chancellory, at the *Mairie*, and at the Bailliage, receivers at the Bailliage, at the Chambre des Comptes, and of the municipality, auditors, correctors, controllers, and saltmasters.

Employees of the King or Town
Civil: bailiffs, tipstaffs, concierges, gatekeepers, jailers, measurers, weighers, *grenetiers*, mintworkers, licensed midwives, bathmaster, brothelkeeper, *Maître des Halles*, trumpeters, criers, and municipal surveyor.

Military: captains, archers, crossbowmen, musketeers, militia officers, and guards.

Professions
barristers (*avocats*), solicitors, *maîtres*, notaries, surgeons, medical doctors, doctor in law, printers/booksellers, scribes and clerks, and schoolmasters/mistresses.

Commerce
merchants, apothecaries, mercers, and resellers.

Transport
carters and couriers.

Hôtellerie
innkeepers, tavernkeepers, and *rôtisseurs.*

Agriculturalists
vignerons, peasants, fishermen, gardeners, and shepherds.

Urban Workers
laborers, loaders, washerwomen and men.

Other
servants, barbers, cooks, musicians, tenniscourt-keepers, churchwardens, a chaplain, a
priest and a curé.

1643:

High Officials
Mayor, *Syndic* of Dijon, aldermen, presidents at the Parlement, the Chambre des
Comptes, and *aux Requêtes, maîtres* at the Chambre des Comptes and *Requêtes,* royal
councillors at the Parlement, *aux Requêtes,* at the Table de Marbre, at the Bailliage, *de
l'Artillerie, du Taillon,* and of the Prince, Guard of the Seal, Commissar of War,
Lieutenants of the *Prevôté,* at the Bailliage, and at the Table de Marbre, *Avocats du Roi*
at the Parlement, at the Chambre des Comptes, *Procureur du Roi* at the Parlement and at
the royal mint, Royal Solicitor at the Chambre des Comptes, *Trésoriers,* royal
mintmasters, *Général de la Gabelle,* and Grand Master of Streams and Forests.

Lesser Officials
Greffiers at the Parlement, at the mint, at the *Tournelle, aux Requêtes,* at the Table de
Marbre, and at the *Prevôté,* receivers at the Parlement, at the Chambre des Comptes, and
of the municipality, paymasters, officials of the seals, correctors, auditors, *essayeurs de
monnaie,* controllers, saltmasters, and postmasters.

Employees
Civil: bailiffs, tipstaffs, *commis,* concierges, gatekeepers, measurers, mintworkers,
secretaries, licensed midwives, coachmen for the governor, the prince, etc., and
bathmasters for the governor, the prince, etc.

Military: captains, archers, musketeers, soldiers, guards, *gendarmes,* and a royal military
engineer.

Professions
barristers, solicitors, *maîtres,* notaries, *praticiens,* surgeons, medical doctors, printers/
booksellers, writers, clerks, and schoolmasters/mistresses.

Commerce
merchants, apothecaries, mercers, pedlars (of flowers, fish, pictures, etc.), and resellers.

167

Hôtellerie
innkeepers and tavernkeepers.

Transport
carters and couriers.

Agriculturalists
vignerons, peasants, gardeners, and shepherds.

Urban Workers
laborers, washerwomen and men, and loaders.

Other
barbers, cooks, bathmasters, tenniscourt-keepers, musicians, churchwardens, a choir-master, a dean, a priest, and an abbé.

1750:

High Officials
Mayor, *Syndic* of Dijon, aldermen, *Syndic* of the Estates, the Governor, *Elus*, Presidents at the Parlement, at the Chambre des Comptes, *aux Requêtes*, and at the Bureau des Finances, *Bailli*, *Maîtres* at the Chambre des Comptes, royal councillors at the Parlement, the Chambre des Comptes, *aux Requêtes*, at the Table de Marbre, *du Taillon*, and at the Bailliage, royal secretaries, war commissars, Intendant, *Subdélégués*, Governor at the Chancellory, Lieutenants at the Chancellory, at the Bailliage, at the *Maîtrise* (of Streams and Forests) and at the Table de Marbre, *Avocats du Roi* at the Parlement, at the Chambre des Comptes, at the Bailliage, at the Table de Marbre, at the mint, at the Bureau des Finances, and at the *Trésor de l'Epargne*, *Procureurs (et substituts) du Roi* at the Parlement, at the Chambre des Comptes, at the Bailliage, at the Table de Marbre, and at the *Grenier à Sel*, *Trésoriers de la France*, *Trésorier Général des Etats*, *Trésorier Extraordinaire des Guerres*, royal mintmasters, royal postmasters, and Guard of the Seals.

Lesser Officials
Greffiers at the Parlement, at the *Trésor de l'Epargne*, at the Seal, at the Bailliage, at the *Grenier à Sel*, at the Chambre des Comptes, at the Table de Marbre, at the mint, and at the *Prevôté*, receivers of the municipality, of the *taillon*, of the royal domain, *des consignations*, and at the Bureau de Tabac, collectors of the *taille*, auditors, paymasters, controllers of the municipality, *des Haras*, of the Post, *des Finances*, *au Tabac*, at the mint, of the Royal domain (forests), at the Chambre des Comptes and *Ordinaires des Guerres*, saltmasters, *Directeurs des Fermes*, *Avocats* and *Procureurs des Pauvres*, and merchandise inspectors.

Employees
Civil: bailiffs, tipstaffs, *commis*, concierges, gatekeepers, jailers, buglers, drummers, criers, *pompiers*, streetsweepers, municipal surveyors, municipal clockmaster, quarter-master, measurers, *grenetiers*, mintworkers, workers *au tabac*, midwives, clerks, secretaries, coachmen for governor, prince, etc., and traffic directors.

Military: archers, crossbowmen, musketeers, soldiers, fifer, cannonier, guards, militia officers, *cavaliers*, and military engineers.

Professions
barristers, solicitors, *maîtres*, notaries, surgeons, dentists, medical doctors, printers/booksellers/bookbinders, writers, schoolmasters/mistresses, grammarians, latin teachers, and university professors.

Commerce
merchants, entrepreneurs, apothecaries, grocers, mercers, resellers, and pedlars of various items.

Transport
carters, couriers, litter-carriers, and liverymen.

Hôtellerie
innkeepers, tavernkeepers, cooks, café-operators, caterers, and restaurateurs.

Agriculturalists
vignerons, peasants, gardeners, and shepherds.

Urban Workers
laborers, washerwomen and loaders.

Other
organists, singers, musicians, violinists, dancemasters, bassoonists, servants, canons, chaplains, deans, choirmasters, sacristans, churchwardens, nuns, monks, priests, abbés, *mépartistes*, and curés.

APPENDIX 4B   NUMERICAL REPRESENTATION OF INDIVIDUAL CRAFTS LISTED ON TAX ROLLS (MALE AND FEMALE)

	1464	1556	1643	1750
WEAPONS/METALWORKING				
Crossbow boltmakers	9	none	none	none
Spurmakers	4	1	3	2
Artillerymakers	1	4	2	none
Armorers	1	8	2	6
Unspecified weapons	1	none	none	none
Swordpolishers	none	8	10	2
Blacksmiths	27	19	8	10
Locksmiths	11	14	13	24
Coppersmiths	9	10	4	8
Cutlers	7	1	3	6
Pinmakers	4	6	1	2
Lanternmakers	3	3	1	none

Appendix 4B   *continued*

	1464	1556	1643	1750
Ironworkers	2	2	2	none
Toolmakers	1	8	5	8
Bellmakers	1	none	none	none
Drillmakers	1	1	6	none
Nailmakers	1	none	1	none
Foundrymen	none	5	2	none
Rivetmakers	none	3	2	none
Gearmakers	none	1	none	none
Copper founders	none	1	none	none
Clockmakers	none	none	3	5
Scrap ironworkers	none	none	none	5
Tinsmiths	none	none	none	4
CONSTRUCTION				
Carpenters	33	35	21	35
Masons	33	58	57	20
Roofers/Tilers	15	17	27	27
Quarrymen	3	7	6	5
Leadworkers	2	none	none	none
Plasterers	1	18	14	12
Paviors	1	2	3	6
Earthmasons	none	8	3	none
Sawyers	none	none	7	3
Stonecutters	none	none	2	46
Tombstonecarvers	none	none	none	11
Marblecutters	none	none	none	1
FOOD				
Oventenders	32	1	none	6
Bakers	20	37	61	62
Butchers	18	39	16	20
Fowlers	8	13	9	2
Butcher's aids	5	6	none	7
Tripers	5	3	3	6
Millers	3	5	5	6
Pastrycooks	3	36	25	12
Oilmakers	2	7	7	12
Cheesemakers	1	none	none	1
Obliers	none	1	none	none
Miller's valets	none	none	none	4
Pig-slaughterers	none	none	none	2
LUXURY				
Goldsmiths	13	17	24	15

	1464	1556	1643	1750
Pewterers	7	9	5	3
Painters	6	4	6	11
Glassmaker/Painters	2	6	6	14
Engravers	1	1	none	2
Copper-potters	1	none	none	none
Illuminators	1	1	none	none
Sculptors	1	2	2	14
Mirrormakers	1	none	none	none
Embroiderers	none	9	5	3
Glaziers	none	5	1	2
Wigmakers	none	none	none	32
Faiencemakers	none	none	none	15
Faiencepainters	none	none	none	1
Carriagemakers	none	none	none	14
Gilders	none	none	none	4
Jewelers	none	none	none	3
TEXTILES				
Clothworkers	55	4	none	none
Linenweavers	53	*	*	*
Weavers	*	46	41	72
Woolcarders	22	11	none	2
Fullers	16	9	none	none
Woolen clothweavers	16	*	*	*
Shearers	14	22	3	5
Dyers	9	10	5	12
Drapers	7	8	12	7
Tapestry/rugweavers	3	2	5	9
Wool and cotton spinners	none	none	1	37
Lacemenders	none	none	none	3
Bleachers	none	none	none	3
CLOTHING				
Tailors and seamstresses	68	73	80	144
Hosiers	22	25	none	none
Hatters	17	15	15	14
Counterpointers	4	3	none	none
Agletmakers	2	none	none	none
Passementiers	none	4	3	1
Doubletmakers	none	2	none	none
Linenseamstresses	none	2	1	4
Buttonmakers	none	1	9	7
Pursemakers (cloth)	none	none	1	8

*On tax rolls of 1556, 1643, and 1750 linenweavers and woolenweavers were classified as simply 'weavers'.

Appendix 4B *continued*

	1464	1556	1643	1750
Knitters	none	none	none	9
Threadmakers	none	none	none	1
Culottesmakers	none	none	none	1
WOODWORKING				
Furnituremakers/Wainscotters	14	39	34	71
Wheelwrights	12	12	12	23
Woodenshoemakers	5	none	none	none
Drillers	1	1	none	none
Turners	none	4	4	13
Coffinmakers	none	none	4	2
Chestmakers	none	none	1	2
Chairmakers	none	none	1	1
LEATHER				
Shoemakers	68	37	45	170
Tanners	14	15	18	10
Furriers	12	16	4	4
Curriers	11	5	6	10
Fur-skirtmakers	10	none	none	none
Cobblers	10	35	85	68
Harnessmakers	9	9	3	15
Parchmentmakers	9	12	6	1
Saddlers	7	10	10	6
Quivermakers	2	1	2	none
Gaitermakers	2	1	5	1
Pouchmakers	1	none	none	none
Glovers	1	2	9	1
Chamoiseurs	none	none	none	4
WINE-RELATED				
Barrelcoopers	40	29	48	51
Vinegarmakers	none	6	11	41
Basketmakers	none	3	1	19
Bottlemakers	none	1	none	none
MISCELLANEOUS				
Ropemakers	8	6	4	17
Candlemakers	7	16	29	19
Spicers	6	none	none	none
Cardmakers	3	3	none	19
Earthenpotters	2	1	none	none
Carbonmakers	2	none	1	none
Makers of unspecified items	3	4	none	7

	1464	1556	1643	1750
Makers of *Bourées*	none	1	none	1
Makers of *Couvères*	none	1	none	1
Makers of *Bouleviers*	none	1	none	none
Tallow workers	none	none	3	8
Combmakers	none	none	none	4
Mattressmakers	none	none	none	3
Umbrellamakers	none	none	none	2
Rapeurs de tabac	none	none	none	2
Rosarymakers	none	none	none	1
Bellowsmakers	none	none	none	1
Organmakers	none	none	none	1
Makers of *Trace*	none	none	none	1
Makers of *Ratoiret*	none	none	none	1

5

The artisans of Aix-en-Provence in the sixteenth century: A micro-analysis of social relationships

CLAIRE DOLAN

Within the cities of the Ancien Régime, artisans formed one of the fundamental elements of the population, their wide variety of skills responding to an urban society whose needs were diverse. Historians have generally focused their attention on the common economic situation and similar position in the social hierarchy shared by the members of this group. In doing so, the elements of diversity that also characterized it have been obscured.

This article will highlight certain differences in behavior between the members of different occupations. But my examination, I should stress from the outset, will be less concerned with groups than with individuals. Choosing the city of Aix-en-Provence as my point of observation, I shall organize my exploration of the contexts in which certain of its artisans lived out their lives by examining one trade after another, yet in the final analysis it is the people within these trades who interest me. This might seem nominalism run amok in the study of urban society. I would argue that such detailed exploration of the artisan world is especially appropriate at the present historiographic moment. The broad contours of early modern French urban society are now well established. What we need to do is to look closer. Doing this requires methods that are slightly different from those that have generally governed the analysis of urban society.

Inevitably, urban history is the history of large numbers of people. Ever since historians recognized that the course of social change could only be illuminated by exploring the fates of large numbers, they have deployed a wealth of imagination in order to confer a certain intelligibility upon the great mass of individual destinies that comprise the history of a given society. New sources have been submitted to statistical examination. The data they contain have been classified, counted, examined for their statistical significance, and used to construct models and typologies. A number of magisterial theses have been particularly influential in determining the methods employed in the study of French cities.[1] These typically have sought to reconstruct the totality of urban society, and necessarily their authors were forced to classify the

174

residents of the cities in question into socio-professional categories, which in turn served as the basis for the analysis of demographic, economic and social behavior. Some historians have sought to isolate specific groups of town dwellers for an intensive investigation of their specific social origins and behavior, but these sorts of studies have been confined overwhelmingly to elite groups, whose members were typically few in number and for whom the sources are often particularly abundant.[2] Whether these studies have dealt with an entire city or a specific group, the sources and methods utilized have been similar. By now, the questions and techniques of urban social history have become so well established that it can appear as though the only originality that can arise from additional studies is the originality that derives from the uniqueness of a specific city or social group.[3]

But statistical analysis and abstract categories are insufficient to do justice to the complexity of the networks of social relationships within which people find their lives woven. Statistics cannot be dispensed with entirely, for they are necessary to identify broad patterns. Equally indispensable, however, are case studies, which can reconstitute the complexity of individual networks of social relations, and which become particularly significant when the recurrence of similar patterns confers upon certain cases the value of models. Recent debates among French social historians have pitted the partisans of quantitative, 'serial' approaches to history against those who stress the value of detailed case studies of individual groups, episodes, or events.[4] I would prefer not to see these as mutually exclusive approaches to the past. Instead, after initially defining certain parameters of Aixois society on the basis of statistical investigation, I will then rely upon the microscopic observation of certain sectors of the city's artisan population, divided into as many individuals as the documents present me with. It is the relations which these people formed among themselves that I shall attempt to follow, linking together the documents about people whom the documents show to be linked.

The sources upon which I shall rely are notarial records. These have hardly been neglected by urban historians; in fact, they have formed one of the chief bases for more than a generation for the statistical analysis of urban society. The kinds of analyses that have become standard, however, have depended upon extracting from the mass of notarized contracts only certain kinds of documents and then recording a few, limited bits of the information that these documents contain. Thus, attitudes toward death have been studied on the basis of the frequency with which certain sorts of clauses recur in long series of wills.[5] The size, wealth, and marital alliances of different groups within the population have been explored by using the indications that marriage contracts provide about the status of partners to a marriage and the sums of money provided as dowries.[6] These sorts of methods were thoroughly original and highly imaginative when they were first developed, and nobody would gainsay the results that their utilization has yielded, but it must be admitted that their repetitive use has gradually deadened the degree of imagination associated with their employment while producing a dissection of the notarial records into detachable bits that robs them of their full coherence. Of course, it can be argued that the examination of carefully delineated samples of selected sorts of documents represented the only way in which urban historians could have summoned up the courage to attack the vast ocean of notarial records that survives for many early modern cities. The notarial archives present any student of early modern cities with a serious case of conscience; they contain exceptional pieces of information that can haunt the researcher's imagination, but they are simply so diverse and abundant that they defy simple utilization, the more so in that they are generally uncatalogued. Since the superabundance of documents can be even more fatal to historical research than their paucity, medievalists have so far been the only historians to undertake the systematic exploitation of all of the notarial records surviving for a single city, the mass of such documents being considerably less great prior to the sixteenth century.[7] And yet, early modern village studies have shown how exceptionally revealing the intensive utilization of notarial archives can be for charting the movements of individuals and families across time and space.[8] Perhaps another approach to the great mass of urban notarial documents can be developed.

WEDDING PHOTOS

The notarial documents that provide the most information about the links between individuals are marriage contracts and wills. Even though the sources do not exist that would enable us to determine the precise percentage of Aixois who were married or who died in the sixteenth century for whom marriage contracts or wills have survived, the notarization of documents was commonplace among all sectors of the population, and such documents survive in massive quantities.[9] They satisfy the criteria of abundance and representativeness demanded by quantitative research. At the same time, they permit the reconstruction of individual destinies on the basis of the picture of social relations that each one provides for the individuals who appear in them.

In order to respect the coherence of the documents, I have considered each marriage contract somewhat like the wedding photographs found in many modern homes. In a wedding picture, the families of the couple pose for posterity around the bride and groom. Subsequent generations then entertain themselves trying to guess who is who on the basis of their place in the picture. Similarly, each marriage contract alludes to between five and twenty close relations of the parties to the marriage – relatives, spiritual kin, friends, and fellow workers – whose precise relationship with the wedding couple may or may not be specified, but who appear in the document because they assisted the couple in drawing up the terms of the marriage contract or offered gifts to be added to the marriage portion. Although I have excluded from consideration the witnesses who signed the marriage contract at the foot, since these were often people used time and again as witnesses by the same notary and who had no necessary personal relationship to the parties to the contract, I have noted the identity of all of the other individuals appearing in the contracts.

The sheer size of a city requires some recourse to sampling. For the purposes of this study, I have consulted 1288 marriage contracts drawn up between 1557 and 1575. My sample includes every surviving contract for the years 1559, 1563, 1567, 1571, and 1575, and an average of 25 randomly chosen contracts per year for the other years between 1557 and 1575.[10] This sample yields 9750 individuals, whom we can begin to situate socially within the network of relationships suggested by the contract in which they appear. Many of these individuals then reappear in other contracts, enabling one to widen the networks defined by individual contracts. I have also examined a sample of wills comparable to that of marriage contracts, which I intend to analyze, using the same principle of respect for the logic of the document itself that I have applied to the marriage contracts. This analysis is as yet incomplete, but some of the evidence provided by the wills about individuals appearing in the marriage contracts has been incorporated into this essay. To these networks can also be added additional information from the notarial archives as well as from other sources, notably wardship records.[11]

Needless to say, the picture of Aixois society that these procedures yield can only be a synchronic one, for nineteen years form too short a time to observe significant changes in the sorts of patterns that these methods reveal. Needless to say, too, the methods employed here can only reconstruct part of the life course of many of the individuals who appear in the marriage contracts, even those who appear in more than one document. Not only are there large gaps both in the documentation itself (not all notarial records from the period have been preserved) and in my sample, but a life simply cannot be inferred from a succession of freeze frames.[12] The arrangement of a series of photographs can pretend to do nothing more than to establish a richer picture of the patterns of relationships linking together different residents of a sixteenth-century city than other methods provide. That in itself is sufficient to shed some new light on urban society and its component groups.

AIX-EN-PROVENCE IN THE SIXTEENTH CENTURY

Aix-en-Provence shared in the post-Black-Death demographic recovery that Europe experienced in the fifteenth and sixteenth centuries and that made it once again, in Pierre Chaunu's famous phrase, a 'monde plein' by the end of the sixteenth century. In Provence, the recovery may have begun somewhat later than elsewhere in France, but it subsequently was extremely vigorous.[13] Between 1471 and 1540, the number of hearths noted on the tax rolls, or *affouagements*, of the province's different communities tripled or even quadrupled. By the middle of the sixteenth century, pre-Black-Death population levels had been re-attained, and the demographic growth was losing the aggressive dynamism that had characterized it for the preceding seventy years. Both the province's cities and its countryside shared the demographic growth, and it does not seem that the percentage of city dwellers within the total population changed significantly. Certain cities were nevertheless profoundly transformed in size and importance, for major population shifts occurred among Provence's towns. Those located in Lower Provence, such as Marseille, Arles, and Aix-en-Provence, rose in prominence, while those – notably Sisteron – located in the interior highlands of Upper Provence, which had still retained considerable importance in the Middle Ages, suffered a relative decline.[14]

These changes in the province's urban network were intimately bound up with regional patterns of migration, which can begin to be glimpsed from the fourteenth century onward. At the beginning of the fifteenth century, the majority of immigrants to the city of Aix came from the southern flanks of the Alps or from the deserted villages of the region immediately surrounding the city. From 1430 onwards, these currents were swollen by a significant number of inhabitants of more distant Alpine regions such as Piedmont, Lombardy, and Liguria, whose numbers augmented steadily until around 1465,

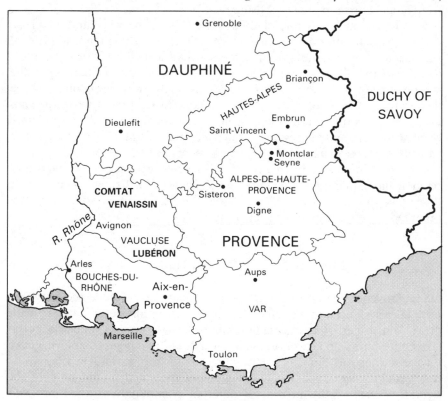

Map 5.1 Aix-en-Provence and its hinterland.

when they began to level off.[15] In the Lubéron region, a quarter of those who drew up wills or marriage contracts between 1460 and 1559 were immigrants, primarily from the Embrunais, Briançonnais or Piedmont. According to Gabriel Audisio, this region's historian, the 'great immigration' here came to an end between 1520 and 1530.[16]

By 1557, the date at which my investigation begins, these interrelated phenomena of demographic recovery and increased long-distance migration may have been largely spent. Aix was now a middling-sized city of ten to fifteen thousand inhabitants. The seat of a Parlement and a Cour des Comptes, it housed large numbers of inhabitants whose destiny was closely bound up with the world of administration and the law, and posterity has particularly retained the city's administrative role. But this should not be permitted to hide its significance as a regional marketplace as well. Aix was located at the bifurcation of the trade routes that led from the Rhône south to Italy and Marseille, and it was actively involved in local economic exchange, especially the wool trade. The single largest sector of its population was engaged in agricultural activities, but artisans were also numerous, forming the second largest sector.[17]

Even though the most rapid era of Provençal population growth was over by the middle of the sixteenth century, certain migratory patterns established in the earlier period of population growth continued to endure and to shape the life courses of many of the city's inhabitants. It was a fundamental characteristic of cities in this era that they depended heavily upon immigration to maintain their population, and later sixteenth-century Aix was no exception to this rule. As Table 5.1 shows, immigrants to the city comprised nearly 60 per cent of the grooms and nearly 50 per cent of the brides whose place of origin is indicated in my sample of marriage contracts. These figures are twice those found by

Table 5.1 Place of origin of those appearing in Aixois marriage contracts, 1557–1575.

	all individuals mentioned		grooms		brides or their father	
	no.	%	no.	%	no.	%
Aix	2945	58	402	43	586	53
Other localities in the Bouches-du-Rhône	756	15	155	17	174	16
Alpes-de-Hte-Provence and Hautes-Alpes	684	13	169	18	190	17
Vaucluse	245	5	56	6	68	6
Var	204	4	61	7	44	4
Italy (incl. Savoyard territories)	38	1	20	2	6	1
Other	136	3	47	5	21	2
Impossible to identify	56	1	23	2	14	1

Note Place of origin is specified for 72 per cent of the grooms, 86 per cent of the brides or their fathers, but only 52 per cent of the other individuals appearing in the contracts.

Audisio in the Lubéron at the height of the 'great migration', a testimony to the especially large place of immigrants within cities.[18] By this period, the Piedmontese, Lombards, and Ligurians who had been so well represented among later fifteenth-century immigrants had largely disappeared once again, but great numbers of immigrants still came from the Alpine regions of Haute-Provence and Dauphiné that today form the departments of the Alpes-de-Haute-Provence, Hautes-Alpes, Isère and Drôme. The relatively few immigrants from what is today the Var highlights the fact that migration in this region tended especially to move southwards towards the coast.[19] Other studies of more recent periods have shown that immigrants to cities often came from clearly defined zones of recruitment that could endure for centuries,[20] and the same appears to have been true for later sixteenth-century Aix, where secular patterns continued to bring to town numerous *gavots*, as the natives of the mountains were known.

FAMILY, MARRIAGE, AND OCCUPATION
The cases of the weavers, leatherworkers, carders, and tailors

Cobblers, tailors, wool-carders and weavers, leatherworkers, and construction workers (masons and plasterers) comprised the most populous groups among Aix's artisans, accounting between them for more than half of all artisan marriage contracts appearing in my sample. Individuals in these trades reappear frequently enough to reveal recurring patterns, and they will consequently form the object of the analysis to follow.

We might begin by considering the extent of intermarriage found among the members of different groups of artisans. The tendency for people to marry others of comparable status has been confirmed time and again by students of early modern France. In the case of urban artisans, studies utilizing marriage contracts have regularly shown that artisans most commonly married the daughters of other artisans or, in certain cases, of those involved in agriculture.[21] But did this pattern of endogamy extend to the specific occupational group of which the individuals in question were members? While Bardet has argued that this simply tended to be less frequent the smaller the trade involved, more precise studies of individual trades have uncovered subtler patterns. As Kaplan stresses, understanding the logic that governed the formation of marriages requires that the problem be approached 'not in a narrowly and abstractly professional framework but in the practical and commercial context of everyday life'.[22]

Doing this requires first of all that we break away from the study of nuclear family units alone and broaden our angle of vision to encompass a wider range of family ties. Given the high mortality rates of the era, it is inadequate to ask simply if, for instance, the wives taken by bakers were themselves daughters of bakers. In many cases, girls' fathers died long before they reached the age where marriage might begin to be contemplated, and if any occupational considerations entered into the choice of a husband in these cases, the trade whose identity it is essential to know could as easily be that of the girl's brother, uncle, or step-father as that of her father. Detailed micro-analyses of individual family networks are thus particularly valuable here, for, by reconstructing more complex patterns of family ties, such a method can take us beyond the simple comparisons between grooms' occupations and those of their brides' fathers that have been the staple of quantitative investigations of urban social structure so far. What we find is that people in certain trades or families intermarried tightly among one another, while among other trades or families networks of marriage extended over a wider area that nonetheless remains intelligible.[23]

Weavers tended to keep things within the family. The occupation was often passed on from father to son, and where weavers did not marry the daughter of another weaver, their new wife generally had some close relative, such as an uncle or former husband, who was himself a weaver. Such tight occupational endogamy was linked to the need for these generally relatively poor artisans to obtain the loom vital to their trade. In three cases out of four, marriage contracts involving weavers include a provision bestowing a loom on the new husband. Thus, Jean Faure's contract stipulates that he will receive from Antoine Chambon, the uncle of his bride, 'a wooden loom for making linen with a comb attached'. The contract allows him to keep the loom in Chambon's house and work on it there, although he can retain the profits of his labor himself. Eight years later, another contract reveals Chambon's widow remarrying another weaver, to whom she grants the right to utlize the shop, loom, and furnishings of her late husband so long as he assumes the responsibility for the two children of her first marriage.[24] In still another contract, we find Jacques Peiron offering the modest dowry of 120 livres to the husband of his daughter, but sweetening the pot with three looms and the tools necessary to make linen. The future husband, too, is a weaver.[25] Finally, four wills of weavers appear in the sample. That of Jacques Bertet indicates that his sole surviving daughter is the wife of a weaver and names as his executor two other weavers, one of whom is his nephew.[26] In this trade, family ties appear to have followed occupational ties very closely, although the sample of weavers is a small one.

The leatherworkers (*curatiers*) behaved very differently. This trade was rarely passed on from father to son; only one of eighteen leatherworkers for whom marriage contracts appear in the sample was the son of another leatherworker, and he, significantly, did not wait for his father's death to marry. Marriages between families of leatherworkers were equally rare. Instead, family ties to carders appear much more frequently. It is not uncommon to find two brothers, one of whom is a leatherworker and the other a carder.[27] Marriages also frequently linked members of these two groups. The son of Pierre Taxil, an Aixois leatherworker, married the daughter of a carder from

Aups; Politre Illary, a leatherworker originally from Dauphiné, married the daughter of a carder from Aix; Marguerite Marguerit married a leatherworker from Digne with the approval of her uncle Pierre, a carder; and Catherine Romier, the daughter of an Aixois leatherworker, married the son of a carder.[28] Carders more commonly passed their trade down from father to son than did the leatherworkers, but they too showed little tendency to marry within the same milieu.

The marriage alliances between carders and leatherworkers reflect a fundamental aspect of Aix's economy: the central role played by those industries based on the transformation of the wool and hides of the sheep and goats raised in the nearby countryside into finished textile and leather products. These economic activities created strong links not only between those who worked in raw wool or unfinished hides, but also between both of these groups and the *nourriguiers* who controlled the herds of sheep and goats that were so plentiful on the hillsides of the region. Leatherworkers and carders can both be found purchasing their raw materials from the same *nourriguiers*. When not forming alliances with one another, both regularly married into families whose occupational activities were practiced in the surrounding countryside. Here, it is worth noting that the dowries of those who married such people were generally small, most often less than 200 livres. Although formally separated into different guilds and different confraternities, the carders and *curatiers* thus appear to have occupied closely overlapping social networks that also linked them to the surrounding countryside.

While, statistically speaking, most leatherworkers were not linked by ties of family or marriage to other leatherworkers, close examination reveals that alliances within the trade were important for a few families. The Laurens family seems to stand at the heart of the leather trades. Simon Laurens wed his daughter to a fellow leatherworker. He also served as the executor of the will of André Lieutaud, another leatherworker, who hailed from the region of Briançon and who bequeathed all of his goods to his brother, likewise a leatherworker as was his father-in-law. Another Laurens, Antoine, whose precise relationship to Simon is not clear, married his eldest daughter Aymes to Raymond Carluoc, *marchand curatier*, in 1559. Widowed a few years later, Aymes married for a second time, again to a leatherworker. The will of her sister Doulce shows that she too married a leatherworker. In her will, she also chooses as an executor Antoine Coquilhat, still another leatherworker.[29]

The wills left by leatherworkers and carders at once modify and enrich the picture provided by the marriage contracts. For the carders, the wills confirm the tendency for the trade to be passed on frequently from father to son and the weakness of ties linking the members of this trade to one another. Although three wives of carders asked other carders to serve as their executors, no carders themselves did so, turning instead to people in a wide variety of occupations with no evident economic links to carding. On the other hand, the leatherworkers demonstrated much more group solidarity as death approached. Three master leatherworkers appear as executors of the will of their fellow guild member, Mathieu Goude: Simon Laurens, Estienne Escoffier, and Bertrand Gueirard. These same men appear as the executors of four other wills made out by leatherworkers, while another leatherworker, Jean du Puchet, appears in the same capacity twice. The reappearance of these same individuals suggests that these may have been the priors of the leatherworkers' confraternity of Saint Claude. The confraternity was clearly a focus of exceptional loyalty among this group, for leatherworkers' wills make provisions for gifts to the lamp of Saint Claude or request burial in the chapel dedicated to that saint in the city's Augustinian church, with a frequency that is unmatched by the rate of similar provisions in any other group's wills. In all, eight of the twelve *curatiers* or their wives whose wills appear in the sample requested burial in the Augustinian church – located, as it happens, near the Rue des Curateries where all of the members of this trade clustered. In this trade, whose need for water and of which the noxious odors led its practitioners to be segregated within a single part of town, a vital confraternity had developed that united its members in the face of death. This confraternity was exclusively devotional and charitable in character; it was not used by the leatherworkers to preserve any sort of trade monopoly. The guild system was weakly developed in Provence, and, at the end of the sixteenth century, it was typical of the province that confraternities provided the chief institutional context uniting members of specific trades. Access to each trade was governed by a system of 'controlled liberty', according to which anyone could open up shop within a trade by paying a moderate fee to the confraternity and promising to hire exclusively journeymen and apprentices belonging to the confraternity. A new set of confraternity statutes drawn up by the leatherworkers in 1589 explicitly reiterates this freedom for newcomers to open up shop.[30] Rather than being institutions devoted to defending craft privileges, Aix's confraternities were thus primarily loci of sociability and mutual assistance. The leatherworkers thus emerge as a group which, although its members tended to be recruited from and to marry outside the trade, nonetheless developed a considerable esprit de corps as a result of its vital confraternity and the close residential proximity that the specific nature of the trade enforced among members.

Aix's tailors were as reticent as its carders or leatherworkers to marry within their trade, but here other forms of associational links between members of the group also seem to have been weak. Not one of the twenty-seven tailors whose marriage contract appears in the sample married the daughter of another tailor. Instead, their fathers-in-law were scattered randomly across the occupational map, from carpenters and *laboureurs* to fencing masters, booksellers, painters, and even a lawyer. Generally speaking, the dowries which the tailors received from their betrothed were anything but spectacular, while the *dons de survivance*, which they had to promise in return in the event of their predeceasing their intended, were considerably higher than the norm.

Clearly tailors' stock in the marriage market was low, perhaps because they formed a highly mobile group that recruited many of its members from outside Aix and the surrounding region. Twenty of the twenty-seven tailors who appear in Aixois marriage contracts were immigrants, nine from Alpine communities and the rest from as far away as the Lyonnais, Burgundy, Franche-Comté, Toulouse, and Picardy – a dispersion unmatched by any other trade in the city. These tailors had few local connections, for their marriage contracts rarely cite the assistance of the brothers, cousins, or 'bons amis' who appear in so many other artisan marriage contracts. Without established family reputations behind them, with few useful kinship ties to offer, these men were clearly at a disadvantage when it came to negotiating a marriage settlement.

Even though so many tailors were immigrants to the city, they did not forge the sorts of links among themselves after settling in the city and marrying that the leatherworkers did. No evidence of a tailors' confraternity has survived from the sixteenth century, and tailors' wills never allude to one. These wills also demonstrate scant group cohesion, for only two call upon other tailors to see that the testator's last will be done. In sum, trade links seem to have been all but insignificant for tailors.

IMMIGRATION AND INTEGRATION
The cases of the cobblers and construction trades

While the tailors were a group characterized at once by a high proportion of immigrants and weak associational links with both one another and the rest of the urban population, we must beware of assuming a more consistent association between immigration to the city and weak integration into its social networks. Certainly, urban historians have detected significant groups of the 'uprooted' in the cities of the era. Jacques Chiffoleau finds such people filling the cities and market towns of the Comtat Venaissin in the fourteenth and fifteenth centuries, dying 'without having had the time to establish any bonds, ... alone in life as in death'.[31] The criminal records of early sixteenth-century Arras indicate to Robert Muchembled the existence of 'a marginal and disorganized world' of 'deracinated beings' whose attempts to integrate themselves into urban life are made even more difficult by the opprobrium bestowed on those without social or family ties by the civic authorities.[32] But in opposition to a long tradition of social analysis, which tended to see social marginalization and disorganization as the inevitable consequence of being pulled from one's place of origin, most recent work on migration has stressed that a great deal of the movement of people from place to place follows regular patterns in which family ties and professional networks bulk large. These ties are crucial determinants of people's ability to integrate themselves into their new surroundings.[33] In the case of the tailors, the fact that so many of them were immigrants to Aix-en-Provence was probably less important than the fact that they tended to come from outside the typical regions from which immigrants to the city hailed. Those who followed better trodden paths to Aix found their way eased by a combination of family ties, ties to other natives of their home villages, and occupational links.

The shoemakers offer a particularly useful group with which to begin examining the special patterns that governed the lives of immigrants into the city, since this was the city's single largest trade. No less than thirty-six cobblers appear in the sample of marriage contracts as parties to a marriage, and another thirty-nine appear in other capacities. Such a large number of cases enables us to see differences between the behavior of those born in Aix and those who moved into the city, which show the particular importance of geographic, family and professional ties for the immigrants.

Like the tailors or the leatherworkers, the cobblers felt little attraction for women whose father followed the same trade that they did. Only three of the shoemakers married daughters, stepdaughters or sisters of shoemakers. In one case, the marriage provided the groom with a way to establish himself in the trade. Guillaume Raynaud's marriage contract specifies that he was to live under his new father-in-law's roof and eat at his table for a year after his marriage. During this period, he was to work as a shoemaker for his father-in-law, who would administer the first 100 livres of the dowry brought him by his wife. It is not clear whether Guillaume already knew the shoe-making business when he first married, but his will, drawn up four years after his marriage, lists him as a shoemaker. In this, while naming his mother as his chief heir, he bequeaths 400 livres to his wife for her 'good services'.[34]

Few discernible patterns can be found governing the marriage choices of those shoemakers whose sole visible links are to other Aixois. In 1575, we find one such master shoemaker marrying the daughter of a master saddler and another engaged to the daughter of a master farrier, each of whom brought with them a substantial dowry (500 florins in the former case, 400 florins to be paid within six months in the latter).[35] Both sons of Barthélémi Ardisson, an Aixois miller, married the daughters of Aixois shoemakers within a few years of one another. Here, however, the dowries were relatively small; the elder son received 80 florins, and the younger 200. Another shoemaker married the daughter of a leatherworker who was also the widow of a cloth shearer.[36] It is difficult in these cases to see any basis in shared economic interests accounting for the marital alliances. For these Aixois shoemakers, considerations of the occupation of their potential father-in-law do not seem to have entered into their choice of a mate.

For the majority of shoemakers born outside Aix, on the other hand, geographic, family and economic connections all clearly came into play. The greater part of these immigrants came from the Alpine uplands. Typically, one member of their family, usually a son, seems to have established himself first in the city. He was then often followed by brothers and sisters, who found, on arriving in Aix, not simply their elder brother, but also cousins and nephews who had followed the same route. Alain Collomp's work on the villages of Haute-Provence has demonstrated how, within the powerful extended families of the region, the family patriarch was often obliged to encourage younger sons and daughters to leave 'la maison du père' and seek their fortunes elsewhere. Yet even in exile from the ancestral house, these children did not leave home empty-handed, and once in town, the extended family was there again to assist them.[37]

Take, for instance, the case of Bertrand Peautrier, a native of the village of Seyne-les-Alpes, who was living in Aix and practicing the shoemaker's trade before he reached the age of twenty-five. When, in 1561, his sister, also in Aix, married a miller's son, he was present to assist her in drawing up the marriage contract and contributed toward her dowry the entire contents of the room in which he lived in Aix, with the exception of 'the furnishings related to his trade as a shoemaker'. Two years later, he in turn married the daughter of an Aixois day-laborer. For this wedding, uncles and aunts on both sides contributed small gifts to help the new couple set up its household.[38]

Bertrand Peautrier was just one of a number of cobblers who came to Aix from Seyne-les-Alpes and the nearby village of Saint-Vincent. Jean Berge was another. When his wife made out her will in 1559, she chose as her executors Berge and a second immigrant from Seyne, a hosier. The will reveals that she had been previously married – to another cobbler from Seyne. Berge also appears in a second contract from 1559, this time assisting his sister (she thus had also moved to Aix) in drawing up her marriage agreement. She married another *gavot*, but he was a linenweaver from Dieulefit. Such marriages did not always remain within the circle of families from the same region.

Among cobblers drawing up marriage contracts in Aix between 1557 and 1575, immigrants such as Peautrier and Berge formed a clear majority. What were the implications of the arrival of so many immigrant shoemakers for the institutional structure of this trade? It is interesting that the members of this trade chose, against some internal opposition, to make it a *métier juré* in 1584, at the same time that other groups such as the leatherworkers and linenweavers opted to remain *métiers libres*.[39] It seems likely that this decision reflects the desire of the established shoemakers to protect them-selves from too much competition from newcomers. It may also reflect a desire to strengthen the cohesion of a *métier* that otherwise apparently had little. Although the cobblers boasted a confraternity dating back to 1453, only one cobbler in the sample requested burial in its chapel. Likewise, only one cobbler had recourse to a fellow shoemaker as the executor of his will.

While the majority of Aix's cobblers were immigrants, natives of Haute-Provence were not represented within this trade in numbers any greater than their overall percentage among those drawing up marriage contracts would

Table 5.2 Occupations of Alpine immigrants to Aix as revealed by Aixois marriage contracts, 1557–1575.

Trades	Natives of Southern Alps	All husbands in sample of marriage contracts
Semi-rural occupations		
Market-gardeners	2	4
Laboureurs	27	162
Day-laborers	52	201
Shepherds	7	10
Construction trades		
Masons	3	11
Plasterers	7	13
Carpenters	1	8
Textile trades		
Carders	4	22
Weavers	1	15
Tailors	3	27
Ropemakers	1	2
Hosiers	1	7
Transport trades		
Mule-drivers	5	17
Blacksmiths	2	5
Leather trades		
Tanners	5	18
Shoemakers	7	36
Metal trades		
Locksmiths	1	9
Food and Drink trades		
Bakers	3	20
Bourgeois and Merchants	3	44
Praticiens	2	14
Total	137	684

lead one to expect. On the other hand, as Table 5.2 shows, natives of this region did tend to concentrate in certain trades more than in others once they moved to Aix. Many became day laborers. Others who could find work guarding flocks of sheep in the outskirts of the city did this, a logical activity for natives of the mountains, although not one for which there was great call in Aix. Those who became artisans went into many different trades, but they demonstrated a particular tendency to become masons or plasterers. The correlation between occupational choice and place of origin becomes if anything even greater as one descends to the level of the individual village. Just as virtually all of the immigrants from Seyne and Saint-Vincent were either cobblers or *laboureurs,* so we find that a number of the immigrant plasterers hailed from another village adjacent to these two, Montclar. Indeed all of the immigrants to Aix from this village in the sample were either plasterers or *laboureurs*. Such traditions evidently were at least a half-century old by the later sixteenth century, for already in 1527 a plasterer from Montclar, who had lived in Aix for at least ten years, can be discovered taking on as an apprentice another young man from the village.[40] Bertrand Peautrier had already learned his trade from his father in Seyne, another shoemaker, but it is probable that, for the most part, the tendency of the inhabitants of the same village to go into the same trade was less a function of the occupations practiced in their native villages, which surely differed little from one another in their socio-economic make-up, than it was of the process of migration itself. Once one or two natives of a given village established themselves in a trade in Aix, others who followed them from the same village drew upon their links with their fellow villagers to move into the same craft.[41]

Among the plasterers, the ties of family, occupation, and place of origin seem to have reinforced each other particularly strongly. Nearly half of all plasterers in the sample came from the Alps, and they commonly married other immigrants from the region as well. These were often the daughters, daughters-in-law, or widows of other plasterers. The case of Honorat Orcel, one of the plasterers from Montclar, is particularly revealing. In 1559 Orcel married the daughter of an Aixois *laboureur* who brought him a dowry of 100 livres, plus the room in which they were to live for the next year. Orcel's father, a *laboureur* himself, made the journey from Montclar to be present at the wedding, but he did not return a year later when his daughter Marguerite also got married in Aix to another *gavot* in the building trades, a mason from the diocese of Grenoble. Honorat was there, however, as were three other brothers, all also residing in Aix, plus a first cousin Cyprien, another plasterer, who served as the guarantor of her modest dowry of 80 livres. Cyprien himself was married to a fellow native of Montclar whose will of 19 April 1575 survives. This document reveals that the couple had two sons and two daughters, one of whom was married to a master shoemaker. This daughter and the two sons were all to receive equal shares of the inheritance, and 125 livres were set aside to constitute a dowry for the second daughter. Named as executors of the will were two plasterers originally from Montclar, including Honorat Orcel. This Montclar native thus was not only married to another native of that village, she also turned to two others to take care of the business of her estate after her death.[42] As for the process of one member of a family moving to the city and then drawing other siblings along behind him, this can be glimpsed from the example of the Vernet brothers. The first to appear in the sample, Jean, another master plasterer hailing from Montclar, wed the daughter of a mule-driver in 1575, assisted only by some 'good friends'. Three months later, a second brother Esprit had come to Aix, for we find him marrying the daughter of a *ménager* of Saint-Vincent, with Jean's assistance.[43]

The close ties that appear to have linked the plasterers together did not stem from residential proximity, for unlike the leatherworkers or even the cobblers, who also tended to cluster in certain streets, the places of residence of the plasterers were scattered throughout Aix.[44] Despite this geographic dispersion, the plasterers remained linked to one another by family relationships, a common trade and shared geographic origins – three different possible sources of social bonds that in this case were all closely interconnected.

CONCLUSION

This essay has been intended as a sort of methodological experiment. Nobody is more aware than the author how time-consuming and painstaking the procedures utilized here are. Nobody is also more aware of their limitations, which have necessitated that the present analysis be restricted to just a few of the larger *métiers* that existed within sixteenth-century Aix. The results obtained nonetheless appear sufficiently important and revealing to justify the time invested.

Particularly striking is the variety of patterns demonstrated even by the restricted sample of occupations examined. Weavers tended to form marriage alliances within their group because possession of a loom was so important to their trade. Carders and leatherworkers demonstrated far less of a tendency toward strict occupational endogamy, but they married instead into families within each other's trades and with *nourriguier* families in a pattern that followed broader patterns of economic interaction. Despite the virtual absence of family interrelationships, the leatherworkers demonstrated many other connections with fellow members of their craft, the result of close residential proximity and a strong religious confraternity. The tailors had few interconnections of any sort. Arriving in Aix from widely scattered and often distant points, they married women whose fathers followed a great variety of different occupations, in the presence of few family members or friends, and only upon promise of large survivorship pensions for their betrothed in case of their early death. They appear to have had a great deal of difficulty inserting themselves into any of the networks of local society. The ranks of the plasterers also included many immigrants, but these men tended to come from villages that were traditional basins of recruitment for Aix's population and to follow family members and neighbors to the city. They consequently were able to recreate strong sets of interrelationships based on family and shared place of origin, even though their trade offered few tangible economic incentives to intermarriage and they lived in *quartiers* scattered across the city.

In sum, sixteenth-century Aix, like any city of the era, was a locus of multiple solidarities. Economic links created by the organization and capital require-ments of specific trades, ties of kinship, *voisinage* and ritual brotherhood, the fact of coming from the same village – all of these could bring individuals together and create the basis for important social relationships. Great diversity, however, existed among different artisan trades in the frequency with which these bonds developed among their members and the extent to which such bonds overlapped with one another. The life experiences and degree of group solidarity typical of members of individual trades were consequently quite different from one craft to the next.

The micro-analysis of the social relationships existing among Aix's artisans also shows that these relationships extended beyond the city walls into the surrounding hinterland, a reminder that urban society cannot be studied in isolation from its larger social and economic framework. Cities and their regions formed tightly connected social and economic units, bound together both by economic exchanges and the constant stream of migration to the city. City dwellers lived their lives within the contexts of these currents of human and commercial exchange, not within the boundaries of a single city's walls. Again, these currents could vary significantly from trade to trade.

Several other studies have also recently looked microscopically at the world of urban artisans and petty shopkeepers, adopting a second, slightly different approach from that employed here, namely investigating specific trades. These have brought our comprehension of the trades in question to a new level of understanding. They too have revealed the complexity of patterns of social relationships among different groups of artisans, as well as a parallel complexity in the organization of labor markets.[45] Whether the micro-analysis of the artisan world continues to advance through the multiplication of case studies or the extensive sampling of documents from a single locale, it seems increasingly clear that such methods hold out the promise of a fuller understanding of the precise contours of artisan social experience than any we have previously been able to achieve.

NOTES: CHAPTER 5

An earlier version of sections of this paper was presented at the annual conference of the Society for French Historical Studies, held in Charlottesville, Va, in 1984. Funding for the project was provided by the Social Sciences and Humanities Research Council of Canada. I would like to thank the student research assistants whose assistance was invaluable for undertaking so large a quantitative study: Marie Thivierge and Richard LaRue, who helped read through the notarial records that form the basis for this study; Christine Métayer, who systematized the data so that they could be entered into the computer; Pierre Grégoire, who checked the data contained in the *sénéchausée* records; and Derek Lamb, who coded and entered the data into the computer.

1   The classic monographs of Maurice Garden, *Lyon et les Lyonnais au XVIIIe siècle* (Paris: Les Belles Lettres, 1970); Richard Gascon, *Grand commerce et vie urbaine au XVIe siècle: Lyon et ses marchands* (Paris: Mouton, 1971); Jean-Claude Perrot, *Genèse d'une ville moderne: Caen au XVIIIe siècle* (Paris: Mouton, 1975); Jean-Pierre Poussou, *Bordeaux et le Sud-Ouest au XVIIIe siècle: croissance économique et attraction urbaine* (Paris: Ecole des Hautes Etudes en Sciences Sociales, 1983); and Jean-Pierre Bardet, *Rouen aux XVIIe et XVIIIe siècles. Les mutations d'un espace social* (Paris: S.E.D.E.S., 1983), all rely on similar sources and display a progressive refinement of the methods of their predecessors.

2   Recent examples of such studies include Maurice Gresset, *Gens de justice à Besançon. De la conquête par Louis XIV à la Révolution française (1674–1789)* (Paris: Bibliothèque Nationale, 1978); Jonathan Dewald, *The Formation of a Provincial Nobility: The Magistrates of the Parlement of Rouen, 1499–1610* (Princeton, NJ: Princeton University Press, 1980); Claire Dolan, *Entre tours et clochers. Gens d'église à Aix-en-Provence au XVIe siècle* (Sherbrooke, Quebec, and Aix-en-Provence: Presses de l'Université de Sherbrooke and Edisud, 1981); Barbara Diefendorf, *Paris City Councillors in the Sixteenth Century* (Princeton, NJ: Princeton University Press, 1983); Monique Cubells, *La Provence des Lumières. Les parlementaires d'Aix au 18e siècle* (Paris: Maloine, 1984). A few recent studies have begun to look at the artisan world in the same way, notably Steven Laurence Kaplan, *Provisioning Paris: Merchants and Millers in the Grain and Flour Trade during the Eighteenth Century* (Ithaca, NY: Cornell University Press, 1984); Jacques-Louis Ménétra, *Journal de ma vie*, ed. Daniel Roche (Paris: Montalba, 1982); Robert Darnton, 'A printing shop across the border', in *The Literary Underground of the Old Regime* (Cambridge, Mass.: Harvard University Press, 1982); Michael Sonenscher, 'Journeymen's migrations and workshop organization in eighteenth-century France', in S. L. Kaplan and C. J. Koepp (eds), *Work in France: Representations, Meaning, Organization and Practice* (Ithaca, NY: Cornell University Press, 1986), pp. 74–96.

3   The thesis of Louis Stouff, *Arles à la fin du Moyen Age* (Aix-en-Provence: Publications de l'Université de Provence, 1986), provides an excellent example of a recent work that emphasizes the originality of its object of study rather than its methods.

4   Michel Vovelle, 'Histoire sérielle ou "case studies": vrai ou faux dilemme en histoire des mentalités', in *Histoire sociale, sensibilités collectives et mentalités. Mélanges Robert Mandrou* (Paris: Presses Universitaires de France, 1985), p. 42.

5   Michel Vovelle, *Piété baroque et déchristianisation en Provence au XVIIIe siècle* (Paris: Plon, 1973); Pierre Chaunu, *La mort à Paris, XVIe, XVIIe et XVIIIe siècles* (Paris: Fayard, 1978); Alain Croix, *La Bretagne aux XVIe et XVIIe siècles: la vie, la mort, la foi* (Paris: Maloine, 1981); Jacques Chiffoleau, *La comptabilité de l'au-delà: les hommes, la mort, et la religion en Comtat Venaissin à la fin du Moyen Age (vers 1320–1480)* (Rome: Bibliothèque de l'Ecole Française de Rome, 1981); Marie-Thérèse Lorcin, *Vivre et mourir en Lyonnais à la fin du moyen age* (Paris: Editions du C.N.R.S., 1981).

6   The classic model of such studies, which has generated imitators too numerous to be listed, is A. Daumard and F. Furet, *Structures et relations sociales à Paris au XVIIIe siècle* (Paris: A. Colin, 1961).

7   Stouff, *Arles*, adopts such an approach, as does Noël Coulet's soon to be published thesis on Aix in the fifteenth century.

8   Particularly exemplary is Alain Collomp, *La maison du père. Famille et village en Haute-Provence aux XVIIe et XVIIIe siècles* (Paris: Presses Universitaires de France, 1983).

9   For the methodological problems involved in the use of the region's early notarial

records, Louis Stouff, 'Les registres de notaires d'Arles (début XIVe siècle–1460). Quelques problèmes posés par l'utilisation des archives notariales', *Provence historique*, vol. 25 (1975), pp. 305–24, is fundamental.

10 The registers of Aix's notaries are preserved in the A.D.B.R., series E.

11 Aix's municipal archives contain a rich series of wardship accounts (A.C. Aix-en-Provence, series CC). Although these accounts are difficult to use by themselves, they provide a useful complement to the data contained in other records.

12 Even for more recent periods, the reconstruction of full life-histories through record linkage is exceedingly difficult. Confronting with one another nineteenth-century birth, marriage and draft records, as well as censuses, Leslie Page Moch was still able to reconstruct only about ten life-histories of immigrants to Nîmes. Moch, *Paths to the City: Regional Migration in Nineteenth-Century France* (Beverly Hills, Calif.: Sage Publications, 1983), pp. 74–5.

13 Noël Coulet notes that the process of reoccupation of land deserted during the difficult years of the fifteenth century began almost thirty years later in Provence than it did in the Quercy. See 'La Provence au temps du Roi René, une "Arcadie de la France"?' in *Aspects de la Provence: Conférences prononcées à l'occasion du cinq centième anniversaire de l'union de la Provence à la France* (Marseille: Société de Statistique, d'Histoire et d'Archéologie de Marseille et de Provence, 1983), p. 21.

14 Edouard Baratier, *La démographie provençale du XIIIe au XVIe siècle* (Paris: S.E.V.P.E.N., 1961), pp. 94, 114.

15 Coulet, 'Provence au temps du Roi René', p. 21.

16 Gabriel Audisio, *Les vaudois du Lubéron. Une minorité en Provence (1460–1560)* (n.p.: Association d'Etudes vaudoises et historiques du Lubéron, 1984), p. 48.

17 For a more detailed discussion of Aix's population and economy, see the collective *Histoire d'Aix-en-Provence* (Aix-en-Provence: Edisud, 1977), pp. 93–7, 104, and 113–14.

18 See above, p. 13. It should be noted here that Audisio's figures refer to the percentage of immigrants among both couples drawing up marriage contracts and individuals making wills. It is possible that the presence of this latter group reduces the percentage of individuals described as immigrants, as, with the passage of time, people came to be less and less identified with their place of origin. It is not uncommon to encounter cases such as that of Josephe Rolland, daughter of a master mason born in Montclar, whose father is constantly mentioned as a native of Montclar in the notarial records until she makes out her will, at which point he becomes an Aixois. A.D.B.R., 303E 104, fo. 620v, 16 June 1571.

19 Baratier, *Démographie provençale*, pp. 114, 122, stresses the particularly rapid growth of the coastal regions around Toulon in the eighteenth century. See also Emmanuel Le Roy Ladurie, *Les Paysans de Languedoc* (2nd edn, Paris: Mouton, 1966), pp. 101 ff.

20 See especially Jean-Pierre Poussou, 'Les relations villes–campagnes en Aquitaine dans la deuxième moitié du XVIIIe siècle: quelques réflexions méthodologiques sur les attractions urbaines et les échanges migratoires', in *Démographie urbaine, XVe–XXe siècle* (Lyon: Publications du Centre d'histoire économique et sociale de la région lyonnaise, [1977]), p. 193.

21 For a good recent overview of marriage patterns during the Ancien Régime, see André Burguière, 'Les cent et une familles de l'Europe', in Burguière *et al.*, *Histoire de la famille*, Vol. 2 (Paris: A. Colin, 1986), pp. 83–90.

22 Bardet, *Rouen*, pp. 226–7; Kaplan, *Provisioning Paris*, pp. 321–3.

23 Ideally, the analysis of patterns of artisan intermarriage ought to take into consideration not only the occupation of those involved, but also whether or not

the people in question are masters or journeymen. Unfortunately, Aix's notaries failed to note consistently whether or not artisans enjoyed the status of master. Some are specifically indicated as being masters, but one encounters other, far richer artisans for whom no such designation is provided.

24 A.D.B.R., 308E 1206, fo. 1876v, 19 November 1567; 302E 516, fo. 2, 1 January 1575.
25 A.D.B.R., 302E 508, fo. 182v, 9 July 1571.
26 A.D.B.R., 307E 755, fo. 756v, 13 July 1567.
27 E.g. A.D.B.R., 306E 646, 1 April 1562.
28 A.D.B.R., 308E 1202, fo. 1231v, 24 October 1563; 308E 1206, fo. 2075, 7 December 1567; 308E 1196, fo. 712, 10 December 1559; 306E 655, fo. 196, 1 April 1571; 308E 1025, fo. 443, 9 August 1571; 309E 912, fo. 485, 12 July 1571; see also 302E 822, fo. 1150, 15 December 1560.
29 A.D.B.R., 307E 775, fo. 167, 29 January 1559; 302E 824, fo. 591v, 11 October 1563; 308E 1138, fo. 718, 28 November 1559; 303E 97, fo. 427v, 25 April 1563; 303E 118, fo. 250, 30 May 1575; 302E 791, fo. 505v, 23 May 1571.
30 J. Billioud, 'De la confrérie à la corporation: les classes industrielles en Provence aux XIVe, XVe et XVIe siècles', *Mémoires de l'Institut Historique de Provence* (1929–30), pp. 252 ff. In 1583, Aix possessed only three fully fledged privileged guilds, those of the surgeons, apothecaries, and goldsmiths.
31 Chiffoleau, *La comptabilité de l'au-delà*, p. 189.
32 Robert Muchembled, 'Crime et société urbaine: Arras au temps de Charles Quint (1528–1549)', in *La France d'Ancien Régime. Etudes réunies en l'honneur de Pierre Goubert* (Toulouse: Privat, 1984), p. 485.
33 John S. MacDonald and Beatrice D. MacDonald, 'Chain migration, ethnic neighborhood formation and social networks', *Milbank Memorial Fund Quarterly*, vol. 42 (1964), no. 1, pp. 82 ff; Charles Tilly and C. Harold Brown, 'On uprooting, kinship, and the auspices of migration', *International Journal of Comparative Sociology*, vol. 8 (1967), no. 2, pp. 139–64; Tilly, 'Migration in modern European history', in William H. McNeill and Ruth S. Adams, *Human Migration* (Bloomington, Ind.: Indiana University Press, 1978), pp. 48–72; Harvey M. Choldin, 'Kinship networks in the migration process', *The International Migration Review*, vol. 7 (1973), no. 2, pp. 163–75; Moch, *Paths to the City*. I would like to thank Professor Bruno Ramirez of the Université de Montréal for kindly furnishing me with many of these references.
34 A.D.B.R., 302E 820, fo. 241v, 6 March 1558; 302E 823, fo. 391v, 21 August 1562.
35 A.D.B.R., 301E 114, fo. 745, 25 July 1575; 307E 784, fo. 2002, 8 November 1575.
36 A.D.B.R., 307E 669, fo. 21, 6 January 1571; 302E 786, fo. 986, 2 October 1567; 301E 110, fo. 1110v, 18 November 1571.
37 Collomp, *La maison du père*, passim, esp. ch. 6.
38 A.D.B.R., 308E 1160, fo. 396v, 26 October 1561; 303E 75, 23 October 1563.
39 Billioud, 'De la confrérie à la corporation', p. 255.
40 A.D.B.R., 309E 813, fo. 181; 309E 761, fo. 520.
41 Apprenticeship contracts which reveal young men from Seyne being placed as apprentice shoemakers in Aix suggest as much. A.D.B.R., 302E 843, fo. 322v, 23 February 1575.
42 A.D.B.R., 303E 91, 5 March 1559; 309E 914, fo. 285, 24 June 1560; 308E 1279, fo. 500, 19 April 1575.
43 A.D.B.R., 309E 956, fo. 189, 20 May 1575; 308E 1279, fo. 1112v, 7 August 1575. In some cases, immigrants relied on fellow villagers who were not relatives to facilitate their integration into urban life, as procuration contracts established by inhabitants of Montclar demonstrate. These call upon merchants or *praticiens* in Aix, themselves natives of Montclar, to have them arrange apprenticeships for children moving to Aix or to collect money owed them by relatives in the city.

A.D.B.R., 301E 153, fo. 161v, 3 March 1567; 302E 839, fo. 558, 3 May 1571.

44 A.C. Aix-en-Provence, CC 157; Jean-Pierre Coste, *La ville d'Aix en 1695. Structure urbaine et société* (Aix-en-Provence: La Pensée Universitaire, 1970), p. 909. It might be observed that no other artisan trade aside from the cobblers and the leatherworkers demonstrated much of a tendency to concentrate in a few streets or sections of the city.

45 See the works cited in note 2 above.

6

Crown and capitoulat: municipal government in Toulouse 1500–1789

ROBERT A. SCHNEIDER

Perhaps nothing distinguishes recent investigation into the structure of the Ancien Régime more than a renewed appreciation of the insights of Alexis de Tocqueville. Indeed, the author of *The Old Regime and the French Revolution* is the godfather of the now burgeoning interest in politics as a key to understanding the causes of the French Revolution. He was the first historian to understand the revolutionary effects of Louis XIV's reign; the first as well to suggest a dynamic relationship between the political and social orders; the precursor of all subsequent research into the corporate structure of the Ancien Régime; the theorist of 'group individualism' as the peculiarly self-destructive mode of political comportment engendered by absolutism; and the master critic of his own class's failure to adapt politically to the demands of modernity.[1]

Central to Tocqueville's dissection of the Ancien Régime is his portrayal of the fate of the realm's municipalities, confronted as they were by the dual challenge of an intrusive intendancy and corruptive venality, together undermining what political autonomy and self-government cities once enjoyed. Here, however, as elsewhere in his analysis, Tocqueville exaggerates both the crown's success in eviscerating local institutions and the speed with which this transformation was accomplished. Upon reading *The Old Regime and the French Revolution*, one gets the sense that in the case of the cities, absolutism was imposed in one fell swoop. 'It was not until 1692 that free municipal elections were everywhere abolished', he writes.[2] Moreover, he conveys a sense that right up until that time the realm's municipalities were blessed with politically robust and independent Hôtels de Ville whose origins date to the feudal past: 'Municipal autonomy survived the feudal system, and long after the lords ceased to administer the country districts French towns retained the right of governing themselves.'[3]

What follows is an episodic account of the relationship between the crown and the municipal government of Toulouse during the last three centuries of the Ancien Régime. My account will emphasize the evolving nature of this relationship, and will suggest that the progress of royal power was not always steady and unbroken; certainly it was not so definitively imposed at the end of the seventeenth century as Tocqueville claimed. Nor were strong municipal governments merely a vestige of some bygone 'feudal' era, as will be revealed by a look at Toulouse's early sixteenth century, when the Hôtel de Ville remained a source of power and prestige within the city, in some domains even managing to extend its authority. Because of its long tradition of municipal self-rule embodied in the town council or *capitoulat*, Toulouse is a good site for such an investigation. Moreover, because the city hosted a Parlement, the sovereign court of Languedoc, we can observe how the dynamics of royal intrusion usually entailed corporate rivalry – how the struggle between crown and capitoulat implicated the Parlement as well, usually, but not always, as the ally of the crown.

THE MUNICIPAL REPUBLIC CHALLENGED

The era of Toulouse's municipal independence effectively came to an end in the thirteenth century with the Albigensian crusade, which devastated the city, leaving it stripped of many of those liberties and privileges that it had secured from the Counts of Toulouse only a century earlier. One privilege that endured, however, was the city's right to choose its own governing council, known as the capitoulat. With twenty-four members, or 'capitouls', at its founding, the capitoulat evolved by the fifteenth century into an eight-man body, each capitoul elected for one year, each representing a section, or capitoulat, of the city. Most important, from 1459 onward the position of capitoul ennobled those who served, their families and descendants.[4]

The promise of automatic nobility made municipal service an attractive opportunity for upwardly mobile men, especially for the rich pastel merchants of the late fifteenth and early sixteenth century, who entered the town council in great numbers. In theory, the capitouls were to be comprised of a mix of lawyers, lesser noblemen and merchants, but in practice, especially after the sixteenth century, merchants were usually excluded or under-represented. The capitulary election took place in several stages during November and December of each year. The procedures for the election, established in the fourteenth century, remained intact, with some adjustments, until the late seventeenth. On 23 November the out-going capitouls each selected six candidates; this group of forty-eight nominees was then halved by a company of former city councillors. The *viguier* (a royal officer who originally served the Count of Toulouse) and *sénéchal* named the final eight, who took their oath of office on 13 December. Afterward, the new capitouls, dressed in their ermine robes of scarlet and black, which the city purchased for them at the cost of 300 livres each, made their traditional 'cavalcade' through the city, only one in a series of ceremonial privileges that the city magistrates flaunted long after their political power was on the wane. Usually the elections were less than tidy civic exercises and were accompanied with much fanfare and backroom dealing. 'The election of the pope has no more ceremony', commented an exasperated intendant in the late seventeenth century.[5] Chicanery and bribes were routine, and the magistrates of the Parlement, as well as other urban notables, managed to meddle in the process, even though they were formally barred from the proceedings.

Men were eager to secure election to the capitoulat not only because they could earn noble status for themselves and their descendants, but also because the position conferred real powers. Collectively, the capitouls, as custodians of the Hôtel de Ville, controlled a major source of urban patronage, for in their hands were more than a hundred municipal jobs, everything from secretaries, councillors, archivists, lawyers, and surgeons, to corps of guards, streetclean-ers, town-criers, musicians, painters, and soldiers. A document from the later sixteenth century lists 164 such appointees, although it is clear that under the supervision of the intendant in the eighteenth century this number was reduced considerably.[6] In addition, the capitouls controlled a large contingent of appointees known as the *dizainiers*, who served as a link between the Hôtel de Ville and the populace. Each *dizainier* was responsible for a *moulon* – an island cluster of houses – whence the name, which probably referred to a block of ten buildings. The *dizainiers* were something like ward-heelers and served on a part-time, ad-hoc basis, performing duties such as searching out the non-resident poor in order to facilitate their expulsion from the city. Most *dizainiers* were craftsmen or laborers who received compensation for their municipal service in the form of tax relief and probably profited as well from routine corruption. The number of *dizainiers* for the city and the suburbs was as high as four hundred.[7]

Beyond this considerable patronage, the capitouls also had formal control over four crucial areas of municipal life: justice, police, 'reparations' (the maintenance of public buildings and thoroughfares) and the city's several hospitals, each area the special responsibility of a pair of town councillors. Indeed, even in the first part of the sixteenth century, a period of both growing royal centralization and increased parlementary power, the capitouls managed to preserve and in some cases extend their powers and responsibilities in each of these domains. There is, for example, evidence that the city was better policed: not only were several unprecedented efforts at poor relief under-taken, but the city's militia was put on a permanent footing and the first Health Board for combating the plague was established as well. The early sixteenth century also saw the first serious attempt to control prostitution. In 1505 the capitouls initiated a reform and reorganization of the city's nine hospitals, which until then had been maintained by several church foundations; now they were placed under the authority of a single municipal administration. And in 1514 the capitouls completed work on a new hospital, the Saint-Sebastian, an institution devoted to the care and confinement of plague victims. The capitouls took particular pride in overseeing the reconstruction of the city, much of it still suffering from the neglect of the period of the Hundred Years' War and the devastation left by a great fire in 1463. The city walls were repaired and completed; the many wells and fountains were finally put in working order; several streets and plazas were enlarged and straightened; in 1540 work was begun on a new bridge crossing the Garonne; and, most important to the capitouls themselves, the Hôtel de Ville was entirely refurbished, transformed into an appropriately splendid showcase for a prideful municipal government. Finally, the capitouls' judicial authority, though increasingly contested by the Parlement, was confirmed by several royal edicts; and in 1554 the crown granted the capitouls the right to prosecute all cases of heresy within the city, thus eclipsing the traditional power of the Inquisition. In short, if a hallmark of successful urban rule is the city fathers' energy and constructive initiative, the first half of the sixteenth century was a time when 'good government' – or at least an active and assertive government – reigned in Toulouse's Hôtel de Ville.[8]

But the capitouls themselves were not the exclusive custodians of Toulouse's city hall and thus were not entirely responsible for the conduct of municipal government. There were in fact three councils, which convened periodically to deliberate on the administration of the city. These were the *Conseil Général*, the *Conseil de Bourgeoisie*, and the *Conseil des Seize*, each of which included the reigning capitouls only as junior members. The *Conseil Général* met infrequently, usually only four times yearly, and comprised a large body of city notables, including the First President of the Parlement (who presided), several parlementaires, representatives of the Archibishop, the major ecclesiastical chapters, and the University, several solicitors, a contingent of 'bourgeois' and merchants, and the old and new capitouls. In mid-sixteenth century the *Conseil Général* assembled almost eighty men and was, in fact, a remnant of the general assemblies held during the period of the medieval commune; but its functions were mostly limited to a ceremonial hearing of the municipal deliberations and the supervision of the capitulary election. The *Conseil de Bourgeoisie*, composed of a more limited number of city notables and capitouls, met more frequently, often without the presence of royal officials, and served as a working committee that oversaw the activities of the capitouls. Finally, the *Conseil des Seize* insured the continuity of municipal government by gathering the previous year's and current capitouls on a board which in the sixteenth century met quite regularly.[9] In the course of the Ancien Régime the composition and relative importance of these councils changed significantly. For example, although churchmen and merchants were heavily represented in the sixteenth-century *Conseil Général*, they all but disappeared in the seventeenth century. The *Conseil des Seize* also declined in importance, an indication that city notables were increasingly unwilling to allow a board of capitouls to deliberate unsupervised by other officials. Most significant was the growing intrusion of the parlementary magistrates. In the *Conseil Général* of

1550 there were no *parlementaires*; by 1556 the royal court was represented by eight officials, including the First President.[10] Indeed, in 1578, the Parlement issued a decree ordering that the assemblies of the *Conseil Général* be attended by the President Latomy and 'certains conseillers du Parlement'.[11] Henceforth throughout the Ancien Régime, the Parlement had its representatives at virtually every assembly held in the Hôtel de Ville. Usually these assemblies were presided over by the First President.

Thus, the fate of Toulouse's municipal government in the sixteenth century was inextricably bound up with the growing hegemony of the Parlement. Indeed, the dramatic growth of the sovereign court since its founding in 1444 reshaped the city as a whole, endowing it with a body of prominent and powerful men whose ranks by the mid-sixteenth century were more than fifty strong, and spawning as well a sub-population of *procureurs* and *avocats* who served in the Parlement. By the mid-seventeenth century there were nearly 100 *parlementaires* in Toulouse, including five presidents, whose collective presence constituted the city's elite, rivaling even the ecclesiastical hierarchs who proliferated in this Catholic bastion.[12] They easily overawed the capitouls and made a point of flaunting their status as privileged royal officers: in 1578, for example, the Parlement decreed that henceforth the capitouls were forbidden to march before the magistrates in public processions.[13] The capitouls, however, did not surrender in the face of such imperiousness and indeed wrestled with the sovereign court on honorific and substantive issues for the duration of the Ancien Régime. But their battle was ultimately a losing one, and it is difficult to fault Zeller's conclusion that 'However glorious the capitouls of Toulouse might have been, they could do nothing without the agreement of the Parlement. They listened respectfully to its remonstrances and yielded to its arguments.'[14]

Still, it would be a mistake to conclude from this that the capitouls were totally eclipsed by the sovereign court in the sixteenth century, shorn of their traditional powers and privileges. In other words, one must not view the relationship between the two institutions as merely a zero-sum game, for this would leave unexplained why the capitoulat survived and often seemed even to thrive for two more centuries. To be sure, the Parlement did encroach on the powers and privileges of the capitouls in conspicuous ways. First, as we have noted, starting in the mid-sixteenth century the court was represented in most assemblies in the Hôtel de Ville and frequently these meetings were presided over by the First President. Second, behind many of the capitouls' actions we can detect the hand of parlementary authority. The capitouls may have boasted in the pages of the 'Annales manuscrits' of their exemplary efforts to repair the city's walls and bridges, but a perusal of the Parlement's *arrêts* reveals that such civic enterprises depended upon the constant prompting, even bullying of the sovereign court. Especially in emergency matters, ranging from policing the city in times of plague to taxing the inhabitants for the relief of the poor, the capitouls, while administrators of these measures, were almost always ordered to the task by the Parlement. Finally, the most blatant form of parlementary interference in city government was the royal court's unilateral naming of the new capitouls. In theory, as we have noted, the Parlement had no role in the capitulary election. But in 1462, eighteen years after the court's establishment, the eight new capitouls were appointed by the Parlement – 'this time only, and without prejudice to custom and tradition', noted the *arrêt*. This avowal notwithstanding, the court violated custom and tradition in like manner sixteen times in the next hundred years (see Table 6.1), on a couple of occasions merely naming two of the capitouls or keeping the town council in office for another year, but most often summarily selecting the entire slate of eight municipal magistrates. Nothing, it would seem, better exemplified the Parlement's power over Toulouse's city government.

But this power was not entirely aimed at negating the capitouls' authority. To think in such terms is to take a seventeenth-century view of French politics, with absolutism often striving, if rarely succeeding, to eviscerate the legitimacy of traditional bodies. In the fifteenth and sixteenth centuries, the dynamics of royal centralization frequently worked to the opposite effect. The establishment of the Parlement and its relationship to local institutions and powers, including the capitoulat, illustrates the point. Here was a body of royal officers created to extend the crown's authority in Languedoc and, in particular, to limit the independence of feudal lords, high churchmen and local judicial corporations. Within the city of Toulouse, this purpose often entailed the defense and support of the capitouls and their authority, if only as a counterweight to other institutions and powers. For example, as early as 1454 the capitouls complained to the court that they could not adequately minister justice in the city because members of the *Sénéchaussée* and other royal officers claimed to escape their jurisdiction. The Parlement thus found itself supporting the Hôtel de Ville in this domain.[15] Again, in 1506, the court ordered several ecclesiastical chapters to contribute towards the construction of a bridge across the Garonne, thus shoring up the capitouls' authority in levying taxes for such enterprises.[16] The Parlement's interference in municipal elections can also be explained in terms of its effort to protect the town council from the meddlesome influence of the *Sénéchaussée*; it was, in other words, not so much a matter of the magistrates' imperious policy toward municipal government as an extension of their ongoing competition with another royal court.

There was another reason why the Parlement, though supreme in the city and region, was not really interested in trampling on the capitouls' authority to

Table 6.1 Years when the Parlement interfered in the capitulary election.

1462	1494	1513	1548
1465	1503	1519	1550
1478	1505	1524	1557
1481	1508	1528	1562

the point of transforming the Hôtel de Ville into a mere vestige of municipal power. Quite simply, the capitouls were needed as the administrators of the city, especially in times of crisis, such as during the plague. When epidemic threatened, the Parlement reserved the right to evacuate the city and hold court in an uncontaminated venue.[17] But before departing, the magistrates would charge the capitouls with policing the city, that is, to institute the battery of health and administrative measures designed to limit the spread of the disease and insure public order. Most important, the Parlement ordered the capitouls to remain in the infected city, while those townspeople who could lost no time in fleeing. To be sure, this order was not always accepted with grace by the town councillors: in 1512 a capitoul was fined 100 livres for cursing the royal magistrates in their presence after receiving the command to remain in the face of the plague.[18] In addition to the need for a dependable administrative apparatus, the royal magistrates, as elite residents of Toulouse, had an interest in preserving what independence and privileges the city still enjoyed, and they realized that this presupposed a reasonably robust municipal government, one that could maintain the loyalty of a cross-section of urban notables and not be sacrificed to corporate rivalries. The benefits of such cooperation across corporate lines were obvious to all concerned, and were demonstrated rather dramatically in 1559 when the collective efforts of the Toulouse elite secured for the city a renewal of its century-long exemption from the royal *taille*.[19]

But it is by no means clear that the capitoulat's authority came solely by way of the Parlement's sufferance. The Hôtel de Ville had its own sources of power and privilege. One dates from the fifteenth century, when Toulouse's position on the frontier of English-held Gascony prompted several royal concessions, not the least of which was the conferral of noble status upon the capitouls. Another relates to the city's new-found wealth in the late fifteenth and early sixteenth centuries, a source of *richesse* that can be summarized in a word: woad. It was then that the cultivation of the pastel plant in the Lauragais region west of the city lured merchants from far and wide, who soon established Toulouse as the world center for the production and distribution of this most important source of indelible blue dye. A community of wealthy *pasteliers* came to dominate the city, transforming its once modest neighborhoods into architectural showcases with the construction of their Renaissance *hôtels*, creating a robust urban economy in what had heretofore been an economically rather sleepy town. Many of these merchants secured election to the capitoulat, bringing their pride and worldliness to the Hôtel de Ville. Municipal government was one beneficiary of this wealth, as the yield from such indirect taxes as the *octrois* increased with the city's growing commercial vitality.[20] In addition, the city fathers also managed to recover some of the city's traditional sources of revenue that had been lost during the wars of the previous century. In 1509, after a long legal contest, two bridges and their tolls, having been usurped by 'several powerful individuals', once again became part of Toulouse's patrimony.[21]

This leads us to another explanation for the vitality and strength of municipal government in mid-sixteenth-century Toulouse, an explanation having to do with the mentality of the city fathers and their supporters, those townsmen who identified with the Hôtel de Ville. In reading the 'Annales manuscrits de la Ville' (a yearly account of municipal affairs drawn up by the outgoing capitouls), one is impressed not only by the capitouls' energy and initiative but also by their purposefulness and high-mindedness. 'The Seigneures of the Capitole represent the Image of the Roman Senate', they proclaimed at one point, somewhat redundantly.[22] Central to their self-image was the myth of 'la république de Toulouse', a myth given currency by a number of writers, many imbued with the tenets of civic humanism. The city's first modern historian, Nicolas Bertrandi, whose *Les gestes des Tholosans* was published in Latin in 1517, argued that while Charles VIII confirmed the municipality's privileges, and in particular the powers of the capitouls, in 1495, its liberties actually pre-date the monarchy, having been granted by the Roman Emperor Theodonius.[23] Indeed, the capitouls were convinced that they were the direct descendants of the Roman consuls. And as 'Senateurs' they easily ranked as equals to their rivals, the magistrates of the Parlement. What distinguished the capitouls – in their own minds – was their noble sense of civic duty and an exemplary willingness to sacrifice their personal interests to the public good. Their honor resides, proclaimed the Annales, in voluntarily 'halting their own business, suspending their commerce, abandoning all particular affections and putting aside their cherished projects in order to augment the Republic, following the precepts of Plato, Aristotle, Xenephon and other philosophers'.[24]

References in the city Annales to the 'municipal republic' for the most part end after 1562, and for good reason: it was then that religious warfare broke out in Toulouse, as it did throughout the realm, and it was then too that the capitouls effectively lost control over the city. The vicissitudes of confessional strife opened the way for a range of political actors, from aristocratic warriors and members of the Parlement to mendicant preachers and self-styled religious leaders. Thus, in so far as the capitoulat played a role in ruling the city during this turbulent period, it had to share power with several other agencies, some popularly based, such as the series of 'leagues', 'associations', and militant confraternities, which proved particularly effective in this Catholic bastion. Because the capitouls elected in 1561 proved to harbor several avowed Calvinists, they were summarily dismissed by the Parlement in 1562 once the religious conflict was ignited, and were replaced with men whose faith was above suspicion; henceforth, the sovereign court closely monitored the capitulary elections.[25] Moreover, the creation of new militias and popular associations for the defense of the faith did not wait for the triumph of the League in Toulouse. As early as 1562, an association of militant Catholics was established, and this 'leaguc' was reactivated several times in the next three decades. Troops were also frequently billeted in the city, for Toulouse served as a Catholic fortress in an otherwise largely Huguenot province. Finally, as such religious orders as the Jesuits and the Cordeliers sought refuge in the city from Protestant persecution, they insisted on playing a major role in its official life, especially now that confessional militancy was the order of the day.[26]

If, however, with the onset of the religious wars, the capitouls were no longer the masters of the urban government, this does not mean that the Hôtel de Ville also lost its centrality in municipal affairs; nor does it mean that the city's political autonomy had forever been sacrificed. In fact, the opposite claim might be made, and nothing supports this claim more than the experience of the take-over of the city by the Catholic League in 1588. It has long been recognized that along with ultra-Catholicism and anti-royalism, the defense of urban autonomy ranked high in many French cities' embrace of the League. In Toulouse this was evident in the city's rejection, not only of the authority of Henry III, his presumptive heir Henry of Navarre, and the politique *gouverneur* Montmorency-Damville, but also of the League warrior the Duc de Joyeuse, whose family had long been regional magnates. From 1588 to 1594 the city was a government unto itself, except for a formal alliance with the national League, and was ruled by an insurrectionary committee called the Eighteen, composed of six *parlementaires*, six capitouls and six clergymen. The seat of the Eighteen was the Hôtel de Ville: it was this bastion of the municipal republic which now served as the storm-center of the general mobilization and defence of the city that was the League take-over. Thus, although the capitouls were relegated to a power-sharing position in the insurrection, municipal government yet remained anchored in its traditional site. In other words, while the ruling personnel of municipal government might have changed, its institutional context was the same. Moreover, the League insurrection clearly drew upon those municipal powers that the capitoulat had accumulated in the course of the sixteenth century. For example, nothing resembles the League take-over more than the policing measures instituted in times of plague, from the closing of the city gates and the systematic monitoring of the populace to the creation of a special ruling committee endowed with emergency powers. And it was in the early sixteenth century that these measures were formalized as an aspect of the city's battery of policing powers, powers vested in the Hôtel de Ville. The capitouls of that era, many of them schooled in the tenets of civic humanism, some of them Calvinists, would hardly have relished the thought that their efforts to police their city better might one day serve the interests of a league of irredentist Catholics, but that in retrospect is what happened.[27]

THE RIVALRY BETWEEN PARLEMENT AND CAPITOULAT

With the close of the era of religious warfare, the Parlement of Toulouse began to assert its authority on the municipal scene in a concerted fashion, and thus what ensued was a period when the sovereign court and the capitoulat were locked in a near-permanent contest for local supremacy. Often this contest spilled into the streets, at times leading to violent clashes between the respective followers of the two corporations, and on several occasions entailing physical encounters between the officials themselves. One of these clashes occurred immediately after Henry IV had established his authority over the city, as if to announce the struggle that was to come: in 1597, during the annual Pentecostal procession, a shoving match broke out concerning which body should escort the Holy Sacrament, during which the vastly outnumbered capitouls ended up being 'manhandled, thrown on the ground and trampled'.[28] In 1644, during preparations for another religious procession, the Parlement ordered the official reviewing stand to be torn down because it did not allow for the required distance between the royal court and the town councillors.[29] And in 1651, the sovereign court's rivalry with the town councillors led to the latter being barred from participating in the Archbishop's funeral obsequies.[30]

What were these contentious displays all about? There was, to be sure, among the officialdom in particular a routine level of hypersensitivity for considerations of rank and honor, which threatened every public ceremony in the Ancien Régime. And the Parlement and capitoulat were not the only official bodies in Toulouse to make a public display of their mutual disdain; contest of this sort was virtually a municipal sport. But they did engage more readily in such violent demonstrations than did others; moreover, one gets the impression that the Parlement never lost an opportunity to aggravate the capitouls' sensitivities, perhaps even making a special effort to do so. Two examples serve to illustrate the magistrates' role as *provocateurs*. In 1638 during the public *fête* celebrating the birth of the Dauphin, both the First President of the Parlement and a capitoul were to participate in the lighting of a bonfire; the parlementary chief, however, made a point of lighting the fire himself, haughtily refusing to relinquish the torch to the waiting capitoul who, with his colleagues, left in anger.[31] In 1646 it was the preaching of a visiting bishop at the parish church of the Dalbade that provided the occasion for the public insult: a *conseiller* of the Parlement not only occupied a seat reserved for the capitouls, but made a point of tearing down their banner marked with the city's insignia and replacing it with his own.[32]

In a sense, these squabblings had to do with the lesson of the religious wars in the city, especially as learned by the Parlement. While many *parlementaires* had supported the Holy League, a large faction in the court had identified with the royalist–*politique* position and indeed fled Toulouse in the early 1590s to set up a rival Parlement in Carcassonne. When peace was restored in 1594, the Parlement regrouped, and, in the early years of the seventeenth century, increasingly asserted itself as a leading force in provincial politics. This required, of course, that its home-base of the city of Toulouse remain secure, never again open to the threat of alternative leadership by a powerful and independent Hôtel de Ville. Indeed, the retrospective analysis of an important local apologist for the Parlement in the seventeenth century, Germain de Lafaille, found that the court's failure to exercise control over the capitoulat had faciliated the League's successful take-over in 1588. Such control was not easy to impose, for the capitoulat had, for example, judicial authority within the city walls that could undermine the sovereign court's legitimacy in criminal matters, something demonstrated in 1637 when the capitouls refused to act upon a parlementary *arrêt* against several duellists, an incident leading to another violent confrontation between agents of the two bodies.[33] But the successful exercise of such control had advantages that transcended urban affairs. The Parlement's major rival in the region was the estates of Languedoc, and among the traditional leaders of the third estate were the capitouls of Toulouse. A means for the Parlement to exert influence within the provincial estates thus lay in control over the selection of the capitouls.

The question, therefore, was how to exercise this control, the surest means being to pre-empt the capitulary elections by unilaterally appointing the eight capitouls. This was done in 1598, 1650, 1652 and 1656.[34] But the Parlement was not the only agent of outside interference in the municipal elections; the crown also intervened with increasing frequency in the first part of the seventeenth century – in 1613, 1621, 1632 and 1644 – and although it is hard to tell, such royal meddling usually came at the behest of the Parlement.[35] Here again, however, we must not conclude that the lines were clearly drawn between the crown and sovereign court on one side and the town council on the other; for the multiple rivalries and shifting coalitions of mid-seventeenth-century French politics had a way of skewing such neat divisions. The events of 1644 illustrate the complicated nature of this matter. Again that year the new capitouls were appointed by the crown, specifically by the royal governor, Gaston d'Orléans, who exercised great authority in the province during the regency. It appears, however, that their selection in this manner was the result of an appeal by a faction within the Hôtel de Ville, which objected to the Parlement's resistance to the crown, especially its refusal to pay the new *joyeux avènement* tax. The new capitouls thus confronted opposition from the Parlement, the old capitouls and a substantial segment of the urban official-dom; indeed, they were prevented from occupying the Hôtel de Ville for four months into their term of office. In this instance it was the Parlement that supported the 'free' capitulary elections and at least some partisans of the Hôtel de Ville who lobbied for royal interference. The city remained divided over this incident for several years, but it was not a division that conformed to the boundaries between town council and sovereign court, for the ranks of each were split.[36]

Thus it was that the power of the crown was not necessarily behind either the Parlement or the capitouls in the period before the Fronde; indeed, each body was capable of using royal interference to its own advantage. In fact, during the Fronde, it was the capitoulat that emerged as the beneficiary of royal favor, largely because the Parlement was implicated in the provincial estates' opposition to Mazarin and was itself, for a time at least, allied with the princely *frondeurs*. In order to guarantee the capitoulat's allegiance during the conflict, the crown was generous in its favor toward the city: it exempted it from several recent fiscal impositions; it affirmed the capitouls' right to select their own delegates to the provincial estates; it ruled to re-enforce the capitouls' authority in several domains, including the policing of markets and craft guilds, areas where the Parlement had asserted its own claims only the year before; and it also granted the capitouls the right on several occasions to take their legal grievances to the Parlement of Bordeaux, thus avoiding the judicial authority of their rivals. In general, it blunted the Parlement's attempt to bully the municipal magistrates.[37] Thus, largely because of its position as a crucial counterweight to a sometimes rebellious Parlement, the capitoulat emerged from the period of the Fronde with many of its powers and privileges intact, although it owed this to royal favor calculatingly proferred.

THE ROYAL ASSAULT ON THE CAPITOULAT

What the crown could grant, of course, it could take away as well. And thus it was that once the Parlement ceased to represent a local threat to the crown's authority, the capitoulat's privileged reign came to an end. The process by which the Parlement was won over to royalism has been masterfully treated in William Beik's recent work, which emphasizes the rewards and advantages that came the way of provincial elites with loyalty to the crown.[38] For the capitouls of Toulouse, however, the process had a less happy outcome: the pacification of the province at the end of the Fronde meant the beginning of a royal assault on their privileges and powers.

The assault commenced in the mid 1650s and was managed by the First President of the Parlement, Gaspard de Fieubet, a royal appointee with connections, through his brother, at court. Fieubet began by insinuating his agents into the Hôtel de Ville: he had Germain de Lafaille named *syndic de la ville*, and this loyal underling, whose municipal service spanned fifty-five years and who at the age of ninety-six penned his 'Testament Syndical' documenting the deterioration of Toulouse's government, served as the First President's spy in the city hall's inner sanctum. Fieubet also arranged the marriage between his *valet de chambre* and the daughter of the Hôtel de Ville's concierge, thus providing him with another channel of information on the inner workings of municipal government. Then in 1659, through the good graces of his brother, who was the Queen's *Secrétaire des Commandements*, Fieubet secured the king's approval of a list of candidates for the capitoulat, all his friends and clients. Two years later, Fieubet received from the crown the power permanently to name the municipal council. In one stroke, therefore, the city was denied a privilege it had exercised, with some exceptions to be sure, since the capitoulat's creation in the twelfth century.[39]

A royal appointee himself, Fieubet was also a local man, and it is likely that his choices were subject to political and family pressures within the city. This was not the case with the royal intendant Basville, who at Fieubet's resignation in 1683, took over the task of selecting the new municipal council.

A word must be said about this particular intendant. Lamoignon de Basville was the quintessential royal servant – efficient, incorruptible, talented and, when necessary, ruthless. Son of a First President of the Parisian Parlement, he had already served as intendant in Pau, Montauban and Poitiers before his assignment to Languedoc. He was, in other words, a career royal agent. Basville was closely connected to the inner circle at Versailles: he was the *créature* of Louvois, a confidant of Madame de Maintenon, and a friend of the influential Jesuit, Père La Chaise, Louis XIV's confessor. His ties to the Jesuits in fact were a factor in his being sent to Languedoc, for the crown wanted an agent who would prove immune to Jansenism, which had many followers in Toulouse. But it is as the persecutor of the Huguenots that Basville gained notoriety, for it was he who was responsible for carrying out the Revocation of the Edict of Nantes in the Midi, and it was he who unleashed the infamous *dragonnades* upon the beleaguered Calvinists of the Cévennes. Religious fanaticism, however, entered little into his actions: Basville was the perfect bureaucrat, combining unswerving loyalty to royal policy with an expert knowledge of the province and its inhabitants. His tenure as intendant of Languedoc was an unprecedented thirty-four years, during which time he came to dominate the provincial elite. Saint-Simon dubbed him the 'King of Languedoc'.[40] He might also be called the boss of Toulouse.

For Basville not only appointed the capitouls, he also controlled the city's treasury. In 1683 a royal edict placed the control of municipal finances into the hands of the intendants throughout the realm, and in 1688 we see this edict being put into effect in Toulouse. In June of that year Basville arrived in town, and his fifteen-day stay produced something of a municipal revolution, or rather a peaceful *coup de ville*. Ensconced in a chamber in the Hôtel de Ville, he assembled the capitouls for daily conferences and proceeded to dictate a new course of municipal government. He scrutinized the new tax rolls and ordered documentary proof for those who claimed fiscal exemptions. He forbade the capitouls to appropriate more than 100 livres – mere pocket money – without his permission. He demanded to examine the receipts of the *octrois* every month. He appointed his own sub-delegate Mariotte to serve as treasurer of the city. He prohibited the capitouls from appointing their own commissioners to attend to the city's business and made sure to enjoin them as well from sending delegates to Versailles to lobby their interests at court. He also prohibited them from convening official assemblies without the presence of an officer of the king, meaning either himself or his sub-delegate.[41]

Basville had established himself and his sub-delegate as the effective rulers of Toulouse, and he had stripped the capitouls of their most fundamental powers. But a man did not seek a place on the town council primarily to become powerful, but rather to become ennobled. In 1691, however, even this most precious of privileges was challenged when the crown imposed a tax on the *noblesse de cloche* of the realm. In Toulouse, all families ennobled through the capitoulat since 1600 were subject to the tax; moreover, the sitting capitouls themselves were charged with the difficult and onerous task of assembling a list of the generations of their predecessors and presenting it to Basville. As might have been expected, the outcry from the capitouls was immense, and they turned in desperation to such powerful figures as the Archbishop of Toulouse and the First President to press their case at Versailles. During the months of negotiation there was even talk of physical resistance. But the capitouls were ultimately saved from such desperate measures and from the tax itself, for the crown was up to its old trick of manipulating privilege in exchange for revenue, of looking for the quick fiscal fix, rather than securing regular sources of taxation. In short, Colbert was probably never serious about taxing the capitouls, but simply wanted to extort the largest possible sum in return for the guarantee of their nobility – and their fiscal immunity. This is precisely what happened. Basville let it be known that, owing to his 'great need', the king would look with particular favor and gratitude on the capitouls if a 'voluntary' amount were forthcoming from the city. The capitouls quickly responded with a 'gift' of 250,000 livres. Three months later the king declared that it had never been his intention to include the capitouls of Toulouse in the royal levy on the *noblesse de cloche*, and assured them that 'their chidren and descendents [would] enjoy in the future as in the past, the same prerogatives and all the other advantages which nobles of extraction and family enjoy'.

The capitouls could congratulate themselves on having rescued, at a cost, their nobility and the fiscal privilege it entailed, but they were not able to savor their victory for long. In August 1692 the crown launched another assault on the structure of municipal government, this time by imposing the office of mayor on the realm's cities. Only Paris and Lyon were spared this humiliating innovation. Like other royal offices, that of town mayor was venal, and in addition it ennobled the possessor and his descendants. In Toulouse, the office went to Jean Daspe, a *conseiller* in the Parlement, who purchased it for 100,000 livres. As the new mayor, Daspe enjoyed privileges and honors that effectively demoted the capitouls in the city's social hierarchy, and piqued their collective pride as well. Although his authority was largely ceremonial – in all substantive matters he was obliged to defer to the intendant – Daspe was intent on milking his office for the maximum *éclat*. He marched ahead of the capitouls in all public processions, and he led the city's delegation to the provincial estates. His name figured first on all municipal ordinances and placards; his personal retinue included four city archers, a sergeant and a valet, and he was also given lodgings in the Hôtel de Ville. To the capitouls, who had just witnessed a drastic erosion of their own authority and prestige, the elevation of Daspe to such honorific heights was insult added to injury.

But they did not have to suffer this indignity for long, for in 1700 the king allowed the city to buy back and retire the office of mayor, and thus the crown was remunerated twice in the transaction, both in the purchase and re-purchase. Like the capitouls' struggle with the crown about their fiscal exemptions, the tug-of-war with Versailles about the office of mayor ended with a costly return to the *status quo ante*. The crown got the funds it needed; the city retained its privileges. But such struggles were bitter object lessons for municipal notables in the ways of Versailles. They were forced to learn that the legitimacy of their offices depended upon royal favor, and that the fiscal demands of the state could destroy time-honored customs and privileges in a single stroke.

Subsequent lessons followed quickly, for the city was next subjected to a battery of innovative taxes, the most notorious being the *capitation*, levied in 1695, a head-tax on all inhabitants, regardless of their privileges. But the city's resources were squeezed as well through a variety of other techniques, several applied directly to the Hôtel de Ville. On two occasions the capitouls were coerced into purchasing shares in royal trading companies, first the *Compagnie des Indes*, for which the sum of 120,000 livres was demanded, and then the *Compagnie du Nord*, where a loan of 80,000 livres was bullied out of the town councillors with the threat of a new tax as the alternative. The most usual form of royal extortion, however, was the creation and sale of offices, from which virtually no corporation or segment of society was spared. In the last two decades of the century royal offices were forced upon each of the city's *corps des métiers* for the total sum of 250,000 livres; upon the Hôtel de Ville, which saw itself saddled with a *procureur du roi*, but which it managed to buy back for a mere 300,000 livres; upon the town merchants, whose compliance was insured with threat of the confiscation of their properties; upon the *officiers de la ville*, whose own tax collectors were summarily dismissed and replaced with twelve new 'assesseurs', each having purchased his office for 6000 livres; upon the city millers, who financed the office with a new tax; and upon the militia, now graced against its will with a royal *lieutenant de police*. The cumulative yield of these burdens was somewhere in the area of two million livres, lending credibility to Lafaille's complaint that it all amounted to a conspiracy to 'strip us down to our nightshirts'.[42] As if these financial sacrifices were not enough, moaned Lafaille, 'there yet came another mortification': in 1692 the crown deprived the city of its artillery and cannons, a move which not only symbolically denied Toulouse's right of self-defence, but also removed its capability to celebrate *fêtes* and *entrées* with the expected *éclat*.[43]

What did the crown accomplish in its assault on Toulouse's municipal government? Like other aspects of French absolutist policy, the results fall into two categories – reform and fiscality. On the side of reform there was much to be done, at least according to Basville, who never ceased complaining about the city's corruption, inefficiency and insolvency, which to his mind was to be blamed on the very nature of Toulouse's government. In short, the capitouls had too much personal power, and used this power in a manner prejudicial to both the public good and the king's will. For example, Basville noted, instead of managing properly municipal charity, 'each capitoul distributes a certain quantity of bread to his shoemaker, to his baker and to other artisans, while the true poor receive nothing'.[44] The city was poorly policed as well, largely because such a task counted for little prestige in the eyes of the capitouls, and 'hence goes to the least distinguished among them'.[45] Most serious in Basville's view was the fact that Toulouse chronically underpaid or stalled on its share of Languedoc's contribution to the *taille*, which by tradition was to amount to one twenty-seventh of the province's 'don'. Even when the city did pay, the capitouls were in the habit of raising only a fraction of the imposition by assessment – sparing, of course, themselves and their friends – taking the balance from the *octrois*, thus depriving the city treasury of funds for other purposes.[46] Not surprisingly, the result was a near-permanent state of municipal indebtedness. Finally, the capitouls themselves, once men of some distinction and commitment, were now likely to have gained access to the municipal magistracy through outright corruption. Lafaille recounts that one disappointed aspirant took his case before the Parlement, where he tearfully expressed his outrage that 4000 livres in bribes had brought him nothing, evoking gales of laughter from the assembled royal magistrates.[47]

Basville's reforms were designed to overcome these and other abuses. As in other cities, the position of *lieutenant de police* was established to relieve the capitouls of a task they neither valued nor performed well. He placed his sub-delegate as treasurer of the city, thus obviating some of the more blatant abuses in the dispensation of municipal funds. He granted the city the right to impose several indirect taxes, but as a condition also severely cut the municipal budget, eliminating, for example, such time-honored expenses as the 200 livres in annual gifts to each minor officer of the Hôtel de Ville. He attempted to put the city's general hospital on a firm financial footing by regularizing the capitouls' contribution; in particular, he insisted that they repay the hospital for a loan its directors had made to the city. And, most important, he placed his own men on the capitoulat.[48]

While it is certain that Basville's reforms injected a measure of regularity and efficiency into municipal affairs, it is also clear that much of what he attempted was undone by fiscal pressures placed upon the city, impositions that the intendant himself carried out and approved. For example, the position of *lieutenant de police*, ostensibly created to improve public order, eventually was repurchased by the city in 1699 for 220,000 livres. The most blatant contradiction to the end of municipal reform was the sale of the position of capitoul. In 1701, according to Lafaille, Toulouse's exhausted credit led to the admission to the capitoulat of only those men prepared to lend the city 10,000 livres.[49] In 1710 Basville reluctantly proposed making the position venal;[50] in both 1711 and 1712, he recommended the selection of individuals who had loaned sums to the city during the recent grain shortage. It seems that increasingly throughout the eighteenth century the position was venal.

Moreover, the intendant was also forced to accept candidates promoted by certain 'grands' of the realm or by various powerful individuals of Toulouse, such as the Archbishop and the First President.[51] Lafaille noted that, by the turn of the century, many men selected as capitouls had never set foot in Toulouse. If the intent of royal reform was to elevate to the capitoulat only those men devoted to public service, it did nothing of the kind.[52]

Indeed, it is difficult to escape Lafaille's observation that 'venality has always been the source of disorder', for especially during the years from 1685 to 1722 the city was forever preoccupied with repurchasing offices that had been imposed upon it by the crown. And this seems to have been the real thrust of the crown's interference in municipal affairs all along: to use Toulouse's Hôtel de Ville as a source of revenue rather than to reform the structure of city government. Such a fiscal strategy was most apparent at the end of Louis XIV's reign, but was also relied upon in 1722 and again in 1734, after which venality proved less successful, owing to the glut of offices for purchase (see Table 6.2).

One result of this policy was to perpetuate the city's indebtedness, another regrettable feature of municipal government which the crown ostensibly wanted to obviate but which it instead ended up by aggravating. There was another result, this one a paradoxical outcome of fiscal pressures placed on many corporate bodies. In borrowing funds to repurchase municipal offices or to defend their noble status, the capitouls relied upon themselves, former town councillors and other partisans of the Hôtel de Ville as creditors. Thus, every royal imposition aimed at municipal government called into action a network of individuals and families who saw their interests as linked to the preservation of the capitoulat and its privileges. A list of creditors for the repurchase of offices created in 1692 illustrates this dynamic. The 250,000 livres were raised through loans from 116 individuals, most for one or two thousand livres. Sixty-one of these names can be identified by title or profession; of them, twenty-six were either current or former capitouls.[53] Others not so identified

Table 6.2 Payments by city of Toulouse to the crown for offices or confirmation of privileges, 1675–1734.

Date	Purpose	Amount (in livres)
1675	capitouls' nobility	100,000
1689	*procureurs du roi*	300,000
1692	craft corporations	250,000
1692	*assesseurs*	72,000
1693	capitouls' nobility	150,000
1699	mayor	112,000
1699	*lieutenant de police*	220,000
1722	various offices	1,390,000
1734	various offices	245,704

Sources: A.N., G 7, 298, 301, 304; A.D.H.G., C 283; A.C.T., GG 287, Testament de Lafaille; Roque, *L'administration municipale.*

were probably related to the town council in some fashion. People associated with the Hôtel de Ville were willing to loan money in these instances, not only because they saw themselves defending an institution they cherished but also because, as insiders of municipal government, they were likely to have their loans repaid. The mobilization of credit in this fashion was a near-permanent feature of municipal life in the late seventeenth and early eighteenth centuries, as the crown continued to hold the city's offices and privileges hostage in return for money. An unintended consequence of all of this was to reaffirm the corporate solidarity of an institution that the crown was doing everything to undermine.[54]

EIGHTEENTH-CENTURY REFORMS

It was not until the eighteenth century that the crown began actually to tamper with the very structure of urban government, in Toulouse and elsewhere. Even then, reform was often intended for fiscal ends. In 1734 a royal edict divided the eight capitouls into two kinds. Four were to be elected, meaning that they would be selected in the manner practiced since 1683, whereby the king chose the capitouls from a slate of candidates nominated by the city. The other four were now designated as 'commissioned' capitouls, that is, men who purchased the position as one might procure any venal office.[55] In 1746 the composition of the town council was again altered: there would be eight permanent 'titulaire' capitouls, each having purchased the office; but only two of them would serve with the six 'elected' capitouls at any given time. The ostensible purpose of this reform was to insure the continuity of municipal government by stipulating the rotation of eight men as councillors, each having accumulated experience in city affairs, each to serve once every four years.[56] But in reality, those who purchased the office seemed to be less than scrupulous in the exercise of their duties: in 1737 the capitouls complained that only the 'elected' among them actually served in the Hôtel de Ville, and the next year it was claimed that six months into his term one commissioned capitoul had not even managed to make it into town.[57] As with the reforms at the end of the seventeenth century, the purpose here seems to have been to regularize the capitoulat's role as a source of revenue for the crown through venality.

In the second half of the eighteenth century the crown's reforming campaign began in earnest. For most of the realm two royal edicts issued in 1764 and 1765 – the so-called Laverdy reforms – were responsible for the reorganization of city governments. Laverdy, who became controller general in 1763, was a *parlementaire* who gained public attention with his role in the court's prosecution of the Society of Jesus. He carried his identification with the Parlement into his new position, for one of his aims in undertaking the reform of the realm's municipalities was to undercut the power of the intendants, who in many cities had attained near dictatorial power over urban affairs. In brief,

Laverdy wanted to revive in town councils a sense of responsibility and independence of action, which the reign of the intendants had pre-empted. His reforms called for the widening of the electoral basis of city councils, the suppression of venality, the regularizing of city finances, and the imposition of some uniformity in municipal administration throughout the realm.[58] In Toulouse, Laverdy's reforms were not enforced, for the Parlement had negotiated with the crown that they would be imposed only on those towns and cities within that part of the court's *ressort* lying outside Languedoc.[59] Municipal reform, however, did finally come to Toulouse in 1778 with a royal edict that entirely recast the structure of city government.

A prelude to this reform was a pamphlet campaign aimed at the weaknesses and failures of Toulouse's municipal government. The authors of these broadsides remained anonymous, although they were undoubtedly partisans of the royally sanctioned reform movement currently taking shape in many domains in late eighteenth-century France. But they also represented the segment of the public that had grown impatient with the conduct of municipal government, with its patent corruption and obvious inefficiency. Their critiques implicated nearly every facet of the capitouls' jurisdiction, from public health to municipal finances. Beggars abounded, disorder and crime were rampant, the streets dirty and ill-lit, they claimed. The city was chronically insolvent and corruption was widespread, nowhere more so than in the Hôtel de Ville. The capitouls themselves were the greatest offenders in this respect, especially when it came to the municipal elections, where fraud and bribery were routine. At fault, these critics declared, was the very nature of municipal government in Toulouse, but especially the capitouls who, because they served for only one year, never acquired the requisite experience for the successful administration of their city. The pamphleteers further repeated what had been a perennial criticism of the capitoulat, at least since the reign of Basville: the fact that ennoblement went with the position not only made municipal service more a matter of self-interest than civic duty, but also tempted merchants to abandon their commercial enterprises for the sake of social promotion, thus stifling the city's economic vitality.[60]

The capitouls and their supporters attempted to refute these and other charges with a series of counter-pamphlets,[61] but to no avail: in June 1778 an *arrêt* of the royal council declared the administrative reform of the capitoulat of Toulouse. Four features marked this reform. First was the elimination of the custom whereby the capitouls represented separate municipal districts. Second was the creation of the position of *chef de consistoire*, appointed by the king, an officer entrusted with ultimate authority over the eight capitouls. The third innovation, the most controversial, called for the selection of the capitouls from three 'classes': noblemen (two), former capitouls (two), and city notables (four). Finally, the entire structure of the Hôtel de Ville was recast into several overlapping councils: a *Conseil Général* of sixty-nine members, fifty-six of whom would be elected for two-year terms and the balance comprised of important lay and ecclesiastical officers; a *Conseil Politique Ordinaire* of forty-six members, of whom thirty-two were elected; and four 'commissions permanentes' devoted to different administrative concerns – disputes, finance, taxation and economic affairs – each directed by urban officials elected for two years from among members of the other two councils. The *Conseil Général* was given the task of electing the capitouls, and the *Conseil Politique* was to oversee the general administration of the city, much as the *Conseil de Bourgeoisie* had done under the previous municipal regime. In addition, service on the capitoulat was extended to two years, and only those men who had been members of the *Conseil Général* for a specified period of time – two years for noble capitouls, eight for those of the other classes – would be eligible for election to the capitoulat.[62]

One of the obvious results of these reforms was to grant the city the right once again to select its own town officials. Since 1683 this had been the prerogative of the King, and it is important to underscore the fact that in the late eighteenth century royal reform meant the relative democratization of municipal government, whereas in earlier years it had resulted in the near-tyrannical tutelage of the intendant. Another result was to widen considerably the number of men who participated, through their membership of one of the councils, in the running of the city, as well as to make many more of these council positions open to suffrage. But most controversy was generated about the division of the capitouls into three classes. The primary purpose here was to attract to the capitoulat men who previously disdained municipal service, specifically noblemen; for the rationale behind royal reform was that one reason why municipal government suffered was its lack of men of the highest stature, and to many in late eighteenth-century France, where the so-called aristocratic reaction was in full swing, this meant gentlemen with noble blood. Accordingly, the capitouls of the first class were granted many ceremonial privileges and some additional powers that, as might be expected, irritated the other town councillors. Several years of public contention and legal contest between the noble and non-noble capitouls ensued.

There was also much complaint from the Parlement. The magistrates correctly perceived that the royal reformers' attempt to woo noblemen to the capitoulat was in part conceived as a means of breaking their influence over Toulouse's Hôtel de Ville; for it made little sense, in the context of a plan to revitalize municipal government, to diminish the power of the intendant while leaving unchecked the hegemony of the Parlement. The court thus launched a campaign against the new regime, and although they eventually had to settle for only minor adjustments, it is interesting to note the language the magistrates employed to defend the traditions of urban government against the 1778 innovations. Their main complaint was against the division of the capitouls into three classes, since it endowed the town council with high nobles, men presumably capable of standing up to the court. But in framing their remonstrance, the magistrates had recourse to language of an elevated sort. It is improper to designate service in government according to profession or station, they noted: rather, 'it is as *citoyen* that one should be selected'. Moreover, they charged that it would be foolish to hope to find such noblemen sufficiently 'enlightened' in the law and civil government, basing their claim on several passages from Montesquieu's *Spirit of the Laws*.[63]

These reforms, of course, barely had a chance: proposed in 1778, they were finally instituted in 1783, leaving a mere seven years before the Revolution radically changed the nature of urban politics. Three features mark them in relation to the upheaval that was to follow. First, the fact that the structure of municipal government was so fundamentally altered served to provide the populace with a model of the possibility of change, with an example of tradition abolished. Second, although municipal government was still limited to the elite, the new selection process was based more on suffrage than in the past and widened as well to include a larger group of men, both as voters and candidates. Finally, the quarrels that followed upon these reforms opened up a Pandora's box of questions concerning the nature of municipal government, the fundamental privileges of various ruling corporations, and the very social categories of the Ancien Régime. The Revolution, of course, had causes that transcended the municipal politics of Toulouse, but the movement to reform urban government unwittingly instructed the populace in both what was wrong with their local regime and what was possible in the way of change.

Despite the fact that in the century before the Revolution, Toulouse's government, like most municipalities, experienced two sets of reform – the first by way of the intrusion of the intendant, the second the structural adjustments just outlined – many traditional administrative prerogatives remained firmly in the capitouls' hands. To be sure, when it came to financial matters – taxation or the dispensation of revenues – the intendant or his sub-delegate were there to restrict the city magistrates' freedom of action. But in two areas the capitouls preserved their autonomy. The first was as judges in criminal affairs within the city's jurisdiction. The capitoulat remained a criminal court down to the Revolution, despite the fact that both the Parlement and *Sénéchaussée* periodically put forth claims to judicial competency within the city.[64] The second was as guarantors of the city's grain supply, a role they were increasingly called upon to fulfil in the course of the eighteenth century, when grain shortages and the attendant threat of riot were constant concerns. Here the capitouls often came into conflict with the Parlement, whose members, nearly all great landlords with a vested interest in the grain trade, were inclined toward a policy of free commerce, as opposed to the municipal mercantilism incumbent upon the town magistrates. When shortages threatened it was the capitouls who scoured the region for available stores and transported them to the city, searched private domiciles for the grain stockpiles accumulated by the ever-suspected monopolists, regulated the public markets, and even established price maximums to placate the hungry populace.[65]

These two roles, as judges and as insurers of the city's food supply, underscore the capitouls' position as the frontline guarantors of public order throughout the Ancien Régime. It was a thankless task and one that they could fulfil only partially, for 'disorder' – crime, rioting, vagabondage and the like – increasingly plagued the city, especially in the eighteenth century. But although they remained formally in control of the instruments of justice and police within the city, ultimately the capitouls were forced to admit that they had lost their authority over public order – and not because the Parlement or intendant had successfully wrested this authority from them. Rather, it was the social conditions themselves, especially grain riots and other public disturbances, that forced the capitouls to turn the city over to outside forces – specifically, royal troops who occupied Toulouse for the first time in 1747 following several days of rioting. The city was occupied in like fashion on several occasions during the next forty years.[66] Nothing else demonstrates the limits of the capitoulats' authority in the eighteenth century and their decline from the once proud masters of the 'municipal republic' – not even the several royal attempts to reform and refashion city government. In the eighteenth century, at least, it was more an urban populace out of control and not so much absolutism that called the city's traditional ruling institution into question and increasingly provoked calls for its reform.

CONCLUSION

Toulouse's municipal government was subjected to a series of challenges in the course of the Ancien Régime, from parlementary interference, the intrusion of the intendant and the pressures of venality, to the structural reforms of the eighteenth century. We could claim that by the end of Louis XIV's reign, the autonomy of the Hôtel de Ville had largely been undermined, but what perhaps should be emphasized rather is how much survived in the way of the city's traditional institutions and practices. The capitouls remained as the chief councillors of the city; the position still ennobled; and although many of their powers had been severely limited, they still controlled an enormous pool of urban patronage, including the several hundred *dizainiers*. Why the crown preserved as much of urban government as it did – that is, why absolutism did not go even farther in eviscerating local institutions – can be explained by three features of absolutist rule itself. First, the capitoulat was useful as a counter-balance to the power of the Parlement: without it, the sovereign court would have reigned uncontested, and thus have been an even greater source of resistance to the crown. Too often absolutism is described in terms of negation: the elimination of traditional powers, privileges and institutions by an imperious monarchy. But it was more often the case that the dynamics of extending royal authority – or rather the limitations on its effective extension – required the manipulation and thus preservation, not elimination, of contending local powers. Second, the capitoulat was useful as well as a source of revenue: the trick of fiscality was to preserve those corporate institutions whose privileges could periodically be held hostage for revenue. Finally, there is a more practical reason why the traditional instruments of urban government remained intact, this being the need for a functioning system for the administration of the city. To be sure, the capitouls' competency on this score was often called into question, especially at the end of the Ancien Régime. But even then, it is telling that the reforms called for the inclusion of more noblemen to the capitoulat. The fact is that the recruitment of elites to public service in the Ancien Régime proceeded almost exclusively on an aristocratic basis: the appeal was to the values of honor and privilege, values still essentially aristocratic in nature. What other basis for public service was there? Civic republicanism was weak in France, mouthed only by select philosophes; and a bureaucracy existed only in the form of the intendancy, hardly a corps of men capable of administering the realm's towns. In short, urban administration required institutions that could, by virtue of their venerability and the privileges they offered, attract men whose aspirations were aristocratic, if not always noble. In Toulouse, the capitoulat was such an institution.

Although Tocqueville consistently overestimated the crown's destructive capabilities, one of his insights was essentially correct: the effect of absolutism was less to change local government than to pit ruling institutions against each other in a manner that ultimately undermined their capacity for real leadership. It would take a political upheaval of unprecedented dimensions to cut through the corporate individualism he described and establish a new basis for public service in France. And it was only in the course of such an upheaval that Toulouse's capitoulat, having survived several centuries of monarchical centralization, would finally disappear.

NOTES: CHAPTER 6

1 Alexis de Tocqueville, *The Old Regime and the French Revolution*, trans. S. Gilbert (Garden City, NJ: Anchor, 1965). Some recent works that emphasize Tocqueville's importance are: Sasha Weitman, 'The sociological thesis of Tocqueville's *The Old Regime and the Revolution*', *Social Research*, vol. 3 (1966); François Furet, *Interpreting the French Revolution*, trans. Elborg Forster (Cambridge: Cambridge University Press, 1981), pp. 132–63; Lynn Hunt, *Politics, Culture, and Class in the French Revolution* (Berkeley, Calif.: University of California Press, 1984), pp. 6–10. See also the comments by Theda Skocpol, *State and Social Revolutions* (Cambridge: Cambridge University Press, 1979), p. 175, note 5.
2 Tocqueville, *The Old Regime*, p. 42.
3 ibid., p. 41.
4 On the capitoulat from its establishment until the late fifteenth century, see Roger Limouzin–Lamouthe, *La commune de Toulouse et les sources de son histoire* (Toulouse: Privat, Paris: H. Didier, 1932), and Philippe Wolff, *Histoire de Toulouse* (Toulouse: Privat, 1974), pp. 183–222.

5 Quoted in L. Dutil, 'La Réforme du Capitoulat toulousain au XIIIe siècle', *Annales du Midi*, vol. 19 (1907), p. 396.

6 A.C.T., BB 113, Rubrique de Police, 1570–1. On the reduction of municipal officers in the eighteenth century, see Barnabé Farmien Rozoi, *Annales de la Ville de Toulouse*, Vol. 4 (Paris: Duchesne, 1776), p. 611.

7 Victor Fons, 'L'Organisation municipale à Toulouse au temps des Capitouls', *Recueil de l'Académie de Législation de Toulouse*, vol. 26 (1877–8), pp. 19–84; Christian Cau, *Toulouse, l'organisation municipale* (Toulouse: Archives Départementales, Haute-Garonne, 1983).

8 On the capitouls' administration in this period, see the Annales manuscrites de la ville, Vol. 2, A.C.T., BB 284, passim; *Reiglement et Ordre des Affaires de la Maison de la Ville et Cité de Toulouse* (Toulouse, 1558); Germaine de Lafaille, *Annales de la Ville de Toulouse depuis la réunion du comté à la couronne*, Vol. 1, pp. 284–326, Vol. 2 (Toulouse, 1701), pp. 2–204; E. Lamouzele, *Essai sur l'organisation et les fonctions de la compagnie du guet et de la garde bourgeoisie de Toulouse au XVIIe et XVIIIe siècles* (Paris: Champion, 1906); Jules Chalande, 'La maison publique au XVe et XVIe siècles à Toulouse', *Mémoires de l'académie des sciences, inscriptions et belles-lettres*, 10th ser., vol. 11 (1911), pp. 65–86; Barbara Beckerman-Davis, 'Poverty and poor relief in Toulouse, 1474–1560', unpublished paper, 1985. For further elaboration on this point, see Robert A. Schneider, *From Municipal Republic to Cosmopolitan City: Public Life in Toulouse 1478–1789* (Ithaca, NY: Cornell University Press, forthcoming), ch. 2.

9 On these various councils, see Philippe Wolff, *Histoire de Toulouse*, p. 384; Henri Roques, *L'administration municipale de 1693 à 1699* (Toulouse: Imprimerie Cooperative Toulousaine, 1908), p. 12; Roger Sicard, *Toulouse et ses capitouls sous la régence* (Toulouse: Université de Toulouse, 1952), pp. 144–5; Victor Fons, 'L'organisation municipale à Toulouse du temps des capitouls', *Recueil de l'académie de législation de Toulouse*, vol. 26 (1877–8), pp. 30–8. See also the series of registers containing the deliberations of the city government: A.C.T., BB 9–58.

10 On these changes see A.C.T., BB 10.

11 A.D.H.G., B 77, parlementary *arrêt* of 11 January 1578; from Charles Roques (ed.), *Inventaire Sommaire des archives départementales antérieures à 1790, Haute-Garonne* (Toulouse: Privat, 1903) Vol. 1, p. 449.

12 On the Parlement of Toulouse, see André Viala, *Le Parlement de Toulouse et l'administration royale laïque 1420–1525 environ* (Albi: Imprimerie relieur des orphelins-apprentis, 1953); Jean–Baptiste Dubédat, *Histoire du Parlement de Toulouse*, 2 vols (Paris: A. Rousseau, 1885); Jean-Claude Paulhet, 'Les Parlementaires toulousains à la fin du XVIIe siècle', *Annales du Midi*, vol. 76 (1964), pp. 37–51.

13 A.D.H.G., B 77, fos. 573–4, *arrêt* of 19 August 1578, in *Inventaire Sommaire*, Vol. 1, p. 456.

14 Gaston Zeller, *Les Institutions de la France au XVIe siècle* (Paris: Presses Universitaires de France, 1948), p. 44.

15 A.D.H.G., B 1, fos. 243–4, *arrêt* of 20 August 1454, in *Inventaire Sommaire*, Vol. 1, p. 6.

16 A.D.H.G., B 13, fol. 155, *arrêt* of 8 July 1506, in ibid., p. 103.

17 Victor Fons, 'Le Parlement de Toulouse en temps d'épidémie', *Mémoires de l'académie des sciences, inscriptions et belles-lettres*, 7th ser., vol. 10 (1878), pp. 39–51.

18 A.D.H.G., B 15, fol. 143, *arrêt* of 8 July 1512, in *Inventaire Sommaire*, p. 120.

19 A.C.T., BB 247, p. 237; Wolff, *Histoire de Toulouse*, p. 232.

20 Gilles Caster, *Le commerce du pastel et de l'épicerie à Toulouse, 1450–1561*

(Toulouse: Privat, 1962); Jules Chalande, *Histoire des rues de Toulouse* (Toulouse: Privat, 1920–1929) 3 vols; Robert Mésuret, *L'Evocation de Vieux Toulouse* (Paris: Editions de Minuit, 1960).

21 Lafaille, *Annales*, Vol. 1, p. 303.

22 A.C.T., BB 274, p. 104 (1548–49).

23 Nicolas Bertrandi, *Les Gestes des Tolosains et d'autres nations de l'environ*, trans. G. de la Perrière (Toulouse, 1555), p. 124. Other sources on local civil humanism include A.C.T., BB 274; Antoine Noguier, *Histoire Tolosaine* (Toulouse, 1556); Antoine Tournier, *Reiglement et ordre des affaires de la maison de la ville et cité de Tolose* (Toulouse, 1558); Guilliaume de la Perrière, *Le Mirror Politique* (Toulouse, 1555).

24 A.C.T., BB 247, p. 50. See also Schneider, *From Municipal Republic to Cosmopolitan City*, ch. 2.

25 On the mobilization of the city before the League take-over see Schneider, *From Municipal Republic to Cosmopolitan City*, ch 3.

26 Lafaille, *Annales*, Vol. 2, p. 250.

27 On the Holy League in Toulouse see Mark Greengrass, 'The *Sainte Union* in the provinces: the case of Toulouse', *Sixteenth-Century Journal*, vol. 14 (1983), pp. 469–96; Jean Loutchitsky, *Documents inédits pour servir à l'histoire de la Réforme et de la Ligue* (Paris: Sandoz et Fischbacher, 1875), pp. 217–79; C. Devic and J. Vaissete, *Histoire générale de Languedoc*, Vol. 11 (Toulouse: Privat, 1889), pp. 769–800. The suggestion that the urban League drew upon the traditions of the municipal republic is derived in part from Robert Descimon, *Qui etaient les Seize?: mythes et réalités de la Ligue parisienne (1585–1594)* (Paris: Klincksieck, 1983), pp. 62–5, 281–5, 295–6.

28 Lafaille, *Annales*, Vol. 2, p. 515.

29 Devic and Vaissete, *Histoire générale de Languedoc*, Vol. 13, p. 200.

30 Devic and Vaissete, *Histoire générale de Languedoc*, Vol. 13, p. 317.

31 Rozoy, *Annales*, Vol. 4, p. 383.

32 ibid., p. 440.

33 A.C.T., BB 279, pp. 145–6.

34 Lafaille, *Annales*, Vol. 2, p. 525; A.C.T., BB 280, pp. 147, 244–5, 337.

35 Devic and Vaissete, *Histoire générale de Languedoc*, Vol. 13, p. 201.

36 William Beik, *Absolutism and Society in Seventeenth-century France* (Cambridge: Cambridge University Press, 1985), pp. 194–5; Rozoy, *Annales*, Vol. 4, pp. 430–5.

37 Rozoy, *Annales*, Vol. 4, pp. 451–5; A.C.T., BB 280, pp. 151–9.

38 Beik, *Absolutism and Society*, pp. 245–339.

39 A.C.T., BB 267, 'Le Testament Syndical de M. de Lafaille', pp. 14–18.

40 On Basville, see Henri Monin, *Essai sur l'histoire administrative du Languedoc pendant l'intendance de Basville* (Paris: Hachette, 1884); J. R. Armogathe and P. Joutard, 'Basville et la guerre des Camisards', *Revue d'histoire moderne et contemporaine*, vol. 19 (1972), pp. 44–67; Beik, *Absolutism and Society*, pp. 115–16; Charles Tilly, *The Contentious French* (Cambridge, Mass.: Harvard University Press, 1986), pp. 164–76.

41 This and the next few paragraphs are assembled from the following sources: A.C.T., BB 267 (Testament de Lafaille); A.C.T., BB 282; Devic and Vaissete, *Histoire générale de Languedoc*, Vol. 13, pp. 603–6, 630–43; Rozoy, *Annales*, Vol. 4, pp. 583–4, 593–8; Roques, *L'administration municipale*.

42 A.C.T., BB 267 (Testament de Lafaille), p. 73.

43 ibid., pp. 73–4.

44 A.N., G7, 299 (letter of Basville, 6 December 1689).

45 A.N., G7, 299 (1 November 1689).

46 A.N., G7, 302 passim.

47 A.C.T., BB 267 (Testament de Lafaille), pp. 32–3.
48 On Basville's various reforms, see A.N., G7, 299–323, passim.
49 A.C.T., BB 267 (Testament de Lafaille), p. 92.
50 A.N., G7, 314 (1710).
51 A.N., G7, 318 (23 November 1712); Roque, *L'administration municipale*, p. 12.
52 ibid., pp. 20–3.
53 A.C.T., CC 1483.
54 This is the argument made by David D. Bien in his article 'The *Secrétaires du Roi*: absolutism, *corps*, and privilege under the Ancien Régime', in Albert Cremer (ed.), *Vom Ancien Régime zu Franzosischen Revolution: Forschungen und Perspektiven/De l'Ancien Régime à la Révolution Française: Recherches et Perspectives* (Göttingen: Vandenhoeck and Ruprecht, 1978), pp. 153–68.
55 Rozoy, *Annales*, Vol. 4, pp. 70–2.
56 ibid., p. 99.
57 ibid., pp. 72, 80.
58 On the Laverdy reforms, see Maurice Bordes, *L'administration provinciale et municipale en France au XVIIIe siècle* (Paris: S.E.D.E.S., 1972), pp. 254–326.
59 In 1766, a 14-page defence of the city's traditional government was published in Toulouse, apparently in response to the Laverdy reforms. See A.D.H.G., C 284: *Mémoire fait en sept cent soixante-six concernant l'administration de la ville de Toulouse*.
60 A.D.H.G., C 284: 'Mémoire sur la necessité de la Réformation de l'administration municipale de la Ville de Toulouse et sur la manière la plus efficace d'y procéder' (1775); *Mémoire prouvé par les Faits sur l'administration vicieuse du Corps de Ville de Toulouse* (Toulouse, 1775).
61 A.D.H.G., C 284: *Mémoire concernant l'administration de la ville de Toulouse, par M. Carrière, avocat et ancien capitoul* (Toulouse, 1778); A.D.H.G., C 285: *Observations sur l'état, l'administration et le pouvoir de Capitouls de la Ville de Toulouse et sur les projects répandus d'une prétendue réformation général touchant ce pouvoir et cette administration* (Toulouse, 1777).
62 On this reform, see note 46, and L. Dutil, 'La Réforme du Capitoulat toulousain', *Annales du Midi*, vol. 19 (1907), pp. 305–63.
63 Devic and Vaissete, *Histoire générale de Languedoc*, Vol. 13, pp. 1315–19.
64 'Les Capitouls, juges des causes criminelles et de police à la fin de l'ancien régime', *Annales du Midi*, vol. 84 (1972), pp. 183–212.
65 On the problem of grain provisioning in the eighteenth century and the conflicting interests among local elites, see Jack Thomas 'Economie politique des marchés: L'ancien régime', an unpublished chapter of a thèse de doctorat, Université de Toulouse–Le Mirail; Charles Tilly, 'Food supply and public order in modern Europe', in *The Formation of National States in Western Europe* (Princeton, NJ: Princeton University Press, 1975), pp. 380–455; idem., *The Contentious French*, pp. 162–200; S. L. Kaplan, *Provisioning Paris. Merchants and Millers in the Grain and Flour Trade during the Eighteenth Century* (Ithaca, NY: Cornell University Press, 1985); L. Viala, *La question des grains à Toulouse au XVIIIe siècle*, thèse de droit, Université de Toulouse, 1909.
66 A.C.T., BB 283, pp. 522, 544 and passim; and Schneider, *From Municipal Republic to Cosmopolitan City*, ch. 10.

7

Economic change, demographic growth and the fate of Dauphiné's small towns, 1698–1790

RENÉ FAVIER

In a petition requesting royal letters of nobility, a merchant from the small town of Gap wrote in 1784, 'Until now, the government has only cast its eyes upon *négociants* established in the seaports or the largest cities of the realm'.[1] In a similar fashion, French historiography has until very recently shown considerably more interest in the larger metropolises and provincial capitals than it has in the small and middling towns that formed the base of the urban hierarchy and contained during the eighteenth century the majority of town dwellers. Only in the last few years has the systematic study of such localities begun to develop.[2] The work done so far has begun to reveal at once the specific attributes and the diversity of the country's smaller towns, as well as the fact that these towns often evolved according to rhythms quite different from those that governed the larger cities. The cities of Dauphiné, a region of marked geographic contrasts, illustrate these points well.

While Dauphiné was one of the few regions of France where all of the major administrative boundaries except those of the church coincided, its rugged topography created an almost infinite variety of landscapes. Elevations within the province ranged from 33 to 4102 meters, and more than three-quarters of the land was hilly or mountainous in character. Settlement consequently concentrated in three regions: the glacial plateaux in the north, near Lyon and its active international commerce; the Rhône valley plain, a major highway for goods moving between northern France and the Mediterranean; and the upland valleys, notably the major ones of the Isère and Durance and the smaller, virtually enclosed basins of the Diois and Baronnies. The variety of the topography was matched by a comparable variety of climates, with the humidity of the northern plains and plateaux giving way to drier heat as one moved southward, while everywhere the higher altitudes brought not only cooler temperatures but also a great diversity of micro-climates according to the configuration of the local peaks and valleys. The result was a province divided into tiny, frequently isolated *pays*, often quite different from one another despite close proximity.[3]

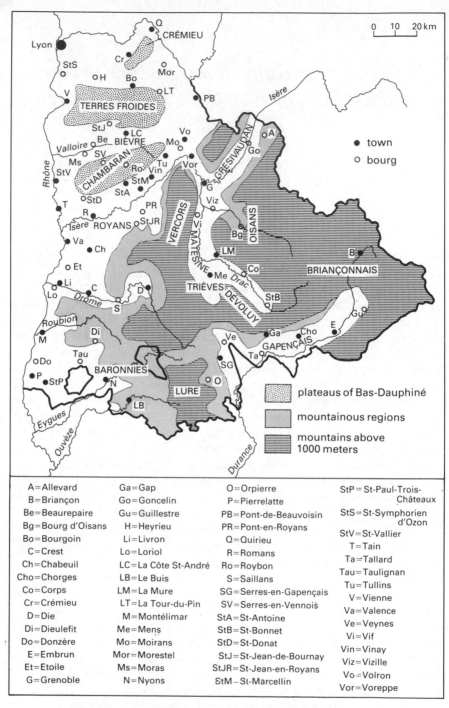

A=Allevard	Ga=Gap	O=Orpierre	StP = St-Paul-Trois-Châteaux
B=Briançon	Go=Goncelin	P=Pierrelatte	
Be=Beaurepaire	Gu=Guillestre	PB=Pont-de-Beauvoisin	StS=St-Symphorien d'Ozon
Bg=Bourg d'Oisans	H=Heyrieu	PR=Pont-en-Royans	
Bo=Bourgoin	Li=Livron	Q=Quirieu	StV=St-Vallier
C=Crest	Lo=Loriol	R=Romans	T=Tain
Ch=Chabeuil	LC=La Côte St-André	Ro=Roybon	Ta=Tallard
Cho=Chorges	LB=Le Buis	S=Saillans	Tau=Taulignan
Co=Corps	LM=La Mure	SG=Serres-en-Gapençais	Tu=Tullins
Cr=Crémieu	LT=La Tour-du-Pin	SV=Serres-en-Vennoiš	V=Vienne
D=Die	M=Montélimar	StA=St-Antoine	Va=Valence
Di=Dieulefit	Me=Mens	StB=St-Bonnet	Ve=Veynes
Do=Donzère	Mo=Moirans	StD=St-Donat	Vi=Vif
E=Embrun	Mor=Morestel	StJ=St-Jean-de-Bournay	Vin=Vinay
Et=Etoile	Ms=Moras	StJR=St-Jean-en-Royans	Viz=Vizille
G=Grenoble	N=Nyons	StM=St-Marcellin	Vo=Volron
			Vor=Voreppe

Map 7.1 Dauphiné: physical features and location of towns.

This rugged land was not conducive to extensive urban growth. Until the end of the Ancien Régime, royal officialdom generally recognized only ten cities in Dauphiné: Grenoble, Vienne, Valence, Romans, Montélimar, Crest, Die, Gap, Embrun, and Briançon. 'All other localities, even if enclosed, should only be reckoned as market towns (*gros bourgs*) because, during the era when the provincial Estates met, only the deputies of the ten cities had the right to take part.'[4] This definition, that of the era itself, understates the density of cities. Certain other documents produced by the intendants grant the status of city to Saint-Marcellin, Le Buis, and Saint-Paul-Trois-Châteaux, while descriptions of the province by travellers, geographers, or cartographers confer this status on as many as thirty localities, although the precise ones mentioned often vary considerably from one observer to another. But even the largest of the localities universally recognized as cities were relatively modest in size. With the exception of the provincial capital, Grenoble, which housed about twenty thousand inhabitants, no city contained more than ten thousand residents at the beginning of the eighteenth century. Only five towns, Vienne, Romans, Valence, Montélimar, and Gap, boasted between five and ten thousand people. All of the rest of the urban network was composed of much smaller places, rarely exceeding two thousand inhabitants. (See Table 7.1.)

These cities were concentrated more heavily in the lower-lying, agriculturally richer regions of the province. Table 7.2, which indicates the percentage of the population living in cities and market towns in each of the province's *élections*, shows the relatively low degree of urbanization in Upper Dauphiné (the *élection* of Gap). Cities were also small and sparse in the *élection* of Vienne in the northern corner of the province, where the proximity of Lyon dampened urban growth. On the other hand, they were particularly dense along the more southerly regions of the Rhône valley. The *élection* of Grenoble contained relatively few towns of importance except the capital itself, which housed 59 per cent of its town dwellers. In no other *élection* did the percentage of town dwellers living in the principal city exceed 41 per cent, while in the *élection* of Montélimar, where the network of smaller towns was particularly dense, this figure was just 24 per cent.

The cities that formed the historic core of the province's urban network all performed significant political, administrative, and religious functions. All six of the largest towns were centers of an *élection*. All but Romans housed a *bailliage* court as well. A *siège présidial* and a small university added luster to Valence, while Vienne's status as an archiepiscopal seat conferred upon it considerable spiritual prestige. The smaller localities mentioned by the intendants as cities, Briançon, Embrun, Le Buis, Saint-Marcellin, Crest, Die, and Saint-Paul-Trois-Châteaux, were also all *bailliage* seats, while Embrun additionally housed an archbishop and Die and Saint-Paul-Trois-Châteaux bishops. The presence of a *bailliage* was especially important, because most judges of seigneurial courts came from the ranks of the *avocats au bailliage*, with the consequence that most seigneurial courts also sat in the local *chef-lieu du*

Table 7.1 The populations of the cities and market towns of Dauphiné in 1698 and 1790.

	1698	*1790*
GRENOBLE	20790	24000
VIENNE	7964	11300
ROMANS	7743	9099
VALENCE	7331	9281
MONTELIMAR	5959	6240
GAP	4313	7019
CREST	3790	4500
BRIANÇON	3100	3180
DIE	2852	3325
CHABEUIL	2747	4135
EMBRUN	2730	3035
TULLINS	2570	3800
VOIRON	2499	5330
LA COTE ST ANDRE	2536	3482
Etoile	2075	2493
NYONS	1999	2700
St Jean de Bournay	1991	2695
VINAY	1975	2380
CREMIEU	1825	2112
St Jean en Royans	1777	2300
PIERRELATTE	1718	2242
Dieulefit	1688	3009
LE BUIS	1651	2215
Taulignan	1621	1630
ST-PAUL-TROIS-CHATEAUX	1592	2055
LA MURE	1575	2146
LIVRON	1575	1953
ST MARCELLIN	1550	1671
Beaurepaire	1483	2244
Loriol	1478	2145
BOURGOIN	1462	3615
St Bonnet	1344	1570
Goncelin	1325	1469
Roybon	1323	2417
ST ANTOINE	1306	1580
Vif	1302	1844
VOREPPE	1302	2620
MENS	1277	1866
Veynes	1243	1780
SERRES EN GAPENÇAIS	1138	1205
ST VALLIER	1125	1606
CHORGES	1105	1900
Donzère	1096	1800

	1698	1790
Allevard	1071	2137
Tallard	1063	1090
SAILLANS	1046	1530
Pont-en-Royans	1046	1083
TAIN	1025	1450
St Donat	995	1535
Vizille	975	1412
Heyrieu	975	1281
Bourg d'Oisans	958	2110
Moirans	911	2133
Serres en Vercors	911	1517
St Symphorien d'Ozon	897	1441
Guillestre	878	1065
Corps	777	921
Morestel	694	892
La Tour du Pin	693	1570
Orpierre	655	805
Moras	600	938
PONT-DE-BEAUVOISIN	550	1544
QUIRIEU	206	281
MONTDAUPHIN		360

This table lists the population of all localities classified as either cities or market towns in the major eighteenth-century administrative surveys of the province. The localities which these descriptions or contemporary maps most consistently identify as cities are indicated in capital letters. Market towns are in lower case. Sources for population figures: B.M. Grenoble, MS U 908, enquête of the intendant Bouchu; A.D.I., J 523, pièce 4, census of 1790. Some corrections have been introduced on the basis of a critical internal analysis and comparison with other contemporary records.

Table 7.2 Degree of urbanization by *élection*, 1698.

Election	Percentage of total population residing in cities and market towns
Grenoble	26.5
Vienne	16.9
Romans	31.5
Valence	31.1
Montélimar	25.1
Gap	20.4

bailliage. These transacted considerably more judicial business than did the royal courts.

The other localities also occasionally classified as cities generally possessed some modest religious and administrative significance as well. Sometimes the memory of past importance was sufficient for a locality to still be considered a city, as Saint-Antoine was because of its abbey and Quirieu, on the border with the Bresse, because it had once possessed military significance. Some, such as Saint-Vallier, were decorated with the privilege of housing on the spot an important seigneurial court. Virtually all had seen one or more religious houses founded within them during the seventeenth century. These functions remained of more prestige than real economic significance, however. These cities existed above all else because of their location at the heart of a small geographic region or on a significant crossroads, a location that generated a somewhat denser concentration of merchants, artisans, and rentiers and a greater, although still modest, control over the surrounding countryside than was typical of most localities. In this, they hardly differed from the *gros bourgs* of the province.

FORCES FOR CHANGE

During the eighteenth century, Dauphiné witnessed a series of significant political, social and economic changes whose overall effect was to modify the balance between its different cities. Although the hierarchy of cities at the beginning of the period reflected the province's administrative hierarchy, these modifications were not primarily the result of transformations within this hierarchy. Such changes were few in number, the most important being the creation of new brigades of the *maréchausée* to police the countryside and the establishment of *subdélégations* to assist the intendants, both of which had little effect upon urban development. The only city to benefit at all significantly from the establishment of new courts was Valence, which saw a new body, the Commission du Conseil, set up within its walls in 1733 to combat smuggling throughout all of southeastern France, while its university underwent a modest renaissance from 1750 onwards.[5] Other forces, instead, were of particular importance in provoking changes in the size of the province's cities. Three particularly important ones can be discerned.

Altered military conditions and improvements in military administration were the first important influence on urban development. As a border province, Dauphiné endured the passage of troops throughout the seventeenth century, and the active campaigning in Savoy that marked the Wars of the League of Augsburg and of the Spanish Succession made the burden particularly intense during the last years of that century and the initial decades of the eighteenth. Gap, Embrun, and Guillestre were all devastated by the duke of Savoy in 1692. The cities that had to lodge soldiers en route to the main theaters of operations or during the winter months found themselves overwhelmed throughout this period. In Vienne, one observer reported in 1702:

> Four to five hundred men have been seen arriving in one night, and the inhabitants obliged to lodge fifteen to sixteen soldiers apiece. There have

been years where not a single day passed when people were not required to billet troops . . . Houses hardly bring any revenue to their owners since most renters only remain in town so long as a large number of soldiers are not passing through. When the troops are on the march, they leave their dwellings and cross the Rhône to Sainte-Colombe in the Lyonnais, where they are sheltered from having to lodge soldiers.[6]

Cases such as this could be multiplied indefinitely. Everywhere in the province, the burdens imposed by the wars of the seventeenth century led to the indebtedness of the communities obliged to billet troops and often to the flight of their inhabitants. In July 1708 the intendant himself attributed the disappearance of Vienne's once thriving swordblade industry to these burdens.[7]

The situation changed as barracks were constructed to house the troops and fighting ceased in the region. As early as 1693 Vauban envisaged lightening the burdens imposed on the cities of the Durance valley by lodging the soldiers in 'some appropriate buildings outside the towns, in imitation of the caravanserais of the Turks; three or four such along this road would do wonders, for where the [current] *étapes* depopulate the region, these buildings would repopulate it through the sales they would generate'.[8] France's loss of Pignerolo in 1697 and of the transalpine valleys ceded to Savoy in 1713 deprived it of the forward outposts that had previously guarded the border and conferred a new strategic importance on the cities of Dauphiné. These now received permanent garrisons, whose deployment hastened the construction of regular barracks within the province. Vienne built its barracks between 1708 and 1716, and Valence, Romans, Montélimar, and Grenoble soon followed suit. Briançon, now a border town, meanwhile saw its fortifications heavily reinforced, while the new town of Montdauphin was created at the strategic confluence of the Durance and the Queyras and endowed with a substantial garrison and walls designed by Vauban.[9]

Once lodged in royal forts or urban barracks, the now more tightly disciplined army units meant more custom for local merchants and tradesmen. A 1787 'Etat des lits militaires' listed the number of permanent beds for soldiers in the province, excepting Grenoble.[10] (See Table 7.3.) Each bed was expected to sleep two soldiers. Even though the beds were not always consistently

Table 7.3 The number of permanent beds for soldiers in towns in Dauphiné in 1787 (Grenoble omitted).

Briançon	1120	Montdauphin	982
Châteauqueyras	28	Montélimar	352
Crest	50	Romans	300
Embrun	280	Valence	516
Fort-Barraux	391	Vienne	732

occupied to full capacity, the presence of so many men who needed to be supplied with food, clothing, and above all drink meant a significant increase in local demand, which local mercantile elites were quickly able to exploit.[11] The benefits of having a local garrison soon came to be recognized, and the smaller towns in particular began to petition for troops to be lodged in their bosom. 'Any inhabitant, whether he be a merchant or of any profession or trade, will find occasion to sell to or work for the troops.... The inhabitants of the neighboring communities will come to town more frequently to sell their produce and make some purchases', affirmed the consuls of La Mure when they appealed in 1743 to have barracks established in their city.[12] The leading citizens of Embrun went even farther in 1764, protesting, 'Our city, whose location renders it incapable of any trade, can only hope to find an outlet for its produce in its garrison, its only way of meeting its public obligations'.[13] In reality, the direct effects of the lodging of troops did not match such inflated expectations. Garrisons remained restricted to a limited number of cities, and the presence of such garrisons seems never to have stimulated much growth in the civilian population of the cities in question. The essential change was that soldiers were no longer a menace and a burden to be feared, as they had been during the preceding century. All of the province's cities benefited from this.

A second determinant of urban development was the productivity of local agriculture. Here, considerable differences existed from region to region. Three broad regions can be distinguished within the province: (1) Upper Dauphiné, where cereal production was generally sufficient to meet the needs of the local population and produced a surplus in the Gapençais, Embrunais, Matésine and Champsaur, although the regions located above 1000 meters such as the Briançonnais and the Oisans had to depend in part upon imports; (2) the plains and plateaux of the Rhône valley and the northern part of the province, where grain was also relatively abundant thanks either to rich local soil (as in the Bièvre plain) or to excellent transportation resources that permitted the easy importation of grain from Burgundy; and (3) the valleys of the Grésivaudan, Romanche, upper Drôme and the Baronnies, all of which always faced a shortfall of grain and were difficult of access. Most cities were deeply implanted in their local agricultural environment, and the concern to raise enough grain always remained paramount. The *terroirs* of most dauphinois cities were not given over to specialized crops appealing to the urban market. Instead, they produced the same crops that were produced elsewhere in their region. Grain dominated, but the hillsides around towns such as Crest were covered with vines, and the landscape was completed by olive trees in the south, walnut trees in the north, mulberry trees for silk production along the Rhône valley, and hemp-fields virtually everywhere. Investigations carried out by the intendants reveal that during the early eighteenth century the province's small towns regularly produced within their own *terroir* over half of the grain they consumed.[14] Such towns as Bourgoin, La Mure, Voiron, Gap, and Embrun were able to meet their entire needs and even produce an occasional surplus. The only cities that needed to import grain from more distant markets were the towns of more than 5,000 inhabitants and the small towns of Le Buis, Nyons, Briançon, and Die, which were located in the least fertile regions. For these towns, the infertility of the local soil was a serious impediment to growth.

The most important changes conditioning the pace of urban development in eighteenth-century Dauphiné were unquestionably those linked to the industrial and commercial growth characteristic of the century. Dauphiné's vocation as an industrial province was longstanding. While the province was not a cloth-making region to rival the weaving centers of Normandy, Champagne or Languedoc, it nonetheless produced ample quantities of woolen and flaxen cloth; per capita woolen output was above the national norm at the beginning of the century. The province also produced important quantities of leather goods; its mineral deposits and fast-moving streams animated papermaking and metallurgical industries; the small quantities of steel turned out here amounted to virtually all of the national production.[15] In the course of the eighteenth century, Dauphiné shared in the general dynamism that characterized so many parts of southeastern France within the economic orbit of Lyon. Although woolen production declined in quantity in the face of intensified competition from Piedmont, the province's woolen manufacturers responded to this competition by orienting their activities toward the production of higher qualities of cloth and managed to increase the total value of their output. Other traditional sectors of the economy, such as papermaking and mining, registered modest increases in production. Above all, the range of industrial activities widened significantly during the century. Stocking production and silk milling were introduced to the province late in the reign of Louis XIV and became major activities, while the spinning, weaving and printing of cotton spread dramatically following the decree of September 1759, which granted *marchands-fabricants* the liberty to establish this industry where they chose. This new activity was concentrated overwhelmingly in a few areas: the northern Grésivaudan, the *seuil de Rives*, and above all the foothills of the Alps and the Rhône plain, close to the major trade routes. Industrial activity remained rare in Upper Dauphiné, with the notable exception of the linen manufactures of the Trièves and some cotton production in the Briançonnais.[16]

In this process of industrial growth, the cities of Dauphiné played a double role, serving as both loci of production in their own right and marketing centers for the output of rural workshops. Crest, for instance, was the place from which wool purchased in the southern part of the province or at Beaucaire was distributed to the inhabitants of the surrounding villages and mountains. They in turn wove friezes and other fabrics, which were brought back to Crest for fulling before being shipped out for sale elsewhere. The entire process was supervised by a small group of local agents working under the supervision of *négociants* of Romans or, increasingly as the century progressed, Lyon and Geneva. Similarly, Voiron was at the center of a web of some sixty villages whose weavers worked for its merchants, while Romans, a major silk market for Lyon, stood at the hub of a silk-throwing region that stretched from the Rhône to the flanks of the Préalpes. In both Crest and Valence, the cotton industry at once established itself in the city and in the surrounding countryside. The Dupont manufactory in this latter city kept more than a thousand workers, primarily female, busy in the surrounding country-side spinning the cotton to feed its looms.[17]

While much of the industrial growth generated primarily rural employment, some cities increasingly emerged as centers of production in their own right. Romans' ancient woolen industry declined during the eighteenth century, but it was replaced by silk-weaving and above all by stocking production, a sector in which the city came to dominate the entire province. Other, smaller cities profited in different ways, usually producing goods in small workshops for powerful outside merchants. Saillans witnessed the growth of silk-throwing for the account of Lyonnais merchants; Beaurepaire produced linens for mer-chants from both Lyon and Marseille; Roybon, Saint-Jean-en-Royans, and Pont-en-Royans all wove woolens for merchants from Romans. Occasionally the workers were assembled under a single roof, as at Vizille, Saint-Symphorien-d'Ozon, and Bourgoin, where manufactories of *toiles imprimées* all employed between 50 and 70 people, or in Valence and Crest, where 155 and 300 people respectively were employed in cotton production.[18]

Two cities grew particularly rapidly as industrial centers: Voiron and Vienne. Voiron represents a virtually unique case in Dauphiné, that of a small town that was almost entirely industrial in character. Its speciality was the production of hempen cloth, the output of which increased by more than 200 per cent between 1730 and 1787. Vienne meanwhile emerged as the province's leading woolen center, thanks to the creation in 1724 of the Manufacture Royale, which grew steadily in size and stimulated imitation by other local producers. In 1754 the Manufacture housed 100 looms within a single building. At the end of the Ancien Régime, some 250 to 300 looms were at work throughout the city.[19]

The acceleration of commerce formed the other half of the century's economic changes. The existence of most small towns was inseparable from that of their markets, which in most cities of the province at the beginning of the century were small, unspecialized, and occasionally merely seasonal. Since the demand for food of so many small towns was limited by virtue of their own production, relatively few inhabitants of the surrounding regions frequented them. Only in cities of more than 3,000–5,000 inhabitants or in those smaller towns located at the boundary of regions of different agricultural character did unspecialized markets generate much activity. Embrun's market, for instance, attracted people from as far away as the Queyras, who came to town to sell their goats, calves, sheep, and butter and to buy grain. Such larger markets offered stiff competition for smaller market towns by virtue of the range of products they could offer. The inhabitants of Chorges, located between Gap and

Embrun, abandoned their own market to buy and sell at these larger towns. Those of La Côte-Saint-André sought to have their market day changed to avoid competition from Grenoble's market, despite their considerable distance from Grenoble.[20]

The eighteenth century witnessed major improvements in the province's road network. River transport was virtually impossible throughout most of Dauphiné and difficult even on the Isère and the Rhône. Beginning in 1730, and accelerating after 1760, a regular program of road construction was undertaken. The policy decisions about where these roads should be constructed were made by bureaucrats from outside the province, and the thinking of the intendants and the officials of the Ponts et Chaussées was governed above all by three imperatives: to improve the linkage between Grenoble as the provincial capital and the main national road system; to facilitate the movement of troops towards the new borders in Upper Dauphiné; and to ease long-distance trade across the province between Lyon and Provence or Savoy on the one hand and between Savoy and Languedoc on the other. Requests for improvements in the connections between regions within the province that did not contribute to achieving these goals were slow to receive a hearing. In 1773, it was decided to construct a major new road linking the Baronnies in the south to the Bresse in the north via Crest, Romans, La Côte-Saint-André and Bourgoin. This plan, however, encountered opposition from the powerful prince of Monaco, whose seigneurial rights encompassed the Rhône tolls, and from Lyon's merchants, who were equally unwilling to see a fraction of the north–south traffic escape from their control. The road was never built.[21] Occasionally, local interests could make themselves felt. In 1785 the engineer of the Ponts et Chaussées for Upper Dauphiné rejected the idea of a direct road between Chorges and Tallard because of its cost and especially the 'irreparable harm' it would do to the city of Gap.[22] But such cases were the exception. By the eve of the Revolution, 161 leagues (approximately 750 kilometers) of new road had been constructed, and these generally followed a course dictated by military considerations, cost, and of course the difficult topography of the province.[23]

The new roads may not have led to a great increase in the speed with which goods circulated, but they certainly lowered transport costs and improved the security and reliability of communications. With the broader expansion of long-distance trade characteristic of the century, they stimulated a sharp increase in traffic moving through the province. New post chaise and coach lines multiplied, and by the end of the century daily departures linked Grenoble to both Lyon and Valence.[24] Along Dauphiné's chief commercial axis, the Rhône valley, the number of carts passing through Vienne increased from 1628 in 1739 to 7378 in 1759. Toll receipts in that city augmented 615 per cent between 1727 and the Revolution, while in Valence they grew by 192 per cent between 1753 and 1788.[25]

The altered road network also stimulated the growth of certain cities at the expense of others. During the century, a number of specialized markets emerged as major centers for trading activity: Bourgoin and Lemps as grain markets, Voiron as a market for hemp and linen, Gap and Veynes as wool markets. Warehouses and entrepôts followed. Commission agencies for grain and flax grew up in Bourgoin. Moirans' cabarets became the point of distribution to the surrounding region for spices brought from Lyon and wool imported from Upper Dauphiné. Gap increasingly profited from its situation as a relay between Dauphiné and Provence to become a commercial center, while Pont-de-Beauvoisin, on the Savoyard border, emerged as a point of sale for goods that had cleared customs. Meanwhile, those cities bypassed by the new construction bemoaned their fate. In 1784 the consuls of Crémieu attributed the decline of their city to 'the establishment of these vast roads which lead to nearby cities . . . Industry and commerce have followed them like water seeking its level . . . The large modern roads, by taking trade and activity to Bourgoin and other localities where these have established themselves, have obliterated all trade in Crémieu'.[26] Similar words came two years later from the consuls of Rozans in the Baronnies:

When roads throughout the province were all roughly comparable and transportation depended upon beasts of burden, Rozans was a much more considerable place; . . . but ever since the main roads constructed far from this *pays* began to attract all commerce because of the ease of transport they offer, its inhabitants, obliged to pay more than others for the shipment of their olive oil . . . have not been able to sell theirs for the same price as those who are held to smaller advance payments . . . The sluggishness of commerce has led to considerable emigration.[27]

In part as a result of these economic changes, contemporaries had a different vision of what defined a city by the end of the eighteenth century. Both size and commercial activity began to enter into account. When on 7 July 1790 the electoral assembly of the newly created department of the Isère decided to rotate sittings of the assembly among the cities of the department, the president of the body raised the question of how it would be determined what a city was. 'The Assembly decided unanimously that a population of two thousand souls enclosed within the same bounds would suffice to have a locality considered a city.'[28]

THE PATTERN OF DEMOGRAPHIC GROWTH

Even though the eighteenth century brought Dauphiné peace, industrial expansion, and a growing volume of commerce, these did not cause the province's cities to grow as a group any more rapidly than the total population. The movement of Dauphiné's population conformed quite closely to eighteenth-century national norms, expanding from 557,307 people in 1698 to 769,962 in 1790 – an increase of 38.2 per cent – with the rate of growth accelerating as the century progressed.[29] (Dupâquier places overall demographic growth throughout France at 32 per cent over the century.[30]) Totalling the number of inhabitants living in 1698 in the cities and market towns listed in Table 7.1, we arrive at 137,581 people, or 24.7 per cent of the total population of the province. By 1730, the absolute number of town dwellers had barely increased at all, attaining only 139,208 people; the weight of military billeting and the serious economic crisis experienced by Dauphiné in these years apparently blocked virtually all urban growth.[31] Thereafter, the urban population began to grow more rapidly, and by 1790 it numbered 186,089. This, however, was still just 24.2 per cent of the province's total population, so slight a difference from the percentage of town dwellers in 1698 that it could easily result from the uncertainties of the data. Paul Bairoch has written that 'The eighteenth century appears to have been for the continent a century in which urbanization ceased or even receded. In France, Germany and Switzerland, urban populations grew at about the same pace or slightly less rapidly than the overall population.'[32] Dauphiné appears to have conformed to this generalization, just as it did to his assertion that, before the industrial revolution, limits to agricultural output tended to prevent urbanization from exceeding 20 to 25 per cent of the total population.[33]

While the percentage of the total population living in cities and market towns remained stable during the eighteenth century, certain categories of towns grew more rapidly than others. The province's six largest cities saw their combined population increase by just 23.7 per cent. Where these housed 9.7 per cent of the province's population in 1698, they sheltered just 8.7 per cent in 1790. If we add to these the other seven primarily administrative towns that were classified as cities at one time or another by the intendants, we find that this 'historic core' of Dauphiné's urban network grew even more slowly as a group, expanding in size by 21.8 per cent in the course of the century. In the same period, the other small towns grew by 54 per cent and the province's *gros bourgs* by 45.7 per cent.[34] Where just eight of these localities boasted over 2,000 inhabitants in 1698, twenty-one did so in 1790. Changes such as these make it easy to understand why contemporaries had such difficulties fitting the geographic realities of their period into traditional categories of what did and did not constitute a city.

Any attempt to explain why urban growth was concentrated primarily in Dauphiné's smaller towns that lacked significant administrative functions must be speculative, but a few hypotheses can be ventured. As we have already seen, the larger towns could not meet their own food needs and were consequently required to depend upon imported grain. Just as this may have driven up living costs and discouraged people from settling in such towns, so too may have the considerable number of privileged individuals enjoying tax exemptions, whose presence would have shifted a heavier tax burden onto the

233

unprivileged. On the other hand, the smaller towns included a large number of people who owned or worked surrounding parcels of land, and the presence of a labor force eager for supplementary activity may have encouraged industrial development in such towns.

Whatever the causes of this broad trend, a close look at the specific towns or regions in which urban growth was particularly concentrated reveals the overwhelming importance of commercial and industrial developments in determining the fate of Dauphiné's different cities. The disappearance of campaigning from the region and lightening of the burdens associated with the billeting of troops created a precondition for the general onset of urban growth after 1730, but those towns that came to house particularly important garrisons were not favored with especially vigorous growth. The fortification of Briançon may have saved it from the outright decline that threatened it when France lost control of both sides of the Montgenevre pass, but the city still saw its civilian population grow by just 80 souls in the course of the century. The attempt to build Montdauphin into a modest center of trade and administration meanwhile met with spectacular failure. Few civilians wanted to move to a cold, windy site that was lacking in good water in order to be at the mercy of the military command in peacetime and enemy attack in case of war. Montdauphin remained throughout the century a miserable hamlet, never able to boast more than 500 civilian inhabitants. On the contrary, the regions where the smaller towns grew most dramatically were those where commerce and industry expanded most rapidly: the Rhône valley and the area to the north of the Isère between Grenoble and Lyon. Voreppe, Bourgoin, La Tour-du-Pin and Le Pont-de-Beauvoisin all saw their population more than double in the course of the century. As Map 7.2 shows, all were located on the major new roads between Lyon, Grenoble, and Savoy. In Upper Dauphiné, whose isolation from the rest of the province made it an exception to the trends found elsewhere, the smaller towns and *gros bourgs* all stagnated or grew at a rate inferior to that of the total population, but Gap's new importance as a commercial node enabled its population to increase by 62.5 per cent. The smaller towns of the Rhône were also consistent beneficiaries of the growth of trade. Many of the other cities that grew more rapidly than the norm were those which, as we have already seen, were centers of rapid industrial growth, such as Voiron, Vienne, Saillans, Roybon, Beaurepaire, and Saint-Symphorien-d'Ozon. But all cities that were located on major commercial routes or witnessed significant industrial growth did not experience especially rapid population expansion. In spite of its commercial and manufacturing importance, Crest only grew from 3,790 to 4,500 inhabitants, largely, it would seem, because its important cotton industry relied heavily on female labor. A growth in employment opportunities for women could bring supplementary income to families, but it does not appear that it sufficed by itself to draw large numbers of new inhabitants to a city and keep them there. In similar fashion, Livron grew less significantly than most other smaller communities on the north–south route along the Rhône because

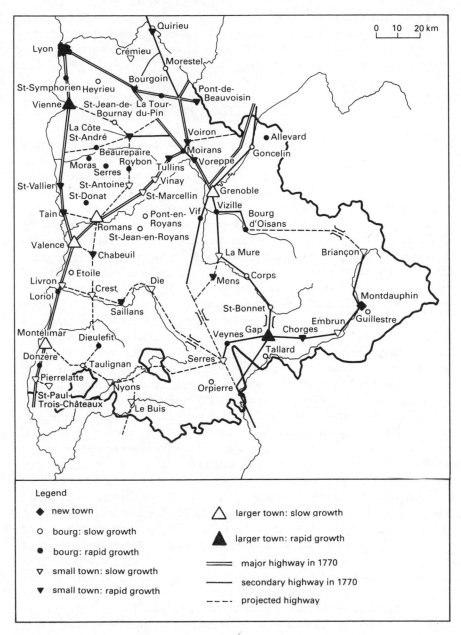

Map 7.2 Evolution of Dauphiné's towns.

Legend

◆ new town

○ bourg: slow growth

● bourg: rapid growth

▽ small town: slow growth

▼ small town: rapid growth

△ larger town: slow growth

▲ larger town: rapid growth

═══ major highway in 1770

——— secondary highway in 1770

- - - - projected highway

the construction of a new bridge over the Drôme there meant that travellers were no longer required, as they once had been, either to wait in the city or to pay its inhabitants to carry them and their goods across the river on their backs when high waters made ferry crossings impossible.

SOCIAL CHANGES

If the economic changes of the eighteenth century thus encouraged particularly rapid growth in Dauphiné's smaller towns, especially those located on major new routes or in dynamic manufacturing regions, how were these towns altered by these changes? My investigation of this question is still continuing, but it is sufficiently far advanced to suggest a few answers.

One thing is very clear. Despite the growth of trade and manufacturing, the rhythms of agriculture still governed the life of most of Dauphiné's small towns at the end of the eighteenth century. Many of the towns in the southern part of the province were virtually 'agro-towns', containing a particularly large number of men employed in agriculture. More than half of those who appear on the tax rolls of Nyons and Livron in the second half of the century are identified as *laboureurs*, *grangers*, or *travailleurs de terre*. More than half of the inhabitants of Nyons, Crest, and Montélimar owned land, which they either cultivated themselves with the aid of day-laborers or let out on share-cropping arrangements.[35] Those involved in agriculture were not only those who lived in hamlets within the *terroir* of a city but outside the main settlement: four-fifths of Montélimar's residents who owned agricultural land and worked it themselves lived within the walls. Such agricultural workers were less numerous in the more northerly regions of the province – *ruraux* represented just 5 per cent of Crémieu's population in 1788[36] – but everywhere in the province even those who worked primarily in artisan or commercial occupations often cultivated a bit of land on the side. When the intendant sought to invoke the *corvée* to compel Gap's inhabitants to work on the roads during the summer, he encountered considerable difficulties because so many of them were busy harvesting their crops.[37] The seasonality of marriage reflected the profound rural imprint on these urban societies. Everywhere in the province, marriages were less numerous during the peak periods of agricultural activity of the late summer and early autumn, with the precise pattern varying from region to region according to the climate. On this score, the rate of growth of different cities made no difference. The same pattern can be observed in sleepy Crémieu, whose population increased by just 16 per cent during the century, and in Bourgoin, which grew by 147 per cent.[38]

Tracing broad changes in the social structure of these towns is a delicate business, not simply because of the unevenness of the survival and quality of the relevant documentation, but also because so many families earned their living from a variety of sources and so much of the industrial change that occurred represented the expansion or contraction of forms of by-employment. Tax rolls or parish registers, which only indicate the principal source of employment for men and rarely mention women's trades at all, are an imperfect guide to the changes that may have occurred. For instance, in Crest, where cotton replaced wool in the course of the century, the capitation roll of 1716 identifies just 15 of 943 people as *grangers* or *travailleurs de terre*, while 207 of 1097 people bore such designations in 1789.[39] Yet the number of men working the land had probably grown little in the interim. What had changed was the disappearance of masculine employment in the woolen industry, which meant that those who previously had been identified as weavers or wool-carders were now identified as agriculturalists. Even if flawed, sources such as these tax rolls remain the best means of obtaining an overview of changing social structures. The figures from Crest do at least suggest that an increasing percentage of the labor of that town's masculine population was devoted to agricultural work, even as female employment in the cotton industry also grew. Livron's tax rolls also reveal an increase in the percentage of people designated as primarily employed in agriculture.[40] In contrast to these two cities, each of which registered less than average growth, Bourgoin witnessed an increase in the percentage of individuals identified as artisans on its tax rolls.[41] These artisans (38 per cent of all heads of household in 1712; 47 per cent in 1786) were engaged in a wide variety of trades, catering primarily to local consumption. The emergence of a substantial concentration of specialized industrial workers was exceptional, but this did occur in Voiron and Vienne. In Voiron, the weavers toiling in the city's workshops comprised nearly a third of the population in 1730 and more than half at the end of the century.[42] In Vienne, the weavers clustered along the valley of the Gère and made up nearly a quarter of the city's population at the end of the century.[43] Here, industrial issues were central to the social crisis that accompanied the Revolution.

The growth of commerce also bred the appearance of merchants of considerable stature, even in smaller cities that experienced only modest demographic growth. One particularly impressive figure, admittedly from a town whose commerce grew exceptionally, Pierre-Daniel Pinet of Gap, traded wool as far afield as Lorraine, sent grain to Marseille, dispatched silk to be milled in communities of both Dauphiné and Provence, and controlled a manufactory of silk stockings in Lyon.[44] Examination of the marriage contracts notarized in eighteen cities during the years 1788–9 reveals that, although merchants' daughters never brought with them dowries comparable to those of the greatest aristocratic families, they nonetheless formed the largest single category of those with dowries in excess of 2,000 livres.[45] Far from being found only in the larger cities, these ample dowries appear in cities of all sizes, although dowries in excess of 10,000 livres were rare in small towns except Voiron.

Many small towns also began to boast a growing range of specialized retail merchants. In the course of the century Saint-Marcellin came to house a *cafetier*, a *liquoriste*, and a *débitant de tabac*. Tobacconists also appeared in Montélimar, Le Buis, La Côte-Saint-André, Crémieu, Moirans, and Bourgoin, while Crest, Nyons, and Tullins came to house *confiseurs*. The number of hostelries and taverns in Bourgoin grew from 15 in 1712 to 34 in 1788.

These changes all bespeak the expansion of commercial horizons and a growing circulation of novel goods. Further intensifying these trends was the development of a regional press from 1774 onward. The *Affiches, Annonces et Avis divers du Dauphiné* linked the smaller towns to the capital. A subscriber in Briançon wrote in July 1774 heralding the appearance of the paper:

> We cannot obtain here all the news which you have the advantage of gaining first in the capital. You will serve to communicate this to us by means of your *Affiches*, which will inform those in one place what occurs or emerges in another place that is new. This, I believe, is the opinion of all your subscribers who are not in the hub of the province.[46]

The newspaper quickly obtained an important circulation.

In sum, while the economic changes of the eighteenth century produced only relatively modest alterations in the social structure of a group of small towns that remained deeply influenced by the rhythms of rural life, they did beget an expansion of commercial horizons, new links to the wider regional and national world, and at least a timid increase in new forms of retail trade and consumption. On the other hand, the new forms of urban sociability characteristic of the eighteenth century had a hard time reaching down to the province's smaller towns. Despite its relatively modest size, Valence became one of the many cities to found an Academy during the eighteenth century.[47] Its university made it something of a center of intellectual life; relative to its population, Valence also provided more subscribers to the Neuchâtel quarto edition of the *Encyclopédie* than any other city in the province, and it saw a public library founded in 1773.[48] The creation of the city's Société Académique et Patriotique owed less, however, to its university traditions than it did to the creation of a school to train artillery officers in 1783. The military officers attached to this school formed the most important and active group within the Academy when it was established in the following year, and the new association attracted few local residents of long standing despite its goal 'to contribute to the progress of the arts, sciences and *belles lettres* so that these may be applied to everything which might be useful for Dauphiné and especially the Valentinois'.[49]

The masonic movement recruited more native Dauphinois. Lodges emerged in the first half of the century in Vienne, Voiron, Romans, and Embrun. Others followed later in the century in Grenoble, Valence, Crest, Die, Briançon and Montélimar.[50] But excluding the ever-exceptional Voiron, which boasted two lodges on the eve of the Revolution, it will be noted that all of the towns that saw these new, Enlightenment forms of associational life establish themselves were the cities that formed the historic core of the province's urban hierarchy and performed significant administrative and judicial functions. Half of the more than sixty members of Valence's Lodge of Wisdom were officials and lawyers, while only a quarter were engaged in trade. In Nyons, the Amateurs de la Sagesse never could obtain the seven members that were the minimum number required to found a lodge. The ranks of the *élites éclairées* remained thin in virtually all of those towns that were not home to large numbers of legal personnel.

In the final analysis, the transformations brought to Dauphiné's small towns were thus limited, despite the economic growth that fueled a somewhat more rapid expansion of these towns than the other communities of the province. Although demographic expansion modified slightly the province's urban hierarchy, it did not radically alter it. Only a few towns such as Bourgoin and Voiron moved up significantly in the rank order of size. It is interesting that these would not see their ascension consecrated in any way by the administrative changes that accompanied the Revolution; it generally reproduced old patterns on this score. But even if the cities that had traditionally dominated the province continued to do so politically and culturally right down to 1800, and even if the life of the smaller towns remained closely tied to agriculture, the equation between urban life and administrative importance was increasingly breaking down. The changes that occurred in the course of the eighteenth century were a forerunner of more dramatic alterations to follow.

NOTES: CHAPTER 7

1   A.D.I., 14J 101.
2   Particularly important are the comparative research project now underway under the joint direction of Jean-Pierre Poussou and Peter Clark on the demographic evolution of small towns in France and Great Britain between 1600 and 1850, and Claude Nières' still unpublished *thèse de doctorat d'etat* of 1987, 'Les villes bretonnes au XVIIIe siècle'.
3   For a fuller introduction to Dauphiné's geography and history, see Bernard Bligny *et al.*, *Histoire du Dauphiné* (Toulouse: Privat, 1973).
4   B.M. Grenoble, R. 5766 (*mémoire* of the Intendant De la Porte, 1754), p. 309.
5   René Favier, 'L'université de Valence et la formation des élites régionales au XVIIIe siècle', in *Le pouvoir régional dans les régions alpines françaises et italiennes. Actes du IXe colloque franco-italien d'histoire alpine, Chambéry 3–5 octobre 1983* (Grenoble: Centre de recherche d'histoire de l'Italie et des pays alpins, 1984), pp. 45–58.
6   A.D.I., II C 318, fo. 1828.
7   A.M. de Boislisle (ed.), *Correspondance des contrôleurs généraux*, Vol. 3 (Paris: Imprimerie Nationale, 1897), p. 34.
8   'Documents inédits relatifs à l'histoire et à la topographie militaire des Alpes', *Bulletin de la Société de Statistique de l'Isère*, 3rd ser., vol. 5 (1876), pp. 132–3.
9   René Bornecque, 'Un paradoxe, la ville citadelle de Montdauphin', in *Vauban*

Réformateur: Actes du colloque de Paris, décembre 1983 (n.p., n.d.), pp. 149–59.

10 A.D.I., II C 715.
11 René Favier, 'Un grand bourgeois à Gap à la fin de l'Ancien Régime: Pierre-Daniel Pinet', in *Bourgeoisies de province et Révolution* (Grenoble: Presses Universitaires de Grenoble, 1987), pp. 43–53.
12 A.D.I., II C 717.
13 A.D.I., B 2315.
14 René Favier, 'Les activités rurales des villes dauphinoises au XVIIIe siècle', in Paul Bairoch and Anne-Marie Piuz (eds), *Des économies traditionnelles aux sociétés industrielles* (Geneva: Droz, 1985), pp. 59–80.
15 Pierre Léon, *La naissance de la grande industrie en Dauphiné (fin XVIIe siècle–1869)* (Paris: Presses Universitaires de France, 1954), Ch. 1; Tihomir Markovitch, *Les industries lainières de Colbert à la Révolution* (Geneva: Droz, 1976), pp. 437–40, 492–5.
16 Léon, *Naissance de la grande industrie*, pp. 188–216; idem, 'L'élan industriel et commercial', in Braudel and Labrousse, Vol. 2, pp. 525–6.
17 Léon, *Naissance de la grande industrie*, p. 260.
18 ibid., p. 258.
19 ibid., pp. 191–2, 259.
20 A.D. Hautes-Alpes, C 23; A.D.I., II C 85.
21 A.D.I., II C 767, nos. 13–14; A.D. Drôme, C 265; Léon, *Naissance de la grande industrie*, pp. 167–8.
22 A. D. Hautes-Alpes, C 127, 10 February 1785.
23 A.D.I., L 479.
24 *Almanach général de la province de Dauphiné pour 1789* (Grenoble: J. L. A. Giroud, 1789).
25 Braudel and Labrousse, Vol. 2, p. 509.
26 A.D.I., II C 767, no. 88.
27 A.D. Drôme, C 258, no. 11.
28 A.D.I., L 201, fo. 9v.
29 The increase was 4.6 per cent between 1698 and 1730, 12.6 per cent from 1730 to 1763, and 17.3 per cent from 1763 to 1790. In calculating population figures, I have relied upon the *enquêtes* of the intendants Bouchu (1698) and Fontanieu (1730), an anonymous *mémoire* of 1763 based upon the *capitation* rolls, and the census of 1790, all corrected as necessary on the basis of a critical confrontation of these documents with other records of the period, notably the demographic data gathered for the years 1690–1701 and 1752–63 at the behest of the abbé Expilly. B.M. Grenoble, MS U 908; B.N., MS Français 8361; A.D.I, J 523, piece 4, and II C 34–42; J. de Font-Reaulx, 'Note sur certaines statistiques et dénombrements ordonnés au XVIIIe siècle par les intendants du Dauphiné', *Revue de Géographie Alpine*, vol. 10 (1922), pp. 429–44; M. E. Martin, *Paroisses et communes de France. Dictionnaire d'histoire administrative et démographique–Drôme* (Paris: Editions du C.N.R.S., 1981); B. Bonnin, R. Favier, J. P. Meyniac, and B. Todesco, *Paroisses et communes de France, Dictionnaire d'histoire administrative et démographique – Isère* (Paris: Editions du C.N.R.S., 1983).
30 Jacques Dupâquier, *La population française aux XVIIe et XVIIIe siècles* (Paris: Presses Universitaires de France, 1979), p. 82.
31 On the economic crisis, see Léon, *Naissance de la grande industrie*, pp. 107–34.
32 Bairoch, *De Jéricho à Mexico: villes et économie dans l'histoire* (Paris: Gallimard, 1985), p. 280.
33 Bairoch, 'Population urbaine et taille des villes en Europe de 1600 à 1970: essai d'analyse statistique', in *Démographie urbaine: XVe–XXe siècle* (Lyon: Publications du Centre d'histoire économique et sociale de la région lyonnaise, 1977), pp. 1–42.

34 Precise population figures by category of town are:

	1698	1730	1763	1790	overall change
six largest cities	54100	54316	60457	66939	+23.7%
smaller cities	49636	51976	60855	69824	+40.7%
market towns	33845	32916	39777	49326	+45.7%
total province	557307	582981	656524	769962	+38.2%
13 traditional administrative cities	71365	70688	80199	86290	+21.8%
others	66216	68520	80890	99169	+49.7%

35 A.C. Livron, CC 44; A.C. Nyons, CC 107; A.C. Crest, CC 75; A.D. Drôme, C 132.

36 A.D.I., IV E 96/43.

37 A.C. Gap, DD4, 25 January 1775.

38 The seasonal movement of marriages was computed for the following communities: Bourgoin, Crémieu, Crest, Die, Le Buis, Montélimar, Nyons, Saint-Marcellin, Saint-Paul-Trois-Châteaux, and Voiron.

39 A.C. Crest, CC 36 and 75.

40 A.C. Livron, CC 31 and 44.

41 A.C. Bourgoin, unclassified capitation registers of 1712 and 1786.

42 A.D.I., Contrôle des actes de notaires, Voiron, C 9 (1730–32) and C 57–8 (1786–90).

43 René Favier, 'La population de Vienne et l'accueil des migrants au XVIIIe siècle', *Evocations*, no. 1–2 (1983), pp. 35–49.

44 Favier, 'Un grand bourgeois', pp. 45–6.

45 Contracts have been examined for the following cities: Grenoble, Vienne, Valence, Romans, Montélimar, Die, Crest, Gap, Embrun, Briançon La Côte-Saint-André, Voiron, Le Buis, La Mure, Crémieu, Nyons, Saint-Marcellin, and Le Pont-de-Beauvoisin.

46 *Affiches, Annonces et Avis divers du Dauphiné*, 1 July 1774. See also René Favier, 'Les "Affiches" et la diffusion de l'innovation en Dauphiné à la fin du XVIIIe siècle (1774–1788)', *Annales du Midi*, vol. 97, no. 170 (1985), pp. 157–67.

47 Daniel Roche, *Le siècle des Lumières en province. Académies et académiciens provinciaux, 1680–1789* (Paris: Mouton, 1978), pp. 57–8.

48 Robert Darnton, *L'aventure de l'Encyclopédie. Un best-seller au siècle des Lumières* (Paris: Perrin, 1982), pp. 412–18.

49 *Almanach général de la province de Dauphiné pour 1789*, p. 319.

50 Alain Le Bihan, *Loges et chapitres de la Grande Loge et du Grand Orient de France (deuxième moitié du XVIIIe siècle)* (Paris: Bibliothèque Nationale, 1967), p. 456.

Index

Melon, Jean-François 42
Melun, size of 9
Mende, size of 9
Mens, population of 224
menuisiers 148, 172
mercers 88, 89, 96, 97
merchant drapers 92
merchants 12, 15, 16, 17, 20, 21, 22, 32, 36, 41,
    43, 71, 91, 96, 97, 98, 99, 100, 115, 117–18,
    120, 123, 124, 125, 126, 135, 139–40, 142–3,
    151–4, 159, 160, 187, 196, 198, 201, 237
Mercier, Sebastien 42, 47
Mercure Galant 37
Mère Folle 18
metal trades 145, 154–5, 169–70, 229
Metz 30, 40
    population of 25
Meulan, population of 25
migration 13–16, 184–8
Milan 16
military in cities 29–30, 40, 141, 227–8
militias, civic 18, 33
Millau, size of 9
millers 12, 88, 170, 185, 186
mining 229
Mirepoix, size of 9
mirrormakers 147, 171
Moirans 232, 238
    size of 225
Monaco, prince of 231
money-changers 125–6
Montagu, Lady Mary Wortley 142
Montargis, size of 9
Montauban 41, 207
    population of 9, 25
Montbrison, size of 9
Montclar 188
Montdauphin 227, 234
    population of 225
Montélimar 223, 227, 236, 238
    élection of 223, 225
    population of 9, 224
Montesquieu, Charles de Secondat, baron de
    215
Montgcnèvre pass 234
Montivilliers, population of 9
Montmorency, house of 93
Montmorency-Damville, Henri de 127, 203
Montpellier 12, 26, 27, 29, 32, 36, 105–28 *passim*
    commerce of 106–7
    geographic situation 105–7
    manufactures 107–8
    municipal government 125–7
    population of 25, 28, 105
    royal officials in 109–28
    social structure 114–18
    University of 108
Moras, population of 225
Morestel, population of 225

Morlaix, population of 25
mortality rates 14–15
Moulins, size of 9
Mousnier, Roland 141
Muchembled, Robert 184
mule-driver 187, 188
municipal surveyors 141
music halls 43
musicians 197
mustard 149–50
mystery plays 18, 27

nailmakers 170
Nantes 40, 43, 44
    population of 9, 24, 28
Narbonne 106
navy 28, 29, 40
neighborhood ties 16–17, 183
Netherlands 39
Neufchâtel 40
Nevers 26
    size of 9
Neveux, Hugues 7
new towns 28
newspapers 37, 238
night watch 23, 33
Nîmes 12, 41, 46, 112
    population of 9, 25
Niort, population of 9, 25
noblesse de cloche 21, 196, 208
Normandy 96
notaries 13, 92, 100, 115, 117, 120, 126, 141
nourriguiers 182, 189
Noyon, size of 9
Nyons 229, 236, 238, 239
    population of 224

obliers 170
occupational differentiation 137–8, 149
octrois, 20, 210
offices, sale of 29, 34–5, 39–40, 45, 121–3,
    208–9, 210–11, 212
oilmakers 170
Oisans 228
organmakers 173
Orléans 41
    population of 9, 10, 24
Orpierre, population of 224
oventenders 170

painters 146–7, 171, 183, 197
Palais de Justice 84, 85, 93
Palais Royal 36, 42, 98
Pamiers, size of 9
Papegaut, companies of 18
parchmentmakers 172
Paris 2, 3, 4, 8, 9, 17, 28, 30, 32, 36, 37, 38, 41, 42,
    43, 45, 47, 48, 69–104 *passim*, 142, 208
    bridges; Pont au Change 87, 91, 99; Pont Neuf